1 Peter

BAKER EXEGETICAL COMMENTARY
ON THE NEW TESTAMENT

ROBERT W. YARBROUGH
and JOSHUA W. JIPP, EDITORS

Volumes now available:

Matthew *David L. Turner*
Mark *Robert H. Stein*
Luke *Darrell L. Bock*
Acts *Darrell L. Bock*
Romans, 2nd ed. *Thomas R. Schreiner*
1 Corinthians *David E. Garland*
2 Corinthians *George H. Guthrie*
Galatians *Douglas J. Moo*
Ephesians *Frank Thielman*
Philippians *Moisés Silva*
Colossians and Philemon *G. K. Beale*
1–2 Thessalonians *Jeffrey A. D. Weima*
James *Dan G. McCartney*
1 Peter *Karen H. Jobes*
1–3 John *Robert W. Yarbrough*
Jude and 2 Peter *Gene L. Green*
Revelation *Grant R. Osborne*

Karen H. Jobes (Ph.D., Westminster Theological Seminary, Philadelphia) is Gerald F. Hawthorne Professor of New Testament Greek and Exegesis, Emerita, at Wheaton College in Wheaton, Illinois. She has written a commentary on Esther (NIVAC) and has coauthored with Moisés Silva *Invitation to the Septuagint*.

1 Peter

Karen H. Jobes

BAKER EXEGETICAL COMMENTARY
ON THE NEW TESTAMENT

Baker Academic
a division of Baker Publishing Group
Grand Rapids, Michigan

Published by Baker Academic
a division of Baker Publishing Group
P.O. Box 6287, Grand Rapids, MI 49516-6287
www.bakeracademic.com

Printed in the United States of America

Library of Congress Cataloging-in-Publication Data

Jobes, Karen H.
     1 Peter / Karen H. Jobes.
          p.   cm. — (Baker exegetical commentary on the New Testament)
     Includes bibliographical references and indexes.
     ISBN 10: 0-8010-2674-1 (cloth)
     ISBN 978-0-8010-2674-4 (cloth)
     1. Bible. N.T. Peter, 1st—Commentaries. I. Title. II. Series.
BS2795.53.J63 2005
227'.9207—dc22   2005004110

          20   21   22   23   13   12   11   10   9

To my husband, Buzz,
who has always exemplified Ephesians 5:25
by his support for my work

Contents

Series Preface

The chief concern of the Baker Exegetical Commentary on the New Testament (BECNT) is to provide, within the framework of informed evangelical thought, commentaries that blend scholarly depth with readability, exegetical detail with sensitivity to the whole, and attention to critical problems with theological awareness. We hope thereby to attract the interest of a fairly wide audience, from the scholar who is looking for a thoughtful and independent examination of the text to the motivated lay Christian who craves a solid but accessible exposition.

Nevertheless, a major purpose is to address the needs of pastors and others involved in the preaching and exposition of the Scriptures as the uniquely inspired Word of God. This consideration affects directly the parameters of the series. For example, serious biblical expositors cannot afford to depend on a superficial treatment that avoids the difficult questions, but neither are they interested in encyclopedic commentaries that seek to cover every conceivable issue that may arise. Our aim, therefore, is to focus on those problems that have a direct bearing on the meaning of the text (although selected technical details are treated in the additional notes).

Similarly, a special effort is made to avoid treating exegetical questions for their own sake, that is, in relative isolation from the thrust of the argument as a whole. This effort may involve (at the discretion of the individual contributors) abandoning the verse-by-verse approach in favor of an exposition that focuses on the paragraph as the main unit of thought. In all cases, however, the commentaries will stress the development of the argument and explicitly relate each passage to what precedes and follows it so as to identify its function in context as clearly as possible.

We believe, moreover, that a responsible exegetical commentary must take fully into account the latest scholarly research, regardless of its source. The attempt to do this in the context of a conservative theological tradition presents certain challenges, and in the past the results have not always been commendable. In some cases, evangelicals appear to make use of critical scholarship not for the purpose of genuine interaction but only to dismiss it. In other cases, the interaction glides over into assimilation, theological distinctives are ignored or suppressed, and the end product cannot be differentiated from works that arise from a fundamentally different starting point.

The contributors to this series attempt to avoid these pitfalls. On the one hand, they do not consider traditional opinions to be sacrosanct, and they are certainly committed to do justice to the biblical text whether or not it supports such opinions. On the other hand, they will not quickly abandon a long-standing view, if there is persuasive evidence in its favor, for the sake of fashionable theories. What is more important, the contributors share a belief in the trustworthiness and essential unity of Scripture. They also consider that the historic formulations of Christian doctrine, such as the ecumenical creeds and many of the documents originating in the sixteenth-century Reformation, arose from a legitimate reading of Scripture, thus providing a proper framework for its further interpretation. No doubt, the use of such a starting point sometimes results in the imposition of a foreign construct on the text, but we deny that it must necessarily do so or that the writers who claim to approach the text without prejudices are invulnerable to the same danger.

Accordingly, we do not consider theological assumptions—from which, in any case, no commentator is free—to be obstacles to biblical interpretation. On the contrary, an exegete who hopes to understand the apostle Paul in a theological vacuum might just as easily try to interpret Aristotle without regard for the philosophical framework of his whole work or without having recourse to those subsequent philosophical categories that make possible a meaningful contextualization of his thought. It must be emphasized, however, that the contributors to the present series come from a variety of theological traditions and that they do not all have identical views with regard to the proper implementation of these general principles. In the end, all that really matters is whether the series succeeds in representing the original text accurately, clearly, and meaningfully to the contemporary reader.

Shading has been used to assist the reader in locating salient sections of the treatment of each passage: introductory comments and concluding summaries. Textual variants in the Greek text are signaled in the author's translation by means of half-brackets around the relevant word or phrase (e.g., ⌜Gerasenes⌝), thereby alerting the reader to turn to the additional notes at the end of each exegetical unit for a discussion of the textual problem. The documentation uses the author-date method, in which the basic reference consists of author's surname + year + page number(s): Fitzmyer 1992: 58. The only exceptions to this system are well-known reference works (e.g., BDAG, LSJ, *TDNT*). Full publication data and a complete set of indexes can be found at the end of the volume.

Robert W. Yarbrough
Robert H. Stein

Author's Preface

Writing a commentary is a challenging endeavor. First, one is constrained by the flow and content of the biblical text itself. Rather than having the freedom to let one's thoughts be structured as they may, the author of a commentary must follow the structure of the biblical text, even where its meaning is difficult or obscure. Second, after about two thousand years of reflection on the New Testament (NT), it is daunting to say something that is new enough to warrant another commentary but not so innovative as to be heretical. Nevertheless, it is truly a great privilege to present the interpretive heritage of the Christian church in a fresh light to today's serious Bible readers.

In this commentary I hope to offer three distinct contributions to that heritage. First, I present a new theory on the historical background of the book of 1 Peter. Interpretive tradition has assumed that the letter was written to indigenous Christians of Asia Minor converted either by the evangelization of the apostle Peter on his travels between Jerusalem and Rome or by anonymous evangelists from the Pauline churches. This commentary presents the scenario that the Christians to whom Peter writes were converted elsewhere, probably Rome, and then displaced to Asia Minor. Peter, with whom they had some previous association, writes to these "foreigners and resident aliens," using their personal situation to lend power to his spiritual application of the motif.

Second, I attempt to make the role of the Septuagint (LXX) for interpreting 1 Peter more accessible to the reader. It was the ancient Greek translation of the Old Testament (OT) that formed the scriptural context in which Peter wrote. Peter does not proof-text when he cites the OT but applies the context of the passage as it occurs in the LXX to his Christian readers in Asia Minor. By interpreting his letter against the context of the passages quoted from the LXX, I seek to utilize an exegetical method that is truer to the historical origin of the letter.

Third, by presenting an analysis of the syntax of 1 Peter based on principles of bilingual interference, this study questions the oft-repeated opinion about the high quality of the Greek of its author. The analysis concludes that the syntax exhibits elements consistent with a Semitic-speaking author for whom Greek was a second language.

I am grateful to Jim Kinney of Baker Academic and to Moisés Silva for the invitation to contribute to this series. Special thanks must go to

Wells Turner and Robert Yarbrough for their oversight and editorial work. Because of their critique, this book is better than it would otherwise have been. I am also grateful to my colleagues Bruce Fisk, Bob Gundry, George Guthrie, Moisés Silva, Frank Thielman, and Diana Trautwein for their time spent reading certain sections of the commentary and for the improvements they suggested. Their timely feedback was a great encouragement to me at just the right moment. Any remaining errors and flaws are of course my own sole responsibility.

Al Pietersma provided the text of the *NETS* quotations before they are available in print, for which I thank him. As we translated 1 Peter together in spring semesters 1999 and 2000, my Greek language students at Westmont College asked many questions that helped me to identify exegetical options for further thought. Classroom discussion with Westmont students in my General Epistles course in spring 2002 allowed me an opportunity to think out loud about the message of 1 Peter. The students in my course on 1 Peter at Regent College in summer 2002 engaged the text with me from the perspective of those long-experienced in church ministry, raising some difficult questions about the significance and relevance of this ancient epistle for the church today. I am grateful to all of these people for their presence in my life, which has helped form this work.

Karin Gluck, the academic secretary for the Religious Studies department at Westmont College, provided much time-saving assistance in tracking down books and journal articles. I appreciate the professional support she has cheerfully provided. I also owe a debt of gratitude to the several Westmont College library staff who offered advice and processed timely interlibrary loans for even obscure titles. Special thanks go to Ruth Angelos, Richard Burnweit, Claudia Scott, and Kristyn Thurman and to their student workers. My faculty colleagues Michael Sommermann and Aleta Anderson provided much-appreciated assistance with some German texts, for which I thank them.

I am grateful to Westmont College for granting the sabbatical time that made completion of this work possible. My dear colleagues in the Religious Studies department covered many tasks in my yearlong absence from departmental responsibilities; I owe them much gratitude. Last, but certainly not least, I express deepest gratitude to my husband for his continual support of my work. It is to him that this commentary is dedicated with heartfelt appreciation for our life together.

into the earlier days of the Christian tradition in the 40s and 50s. The alleged contrast between the earlier Paul, who made a sharp break with Judaism as reflected in Galatians, and the later Paul in Romans, who takes a more moderate stance toward the conservative Jewish Christian tradition, is probably overvalued by Brown (Brown and Meier 1983: 134–36). For it is not clear that Galatians and Romans reflect a substantial difference in Paul's thought, especially since the situation in Galatia was quite different from that in Rome and called for a sharp demarcation between the truth of the gospel and the practices of Judaism.

Therefore, the nature of the affinities between 1 Peter and Paul's writings does not compel the conclusion that 1 Peter is dependent on Paul's writings, even if Peter knew of them (cf. 2 Pet. 3:15–16).

Two other considerations. In addition to the question of the quality of the Greek and to the three arguments related to the book's *Sitz im Leben*, two other factors have contributed to a late-first-century date for 1 Peter. Unless Peter himself brought the gospel to Asia Minor (for which there is no compelling historical evidence), it is argued that the spread of the gospel from the Pauline churches to the remotest areas of Asia Minor would have taken decades. The even further time it would have taken for persecution of Christians to develop would place the setting for the letter well beyond Peter's lifetime. Furthermore, it is argued that the code word "Babylon" in 5:13 suggests a date after the destruction of Jerusalem in AD 70.

The origin of Christianity in Asia Minor. In the absence of any historically grounded tradition associating any known apostle with the churches of remote Asia Minor, it has been assumed that Christianity spread only gradually to these remote areas through indigenous evangelization by unknown persons, probably from the Pauline churches in the south. This assumption has led to the inference that it would have taken a decade or more after the lifetimes of Peter or Paul for Christianity to have become adopted by enough people to attract the kind of social persecution that 1 Peter addresses (Beare 1970: 30; Goppelt 1993: 46).

Because Pliny's correspondence (AD 109–111) to Trajan mentions that persecution of Christians in Bithynia had been going on for about twenty years, it is inferred that 1 Peter could not have been written much before 80. The gradual growth of the church in these regions over decades is usually presented as a conclusive argument for pseudonymous authorship. If, however, Christianity came relatively quickly to these regions through Roman colonization of Asia Minor, then that assumption is removed and an earlier date, even during Peter's lifetime, becomes more plausible (see a detailed discussion of this theory under "Recipients" below).

Babylon in 1 Peter. The reference to Babylon in 5:13 is often read as the code word for Rome that is found in Jewish and Christian apocalyptic writings such as the NT book of Revelation. If so, this is offered as evidence for dating 1 Peter in that period of time when Rome had become such a threat that subversive writing must use an encoded reference to it, a time generally regarded as after the destruction of Jerusalem in AD 70. This would place the letter beyond Peter's lifetime and corroborate the theory of pseudonymous authorship (Brown and Meier 1983: 130). However, 1 Peter is not apocalyptic in genre and portrays Rome as neither a great threat nor a great evil. It could hardly be viewed as politically subversive, since it admonishes submission to the governors (2:13) and honor to the emperor (2:17).

The association of the code word "Babylon" with later apocalyptic literature has been confused with a different purpose for its presence in 1 Peter. The reference to Babylon is motivated by the Diaspora framing of the letter (1:1) and functions as the closing inclusio of that motif. Just as the Babylonian exile marginalized the religion of the Jews with respect to the dominant society, Roman society of Peter's day was marginalizing the Christian faith (see comments on 5:13). Thus, Rome could have been referred to as "Babylon" at any time after it gained dominance over Palestine in 63 BC, and the terminus a quo of AD 70 is eliminated (Thiede 1986). A more personal reason may have involved Peter's desire to avoid calling attention to his actual location, if Rome was in fact the "other place" to which he fled after being arrested in Jerusalem and narrowly escaping execution (Acts 12:17; see discussion under "Recipients" below).

Evidence for Peter's Authorship

If the evidence traditionally used to point to a late date and pseudonymous authorship is actually inconclusive because it could pertain to any period of the Christian church in the first century, then it becomes more difficult to avoid a more direct association of the letter with the apostle Peter himself. And there is substantial evidence that would point to a very close association of the apostle Peter with the letter.

First, the letter indisputably claims to be from the apostle Peter (1 Pet. 1:1). In today's scholarly milieu, this may seem a naive point. But under the assumption that epistolary pseudonymity was frequently practiced and widely accepted in antiquity, the text's own claim is sometimes not given its due in favor of inferred evidence of questionable weight. The insistence that the letter's claim to be from the apostle Peter be given its due weight is not an appeal to inspiration and inerrancy. For those doctrines cannot rule out pseudonymous authorship a priori, since any legitimate literary form of the time must be allowed a biblical author when so moved by the Holy Spirit to adopt it. Therefore, the question of pseudonymity becomes a question of genre. What genre is 1 Peter, and was pseudonymity a legitimate characteristic of that genre? Specifically, was *epistolary* pseudonymity a recognized and accepted literary form at the time the NT was written?

While it is likely true that pseudonymity was an accepted literary trait of certain genres, particularly Wisdom literature (e.g., Wisdom of Solomon) and apocalyptic (e.g., 1 Enoch), it is much more questionable whether it was acceptable in personal correspondence, especially since there is some evidence to the contrary. Proponents of epistolary pseudonymity claim that it need not be troubling, for the "feeling that it is somehow fraudulent is a purely modern prejudice" (Beare 1970: 48).

Even though Schlatter (1999: 356), in his discussion of 2 Peter, rejects pseudonymous authorship for 1 Peter, he puts the best spin on how a writing can nevertheless be understood as apostolic even though pseudonymous:

> By writing not in his own name but in the name of Peter, a Christian here indicates that the weight of the apostolic word transcends all that is owned by the present community. No message of a contemporary possesses similar authority. This reveals a certain amount of the community's despair of its own vigor remaining after the death of the apostles, as well as the realization that nothing the community produces can be compared with the apostolic word. By seeking to remind the community in the name of Peter of what it has received, the writer calls the memory that continually draws on the apostolic word the condition for the church's existence (2 Pet. 1:13).

Such a spin may be a helpful way for understanding a work attributed to an apostle that otherwise bears all the marks of pseudonymity, but 1 Peter does not (Achtemeier 1996: 43; Marshall 1991: 23–24). Furthermore, the claim that the book, though pseudonymous, preserves authentic apostolic teaching is unverifiable when the direct link to apostolic authority is merely inferred. Moreover, even a motive of honoring the apostolic memory may not have been enough to excuse pseudonymous personal correspondence in the early church. The spurious letters to the Laodiceans and to the Corinthians (3 Corinthians), both attributed to Paul, enjoyed some period of acceptance because Pauline authorship was assumed, but were rejected when their pseudonymous origin was recognized (Guthrie 1970: 675–77). Tertullian notes that love for Paul motivated the production of 3 Corinthians (Metzger 1972: 14). Nevertheless, when a presbyter of Asia Minor was discovered as its author, he was not congratulated for honoring Paul but censured for his action and removed from church office, even though his work apparently contained nothing heretical. Such examples of pseudonymous personal correspondence indicate that epistolary pseudonymity was not clearly a recognized literary device acceptable to the church.

Nor was it only Christian sensibilities that rejected pseudonymity for some genres. The learned second-century physician Galen felt incensed, not honored, to discover that medical works were being published pseudonymously in his name. He therefore was compelled to publish an essay entitled *On His Own Books* to set the record straight (Metzger 1972: 6).

Pseudonymity appears to have been an acceptable literary device when the alleged author had been dead for centuries, as in the case of Enoch and Solomon. However, when generated relatively soon after the alleged author's death (or during his lifetime as in the case of Galen!), it appears to have been viewed as a forgery and rejected when its true origin was discovered. It is therefore difficult to see how the pseudonymity of NT epistles could have been so clearly understood and widely accepted as a literary device in the first century. Moreover, the wide range of words in Greek vocabulary used to condemn forgery and plagiarism, and the practices used to detect them, show that they were moral offenses even in antiquity (Metzger 1972: 12–13). Metzger (1972: 19) points out that literary forgeries in antiquity "were of many kinds, from the amusing hoax to the most barefaced and impudent imposture, and that the moral judgment to be passed on each must vary accordingly." Therefore, Beare's facile remark that resistance to pseudonymity is a "modern prejudice" must be seriously challenged. The assumption that pseudonymous personal correspondence, such as 1 Peter, was a completely legitimate practice that carried no moral implications must be critically reexamined.

Aland (1961: 41), who argues for the legitimacy of canonical pseudonymous books, seems to appreciate the problem of pseudonymous personal correspondence when he distinguishes "an epistle from a real letter" and defines "the Catholic epistles" as the former, therefore qualifying them for pseudonymous authorship. But Aland gives no reason for distinguishing a real letter from an epistle except that the personality of the writer clearly appears in real letters: Real letters "have to introduce their writers," who "wanted to utter their own opinion on concrete problems to individual addressees and to answer their questions, just as all letters do any time. Here the person of the writer was exceedingly important." But is this not exactly what the author of 1 Peter intended to do? Therefore, the question of the pseudonymity of 1 Peter turns on the identification of its genre. Was it actual personal correspondence from the apostle to a target audience he had in mind, or an open rhetorical form that was a literary creation intended to bring the first-century voice of Peter to Christians of another time and place? Given that it bears the Hellenistic form of actual personal correspondence (1:1; 5:12–14) and that the themes of the epistolary framework cohere with those in the body of the letter, the former seems more likely (see discussion under

"Literary Unity and Genre" below). If it is personal correspondence, the claim of legitimate pseudonymity becomes quite suspect.

The reasons for rejecting Peter's authorship in favor of a pseudonymous author, other than the quality of the Greek, depend on the evidence (discussed above) that dated the letter beyond the apostle's lifetime. If that evidence is found to be less than compelling, the motivation for accepting pseudonymous authorship is substantially reduced. Furthermore, if there is historical evidence that points to a date before the mid-60s, it would be hard to imagine a pseudonymous author successfully writing in Peter's name while Peter was still alive. This study has found new evidence that such a historical link may in fact exist (see discussion under "Recipients" below).

A second consideration of evidence for Peter's authorship of the letter lies in its allusions to the teachings of Jesus. The value of these allusions for the question of authorship is debated (Gundry 1966–67; Gundry 1974; Best 1969–70). Selwyn (1958: 23–24) identifies in 1 Peter at least thirty allusions to words of Jesus, which he believes represent the author's dependence on Q. He labels these words of Jesus the *verba Christi*, using Latin to denote their ecclesiastical status. Gundry (1966–67) examines fifteen *verba Christi* in 1 Peter that he observes had parallels in the Gospels, including John's Gospel. The phrases in 1 Peter do not quote the Gospels and so do not indicate a literary dependence. Gundry (1966–67: 345) observes:

> The most striking feature about the *verba Christi* in I Peter, however, is that they refer to contexts in the gospels which are specially associated with the Apostle Peter or treat topics that would especially interest the Apostle Peter according to the gospel tradition concerning him. There is, so to speak, a "Petrine pattern" in the *verba Christi* reflected in I Peter.

Gundry (1966–67: 349) further declares that the *verba Christi* are "worked into the context of the epistle far too allusively to be a deliberate fake for the verisimilitude." Thus, he concludes that the *verba Christi* both point to Peter as the author of the epistle and authenticate the sayings of Jesus as preserved in the Gospels.

Best (1969–70) contradicts Gundry's conclusions with a number of observations. By way of disagreeing with Gundry on the number of allusions present in 1 Peter, he argues that the contacts between 1 Peter and the gospel tradition lie only in two blocks of material in Luke. If Peter had actually authored 1 Peter, one would expect "a more haphazard distribution of contacts" (Best 1969–70: 111). Moreover, knowledge of the *verba Christi* does not imply a personal presence when Jesus originally spoke the words if those words had subsequently become codified in some form, whether written or oral (Best 1969–70: 113).

In response to Best, Gundry (1974) points out that they disagree first on how to identify an allusion to Jesus' sayings. Furthermore, because the apostles would have played a part in the subsequent codification of the Jesus sayings, the existence and even use of a codified tradition in no way counts as negative evidence against Peter's authorship of the epistle.

The *verba Christi* in 1 Peter as evidence of authorship will no doubt be valued differently by different minds. Intriguing are the echoes of Jesus' teachings that clearly are not dependent on the literary publication of the Gospels but reflect episodes from Jesus' life when the apostle Peter was present. When combined with other evidence that points the epistle to the lifetime of the apostle, they form a striking feature that is consistent with Petrine authorship (as also Hillyer 1992: 1).

A third important consideration for the authorship-date question is that the theology of 1 Peter appears to reflect an earlier stage of development rather than a later one (see "Major Themes and Theology" below). The suffering of Jesus Christ and the single-point eschatology that God will one day judge everyone contrast with the more highly developed Christology and eschatology such as that found in the later writings of John's Gospel and the Revelation of John. Moreover, 1 Peter seems unconcerned with the problem of heresies, such as incipient Gnosticism, that receives so much attention in the last third of the first century, particularly in Asia Minor. Nor is the theology of 1 Peter developed in the direction of later Catholicism. If Schutter (1989: 35) is correct, his conclusion that 1 Peter depends more on oral Christian sources than on written also points in the direction of earlier composition rather than later.

A further historical footnote should be considered in the dating of the book and therefore indirectly in determining the authorship question. The names of the areas listed in 1:1 may suggest that the letter was written before AD 72, when Galatia and Cappadocia were combined into one military command marked by a change of terminology in the inscriptions. Hemer (1977–78: 242) concludes from the separate mention of Galatia in 1:1 that "there is some indication to favour an earlier date [i.e., before AD 72] . . . if one accepts that 'Galatia' here denotes the eastern district without qualification." However, his reluctance to press the point is well taken: the areas of Bithynia and Pontus had been one Roman province since Caesar's conquest of them in 65 BC, yet they are listed separately in 1:1—with one at the head of the list and the other at the end, no less.

This study offers further historical evidence that may link the letter of 1 Peter to circumstances that arose during the apostle's lifetime (see "Recipients" below). If so, the accumulating weight of positive evidence that brings the book into the time of Peter must be reconsidered against the traditional scholarship for late and pseudonymous authorship.

Summary of evidence for date and authorship. The rejection of Peter's authorship of 1 Peter is a relatively recent development in the history of interpretation, dating from work in the nineteenth and early twentieth centuries by scholars who included von Soden, Gunkel, Knopf, Loisy, Windisch, Renan, and Harnack. Prior to that time Peter's authorship was uncontested in the history of the church, and that position continued to be supported by Weiss, Zahn, Lightfoot, Hort, Hatch, Moffatt, and Schlatter. Although the late date for 1 Peter arose from source-critical assumptions that have subsequently been rejected, the theory that 1 Peter is a pseudonymous work that dates to between AD 70 and 90 has nevertheless largely been retained. This is primarily because the quality of its Greek remains at issue. However, the pseudonymous hypothesis generally ascribes authorship to a native-Greek speaker of the Petrine school in Rome. If syntax criticism has uncovered Semitic interference in the Greek of 1 Peter that is consistent with a native-Semitic speaker for whom Greek is a second language, then the pseudonymous hypothesis must be modified accordingly (see excursus). If, however, a pseudonymous Semitic author in Rome is proposed, then further consideration must be given to Silvanus or Mark, and certainly even to Peter himself.

The number of prominent interpreters who continue to favor pseudonymous authorship may suggest that the issue has been settled (Achtemeier 1996: 43; Best 1971: 63; Beare 1970: 47; Bechtler 1998: 46; Bigg 1956: 33; Boring 1999: 30; Brown and Meier 1983: 130; J. H. Elliott 2000: 118–30; Goppelt 1993: 51; Horrell 1998: 2; R. P. Martin 1994: 94; Perkins 1995: 10; Schutter 1989: 17–18). Although the case against Peter's authorship may at one time have seemed "overwhelming" (Beare 1970: 48), it no longer appears to be so. Because the evidence used against Petrine authorship is not conclusive and because of further evidence that points the letter to the lifetime of Peter, many other prominent interpreters believe that an amanuensis wrote under Peter's personal direction (W. Barclay 1976: 163; Carson, Moo, and Morris 1992: 423; Clowney 1988: 21; Congar 1962: 175; Cranfield 1958: 10; Dalton 1974: 265; Davids 1990: 10; Davidson 1981: 318; Grudem 1988: 37; Gundry 2003: 480; Guthrie 1970: 796; Hillyer 1992: 3; Kelly 1969: 33; Kistemaker 1987: 9; Marshall 1991: 20; McKnight 1996: 29; Michaels 1988: lxvi–lxvii, with hesitation; Reicke 1964: 71; Robinson 1976: 169; Selwyn 1958: 62; Stibbs 1979: 23; Thiede 1988: 177; van Unnik 1954–55: 93; Wendland 2000: 25).

Destination

The letter of 1 Peter is addressed to Christians residing in Pontus, Cappadocia, Galatia, Asia, and Bithynia, a vast area of approximately 129,000 square miles (J. H. Elliott 2000: 84). (As a comparison, the state of California covers about 159,000 square miles.) The regions addressed in 1 Peter comprised the area of first-century Asia Minor that lay west and north of the Taurus Mountains. Tite (1997: 30) has suggested that the specification of these five provinces is merely metaphorical, but his proposal is unconvincing because he offers no explanation for why these particular provinces would be cited.

Asia Minor, now known as Turkey, is a peninsula bordered on three sides by great seas: to the north the Euxine (now called the Black Sea); on the west the Aegean; and to the south the Mediterranean. Its east–west extent was about 1,000 miles, and north–south about 350 miles. A great salt lake and desert occupied the center of Asia Minor, separating the northern Royal Road (built during the Persian period) from a more southern passage that became the great commercial route of the Greco-Roman period, for it was the shorter and less difficult route to travel. Along this southern route, Roman colonies first appeared, one of which was Antioch in Pisidia, established during Augustus's reign and not long thereafter visited by Paul, as recorded in Acts 13 (Goodman 1997: 238). The outstanding feature of the geographical destination of 1 Peter "is the enormous diversity of the land, peoples, and cultures" (J. H. Elliott 1981: 61).

The westernmost region of Asia Minor was the point of the Asian continent closest to both Greece and Rome—hence its provincial name of Asia. It was the first region of Asia Minor to be annexed as a Roman province in 133 BC. Within a few decades, the first 173-mile segment of the great southern road from Ephesus to the eastern Cilician Gates had been reconstructed to Roman standards (Ramsay 1890: 164). This route would later become the conduit of the gospel.

The westernmost province of Asia was the most populated area of Asia Minor, with at least forty-two cities in the Roman period, and was also the most Hellenized region of the peninsula (Ramsay 1890: 95). Here the great Pauline mission took root in Ephesus, Colossae, Laodicea, and other locales where the seven churches of Rev. 2–3 were located. Of all the Roman provinces, Asia most wholeheartedly embraced the Roman imperial cult (Alston 1998: 310; S. Johnson 1975: 93; Magie 1950: 1.544). Because of their indigenous religious tradition, the peoples of western Asia Minor easily accepted the emperor as both a monarch and a god (Momigliano 1934: 28–29). Most of the thirty-four cities in Asia Minor with temples dedicated to Augustus were located in this western province of Asia.

Because of its relative proximity to Greece and Rome, more of the population of the province of Asia was urban and Hellenized than that of the rest of Asia Minor. The educated spoke the Greek language, assimilated the Greco-Roman culture, embraced emperor worship, and traveled freely to the west. It would, however, be a great mistake to assume that the sociopolitical situation of Asia applied equally to Pontus, Cappadocia, Galatia, and Bithynia, where Hellenized urban centers were few and far between and where Greek or Latin was spoken only by administrative officials.

East of the province of Asia lay the region of Galatia, which became an imperial province in 25 BC (Frank 1927: 375). The boundaries of Galatia were redrawn during the first century, making it difficult to know with certainty the exact area to which the name referred at a given time. Roman colonization was concentrated along the major southern route in Galatia, leaving the Celtic tribal lands of the northern interior relatively unaffected. Emperor Augustus planted several Roman colonies, among them Pisidian Antioch in 25 BC, which he colonized with "veterans of the fifth Gallic legion—presumably thinking that they might find congenial company near the Galatian country" (Frank 1927: 376). For the first-century emperors, Galatia was important only for military purposes, and the diverse peoples of the province of Galatia were never unified culturally or linguistically during Roman rule.

The annexation and expansion of the province of Galatia completed the Roman domination of Asia Minor that had begun with the province of Asia. Between the annexations of Asia and later of Galatia, Julius Caesar had conquered northern Asia Minor on the fifth day after his arrival in its major seacoast city Sinope after only four hours of fighting. This battle has been memorialized by his now famous words *Veni, vidi, vici*—"I came, I saw, I conquered" (Suetonius, *Julius* 37; Magie 1950: 1.412). Apart from the narrow riviera along the Euxine coast (the legendary home of the Amazons), the Romans found in the interior of Pontus a region more untouched by Western influence than any in Asia Minor except for the adjacent region of Cappadocia (Magie 1950: 1.179). There were only four towns of any size in the entire province (Jones 1971: 155).

The task of organizing these newly conquered lands was given to the great Roman general Pompey, who established eleven urban administrative centers (*politeiai*), which included the three Greek ports of Amisus, Sinope, and Amastris and the ancient captial, Amaseia, as well as seven new Roman colonies (Magie 1950: 1.369–70). In 65 BC Pompey combined his eleven *politeiai* of western Pontus with the province of Bithynia, which had been annexed to the Roman Empire in 74 BC (Ramsay 1890: 191). "On the whole the kingdom of Bithynia remained isolated from the general development of Asia Minor" (Ramsay 1890: 44). According to Pliny, in his time there were but twelve cities in Bithynia, but among them were the cities that would later figure so prominently in Christian history: Chalcedon, Nicaea, and Byzantium (Jones 1971: 164).

Cappadocia, the region farthest east in Asia Minor, remained sparsely populated and culturally separated from the western provinces, making it a place congenial to the monastic life of the eastern Cappadocian fathers even into the fourth century.

According to Strabo, there were only two cities in Cappadocia, one of which, Caesarea, was the major administrative city in the first century (Jones 1971: 174–79). Evidence from inscriptions indicates it had a long-standing Jewish population (Juster 1914: 193). The isolation of Cappadocia from the dominant Greco-Roman culture is evident in the populace's use of the Cappadocian language rather than Greek even well into the fourth century AD. Basil observes that "the divine providence had saved his countrymen from a somewhat obscure heresy, since the grammatical structure of their native tongue did not permit the distinction between 'with' and 'and'" (Jones 1971: 175). Jones notes further that in Cappadocia "even high officials still used Aramaic beside Greek in the first century BC." There were, however, three Roman colonies in Cappadocia: Archelais, founded by Claudius; Arca, probably founded by Hadrian; and Faustiniana, founded by Marcus Aurelius (Jones 1971: 179).

The picture that emerges of the regions to which Peter wrote is one of a vast geographical area with small cities few and far between, of a diversified population of indigenous peoples, Greek settlers, and Roman colonists. The residents practiced many religions, spoke several languages, and were never fully assimilated into the Greco-Roman culture (Frank 1932: 374; S. Johnson 1975: 143; Yakar 2000: 61–65). The problem of linguistic diversity would have been an obstacle to any evangelistic efforts of the indigenous peoples, since Greek and Latin are poorly attested in vast areas of Asia Minor except among officials in the cities that became Roman administrative centers.

And yet this untamed region became the cradle of Christianity. From Asia Minor emerged people whose names are immortalized in Christian history. From Pontus came Aquila, the Jewish tentmaker and husband of Priscilla (Acts 18:2), as well as Marcion, the wealthy shipowner and Christian dissident of the second century who resided in the prominent city of Sinope (S. Johnson 1975: 124). Aquila, the famous translator of a Greek version of the OT, hailed from Sinope as well (Juster 1914: 194n6). From Hierapolis in Phrygia (in Roman Galatia of the first century) came Epictetus, the famous Roman slave and Stoic philosopher (S. Johnson 1975: 91), as well as Papias, bishop of Hierapolis, repeatedly quoted by Eusebius (S. Johnson 1975: 109). In the fourth century came the Cappadocian fathers, such as Basil, bishop of Cappadocia's capital city, Caesarea; his brother Gregory of Nyssa; and Gregory of Nazianzus, bishop of Constantinople—all three defenders of the Nicene Creed against the heresies of Arius.

To this remote and undeveloped region, the apostle Peter writes his letter to Christians whom he addresses as "visiting foreigners and resident aliens" (1:1; 2:11), scattered across the vast reaches of Asia Minor. We may surmise that, in no small part because of this letter and the faithfulness of those who received it, well-established churches flourished in all five of these regions by AD 180. Their bishops attended the great councils of the second through fourth centuries, where the doctrines were forged that Christians hold dear yet today.

Recipients

Most discussion about the original recipients of 1 Peter has focused on whether the majority of Christians addressed were of Jewish or of Gentile origin (the consensus is Gentile) and whether Peter's description of them as παρεπίδημοι (*parepidēmoi*, foreigners, 1:1) and πάροικοι (*paroikoi*, resident aliens, 2:11) should be taken literally or metaphorically (the consensus is metaphorically).

Jewish or Gentile? In contrast to modern interpreters, most ancient exegetes except Augustine and Jerome understood the recipients of the letter to be converts from Judaism. Calvin continued the tradition that this letter was addressed to Jewish converts, and took the phrase *parepidēmois diasporas* (foreigners of [the] scattering) in 1:1 to be a literal reference. This is plausible, since there was a sizable Jewish population in Asia Minor by the time of the first century (Trebilco 1991: 32). The Jewish Diaspora in Asia Minor dates at least from the end of the third century BC, when Antiochus III sent two thousand Jews from Babylon to colonize Lydia and Phyrgia (Mitchell 1993: 2.32).[3]

On the basis of 1:18, most modern commentators disagree that the audience was primarily Jewish Christian; that verse refers to the "the useless way of life you inherited from your ancestors" (for an opposing view see Stewart-Sykes 1997). This understanding is reinforced by the further description in 4:3, "For the time past was [more than] enough to do what the Gentiles like to do, as you went along with acts of abandon, lust, drunkenness, revelry, carousing, and licentious idolatries." It is argued that Diaspora Jews of the first century could never have been described in such spiritually bankrupt terms and that the ways of Judaism would never have been described as a "useless way of life." Therefore, most interpreters today conclude that the original recipients must have been Gentile converts.

However, this argument may not be as compelling as it sounds at first. The context is redemption, as 1:19 goes on to say: "Rather, you have been redeemed by the precious blood of Christ, as of a blameless and spotless lamb." The reference to Christ's blood as "of a blameless and spotless lamb" clearly alludes to the old covenant's sacrificial system, which *was* in fact empty of ultimate redemptive value in comparison with the blood of Jesus Christ. The apostle Paul expresses similar thoughts in Eph. 2:3 and Phil. 3:7–9, where he admits that "all of us"—apparently

---

3. In fact, there may have been Jews in Sardis much earlier, when Obadiah was written, if *Sepharad* in verse 20 may be so understood. There is also a possible reference to Jews in Asia Minor in Herodotus (S. Johnson 1975: 97).

including Jewish people—once lived to gratify the "cravings of our sinful nature." Paul further describes all of his achievement in Judaism as "garbage" (Phil. 3:8 TNIV).

Calvin (1963: 50) points out that when the NT declares that the true revelation of God is known through the Jews, it is with specific reference to the law, commandments, and temple and does not validate the practices of the contemporaneous Jewish people. Moreover, the possibility that numbers of Diaspora Jews had assimilated pagan values and adopted corrupted lifestyles to a greater or lesser extent is not out of the question. Even synagogues in Galilee were decorated with mosaics representing the zodiac with the sun-god at its center, depictions of Hercules, scenes reminiscent of the Dionysus cult, and other pagan symbols (Baumgarten 1999: 73, 80). To what extent such decoration is evidence of a syncretistic assimilation is highly debated, but the fact that other Jews defaced many such symbols in ancient times suggests their passionate disapproval. The impulse for the incorporation of Hellenistic symbols into synagogue decor came from wealthy Jewish donors as a display of "their acculturation in the Hellenistic world" (Baumgarten 1999: 82). Even though a penchant for decorative artwork does not necessarily imply Hellenistic Jews practiced the pagan vices that Peter lists in 4:3, assimilation to pagan cultural norms and practices cannot be ruled out in the reference to doing what the "Gentiles like to do." To some extent and in various ways, some Diaspora Jews, though God's covenant people, may have lived like pagans and were in any case as needy as Gentiles of renewing a covenant relationship with God in Christ.

Understood this way, it makes little difference whether the original readers were Jews or Gentiles. Both spiritual systems were empty in that in themselves they offered no redemption, and both people groups were equally guilty in God's sight. Whether converts from paganism or Judaism, the letter's recipients needed to understand their new covenant relationship with God in Christ and the implications of that relationship for transformed living. Nevertheless, faith in Jesus, the *Jewish* Messiah, brought converts into the religious world of Judaism, not of pagan religions. Therefore, whether Peter's readers were formerly Jews or Gentiles, Peter addresses them indiscriminately from within the traditions of biblical Israel, in which the author was thoroughly steeped.

Foreigners and resident aliens: literal or metaphorical? Modern commentators almost unanimously take the description of the recipients as *parepidēmoi* (visiting foreigners) and *paroikoi* (resident aliens) to be a metaphor for the Christian journey through this earthly life and seek no further explanation. Most have not been persuaded by J. H. Elliott (1981; 2000), who argues that these terms are not metaphors but socioeconomic descriptors. When they are understood as figurative language, there is no agreement about the controlling metaphor of the book. T. Martin (1992a) understands *diaspora* to be the controlling metaphor (also Tite

1997: 32), Feldmeier (1992) presents *der Fremde* (the stranger), Seland (2001) argues for the *proselyte* as the key, and Achtemeier (1996) offers the quite general *Israel as the people of God*.

The view that the terms *parepidēmoi* and *paroikoi* are used metaphorically of Peter's Christian readers is justified because these terms occur in the LXX to describe God's ancient people Israel in their various historical situations.[4] First Peter 2:9–10 uses other terms from the OT as well—chosen people, royal priesthood, holy nation, God's special possession—to describe Peter's Christian readers who are now understood to be the people of God. The terms *parepidēmoi* and *paroikoi* are similarly understood as descriptions applied metaphorically first to ancient Israel and now to Christians. Clowney (1988: 228), for instance, believes "the figurative meaning that is clearly present offers ample ground for setting aside the literal meaning" of the terms. Achtemeier (1989: 228), arguing against J. H. Elliott, concludes that "this phrase [*paroikoi*] is drawn not from the political arena of the Greco-Roman world to describe the political status of the readers . . . but rather is again chosen under the influence of the controlling metaphor, the chosen people, and applied to Christians." While the figurative sense of the description of the addressees is apt, the letter must nevertheless have had some particular social and historical setting, and there must have been some precipitating occasion for its writing. Whatever metaphorical sense these terms carry for the Christian life need not exclude some literal sense related to the letter's original historical circumstances. This study presents an alternative sociopolitical background from which the metaphorical sense derived its power for this particular group of people to whom the letter was originally addressed.

Discussions of Jewish or Gentile Christians and literal or figurative foreigners have proceeded from the unquestioned assumption that the Christians addressed were native to Asia Minor and had been converted to Christ in their native residence. This assumption raises the issue of how conversions over such a vast area of about 129,000 square miles occurred when there is not a shred of extant historical evidence of first-century evangelism in most of the regions mentioned, much less of apostolic evangelism. The assumption has been that Christianity came to northern Asia Minor by one or more unknown traveling evangelists. Some speculate this was possibly Peter himself or his associates from Jerusalem (Brown and Meier 1983: 131). Others propose a gradual evangelization through believers from the Pauline churches, since Paul himself was explicitly forbidden by the Spirit to enter Bithynia (Acts 16:6–10), and there is no evidence he ever traveled most of the area addressed.

4. See in the LXX: Gen. 15:13; 23:4; Exod. 2:22; Lev. 25:23; Deut. 23:8 (23:7 Eng.); 1 Chron. 29:15; Ps. 38:13 (39:12 Eng.); 104:12–13 (105:12–13 Eng.); 118:19 (119:19 Eng.).

The assumption that Christianity came to northern Asia Minor through the conversion of indigenous people has led to the inference that Christianity spread gradually throughout this area. Thurén (1990: 31) writes that 1 Peter "presupposes a *situatio* in the Christian mission which was hardly achieved before 60 AD." The gradual evangelization of these areas of Asia Minor demands a date for 1 Peter much later than the mid-60s (the death of Peter) and possibly as late as the time of Domitian (S. Johnson 1975: 116). On the other hand, Pliny's writings (ca. AD 110) imply persecution of Christians by the Roman authorities that had been present to some extent for at least twenty years (Pliny, *Letters* 10.96.6). This implies that by the late 80s or early 90s there must have been a critical mass of Christians who had come to the attention of society and of the authorities.

Those who speculate that the apostle Peter himself evangelized these areas often raise the concern about Peter working in areas that may have overlapped with Paul's mission work in the provinces of Galatia and Asia, although most of the regions addressed lie outside Paul's area of activity. Selwyn (1958: 61) has theorized that Paul was forbidden to enter this area (Acts 16:6–10) specifically because Peter was already at work there. Perhaps as Peter gradually made his way westward from Jerusalem toward his death in Rome twenty-some years later, he passed through these remote areas and later wrote to the Christian converts he left behind there. If so, it is strange that nothing in 1 Peter alludes to such travels or to a firsthand knowledge of any of the areas addressed. Furthermore, 1:12 seems to imply that others had preached the gospel to Peter's original readers. Moreover, if Peter did travel to these places, his effort would have to have been quite extraordinary, for the shortest route across Asia Minor from the east to the major western port of Ephesus, and on to Corinth or Rome, was the southern Roman road traveled by Paul. That route would have taken him south of the Taurus Mountains, bypassing most of Galatia and avoiding Bithynia, Pontus, and Cappadocia altogether. Furthermore, if the apostle Peter had been the founder of Christianity in northern Asia Minor, it is more than curious that not even a hint of that apostolic heritage has survived in textual form from such a vast area that later became a center of Christianity.

Given the complete lack of historical evidence, the conversion of these regions through evangelization in situ is inference based on sheer speculation. Perhaps the alternative possibility should be considered: that the Christians to whom Peter writes had become Christians elsewhere, had some association with Peter prior to his writing to them, and now found themselves foreigners and resident aliens scattered throughout Asia Minor. Peter writes a word of encouragement, using their life experience to explain that all Christians, regardless of their geographical residence, become foreigners and resident aliens in some sense by virtue of their conversion to Christ. If so, Peter would be transforming the

Not only were those deported from Rome often "foreigners" (i.e., not citizens of Rome), but they were often viewed as foreigners at their destination as well. Because colonists immigrating from Rome generally benefited from resources often confiscated from the local indigenous population and because colonists enjoyed the official sanction of Rome, they were naturally viewed as foreigners by the native populations, and at times with great resentment (Mitchell 1993: 1.178; Salmon 1970: 150). Sometimes colonists even became a target of violence and persecution by the native population (Magie 1950: 1.548; Salmon 1970: 150). By virtue of being Roman colonists, the people who settled in the colonies were granted some category of Roman rights (often Latin rights), if not full Roman citizenship (Goodman 1997: 136–37; Momigliano 1934: 66–67; Scramuzza 1940: 143; Stevenson 1939: 166). However, because cities reserved the right to bestow local citizenship, even colonists with Roman citizenship were not automatically made citizens in the city in which they found themselves living as colonists until they earned it or bought it through benefaction. And even Roman citizens could be quite poor, since citizenship provided a legal status that did not reflect economic or social standing (Alston 1998: 215). Moreover, upper-class provincials who were citizens of their city but were foreigners with respect to Roman citizenship nevertheless tended to acquire privileges of Roman status even though they may never have technically achieved Roman citizenship (Goodman 1997: 136–37; Sherwin-White 1974: 254). Hence, citizenship in the Roman period was a complicated issue, and therefore the word "foreigner" could be applied in various contexts to various people depending on the reference point. This resulted in complex social relationships accompanied by serious tensions that played out differently between citizens and noncitizens, free and slave, rich and poor in each city (Garnsey 1974: 159–65; Sherwin-White 1974: 254; Levick 1967: 189; MacMullen 1974; Mitchell 1993: 1.177–78; Rostovtzeff 1971: 318–19).

Disputed entitlements, such as land rights, were one way the problem of foreignness played out (Rostovtzeff 1926: 255, 319). From the perspective of Roman colonists, native inhabitants of the territory around the colonized cities had no share in the form of government recognized as Roman and were therefore viewed as "by-dwellers" (Latin: *incolae*; Gk.: *katoikoi*, or possibly *paroikoi*) with respect to the newly established Roman colony (Clausing 1925: 203, 217–18; Rostovtzeff 1971: 250, 334). J. H. Elliott (1981: 2000) has argued that, as *paroikoi* (2:11), all the recipients of 1 Peter were converted to Christianity from among these rural, disenfranchised native populations, who lived in relative poverty. The primary objection to Elliott's specific social reconstruction has been that the relationships between the social and economic classes in first-century Asia Minor are too complex, and the terms that refer to them are understood too imprecisely, to validate Elliott's hypothesis

(Achtemeier 1984: 130–33; Achtemeier 1989: 216–17; Bechtler 1998: 17, 206; Dalton 1983: 442–44; Danker 1983: 84–88; Hemer 1985: 120–23). Furthermore, Peter's exhortation that their women not adorn themselves with gold jewelry and fine clothes (3:3) would seem a cruel mockery if addressed to subsistence peasants. Clowney (1988: 227–28) objects that *parepidēmoi* "cannot serve as a primarily sociological description of all the Christian churches over such a vast area." Moreover, it cannot be assumed that the *paroikoi* inhabiting the rural regions could read Greek, for most people in these regions retained their own languages (Rostovtzeff 1926: 346). Although Elliott's theory has not gained wide acceptance, it does rightly call attention to the largely overlooked issue of the historical and social realities that motivated the letter, especially if the later dating during Trajan's reign has been abandoned (see "Date and Authorship" above).

Expulsion from Rome under Claudius. Claudius was not only aggressive in colonization; for political reasons he was also a champion of the Roman gods and a conservative when it came to religious policy (Scramuzza 1940: 145, 150). Beginning with Augustus, the expansion of the empire over other cultures and the need for imperial unity forced a certain official tolerance of "superstitions" and other religions. "The cardinal point of that policy was to grant hospitality to foreign religions, but to consider them a menace the moment they took advantage of that courtesy to disturb the public peace, offend accepted morals, or *engage in converting native Romans*" (Scramuzza 1940: 151–52, emphasis added). When the empire expanded under Claudius to Gaul and Britain, Claudius warred against Druidism, outlawing it as an unacceptable religion because of its practice of human sacrifice (Levick 1990: 170–72). Astrology for divination was gaining great popularity in Rome, and the seers of Egypt and Babylon were being preferred to the native Italian diviners. These foreigners were expelled from Italy time and time again, and once more by Claudius (Scramuzza 1940: 147–48; Momigliano 1934: 28).

The most famous Roman expulsion occurred during the reign of Claudius toward the end of the fifth decade AD. As the Roman historian Suetonius tells us, *Iudaeos impulsore Chresto assidue tumultuantis Roma expulit* ("since the Jews constantly made disturbances at the instigation of Chrestus, he [Claudius] expelled them from Rome"; Suetonius, *Claudius* 4; Rolfe 1939), an event corroborated by Acts 18:2. The name *Chrestus* has been taken as a reference to Christ, but some historians argue against this understanding (e.g., Slingerland 1989b). Current knowledge does not allow the issue to be decided with certainty, though the corruption of the same vowel also appears in early anti-Christian graffiti (Marucchi 1949: 21). The exact year of this expulsion is debated, but it apparently came several years after Claudius forbade "the Jews" to assemble in AD 41, according to Cassius Dio (*Roman History* 60.6.6).

An expulsion of Jews from Rome in AD 49 fits well the chronology in Acts 18:2, which mentions Priscilla and Aquila's arrival in Corinth after being forced to leave Rome. However, Slingerland (1992) argues that Jews were expelled from Rome by Claudius more than once. The historical evidence suggests that the fourteen-year reign of Claudius was a difficult time for Jews living in Rome.

The problem among "the Jews" in Rome was happening about the same time Claudius was upholding the Jews' right to city citizenship in Alexandria (AD 41) and while he was relieving Jews throughout the empire of the oppressive edicts of his predecessor Gaius Caligula (Josephus, *Ant.* 19.280–87). For this reason some historians call Suetonius's historical accuracy into question, believing that Claudius actually held a pro-Jewish policy, which might have prevented the kind of expulsion that Suetonius records. Claudius, however, upheld the Jews' entitlements to freedom of worship, residence, and business in Gentile cities provided that they did not undermine the religious and political rights of their Gentile neighbors (Scramuzza 1940: 151; Momigliano 1934: 34–38). Evangelistic Christians, whether of Jewish or of Gentile origin, could be accused of violating all three points of Claudius's policy on religious tolerance: disturbing the public peace, possibly by their street preaching (as Paul seemed to do wherever he went); offending accepted morals (biblical morals being so different from those accepted by pagan society); and engaging in converting native Romans (which was the hallmark of first-century Christianity, as attested by the explosion of the church in those early decades).

Scramuzza (1940: 151), who is a historian and not a biblical scholar, understands the expulsion of the "Jews" from Rome in the late 40s to have been the expulsion only of prominent Christians. There were about fifty thousand Jews in Rome at that time, probably too many for Claudius to expel en masse, and so some selected group of lesser numbers was probably targeted (Momigliano 1934: 31). Moreover, in the 40s Christianity was still viewed by Romans as a sect of Judaism. This might explain how Suetonius's reference to the expulsion of "Jews" could have included Christians, whether they were of Gentile or Jewish origin. But Acts 18:2 refers to the expulsion of "the Jews," and Luke would certainly have distinguished between Jews and Christians. The example of Gallio indiscriminately driving away both Jew and Christian in Corinth when charges were brought against Paul may indicate the indifferent treatment that Jewish-Christian tensions provoked (Acts 18:12–17). Similarly, Claudius's expulsion of the Jews, for whatever reason, could have included Christians, but was probably not specifically targeted at Christians *as Christians*.

Peter in Rome? Recently, Botermann (1996: 127) has argued that Claudius became more hostile to the Jews of Rome because of trouble among them that resulted specifically from the preaching of the apostle

Peter in the early 40s. Tradition does associate Peter with Rome long before his death there during the reign of Nero (see O'Connor 1969 for an extensive discussion of the literary, liturgical, and archaeological evidence). A reference in Ignatius (Ign. *Rom.* 4.3) is sometimes cited as early-second-century evidence that Peter not only died in Rome but had also resided there, yet it actually says nothing to the question. It was not until the third century that the tradition of Peter's twenty-five-year episcopate in Rome developed (O'Connor 1975: 147). Since the time of the Reformation, Protestants have rejected this tradition because it has been used to validate apostolic succession for the Roman papacy. Moreover, both Catholic and Protestant scholars view the tradition with skepticism, since neither the NT nor any other contemporary, extant documents directly validate its historical accuracy, and the later Christian documents, such as Eusebius's *Ecclesiastical History*, seem to be based more on inference than on historical knowledge. However, the absence of extant historical validation does not necessarily disprove that Peter had an early association with, if not residence in, the imperial city. Furthermore, even if Peter arrived in Rome in the early 40s, it does not mean that he held a supreme bishopric there or that Peter was founder of the church at Rome.

Wenham (1972), following Balleine, argues that when Peter was released from prison in Jerusalem and fled to "another place" about AD 42 (Acts 12:17), that place was Rome (also Thiede 1988: 155). The almost unanimous opinion of scholarship, both Catholic and Protestant, has dismissed this scenario as "wholly unhistorical" and "quite inconsistent with known facts," as J. B. Lightfoot concludes (cited in Wenham 1972: 95–96). Nevertheless, Wenham (1972), Thiede (1988), and Botermann (1996) are recent scholars who argue in similar terms for Peter's early arrival in Rome during the reign of Claudius.

Following Harnack's dating of Acts to AD 62, Wenham (1972) argues that Luke cryptically refers to Peter's fleeing to "another place" (Acts 12:17) to avoid disadvantaging his defense of Paul to Roman authorities (also Thiede 1988: 154). Moreover, a cryptic reference would also protect the knowledge of Peter's whereabouts, given that he was a fugitive from Roman law in Jerusalem, though this was probably less necessary by the time Acts was written. O'Connor (1969: 10) argues that the term could simply refer to another house in the same area, but agrees that the cryptic nature of the reference could be a security measure. Moreover, Peter's covert presence in Rome does give a reason for his cryptic reference to "Babylon" in 1 Pet. 5:13, if he was intending to avoid revealing his personal location. (The association of "Babylon" with Rome that is found in later Jewish apocalyptic literature is arguably not the same reason for its use in 1 Peter. See "Date and Authorship" above and comments on 5:13.) Just as the Jews had been driven out of Jerusalem and sent into exile in Babylon by their oppressors, Peter had also been driven out of

Jerusalem by persecution and is sojourning in exile in the capital city of his oppressors. Given the good Roman system of transportation, Peter could have fled to any number of places around the Mediterranean, but in fact the only place that claims any association with Peter is Rome.

The primary argument against Peter's presence in Rome in the 40s is silence. There is no early historical evidence that would indicate his presence, but there is also no historical evidence that contradicts the possibility or that offers an alternative. R. Brown is among those scholars who consider the absence of any mention of Peter's early presence in Rome by Luke in Acts or by Paul in Romans to imply that Peter did not first reach Rome until the early to mid-60s (Brown and Meier 1983: 103). Even J. B. Lightfoot bases his conclusion on silence: "If silence can ever be regarded as decisive its verdict must be accepted in this case" (quoted in Wenham 1972: 96). Inference from silence is always precarious, and while the silence in Acts about Peter's whereabouts is curious, it does not disprove Peter's early presence in Rome, especially if there is now some possible historical connection between Claudius and the original destination of 1 Peter.

As Wenham (1972) points out, a twenty-five-year period of Peter's association with Rome fits neatly between the period from Agrippa's reign in Palestine (AD 41–44) and Nero's death in AD 68, corresponding respectively to Peter's flight from Jerusalem and his execution by Nero. In the absence of a competing theory, most NT scholars at least acknowledge the strong tradition that Peter died during Nero's reign in Rome about 66–67. Ramsay (1893: 283) alone argues that Peter actually survived Nero's reign and lived to write 1 Peter about AD 80, but his theory is merely noted as a curiosity by other scholars.

Moreover, Peter's first arrival in Rome in the early 40s would explain how the tradition of a twenty-five-year Roman episcopate from AD 42 to 67 arose. Eusebius may only be inferring that Peter resided and held office in Rome for the full extent of the apostle's traditional association with Rome. However, the earliest use of the term ἐπίσκοπος (episkopos, overseer) referred not to the ecclesiastical office of bishop, as it later came to mean, but to leadership of the church more generally (as the related participle is probably used in 5:2; see comments). As Wenham (1972: 97) points out, "If Peter twenty-five years before his death worked for a time in Rome and kept in touch with the church thereafter, he could rightly have been regarded as its overseer." While Peter's association with Rome may have begun shortly after he fled Jerusalem, and ended with his death there, it is not necessary to conclude that he spent the entire twenty-five years in residence or that he held any position resembling the later bishopric. Neither the fact that Peter was not in Rome at the end of the decade of the 40s, when he was in Jerusalem and Antioch, nor his apparent absence from Rome in 57, when Paul wrote to the Roman church, proves that he could not have been in Rome previously. It is well documented that people traveled between Rome and the East with relative speed and ease, especially by sea (Casson 1974; Noy 2000: 56). Repeated trips were not uncommon, as documented even among less prosperous Christians. The inscription on the tomb of the craftsman Flavius Zeuxis in Asia Minor records that he had sailed seventy-two times to Rome (Casson 1974: 128; Noy 2000: 56)! The crisis in the early church that created tensions between Jerusalem and Antioch would have provided a motivation for Peter to leave Rome and to make an extended visit to both cities. Moreover, Agrippa's death in 44 would have made it relatively safe for him to do so. Given the time span in view, Peter could have traveled to be present at the Jerusalem Council (Acts 15), in Antioch (Gal. 2:11), and possibly in Corinth as well (1 Cor. 1:12). From consideration of literary and archaeological evidence, Marucchi (1949: 22) concludes that Peter most likely arrived in Rome during the reign of Claudius, between 41 and 54, left when the edict of Claudius was published in about 49, and did not return to Rome again until shortly before his death.

Concerning Peter's association with Corinth, it is worth noting that Priscilla and Aquila arrived in that city after being expelled from Rome by Claudius (Acts 18:2) and that at a later time some in the Corinthian churches had loyalties to Peter (1 Cor. 1:12). Whether Priscilla and Aquila became Christians in Rome or only as the result of Paul's ministry in Corinth is unknown, but the theory that some Christians in Rome who previously knew Peter there ended up in Corinth after the expulsion provides another explanation of Peter's following in the Corinthian church.

But was not Peter in Rome when he wrote the letter? And would that not be unlikely following Claudius's edict? Since most Roman expulsions did not impose a permanent ban, the expelled sometimes returned at a later date after the precipitating crisis had passed. The career of Priscilla and Aquila is one example of the extent of personal travel possible to people who were in the socioeconomic class occupied by tentmakers. Originally from Pontus in Asia Minor, they were expelled from Rome, resided in Corinth, traveled to Ephesus, but were apparently back in residence in Rome when Paul wrote Romans (Rom. 16:3). And so Peter's return to Rome sometime after Claudius's edict would not have been impossible.

A similar problem is the whereabouts of Mark and Silvanus, who are both mentioned as with Peter when he writes (1 Pet. 5:12–13). When and where would all three of them have been together? Some speculate that the three were almost certainly in Rome in the early to mid-60s, possibly soon after Paul's execution. However, the three were also together in the late 40s or early 50s. Both Mark and Silvanus (Silas) resided in Jerusalem before and immediately after the Jerusalem council (Acts 15:22, 36–40). Silas was one of those sent to Antioch from the Jerusalem Council (15:22, 32). Moreover, on one reading of the itinerary in Galatians, Paul's reference to Peter's visit to Antioch would have occurred during the same general time frame (Gal. 2:11–14). Peter, Mark, and Silvanus were in the same location in the early 50s in Jerusalem or Antioch and in the early to mid-60s in Rome, providing two opportunities during Peter's lifetime for 1 Peter to have been written.

A further lexical consideration. In addition to the historical considerations, a lexical point from the text of 1 Peter must be considered in light of this theory. The major "qualification" for deportation from Rome was the lack of Roman citizenship (although citizenship was sometimes granted to some colonists who volunteered to relocate). Roman citizenship was such a key to entitlements that Claudius made it a capital crime to impersonate a Roman citizen (Levick 1990: 165; Noy 2000: 24). People who were not Roman citizens were referred to in Latin as *peregrini*, usually translated in English as "foreigners." However, the semantic range of the English word does not fit the semantic specificity of the Latin term. *Peregrinus* "was primarily a legal term for someone who was free but not a Roman citizen," but it said nothing about one's social class, economic standing, or place of origin (Noy 2000: 1). As Noy points out, a *peregrinus* could be from a family who had lived in Rome for generations and spoke only Latin but still lacked citizenship. Conversely, a Roman citizen might not speak any Latin and might never have set foot inside the city of Rome but have acquired citizenship in the imperial city by inheritance, purchase, or manumission. Moreover, "people who were born at Rome could still be considered 'foreign,' by themselves and others, if their attachment to another place (the birthplace of their ancestors, or the centre of their religion) seemed greater than their attachment to the city of Rome" (Noy 2000: xii). But when push came to shove in Rome or other urban areas during times of famine or other duress, it was the *peregrinus* who was in jeopardy of being expelled, regardless of how long he had lived there. Eventually, in the fourth century, the term *peregrinus* was used as the label to refer specifically to the "foreigners" (noncitizens) who were expelled (Noy 2000: 1). To confuse the sense of the term with the semantic range of the English word "foreigner" even further, within the Christian context, *peregrinus* later came to be vested with the sense of "pilgrim." Interestingly, the Greek equivalent of the Latin term *peregrinus* is παρεπίδημος (*parepidēmos*, foreigner), the very term used to describe those addressed in 1 Pet. 1:1.[6]

While the use of *parepidēmos* in 1:1 does not prove that the original recipients of 1 Peter had been deported from Rome, it is certainly consistent with the colonization theory. Moreover, by suggesting that not all Christians of Asia Minor would have been described by the same sociological term, it answers the objection Clowney (1988: 228) raises

---

6. Scapula 1820: s.v. *peregrinus*; Bergren 1991: 116; Schmoller 1989: 386.

to taking the term literally. Because Peter's original readers were not citizens of the dominant power, they had been displaced and consequently found themselves outsiders both in Rome and in their new location. In effect, they were outsiders in their world, which is exactly the point that allows the metaphorical interpretation of Christians as sojourning pilgrims to emerge. This understanding may have actually contributed to the semantic shift of *peregrinus* to "pilgrim" in Christian contexts, reinforcing the metaphorical reference to the Christian life as a journey toward heaven, even though the word apparently did not bear that sense in the first century.

Roman colonization and 1 Peter. If the theory of Roman colonization is correct, Peter uses the sociohistorical situation of his readers to explain their sociospiritual situation. In 1:1 they are addressed as "foreigners," noncitizens, with respect to their society, but as *chosen* by God. In 2:11 Peter begins to exploit the sociopolitical situation of his readers in such a way as to describe Christian living more generally (see comments on 2:11). Once the letter circulated away from its original historical destination, the figurative sense naturally emerged as the predominant understanding. Although Peter's readers may in fact have been resident aliens and strangers in Asia Minor, the cause of their deeper alienation from society is their faith in Christ (which may have been why they were deported from Rome as disruptive "Jews" in the first place). Because they are citizens of the kingdom of God, they are to understand themselves as resident aliens and foreigners wherever they may be residing.

Peter explains to these socially alienated Christians that although they may be rejected in the eyes of their society because of their commitment to Christ—perhaps doubly so, if that was the cause of their expulsion from Rome—they are in fact chosen by God and fully entitled to the promise and inheritance of his kingdom. Moreover, these two concepts are concomitant in 1 Peter: to be chosen by God and committed to Christ is *by definition* to become a visiting foreigner and resident alien in the world and thereby disenfranchised from its entitlements that are based on undivided allegiance to its gods.

According to Peter, however, because they are Christians, their disadvantaged social status does not really matter. Having been chosen by God, they are participants in the new birth (1:3) that brings them into a new family and consequently bestows a new citizenship that is privileged beyond anything Rome or its provinces can offer. For all the glory of Rome is but as the grass and the flower of the field, which fades and falls (1:24). But the word of God, which has germinated within them their faith in Christ, stands forever. One need only look at the ruins in Rome today and the vitality of the Christian church throughout the world to see this truth in historical perspective.

The explanatory power of the theory of Roman colonization. Could it be, then, that a sizable number of Christians went, either voluntarily or by force, to help populate Claudius's newly established colonies in Asia Minor? Because of Peter's association with Rome, he writes to them after their emigration to encourage them in the faith and to instruct them how to live as Christians in their new and trying situation.

This theory is based on several points of historical evidence: (1) Claudius, and perhaps only Claudius, established colonies in *every one* of the five regions to which 1 Peter is addressed. (2) Colonies were typically populated by deportations from Rome and other urban centers. (3) There is the historical evidence of Roman writers of the first and second centuries indicating that Claudius did expel people in some way associated with "Chrestus." (4) Peter is the stated author of 1 Peter. (5) The ancient tradition that places Peter in Rome during the reign of Claudius continues to be cogently argued (Botermann 1996; Thiede 1988; Wenham 1972). Even if Peter wrote in the 60s, the colonization of Roman Christians still provides a motivation for a letter to these remote regions.

Most commentators seem quite content to see the motif of foreignness to the world in 1 Peter as simply and exhaustively a metaphor for the Christian pilgrimage through this life. They feel that the spiritual application is sufficient to motivate and justify the metaphor. Perhaps that is true, but it seems odd that the entire book of 1 Peter is both framed (1:1; cf. 5:13) and saturated with the terms of exile and foreignness (e.g., the extensive use of Ps. 33 LXX [34 Eng.], a psalm of deliverance from sojourning as a foreigner). Moreover, 1 Peter is the only NT book to use the motif of foreignness to explain the life of the Christian with respect to society. Paul's use of the foreigner motif in Eph. 2:19 is somewhat different, since it refers to Gentiles, who as Christians are no longer foreigners with respect to God's people. This is a different thought, though not incompatible with the concept that as Christians Peter's readers have become foreigners with respect to the larger reference group of society. The nature and extent of the "foreigner" metaphor in 1 Peter are better explained if it was triggered by a real event or experience instead of just being pulled out of thin air.

One of the tests of a new theory is how well it explains issues that were puzzling or not addressed under the old theory. Looking at 1 Peter in the context of Roman colonization explains a number of issues. The strong Jewish character of 1 Peter would be explained not only because the author was himself a Jewish Christian but also because the defining experience of his original readers was their expulsion from Rome as "Jews" regardless of whether they were previously Jewish or Gentile. Peter addresses them as of the "Diaspora" of Asia Minor (1:1) because they literally have been scattered and because as Christians they are now, both in the eyes of the pagans who expelled them and in spiritual reality, joined to the ancient people of God. If his readers were Jewish Christians from Rome but perhaps included Gentile converts among them, the puzzle is solved of how indigenous Gentiles of Asia Minor could be expected to understand Peter's theology based on the presumption of familiarity with the LXX. Otherwise, it is difficult to imagine that before the NT existed, scattered people who had come to faith in Christ without the presence of an apostle could be well enough acquainted with interpreting the Scriptures to have caught the theological relevance of Peter's many allusions to, and quotations from, both the OT and the teachings of Jesus. Greek would have been the common language of Peter and the Roman Christians, which eliminates the obstacle of the diverse indigenous languages of Asia Minor. Moreover, if Peter resided in Rome for a time, his own Greek proficiency would have increased markedly by using that language daily, and his exposure to Roman rhetoric would have presented opportunity for his own writing to be generally shaped by its structure. It would also more easily explain Peter's familiarity with Seneca's proverb alluded to in the fiery trial image, since Seneca was the most public literary figure in Rome during the middle of the first century (see comments on 1:7 and 4:12).

If Peter wrote in the early 50s, that would have been the period between Paul's first and third missionary journeys. This may explain why 1 Peter does not address regions visited on Paul's first missionary journey but seems to include some of those in western Asia Minor that were later evangelized on Paul's third journey. It also explains how Peter could write to residents of Asia Minor without violating the agreement to be an apostle to the Jews (Gal. 2:8–9), though that distinction cannot be pressed absolutely. It also may explain why Peter does not write to the ἐκκλησία (ekklēsia, church) of specific cities, for his letter reflects a time when only unstructured groups of Christians resided as scattered enclaves throughout these regions. The knowledge of where the Roman colonies were located would have provided a sufficiently specific destination for a messenger to know where to deliver the letter, since no specific destinations or names are given in the letter itself. Moreover, the somewhat odd reference to elders "among" you in 1 Pet. 5:1 could reflect the same undeveloped structure (see comments on 5:1). Perhaps these individuals had been elders in their previous location but were uncertain of their role and responsibility now that they found themselves living among fellow-Christians but without a well-organized church to oversee. This would explain Peter's somewhat unusual instructions that elders should "shepherd" the believers (which would have been stating the obvious in a well-established church) and why he must instruct the younger to respect their leadership (see comments on 5:1–5).

If Roman colonization were the means by which Christianity first came to these regions, it would also explain why no evangelist's name is associated with the church in northern Asia Minor. If Peter had an

munal identity as the elect and holy people of God which sets it apart from its society" (J. H. Elliott 1998: 183). Their abandonment of socially acceptable but morally bankrupt practices incarnates the Christian's new identity as God's chosen, providing the opportunity for society to view them with suspicion, mistrust, and disapproval. Nevertheless, they are not to feel shame or doubt because of the way their society responds to them, for the kind of suffering they are experiencing is God's will (4:19) and an indication that the Spirit of God rests upon them (4:14). Thus, the Spirit's sanctifying work (1:2) sets the chosen apart by their acceptance of the word of God preached to them (1:12). Consequently, they are willing to distinguish themselves from the values and customs of their society even though it may mean suffering for their convictions.

2. *Suffering for being a Christian*. When God's call to holiness (1:15) conflicts with the values and morals of social practice, Christians devoted to that call may expect to experience verbal abuse, slander, malicious talk, and other forms of persecution that Peter summarizes as "to suffer grief in all kinds of trials" (1:6). Christians rejoice greatly in the living hope secured by the resurrection of Jesus Christ, which will eventually and certainly be theirs. Even so, Peter sees an inevitable suffering in this life as one lives by new, eschatological values in this old, fallen world. Peter's exhortation to trust in God as Father and faithful Creator in the midst of suffering may be more broadly applied to those suffering from all sources, such as bereavement, illness, the vicissitudes of aging, and even the consequences of sin. However, to address the specific issues of the original readers, the apostle carefully delimits the type of suffering in view to that caused by persecution for nothing other than bearing the name of Christ (4:14–16).

The problem of suffering this kind of grief in the workplace, the public forum, and even the home motivates Peter to explain why suffering grief for being a Christian should not be surprising but is to be expected as a normal part of Christian life. The destiny of Christ is the destiny of the Christian in 1 Peter. A godless society can be expected to reject the Christian for the same reasons it rejected Christ. Therefore, the Christian community is to be an alternate society, a Christian colony, where believers find brotherly love, compassion, and sympathy (3:8). Together, Christians are the living stones that form the spiritual house of God, offering spiritual sacrifices to him (2:4). Christian calling, identity, and purpose are all therefore found in God's redemptive plan, which transforms the believers' relationship with the world and their self-understanding of their place within it.

3. *First Peter's concept of God*. Though Peter's readers are foreigners in their society, the trinitarian God has chosen them according to the foreknowledge of the Father, through the sanctifying work of the Spirit, and for the purpose of participating in the covenant based on the blood of Jesus Christ (1:2). Jesus Christ is the central focus of 1 Peter's theology.

Even the Godhead is introduced in relation to Jesus Christ: God is the God and Father of Jesus Christ (1:3), and the Spirit is the Spirit of Christ (see comments on 1:11). Although 1 Peter is certainly a theocentric letter, it is nonetheless true that it is just as much a christocentric work.

Divine fatherhood is the controlling concept of God in 1 Peter. God is first introduced as the Father of our Lord Jesus Christ (1:3). God has become the Father of Christians by virtue of the new birth generated by his imperishable seed, which is his living and enduring word (1:3; 1:23). God's nature is introduced as merciful (1:3). God's redemptive work to create a redeemed people flows from his mercy (2:10). The existence of the Christian church is, therefore, the evidence of the effectiveness of God's mercy.

God the Father is nevertheless God the impartial Judge of each one's life (1:17). Therefore, those who reject his mercy will one day face him as the Judge of their deeds. Christians, however, have already received God's mercy by virtue of their faith in the redemption Christ has won and therefore face God's judgment confident of their deliverance from his condemnation. The new birth, however, does not give believers license to live as they wish but enjoins them to live as obedient children of God the Father, who will judge each one's life impartially (1:14; 2:1). Strangely enough, Peter teaches that God's judgment of all humanity begins with those of God's own house (see comments on 4:17–18).

Although, by virtue of their faith in Christ, believers have received God's mercy, for that same reason they should not be surprised if they are scorned by the world. This kind of suffering because of their new identity is not outside God's will for his people (4:19). Because God is also Creator, and therefore sovereign over all people and situations, suffering Christians are to entrust themselves to their faithful Creator and continue to do good and to live as obedient children of the Father, who will have the final say (4:19). For God has called the Christian ultimately not to suffering but to eternal glory, which will vindicate and establish those who live by faith in Christ (5:10).

4. Jesus Christ in 1 Peter. The work of the trinitarian God in 1 Peter extends people mercy, which delivers them from final condemnation. Peter's concept of deliverance from God's condemnation rests upon the sacrificial system of ancient Israel. Christian redemption has been provided not with perishable things that have limited value but with the precious blood of a perfect lamb, Jesus Christ (1:18–19).

The work of the Holy Spirit is presented in relation to this sacrificial death of Jesus Christ. First, it was "the Spirit of Christ" who revealed to Israel's prophets in ages past that the Christ would have to suffer before entering into his glory (see comments on 1:10–12). Peter reassures his readers that Jesus Christ is integrally related to the work of God's Spirit throughout the history of ancient Israel. The gospel of Jesus Christ is not a new religion or something separate from the redemptive work of

Israel's Yahweh. Rather, Jesus Christ is foundational to God's redemptive work because the Father's foreknowledge and the Spirit's sanctifying work terminate in the covenant between God and people that was established by Christ's blood (1:2). The sanctifying work of the Holy Spirit does not draw one into some generic spirituality but into the covenant with God in Jesus Christ that stands as the culmination of God's work and revelation throughout all history. By raising Christ from the dead, God created the eternal new life into which he gives people new birth (1:3). To believe in the resurrected Christ is therefore to have faith and hope in God (1:21).

Christ is not only essential to the new birth but is central to the Christian's new life. In 1 Peter, Christ's response to suffering at the world's hands is the exemplar of godly suffering, which all Christians are called to accept (2:21–25). The call to follow in the footsteps of Jesus is a call to choose in every decision not to disobey God, even though certain suffering may result. As Schlatter (1999: 52) writes, "The cross does not merely set the community free from punishment; it turns it away from evil, providing it with the norm to which it must remain obedient. For Jesus showed believers by his death how they too should serve and suffer (1:17–20; 2:21–24; 3:18)." In 1 Peter the Christian life is very much the way of the cross.

Therefore, the theology of 1 Peter does not highlight the preexistence of Jesus as in John's Gospel, or the teachings of Jesus as in the Synoptic Gospels—although these concepts are assumed. It is specifically the rejection that Jesus suffered unto death that is the focal point of Peter's Christology, presented as (1) the basis of the new covenant (1:1–3), (2) the price of redemption (1:18–25), (3) the substitution of himself in death for the sins of others (2:21–25), and (4) reconciliation with God (3:18).

But the footsteps of Jesus do not end at the tomb—hallelujah! They continue on to the glory of eternal life. God vindicates Jesus by raising him from the dead (1:21), and that vindication of Jesus to resurrection life is the assurance that those who follow him will also be vindicated despite the mockery and scorn of the world. Christ's resurrection and ascension find a central role in Peter's Christology as the proclamation of victory over all the powers that oppose God (see comments on 3:18–22). In Christ's resurrection the endgame has been played. Christ ascends alive forevermore to take his rightful place over all angels, powers, and authorities in submission to him. Though rejected and executed by the world, Christ's vindication by his resurrection secures the vindication of those who are rejected by the world because of their belief in him. He is the great Shepherd of God's sheep (2:25), who love him and rejoice in his victory (1:8–9).

The resurrected Jesus, Messiah of Israel, is the stone God has placed in Zion, a cornerstone of his redemptive building project, into which believers are built as living stones (2:4–5). However, those who reject

God's mercy in Christ are building on another foundation. To them, Christ becomes a stone of stumbling and condemnation (2:6–8). In the theology of 1 Peter, God's relationship to all humanity, not just to Christians, is centered on relationship to Christ. Rejection of Christ does not excuse one from the purview of God's judgment. God calls those who accept the gospel of Christ's victory to glory in eternity (5:10).

5. *Salvation in 1 Peter: The christological pattern of the Christian life.* For Peter, salvation is the goal of faith (1:9). Christians are living between the time when God's redemptive work in Christ has been completed by the cross, resurrection, and ascension of Jesus, and the time of final vindication, when God will judge all people based on their response to Christ's gospel. The salvation that comes to Christians through belief in Jesus Christ is, according to Peter, the same salvation foretold by the prophets of ancient Israel who foresaw the sufferings of the Messiah and the glories that would follow (1:10–12). Those prophecies were given ahead of time to confirm the message of the gospel of Jesus Christ, which would come to a later generation (1:12). One of the marks of God's sovereignty is his ability to bring to pass what he has previously announced so long before (Isa. 48:5).

According to Peter, salvation begins with the new birth that occurs when the message of the gospel of Jesus Christ is heard and believed. However, salvation as 1 Peter presents it is not at that point complete. The accomplishment of redemption in the resurrection of Christ *is* a done deal, and that is the objective historical act upon which salvation is based. But in Peter's thinking, the believer's salvation yet lies ahead, to be revealed at the last time (1:5), at God's last appointment with humanity, when he judges all (see "First Peter's Eschatology" below). God's power shields his children by faith until judgment day has passed, when they will claim their final inheritance and enter into eternal glory. Only then would Peter concur that we are indeed saved. As Kendall (1986: 108) observes: "'Salvation,' therefore, embraces past, present, and future. Though salvation is the goal of Christian life, it has been manifested historically in the sufferings and glories of Jesus Christ and constitutes a present reality for those who have received grace in the proclamation of the gospel."

Until then, the grievous trials of this life present opportunities at every turn for the genuineness of faith that leads to salvation to be tested and, hopefully, confirmed (1:7). Faith that is genuine chooses to follow Christ in holy obedience rather than to take the path of least resistance, which results in sin. Suffering for no reason other than for being Christian presents the opportunity for the professing Christian to continue to choose allegiance to Christ even when it means that suffering will continue. Each such opportunity is in effect a reembracing of the gospel. In his forthcoming NT theology, Thielman (2005: 578) writes of 1 Peter:

Willingness to suffer is, therefore, an expression of a far-reaching commitment to a world view different from that of the societies around them. They are focused not on present pleasures but on the end of the present period of time, when their sojourning will be complete . . . and God will bring justice to their oppressors.

Although the way of the cross that leads to salvation is admittedly difficult in a world that scorns the gospel, what, Peter asks, will happen to those who have rejected that hard way for the easier path (4:17–19)? Peter admonishes his readers not to be among them but to continue to persevere in following Christ by doing the right thing and leaving the outcome to God.

Therefore, the "themes of suffering and glory, representing the contours of the Christ-event, offer the framework for the author's understanding of the Christian's life in the world" (Richard 1986: 134). Christ obeyed, suffered, died, was resurrected, and ascended to eternal glory with the Father. Following in Christ's footsteps, the Christian's life is shaped by the same pattern. As named by theologians, all three components of salvation—redemption as past event, sanctification as ongoing process, and glorification as future reality—are present in 1 Peter.

6. First Peter's eschatology. Peter's perspective that salvation is the calling to future eternal glory, based on the past resurrection of Christ and yet to be revealed at the final judgment, structures his eschatology. He goes no further in his description of what lies ahead than the fact that an impartial God will someday judge humanity. One's response of faith to Christ's gospel is the key to deliverance from God's condemnation on that day, for it attests that one has been given new birth.

Parker (1994) has argued that the verses in 1 Peter that have been understood to refer to the eschatological future (1:4b–5, 7, 13; 2:12; 4:13; 5:1) have been misunderstood. In fact, he claims they refer not to the future but to the revelation of Jesus Christ in the *present* life of the Christian: "The important thing about [these] passages . . . is that they all emphasize, not the wonders of a future glory, but the significance of the present possession of Christ" (Parker 1994: 31). While his argument is not convincing, his point about the present relevance of Peter's eschatological perspective is well taken. For Peter is not saying that Christians should complacently suffer through this life because the afterlife will be so much better. Peter's eschatology is not "pie in the sky by and by." Rather, it imparts an ethical quality of life *now* by setting present Christian experience within an eschatological perspective.

Christian ethics must be grounded in a rightly conceived eschatology, for what one believes about the future will largely shape how one will live today. Two reference points frame Peter's eschatology: the new birth based on Christ's resurrection is the alpha point; the final judgment and the glory that follows is the omega point. In between, the new life that

Christians are called to live is a quality of life that is authentically and fully human as God, the Creator and Judge of humanity, has defined it. Such a life is characterized, to borrow a thought from Selwyn (1958: 64), by freedom and responsibility that "are exercised within a cosmic order which has God for its source, its sphere, and its end." The life lived in sin is a subhuman life, deformed by the powers of darkness and failing to achieve its full human potential. The fully human Jesus Christ lived the life that authenticated the relationship of a human being to God at its best. Peter therefore calls Christians to follow in Jesus' footsteps, even though living such a life will no doubt attract the scorn and rejection of those who do not live so, just as Jesus' life did.

For Peter, the persecution of the Christian by the unbeliever is in fact an opportunity for God's judgment to be a present reality (see comments on 4:17). The eschatological judgment begins with God's house because those who profess faith in Christ are the first ones to be tested in God's eschatological sifting of humanity. The testing of persecution that Christians experience throughout history is of one piece with the final eschatological judgment, because it sorts out those who are truly Christ's and remain faithful from those who are not. Eschatological glory is also present in suffering. When insulted because of the name of Christ, the believer is blessed now because the Spirit of glory and of God is present (4:14). Both eschatological judgment and glory are a present reality in the suffering of Christians for the name of Christ.

The resurrection of Jesus Christ's human body to eternal life assures that he has survived the worst that this world can do and that he has outlived the world. Peter seems to expect a reappearance of Christ associated with God's final judgment, for he writes that when the "Chief Shepherd" appears, elders who have faithfully served their calling will then receive the eternal crown of glory (5:4). Not only the elders but all believers will receive the imperishable, unspoiled, and unfading inheritance that is now kept in heaven until "the last time" (1:3–5). This eschatological perspective is to be the source of Christian joy *now* and the motivation for Christian living *now*.

Peter understands the end of all things to be near (4:7). His statement is not so much one of timing as it is a warning of urgency. Because God's judgment is near, Christians must be clear-minded and self-controlled for the purpose of prayer. This is no time to be distracted and captured by the things of the world that have no permanent value. Therefore, Peter's eschatology of the judgment and vindication that lead to the eternal glory secured by Christ serves his exhortations to Christian living now. Christians can now bear the ridicule and injustice that may come to them for believing that Jesus is resurrected, because in the end it will be shown to all people to be true. Christians can bear any disadvantage now because of the certainty of their eternal inheritance. For the willingness to persevere through injustice now can be sustained only when ultimate justice is certain. For this reason, Peter emphasizes that God will condemn those who, by persecuting Christians for their faith, show that they reject the gospel that Christians embrace as Truth.

These promises of the living hope provide incentive for persevering in faith when the attractions or the ridicule of society tempt one to deny the new birth in Christ and live as unbelievers do, without godly hope and without a moral compass. Peter's eschatological perspective motivates a Christian life of witness and engagement, not of withdrawal and nonparticipation, so that "Gentiles" may be won before the day of God's judgment (2:12). Therefore, in 1 Peter, how the Christian is to live in the historical situation of the moment is viewed from the eschatological perspective, which has already been realized in the resurrection of Jesus and has begun to be realized in individual lives through the new birth.

7. *The early and creative nature of 1 Peter's theology.* One of the complaints made by scholars examining 1 Peter is how Peter's theological interests have so often been subsumed and read through the lens of Paul's theology (Parker 1994: 31; Thurén 1995: 210). In fact, when the literary dependence of 1 Peter upon Paul was assumed, Peter's epistle was viewed as a mere footnote to Pauline theology. Many scholars now contend that the affinities between Peter and Paul are best explained as both authors independently drawing upon common Christian tradition (see "First Peter's Dependence on Paul" above). This move has allowed the creativity of Peter's theology to be appreciated.

First Peter offers some ideas that are unique to the NT and demonstrate the theological and interpretive creativity of its author (Schlatter 1999: 65). The most striking contribution to Christology is Peter's identification of Jesus with the Suffering Servant of Isa. 52:13–53:12 (hereafter referred to simply as Isa. 53). Although this passage of Isaiah is quoted numerous times in the NT, we can thank Peter alone for the familiar Christian tradition that identifies Jesus with the Suffering Servant of Isa. 53 (cf. 1 Pet. 1:10–12). (The identification of Jesus and Isaiah's Suffering Servant is implied in Acts 8:32–35, but it is not developed there.) Peter exegetes Jesus' death in light of Isa. 53—and not vice versa—for the sequence of 1 Pet. 2:21–24 follows the passion story of Jesus and not the sequence of Isa. 53 (Achtemeier 1996: 193; Goppelt 1993: 211).

This focus on the suffering of Jesus and the need to explain it in terms of the OT Scripture may suggest a time when the crucifixion still remained a vivid memory in the church. As Selwyn (1958: 91) notes: "St. Paul has nothing corresponding to those intimate touches of detail with which St. Peter describes Him, 'who, when he was reviled, reviled not again; when he suffered, he threatened not.' Nor is anything similar to be found in any other Epistle."

Another unique contribution to Christology is Peter's statement in 3:18–22 that presents Christ's victory in his resurrection and ascension in relation to the imprisoned spirits of Noah's generation (see comments on 3:18–22). R. P. Martin (1994: 94) cites this as a "rudimentary version of the more elaborated Christological saga in I Tim. 3.16."

Third, the use of the OT stone passages understood to be references to the Messiah are extended to present a concept of Christian believers as living stones being built into a spiritual building with Christ as the living cornerstone (2:4–8). This beautiful image is unique to 1 Peter in the NT.

All of these concepts and images contribute to the development of early Christian theology and can be attributed to Peter's reinterpretation of the OT, which he understands to have been inspired by the Spirit of Christ (1:10–12). As Achtemeier (1993: 187) observes, the hermeneutic employed in 1 Peter differs from the prefiguration that we find in Hebrews, the typological events noted by Paul, and the fulfillment of specific OT prophecies in the life of Jesus that are pointed out by Matthew. Peter's insight that Jesus Christ himself was in some form present to the prophets of ancient Israel is a unique contribution of the apostle Peter. This allows Peter's immediate identification of the Suffering Servant with Jesus as well as his unqualified appropriation of the language for ancient Israel to the Christian community. In Peter's thinking, there is continuity between Israel and the Christian church because, according to Peter's hermeneutic, from the very beginning of their existence God's chosen people had been informed by the Spirit of Christ. This hermeneutic also explains why Peter is unconcerned to address Gentile Christians in any way different from Jewish Christians, for from the time of Abraham there is but one chosen people of God, and they are Christ's.

The emphases in Peter's theological concepts, such as the suffering of Jesus, may reflect an earlier rather than later time of origin. R. P. Martin (1994: 94) points out that the Suffering Servant of God "represents a kind of early Christology that quickly dropped out from developing Christian thought." Schlatter (1999: 64) observes, "Set beside Paul's statements regarding Christ and the Spirit, Peter's statements appear antiquated." This means not that Peter's theological understanding is inferior and has been superseded but only that it reflects a stage of theological development closer to the crucifixion rather than later. In comparison, for instance, with Paul's thought on the rapture of the church (1 Cor. 15:12–54; 1 Thess. 4:13–18) or John's images of the eternal state (Rev. 21:1–22:6), Peter's eschatology, though not contradicting the other apostolic writings in any way, is less developed. Its simple eschatological point that God will judge all stands close to Jewish eschatology. If 1 Peter does indeed reflect an expectation of an imminent parousia, that too is usually taken as the thought of the earliest stage of Christianity. Marshall (1991: 24) further notes that the letter lacks several signs of late composition, for instance, a concern with heresies such as incipient

Gnosticism, a characterization of the Roman state as a malevolent beast, the posthumous glorifying of Peter, and the "developed apparatus of pseudonymity." Nor is the theology of 1 Peter developed in the direction of early Catholicism. The absence of concern with heresy and the rather positive attitude toward the Roman state are particularly striking when compared with the Johannine Epistles and Revelation, also written to Christians in Asia Minor at the end of the first century.

The theological contribution of 1 Peter shows that its author is not simply mimicking the doctrines of Paul but is reflecting creatively in a manner consistent with the early apostolic teaching on the significance of Jesus' death and resurrection and how they are related to God's final judgment.

Literary Unity and Genre

Unity of the text. The weight of scholarship today understands 1 Peter to be a unified text written by one author for one purpose at one time (Achtemeier 1996; Boring 1999: 37; Dalton 1965: 68; J. H. Elliott 2000; Goppelt 1993: 21–24; Hillyer 1992: 6; Horrell 1998: 12; Kendall 1986: 103; Marshall 1991: 20; R. P. Martin 1994: 96; T. Martin 1992a; Michaels 1988; Schutter 1989: 82; Thurén 1990; Thurén 1995). This view rejects the conclusions of an earlier time when source critics argued that the doxology at 4:11 signaled the end of one work and when they perceived a different emphasis on persecution in the text that followed. These observations led Streeter (1929: 128–31), following earlier German form criticism, to propose that 1 Peter was composed of two letters, the former written when persecution was threatening, the latter some years later, when persecution was a pressing reality. When Preisker (1951: 156) revised Windisch's earlier commentary, he argued, following Perdelwitz (1911: 37), that 1 Peter was a baptismal homily later put in epistolary form, with the baptism occurring between 1:21 and 1:22. Cross (1954: 31) further embroidered that theory by proposing that the baptism was part of the paschal liturgy of Easter, which occasion, and not persecution, explained 1 Peter's emphasis on suffering.

More recent scholarship has reconsidered the evidence of a composite nature and found it unconvincing (Achtemeier 1996: 60; Bechtler 1998: 19; Dalton 1965: 68; J. H. Elliott 2000: 9–11; Goppelt 1993: 21–24; Hillyer 1992: 6; Horrell 1998: 12; Marshall 1991: 20; T. Martin 1992a: 78; Michaels 1988: xxxvii–xxxix; Thurén 1990; Thurén 1995). There is no manuscript evidence for such composite theories, and later interpreters of 1 Peter have found evidence of its unity that outweighs any suspicions about its literary coherence (J. H. Elliott 2000: 9–11; Hillyer 1992: 6; Horrell 1998: 12; Marshall 1991: 20). The themes of the epistolary framework (1:1–2 and 5:12–14) introduce, and are consistent with, those in the body of the letter (Goppelt 1993: 21–24; Michaels 1988: xxxvii–xxxix; Schutter

1989: 55). The opening statements of the letter in 1:3–12 introduce in general terms the themes that will be applied to the specific situation of the readers in the body of the letter (Kendall 1986). The doxology in 4:11 functions to punctuate the closing of a unit of thought, as doxologies have been found to do in other NT books (Achtemeier 1996: 60). The intensity of the persecution following 4:12 has been exaggerated under the influence of the theory it is called upon to support. In addition to thematic and stylistic unity, rhetorical analysis of the text has demonstrated its coherence (T. Martin 1992a; Thurén 1990; Thurén 1995; Tite 1997). This study has found no reason to reject the original unity of the letter. First Peter is presented as a literary unit in its extant and canonical form, which is sufficient reason to legitimize its study as one literary composition.

Genre of 1 Peter. Rejection of the composite nature of 1 Peter implied rejection of its original form being a baptismal homily or liturgy to which an epistolary framework was later added (Dalton 1965: 69; Hillyer 1970: 56; R. P. Martin 1994: 99; T. Martin 1992a: 269; Thurén 1990: 177). The idea that this text was originally a baptismal liturgy suffers from the fact that baptism is mentioned only once (3:21), and discourse analysis shows that this reference to baptism is not a prominent thought within its larger unit of discourse. "To say that the letter, or most of it, is a baptismal homily or liturgy is to treat as explicit, direct and prominent what is only implicit, presupposed, and subsidiary" (Hill 1976: 189). Although the letter's origin was not directly linked to the ritual of baptism, Hill (1976: 185) has rightly stated the importance of baptism as presumed in 1 Peter:

> Since baptism was the occasion and the sign of voluntary self-commitment to the Christian way, those who offered themselves for the rite were aware, through their knowledge of what Christians endured, that this way on which they were embarking would inevitably involve suffering. Acceptance of consequences of becoming and being known as a Christian was implied in the acceptance of baptism. In short, a Christian's suffering and his baptism are linked because, in accepting baptism, he is affirming willingness to share in the known experience of baptized persons who were commonly, if not constantly, treated with suspicion and hostility.

If the unity of the extant form of 1 Peter is accepted, its genre is clearly that of personal correspondence. Many refer to it as a "Diaspora letter," which is an apt designation of its content and purpose. Extant Jewish writings attest to other Diaspora letters. J. H. Elliott (2000: 12) observes that 1 Peter is closest in form to the Epistle of Jeremiah, a pseudonymous work translated into Greek not later than 100 BC and addressed to exiles in Babylon. Other Diaspora letters include 2 Macc. 1:1–9 and

2 Bar. 78–87. As a distinctively Jewish form, the Diaspora letter was written by a recognized spiritual authority who urges a distinctive and holy way of life for those living in a society not conducive to it. Given the situation of the Christians in Asia Minor, a Diaspora letter is a very appropriate form in which the apostle Peter should choose to communicate, and quite in keeping with the Jewish tenor of the letter. However, there is no reason to believe that the Diaspora letter formed a distinct, indigenous literary genre. Other than being addressed to a scattered people for whom the author assumed spiritual authority, there are no distinct markers of a common genre, and the content of Diaspora letters could be quite varied. While the content of 1 Peter is clearly paraenetic, Holloway's (2002: 448n75) suggestion that it may be a letter of consolation deserves further study.

Sources. The rejection of the composite theory in favor of the view that 1 Peter is a work of personal correspondence because of the literary coherence and unity of its extant form does not, of course, prejudge the author's use of sources. Peter obviously draws extensively from the Greek version of the OT, which must be considered his primary source and the primary literary and theological context of the letter. Apart from its use of the OT, Schutter (1989: 35) has concluded that 1 Peter is demonstrably more dependent on oral Christian sources than on written.

The question of whether Peter used preexisting hymns or liturgical material is open to debate. Two christological passages, 2:21–25 and 3:18–22, have been identified as the most likely preexisting material, though Boismard (1961) has proposed that 1:3–5 and 5:5–9 also reflect previously existing hymns. J. H. Elliott (2000: 31) lists nine passages that may include at least fragments of preexisting material. Perhaps the greatest difficulty with concluding that Peter used preexisting hymns within his letter is that those who most studiously propose their existence cannot agree on which material can be so identified or on the markers that would indicate such material. Furthermore, the nature of the christological content identified as hymnic seems to be so general that it could reflect common Christian teaching about Jesus (J. H. Elliott 2000: 30–31; Prigent 1992: 59; Richard 1986: 130). Moreover, attempts to reconstruct a hymn from its form in 1 Peter have been given up as futile (Achtemeier 1996: 242; Richard 1986: 129).

There is no consensus on the origin of even the two passages that all agree are the most likely candidates to have been preexisting hymns, 2:21–24 and 3:18–22. This study concurs with Osborne (1983: 408), who expresses the opinion that the evidence offered that 2:21–24 originated as a hymn indicates only that it came from a source, and that source is adequately identified as the Greek text of Isa. 53 (as also Achtemeier 1996: 192–93; Michaels 1988: xliii). With reference to 3:18–22, J. H. Elliott (2000: 697) reviews the work of Windisch, Cullmann, and Bultmann and concludes that there is "no convincing case at hand for the existence and use of a fixed creed or hymn in vv. 18–22" (as also Achtemeier 1996: 242–43; Goppelt 1993: 249; Michaels 1988: xliii). Concerning the use of hymns or creedal material in 1 Peter, J. H. Elliott (2000: 32) concludes: "The most that can be stated with certainty is that 1 Peter incorporates isolated phrases and formulas of christological and kerygmatic tradition but not that this material was embodied in demonstrable hymnic or creedal sources." Even if the author of 1 Peter used preexisting material, that material was so thoroughly integrated into his own thought that its original form cannot be reconstructed. Therefore, that material must be understood within the overall context of the letter as contributing to the flow of thought originating with Peter.

Outline of the Discourse

   I. A greeting to the Christian Diaspora of Asia Minor (1:1–2)
   II. The opening of the letter: reassurance for God's people (1:3–2:10)
    A. Doxology as the basis for the Christian life (1:3–12)
       1. The opening doxology (1:3–5)
       2. Joy and suffering in the new life (1:6–9)
       3. The Christian's advantage over the prophets and even the angels (1:10–12)
    B. Be what you are (1:13–2:3)
       1. Be children of the Father (1:13–21)
       2. Christian love means moral transformation (1:22–2:3)
    C. The identity of God's people (2:4–10)
       1. A spiritual house and a holy priesthood (2:4–8)
       2. Now you are the people of God (2:9–10)
   III. As God's people, live godly lives (2:11–4:11)
    A. Commendable social behavior as God's people (2:11–3:7)
       1. Lifestyle evangelism (2:11–12)
       2. Submit even to pagan authority (2:13–17)
       3. Christ's example in society's most basic unit (2:18–3:7)
          a. The slave as the paradigm for believers (2:18–25)
          b. Instructions to Christian wives and husbands (3:1–7)
    B. The inner qualities of righteous living (3:8–12)
    C. Suffering unjustly for the name of Christ (3:13–4:11)
       1. Suffering for doing good (3:13–17)
       2. Christ's victory over unjust suffering (3:18–22)
       3. Living out Christ's victory in an unbelieving world (4:1–6)
       4. Living out Christ's victory in the Christian community (4:7–11)
   IV. Consolation for the suffering flock (4:12–5:11)
    A. Two final thoughts about suffering for Christ (4:12–19)

B. Final exhortations to the community (5:1–11)
   1. Christ shepherds his flock through the elders (5:1–5)
   2. Accepting difficult times, standing fast, and trusting God (5:6–11)

V. The letter closing: final words and greetings (5:12–14)

I. A Greeting to the Christian Diaspora of Asia Minor (1:1–2)

The Christians of Asia Minor were facing troubling times. Because of their faith in Christ, they were being persecuted through social ostracism. Slander and malicious talk undermined their relationships with associates and family, threatened their honor in the community, and possibly jeopardized their livelihood. The issues of how to maintain a vital Christian faith in such circumstances and how to respond to such unjust treatment pressed upon them. Peter writes to give these Christians hope, consolation, and encouragement by explaining their identity in Christ and how even suffering is an integral part of that identity. In his opening salutation the apostle uses terms that describe the Christian's relationship to God, to society, and to God's historic people, ancient Israel.

A. The author and recipients (1:1)
    1. Foreigners (1:1a)
    2. Foreigners of the Diaspora (1:1b)
    3. Pontus, Galatia, Cappadocia, Asia, and Bithynia (1:1c)
B. Chosen by God (1:2)
    1. According to the foreknowledge of God the Father (1:2a)
    2. By the consecration of the Spirit (1:2b)
    3. For obedience and sprinkling of the blood of Jesus Christ (1:2c)
C. The greeting (1:2d)

Exegesis and Exposition

[1][This letter is from] Peter, apostle of Jesus Christ to the chosen, foreigners of the Diaspora of Pontus, Galatia, Cappadocia, Asia, and Bithynia, [2][chosen] according to the foreknowledge of God the Father, by the consecration of the Spirit, for [the purpose of] obedience and sprinkling of the blood of Jesus Christ. Grace to you and may peace be multiplied.

A. The Author and Recipients (1:1)

Peter addresses his readers using terms from the OT tradition that describe them as God's covenant people. In this salutation, he applies to them the covenantal language of (1) election and (2) Diaspora, as well as (3) adjectives used in the Greek OT to describe Abraham, Moses, and the Israelites in Egypt. Moreover, he alludes to the ancient covenant made on Mt. Sinai by referring to the "obedience and sprinkling of the blood" (cf. Exod. 24), yet he defines the covenant in which his readers participate as the covenant established by the blood of Jesus Christ.

Although he uses the standard form of the Hellenistic letter, Peter further addresses his readers as foreigners (παρεπίδημοι, *parepidēmoi*). By drawing an analogy between the Jewish Diaspora and the situation of his readers, he implies they should understand themselves as Christians in terms of God's people of the old covenant who were foreigners in the lands to which they had been scattered. The Diaspora experience provides a perspective through which they are to frame their experiences. Peter grounds his readers' identity in terms of their relationship to God by defining the role of the Father, Holy Spirit, and Jesus Christ in their conversion and inclusion as people of the covenant. In the very opening sentence of his letter, Peter introduces a concept of Christian identity that is based first on relationship to God and then on relationship to the world.

All of the formal elements that opened a personal letter of the Hellenistic period are found here: the name of the sender (Peter, apostle of Jesus Christ), the recipients to whom the letter is addressed (the chosen, foreigners of the Diaspora of Pontus, Galatia, Cappadocia, Asia, and Bithynia), and a greeting that is framed as a Christian prayer for grace and peace. This salutation and the closing of 1 Pet. 5:12–14 indicate that the author intends this work to be read as personal correspondence.

The opening of the letter states it is from Peter, apostle of Jesus Christ (1:1), and should therefore be read as such (see "Date and Authorship" in the introduction). Peter writes with the confidence that he is presenting the "true grace of God" (5:12) and that his words come with apostolic authority. In the first century of the Christian church, the primary characteristic of an apostle was his authority to bear authentic testimony to the life and significance of Jesus Christ. An apostle was recognized to have an authority distinct from even the great early church leaders such as Ignatius, Polycarp, and Clement of Rome. Ignatius (Ign. *Rom.* 4.3) writes in his letter to the Romans, "I do not enjoin you as Peter and Paul did. They were Apostles; I am a convict" (Lightfoot 1893). And again he writes (Ign. *Trall.* 3.3), "But I did not think myself competent for this, that being a convict I should order you as though I were an Apostle" (Lightfoot 1893; similarly also Ign. *Eph.* 3.1; Ign. *Magn.* 6.1). Furthermore, the apostles were recognized as equal in authority to the prophets of the OT era. Polycarp (*Phil.* 6.3) wrote, "Let us then serve him in fear, and with all reverence, even as he himself has commanded us, and as the apostles who preached the gospel unto us, and the prophets who proclaimed beforehand the coming of the Lord [have alike taught us]" (Lightfoot 1893). It is with such apostolic authority that the author of the letter of 1 Peter wishes to be understood.

Some have argued that the original recipients of this letter were Jewish converts because Gal. 2:8–9 indicates that Peter was the apostle to the Jews. For instance, Stewart-Sykes (1997) argues that a pseudonymous author of this letter adopted the pseudonym of the apostle Peter because he was writing to Christian converts from Judaism. However, the Galatians statement should not be perceived as an absolute and inviolable agreement between Peter and Paul. Though his ministry was perceived primarily as a mission to the Gentiles, Paul continued to preach to the Jews during his second journey in Thessalonica (Acts 17:2), in Berea (17:10), in Corinth (18:4), and on his third journey in Ephesus (19:8). Similarly, Peter could well have preached to Gentiles and ministered to converts from the Gentiles (10:1–11:18).

The apostle of 1 Peter identifies himself by his Greek nickname, πέτρος (petros, rock), the name given to him by the Lord Jesus himself upon Peter's call to discipleship (John 1:42) and reasserted upon his recognition that Jesus was the Christ (Matt. 16:18). The Greek word for "rock," πέτρα (petra), is grammatically feminine but, when used in reference to a man, would be written with the masculine ending as πέτρος (petros). There may be evidence from Qumran (4QM[ilik]130) that this was a Jewish name in use before Christ and not a nickname created by Jesus uniquely for his apostle (Charlesworth 1992).

The nickname was probably given by Jesus in Aramaic as כֵּיפָא (kêpāʾ, rock), for Peter's name is sometimes given by the Greek transliteration κηφᾶς (kēphas).[1] This Aramaic form has been preserved in John 1:42 and is frequently used by Paul to refer to Peter (1 Cor. 1:12; 3:22; 9:5; 15:5; Gal. 1:18; 2:9, 11, 14), attesting to its use in the early church. Peter's given name at birth was the Aramaic name Simon. His given name is combined with his nickname, Simon Peter, only in the Synoptic Gospels and 2 Pet. 1:1 (Simeon). By far he is most often called simply "Peter" throughout the NT. The Lord gives him a new name to symbolize Peter's new role as the apostle of Christ, a role so foundational in the early church. This apostle's fame in the earliest days of the church as the "Rock" is attested by being named in the early kerygma as the first apostle to whom the resurrected Christ appeared (1 Cor. 15:5).

Peter, apostle of Jesus Christ, writes to the chosen (ἐκλεκτοῖς, eklektois) who are foreigners (παρεπιδήμοις, parepidēmois) of the Diaspora (διασπορᾶς, diasporas) of regions that comprise a vast area of the central and northern plateau of Asia Minor, now the modern nation of Turkey (see "Destination" in the introduction). Peter's description of the recipients

---

1. For a discussion of the occurrence of this name in its various forms throughout the NT, see J. K. Elliott 1992: 126–38.

as both chosen and foreign defines their identity in relationship to God and to the society in which they live, respectively.

1. Foreigners (1:1a)

Most modern interpreters understand the address to Peter's readers as "foreigners" to be a metaphor that describes the Christian's relationship to the world. By virtue of faith in Christ, home is heaven, and Christians therefore are just passing through this world as foreigners (see "Recipients" in the introduction). The term *parepidēmos* (plural, *parepidēmoi*) was used in the first century to designate someone who did not hold citizenship in the place where he resided and was therefore viewed as a foreigner. The lack of citizenship implied that such people did not enjoy all the rights and privileges of citizens. Moreover, as foreigners, they were not necessarily expected to hold the values and practice the customs of their host culture. Because of such differences, foreigners were often looked upon suspiciously as potentially subversive to the established social order, an attitude not unfamiliar even today.

J. H. Elliott (1981) argues that this term should be understood as describing the actual sociopolitical situation of the people to whom Peter was writing before their conversion to Christ, a conversion that only further marginalized them from the dominant society. Although Elliott's argument has been unconvincing to most interpreters, it has called attention to the issue of the social and historical setting of the addressees and the occasion that prompted the letter to be written (Achtemeier 1984; Chin 1991; Clowney 1988: 228; Dalton 1983; Danker 1983; Hemer 1985; Porter 1993. McKnight 1996: 48–51 stands alone in following Elliott).

This commentary presents the possibility that the people to whom Peter writes were Christians from Rome who were deported to Roman colonies in Asia Minor during one of the several expulsions in the first century (see "Roman Colonization and the Origin of 1 Peter" in the introduction). Peter, the apostle associated with Rome, uses their disorienting experience to instruct and encourage them with his insight that all Christians are in a real sense foreigners to their place of residence, regardless of where they are living, whenever Christian values and customs conflict with those of the dominant society.

Peter again describes his readers as *parepidēmoi* in 2:11: "Dear friends, I urge you, as resident aliens [*paroikoi*] and foreigners [*parepidēmoi*], to abstain from the carnal desires, which war against your soul." Other than these two occurrences in 1 Peter, the word *parepidēmoi* occurs elsewhere in the NT only in Heb. 11:13: "All these people were still living by faith when they died. They did not receive the things promised; they only saw them and welcomed them from a distance, admitting that they were strangers and foreigners [*parepidēmoi*] on earth." The word occurs only twice in the LXX. In Gen. 23:4 LXX Abraham describes himself as an alien (*paroikos*) and a foreigner (*parepidēmos*) while living among the Hittites. In Ps. 38:13 LXX (39:12 MT/Eng.), the psalmist likewise refers to himself as a foreigner (*parepidēmos*) as well as an alien (*paroikos*) with respect to the Lord. These two OT occurrences of *parepidēmos* do not seem to constitute a biblical metaphor that Peter is extending to his readers. (A different case may perhaps be made for *paroikos*, but that word does not appear in the opening address. See comments on 2:11.)

Rather than understanding *parepidēmos* in 1:1 as describing the believers' transitory life on this earth as a journey toward their heavenly home, it should be understood primarily as defining the relationship between the Christian and unbelieving society. Goppelt (1993: 67–68) explains:

> The sociological effect of being a foreigner is in view: Christians distance themselves as nonconformists from handed-down life-styles (1:17f.); therefore, those around them are "estranged" regarding them (4:3f.). In both Christians and those around them the effects of this foreignness can or should be felt—the letter speaks of this in the parenesis—but the foreignness is established by election.

These foreigners are not addressed as a single group. That is, in contrast to Paul, Peter notably does not address his readers as the ἐκκλησίαι (*ekklēsiai*, assemblies, churches) in the named provinces. Goppelt (1993: 64) sees this as

> characterizing them in the horizontal dimension in light of their relationship to the world around them: They have been set apart from the nations of the world by election and live scattered among them as foreigners who have no homeland here. The very address thus envisages the theme of the letter: Christians in society. It does not have particular churches in mind, but Christians in the everyday world living among their fellow human beings.

Peter uses the term "foreigner" to distance his readers from the hold their society may have over them. Nevertheless, Peter does not call them to withdraw from society but will instead present Christian engagement with society in the mode that might be expected of foreigners who wish to maintain their identity of origin. That is, foreigners dwell respectfully in their host nation but participate in its culture only to the extent that its values and customs coincide with their own that they wish to preserve. In this way the salutation of the letter introduces a concept of a differentiated engagement with society that subsequently will be expanded in terms of neither full assimilation nor complete withdrawal.

2. Foreigners of the Diaspora (1:1b)

The addressees of 1 Peter are not only foreigners; they are foreigners "of the Diaspora" (διασπορᾶς, *diasporas*) of Pontus, Galatia, Cappadocia, Asia, and Bithynia. This should probably be read as a qualitative or epexegetical genitive, rather than a partitive, making the Christians of Asia Minor constitutive of the Diaspora of these regions. The noun "Diaspora," though linguistically related to the Greek verb διασπείρω (*diaspeirō*, scatter), was a technical term found only in Jewish literature of the Hellenistic period to refer to the Jewish population living outside Palestine since the Babylonian exile.[2] Since the time of the Seleucid king Antiochus III in the third century before Christ, a large part of the Jewish Diaspora was resident in Asia Minor, which ranked third behind Babylon and Egypt as a center of Jewish population (Mitchell 1993: 2.32; Davids 1990: 46n3). The term "Diaspora" can generally refer to any displaced people group. However, the reference to "Babylon" in 5:13 forms an inclusio with the term "Diaspora" in 1:1 and makes it perfectly clear that Peter is alluding to the Diaspora of the Jews.

Should this reference to the Jewish Diaspora be taken to mean that the Christians to whom Peter writes were converts from Judaism? Or does it describe metaphorically the character of the Christian church as a community scattered among the nations and on pilgrimage in this world until the Lord returns? Although the latter, metaphorical interpretation is the consensus of modern commentators, most ancient interpreters, except Jerome and Augustine, understood 1 Peter to be written to Christians who had been converted from the Jewish Diaspora population living in Asia Minor (Kelly 1969: 40). Calvin (1963: 230) continued that tradition and also argued against a metaphorical sense of "foreigner" in 1:1:

> Those who think that all the godly are so called [foreigners], because they are strangers in the world, and are going on metaphorically towards the celestial country, are greatly mistaken, and this mistake can be refuted by the word *dispersion* which immediately follows. This can apply only to the Jews. (italics original)

More recently, van Unnik (1980: 95–105) vigorously argues that "Diaspora" is not a term that can be appropriately applied to the Christian church as an entity and must therefore refer only to converts from Judaism. This view makes it difficult to understand why Peter would address converts from Jewish communities who had lived in Asia Minor

---

2. Neither Josephus nor Philo use the noun *diaspora*, but in the LXX it refers to the scattering of God's covenant people outside the land of Palestine: Deut. 28:25; 30:4; Neh. 1:9; Ps. 146:2 (147:2 Eng.); Isa. 49:6; Jer. 15:7; 41:17 (34:17 Eng.); Dan. 12:2; and in the Apocrypha: 2 Macc. 1:27; Jdt. 5:19.

for centuries as "foreigners," when addressing them as the chosen "of the Diaspora" of Asia Minor would have sufficed if it were his intent only to acknowledge them as Jewish converts. The collocation of "foreigners" together with "Diaspora" raises the possibility that Peter's readers had indeed been scattered, not by the Babylonians or the Seleucids, but by their successors, the Romans (cf. 5:13; see "Roman Colonization and the Origin of 1 Peter" in the introduction).

The framing of the letter with a reference to "Diaspora" in 1:1 and "Babylon" in 5:13 invites the Christian "foreigners" of Asia Minor to see their own situation as parallel to the history of God's people, ancient Israel. Thus, "Diaspora" in 1:1 has a double purpose: first, possibly alluding to the actual experience of Peter's readers; second, interpreting that experience from the perspective of God's chosen Israel as a way of identifying his readers as God's chosen people. Once the letter circulated away from its original readers, the first sense necessarily receded and the metaphorical sense of "foreigners of the Diaspora" became primary.

Although God's chosen people, to what extent can Christians understand their life experience through the lens of the Jewish Diaspora? Throughout history the Jews left Palestine for various reasons and many destinations, but the original impetus for the Diaspora was God's judgment on their sin as a nation when Jerusalem and Judea went into exile in the sixth century BC. The words "exile" and "Diaspora" were at one time virtually synonymous in Jewish history.[3] As a symbol, "Diaspora" denotes covenant failure. Hence, in what sense is the Diaspora experience of the Jews an apt concept for the Christians' self-understanding? As Danker (1967: 100) puts it,

> In the case of OT Israel, sufferings were often viewed as the result of disobedience and Israel's validity as God's people was called into question. Is the same inference to be made in the case of the new [Christian] community? The writer [of 1 Peter] denies this emphatically. The sufferings of the new community come about not because of disobedience but *in spite of obedience.* (emphasis added)

T. Martin (1992a) considers Diaspora to be the controlling metaphor in Peter's paraenetic letter. One aspect of Diaspora he identifies as relevant to Christians is that it conceptualizes them as "the wandering people of God on an eschatological journey" that commences with their new birth (T. Martin 1992a: 154). While this is consistent with the modern metaphorical interpretation of the symbol, it is not obvious that the Diaspora motif necessarily involves the idea of journey, for once the Jews had resettled in their Diaspora place, they remained in residence

3. It is this linguistic bleed that causes some (e.g., NRSV) to translate 1:1 as "to the exiles of the Dispersion."

there indefinitely. The second aspect of Diaspora relevant to the Christian life is "the danger of assimilation to the pagan environment" and consequent defection from the faith (T. Martin 1992a: 156), which is more to the point of Peter's concerns revealed in the letter.

Seland (2001: 256) wishes to refine Martin's Diaspora concept further by arguing that Peter's addressing readers as *parepidēmoi* and *paroikoi* shows that "in his perception of the social world of his Christian recipients, their social situation had become similar to that of the Jewish proselytes [converts to Judaism]." He argues that this description should be read not as describing a heavenly pilgrimage on earth but as drawing an analogy between the social situations of the Asian Christians and the Diaspora Jewish proselytes to dramatize how society reacted to converts from paganism to Judaism. Seland (2001: 261) looks to Philo's works, which emphasize "leaving polytheism for monotheism; leaving one's country, family, and kinfolk and becoming enemies of families and friends at the risk of one's life; and entering a community of fictive kinship and brotherly love." While some of these emphases may indeed be applicable to converts to Christianity, 1 Peter does not in fact even once address or refer to its readers as προσήλυτοι (*prosēlytoi*, proselytes). Furthermore, Seland's reliance on Philo and his questionable use of lexical evidence from the LXX to claim that the terms Peter uses were nearly synonymous with *prosēlytoi* cast doubt on his argument. Nevertheless, his point that Peter uses the terms *parepidēmoi* and *paroikoi* in reference to his readers' social situation, and not their earthly pilgrimage, is well taken.

Although "Diaspora" is an apt symbol for covenantal judgment on sin, nothing in the use of the motif in 1 Peter suggests condemnation. For, as Peter will immediately explain in 1:3–9, the negative connotations of judgment associated with the Diaspora have been swallowed up in the death and resurrection of Jesus Christ. It is the resurrection of Jesus that has given them new birth (1:3), and new birth implies a new identity and a new "citizenship" (though Peter does not use the phrase "kingdom of God"). For the Christian readers of 1 Peter, therefore, the concept of Diaspora indicates their heritage in Israel's history and provides the religious perspective from which their social situation is to be understood. Goppelt (1993: 65) explains:

> The Diaspora Jews participated in the commerce and life of their environment in accord with the picture given by the legends in . . . Daniel: Life in a society holding a different worldview motivates Jews to formulate an apologetic that represents conceptually the universal claim of "the Lord" on global society.

And so, as members of the Diaspora of Asia Minor, the Christians Peter addresses are foreigners with respect to first-century society. Whether or not this alludes to an actual experience of displacement, Peter uses it to explain their identity as God's chosen and to conceptualize their resulting experience of sociopolitical alienation.

3. Pontus, Galatia, Cappadocia, Asia, and Bithynia (1:1c)

The Diaspora addressed is "of Pontus, Galatia, Cappadocia, Asia, and Bithynia," the regions of Asia Minor in which Peter's original recipients resided (see "Destination" in the introduction). These areas addressed are predominantly regions not evangelized by Paul or by any other known apostle (though the existence of 1 Peter has led some to infer that Peter must have traveled through these lands). Paul evangelized areas of Galatia on his first mission; whether in northern Galatia or southern is still a matter of some debate. However, Galatia was a large area, and if Peter was writing to Christians residing in a colony Claudius had established there, it would not necessarily have been in the area of the Pauline churches (see "Roman Colonization and the Origin of 1 Peter" in the introduction). Paul did not spend time in the province of Asia until his third journey, in the latter half of the 50s. Luke describes Paul as having been kept by the Holy Spirit from preaching in Asia on his second journey and forbidden by the Spirit of Jesus from entering Mysia and Bithynia (Acts 16:6–7), raising the intriguing question why. Selwyn (1958: 61) has theorized that Paul was forbidden to enter Bithynia because Peter was already at work there. However, the absence in 1 Peter of specific names, locations, and references to a former time there argues against this theory.

Since the time of Hort (1898), some commentators have understood the order of the list—Pontus, Galatia, Cappadocia, Asia, Bithynia—to have something to do with the route taken to deliver the letter. The most obvious feature of the list is that it does not follow a west-to-east route that one might expect if the letter arrived from Rome through one of the large ports of western Asia Minor, such as Ephesus. Although various proposals have been made, none seem able to describe an itinerary that both follows the list and is consistent with what is known of the network of roads in first-century Asia Minor—unlike the order of the seven churches of Revelation, which were on a known major route of travel in the sequence given. Moreover, such an attempt presumes that only one copy was taken *ad seriatim* throughout the regions named. That may be likely if only one person, namely, Silvanus (1 Pet. 5:12), was personally responsible for delivering the letter, but his exact role in the origin and delivery of 1 Peter is not known with certainty. Instead of describing an anticipated delivery route, it seems more likely that the list of regions simply represents the author's mental map of Asia Minor, probably using the names of regions as he first learned them, even if Roman administration had subsequently altered the map.

B. Chosen by God (1:2)

The original recipients of this letter may have been foreigners with respect to their society and scattered throughout the vast area of Asia Minor, but with respect to God, Peter says they are chosen (ἐκλεκτοῖς, *eklektois*, 1:1 in the Gk. text). In fact, Peter goes on to explain that it is *because* of their relationship with God in Christ that their relationship with their society has become troubled.

Both ἐκλεκτοῖς and παρεπιδήμοις (*parepidēmois*, foreigners) can be either adjectival or substantive (see the second additional note on 1:1). These words are best understood as substantives in apposition, with *parepidēmois* in apposition to *eklektois*. As a substantive, *parepidēmois* refers to those who live in a place where they do not hold citizenship, even if residing there for an extended time. Taking *parepidēmois* in apposition to *eklektois* (the chosen who are also foreigners) highlights both the vertical and the horizontal dimensions of their identity as Christians. On the one hand, they are chosen with respect to God (the vertical dimension), but at the same time, they are foreigners with respect to their sociopolitical world (the horizontal dimension). Moreover, this description of people who are both chosen by God and foreigners in the place of their residence lends itself to the spiritual understanding of *parepidēmos* as describing the Christian's earthly life as a temporary residence in this world, on the way to the Christian's ultimate home in the realized kingdom of God (Achtemeier 1996: 82; W. Barclay 1976: 167–68; Beare 1970: 75; Best 1971: 70; Bigg 1956: 90; Blum 1981: 219; Clowney 1988: 228; Cranfield 1958: 14; Davids 1990: 46–47; Goppelt 1993: 67; Kelly 1969: 41; Michaels 1988: 6; Reicke 1964: 76; Stibbs 1979: 72).

Three prepositional phrases in 1:2 further describe the recipients of this letter. They are

- chosen according to the foreknowledge of God the Father,
- chosen by the consecration of the Spirit, and
- chosen for obedience and sprinkling of the blood of Jesus Christ.

Some commentators take these three prepositional phrases to qualify *apostolos* in verse 1 or the entire thought of verse 1, which can be supported theologically by a broad view of God's purpose and providence (e.g, Beare 1970: 75; Grudem 1988: 50; Selwyn 1958: 119). However, such a view diffuses the focus of these phrases as the basis on which the addressees are to place their hope and be encouraged. Peter does not dwell on a defense of his apostleship or on the geographical situation of the recipients. He does address their discouragement because of the sociopolitical alienation they experience, which is a direct consequence of their relationship to God in Christ. Therefore, it is exegetically preferable to understand these three phrases as modifying the term that most fundamentally defines who these Christians are: the *eklektoi*, the chosen.

This triadic structure describes the relationship of the Christians to whom Peter writes to each member of the Godhead, particularly in reference to their conversion. The order—Father, Spirit, Christ—perhaps reflects the logical *ordo salutis*[4] of conversion that finds its ultimate origin in the heart of God, is made operative in human lives by the Holy Spirit, and is evidenced through personal expressions of faith in Jesus Christ. Although it would be anachronistic to call this a reference to the Trinity, surely such verses as this one later issued in the orthodox doctrine of the Trinity at the First Council of Nicaea (AD 325), which was located in Bithynia, one of the regions to which Peter writes.

Two major points are made about God's role in the election of the Christians to whom Peter writes: (1) their election is according to God's foreknowledge, and (2) God is described to them as "Father."

1. According to the Foreknowledge of God the Father (1:2a)

The attribute of God primarily in Peter's mind is his eternal foreknowledge, which effectively issues in the circumstances of history. These Asian Christians were chosen according to the foreknowledge (πρόγνωσις, *prognōsis*)—not simply the knowledge—of God the Father. In the NT the noun occurs in only one other verse in reference to Jesus, who was handed over for crucifixion by God's will and foreknowledge (Acts 2:23). The verbal form *proginōskō* occurs twice in the NT in the active voice with God as subject (Rom. 8:29; 11:2), and in both occurrences with God's people as the object of his foreknowledge. The NT understanding of God's foreknowledge of his people indicates that God did not simply observe them or have information about them at some prior time in history. Instead, God chose them according to (κατά, *kata*), or consistent with, his plan and purpose long before God formed a people to be his own. First Peter 1:20 states that the redemptive role of Christ was also foreknown (*proginōskō*) to God before the creation of the world. Therefore, verses 2 and 20 express correlating thoughts that even before creation God had chosen both the people who would be redeemed and the agent who would redeem them. Regardless of whether one accepts the idea of individual election before creation, "the essential point is that Christians are in the church not merely by their own decision, but by the initiative of God who has called them" (Boring 1999: 55). Peter here instructs his readers that God's divine initiative has operated in their lives even before they were aware of it. It is this purposeful plan of God, larger than an individual's life, that forms the ultimate foundation for the hope and encouragement that Peter is about to offer.

---

4. *Ordo salutis* (order of salvation) is a Latin theological term that refers to the sequence of God's redemptive work in an individual's life.

Peter describes his readers' relationship to God by referring to him as God the Father. Contrary to the popular idea that all people are entitled to call God "Father" because he is the Creator of all, Peter's use of the term is anchored to two reference points. Of first importance, the God to whom Peter refers is the Father of the Lord Jesus Christ (1:3). God's fatherly relationship to Christ is the theological foundation for his fatherly relationship to believers in Christ. Second, Peter develops and expands the father-child paradigm throughout his letter. The Christians to whom Peter writes have been regenerated, or reborn (ἀναγεννήσας, *anagennēsas*), by the imperishable seed of God's word (1:3, 23). God has therefore become their Father, though in a different sense than he is the Father of Jesus Christ.

With this prepositional phrase, "chosen according to the foreknowledge of God the Father," Peter reminds his readers that the God who took the initiative in their lives has drawn them into an intimate, loving, and redemptive relationship with him, but also one in which God claims supreme authority over their lives. Such a reminder is apt at times when Christians are troubled by the circumstances in which they find themselves, confused about how to live, and tempted to doubt God's goodness or faithfulness.

2. By the Consecration of the Spirit (1:2b)

These chosen, who are foreigners of the Asian "Diaspora," have also been chosen ἐν ἁγιασμῷ πνεύματος (*en hagiasmō pneumatos*, by the consecration, or sanctification, of the Spirit). A few questions concerning syntax and sense arise among commentators: (1) Is the *en* locative or instrumental? (2) Does *pneumatos* refer to the human spirit or the Holy Spirit? (3) Is the sense of *hagiasmō* to be understood as a transformation of character (what theologians call sanctification) or a setting apart for a purpose (consecration)?

Following Selwyn (1958: 119), Grudem (1988: 52) takes the phrase *en hagiasmō pneumatos* to be locative, in the sense that the whole existence of the chosen foreigners "is being lived 'in' the realm of the sanctifying work of the Spirit." Selwyn takes the location to be the inner person, where the "inward part of the sacrament of baptism" occurs. Both Selwyn and Grudem take the whole of verse 1 as the governing thought of these three prepositional phrases, but if *eklektois* is the more specific antecedent thought, then an instrumental dative is more apt here. To be chosen *by* the instrumental agency of the Spirit is a more natural thought than to be chosen *into* a location, even if the location is a "spiritual" one.

Because God the Father and Jesus Christ in the other two prepositional phrases clearly refer to the divine initiative, "spirit" (*pneuma*) here is almost certainly to be understood as the Holy Spirit, who is the instrument, or agency, by which God makes his electing foreknowledge operative in the lives of those who come to faith in Christ (Achtemeier 1996: 86; Beare 1970: 76; Clowney 1988: 31; Cranfield 1958: 17; Davids 1990: 48; Goppelt 1993: 73; McKnight 1996: 73; Michaels 1988: 11; Stibbs 1979: 72). Goppelt (1993: 73–74) synthesizes the locative and instrumental ideas: "The Spirit is a power from beyond this world; through it God or the Exalted Christ takes hold of a person from the inside by addressing that one in a convincing way. Whoever is taken hold of by the Spirit is thus taken from the realm of the profane and placed into the sphere of the holy."

When the purpose of the work of the Spirit—given in the third prepositional phrase—is considered, the sanctification in view here is first the consecration of these people that occurred when they heard and responded to the word of God effectively preached in the power of the Spirit, which brought forth their new birth (1:23). Boring (1999: 55) explains:

> This refers . . . to the work of the Spirit in the preaching activity by which the readers were converted. . . . To declare that the readers are elect means that they belong to the holy people of God, that is, not that they are more pious or that they are morally superior to others, but that they have been called to form a distinctive community with a singular mission. To be called "holy" means that they, like Israel, have been set apart for a special purpose in God's saving plan.

Peter points to his readers' belief in Christ as the evidence that they have been chosen according to the foreknowledge of God. He later develops the ideas of both their consecration as a royal priesthood (2:9) and their transformation into obedient children conforming themselves to the holy likeness of their Father, God (1:14). The two components of consecration and sanctification cannot truly be separated: the transformation of character away from conformity to the world is constitutive of consecration.

When Martin Luther explains the third article of the Apostles' Creed, "I believe in the Holy Spirit," he writes, "I believe that by my own understanding or strength I cannot believe in Jesus Christ my Lord, or come to him" (Wengert 1996: 23). The electing purpose of God is made real by the faith of believers, but that faith is itself a completely gracious act of the Holy Spirit. It is the Spirit who first stirs in the heart a reaching toward God, quickens one's understanding of the gospel, convicts of sin, reassures of pardon, and transforms the character by his fruit of virtues.

3. For Obedience and Sprinkling of the Blood of Jesus Christ (1:2c)

This consecrating work of the Spirit has a specific goal. He does not bring a person to some generic spirituality, such as is currently popular in much of Western culture, but more specifically into the new covenant founded on the blood of Christ Jesus. The Christians to whom Peter writes were chosen in God's foreknowledge by the work of the Spirit for a purpose. In our spiritually pluralistic society, many today believe in a supreme God and speak of his Spirit working in the lives of people. But Peter drives home the point that the people to whom he writes were chosen for the distinct purpose of "obedience and sprinkling of the blood of Jesus Christ," not simply for some generic form of spirituality.

The syntax of this prepositional phrase is somewhat problematic to translate for three reasons: (1) the sense of the preposition εἰς (*eis*), (2) the relationship of obedience (ὑπακοήν, *hypakoēn*) to sprinkling (ῥαντισμόν, *rhantismon*), and (3) the sense of the genitive Ἰησοῦ Χριστοῦ (*Iēsou Christou*, of Jesus Christ) with respect to both. Most commentators read *eis* to have a telic sense, yielding the sense that the recipients of the letter have been chosen for the purpose of "obedience and sprinkling." (Agnew [1983] argues that the sense of the preposition is causal. See additional note on 1:2.) The phrase is properly understood as an allusion to the establishment of God's covenant with Israel in Exod. 24:3–8. Furthermore, the exhortations subsequently developed in 1 Peter suggest that Peter's point is that the Christians of Asia Minor have been chosen for a purpose, and that purpose is their own obedience after the example of Christ (cf. 1:14; 2:21).

Most commentators also take the genitive *Iēsou Christou* as an objective genitive with respect to "obedience": the recipients were chosen for the purpose of obeying Jesus Christ, in the sense of either an initial response to the gospel (so Best 1971: 71; Davids 1990: 48) or ongoing obedience to the law of God as Christ embodies it (e.g., Bigg 1956: 92). It is, however, difficult to take the genitive *Iēsou Christou* as objective with respect to the second noun phrase, "sprinkling of blood," and so most understand it as possessive, meaning Christ's blood, a metonymy for Christ's death (so the TNIV, NIV, NLT, and NRSV). However, grammatically it is difficult to defend taking one and the same phrase as an objective genitive with respect to the first noun but as possessive with respect to the second. Those who do so see the two nouns as referring to sequential phases in the Christian life: first, one obeys by responding in faith to the gospel, and then one is sprinkled. "Here the 'sprinkling,' following obedience, seems to impart the spirit of readiness, not so much to do God's will as to suffer for Christ's sake. This is the highest stage in the progress of the Christian life on earth" (Bigg 1956: 93).

This grammatical difficulty can be avoided if the phrase "obedience and sprinkling" is understood as a hendiadys (expressing a single idea by two words) alluding to the establishment of the Mosaic covenant (Exod. 24:3–8). There the newly formed people of Israel first pledge their obedience (24:3, 7) and then are sprinkled with the blood of the sacrifice (24:8). In this ceremony both sides of the essential nature of the covenant are represented: the people pledge obedience to God, and the blood of the covenant is applied to them. Thus the phrase "obedience and sprinkling of blood" can serve as a hendiadys to refer to God's covenant relationship with his people.

This allusion to the covenant ceremony in Exod. 24 is well recognized by most commentators, though its force is construed differently. Goppelt (1993: 74) considers the language only "remotely" related to covenant making, and Michaels (1988: 12) considers Num. 19 (the red-heifer passage) to be the primary background. Beare understands the phrase in 1 Pet. 1:2 to be a hendiadys alluding to the covenant in the context of Christian water baptism, where "the sprinkling with water in baptism is treated as figuring the sprinkling of the community with the blood of the sacrifice" (Beare 1970: 77). Similarly, an allusion to water baptism is understood by Goppelt (1993: 71) and Reicke (1964: 77). However, "sprinkling" as an allusion to water baptism made better sense when 1 Peter was previously understood to have originated in the liturgy of water baptism (see "Literary Unity and Genre" in the introduction).

In Exod. 24, animal blood was sprinkled on the people to establish that first covenant. Just before the sprinkling with blood, Moses told the people all that the Lord had said. In light of the subsequent history of Israel, the people's twice-repeated response, "Everything the Lord has said we will do" (24:3, 7; cf. 19:8), seems naive at best, if not even farcical. However, their response to God's word is telling. Even though the human heart is undeniably depraved, there is nevertheless at the same time a deep urge within people to obey God. The inability to do so is frustrating to the point of despair, but because human beings bear the image of God, there is an impulse to be what he created us to be. The old covenant was powerless to bring that innate desire to complete realization. But through Jesus "everyone who believes is set free from every sin, a justification you were not able to obtain under the law of Moses" (Acts 13:39 TNIV). The new covenant in view in 1 Pet. 1:2 is the one that has been established by the blood of Jesus Christ. What the law was powerless to do—transform the hearts of people so they can obey the word of the Lord—has now been made possible by the blood of Jesus Christ. Christ brings to realization that innate desire to obey God. It is for this new covenant that Peter's readers have been chosen and called.

The concept of obedience and sprinkling is also joined with the Diaspora motif in the eschatological prophecy of the OT. God promises to call his people out of the Diaspora of the nations, to sprinkle clean water on them, cleansing them from impurities and from idolatry, and to put his Spirit in them so they will obey his decrees and laws from their hearts (Ezek. 36:24–28). When Peter refers to "Diaspora" followed by a reference to the foreknowledge of God, the sanctification of the Spirit, and the obedience and sprinkling, he may be echoing Ezekiel's prophecy to indicate that God is fulfilling that promise of the Diaspora prophet through the gospel of Jesus Christ.

C. The Greeting (1:2d)

Peter's salutation follows the conventional Hellenistic form by conclud-ing with a greeting. The standard form attested in documents from the third century BC to the third century AD is simply χαίρειν (*chairein*, to rejoice), an infinitive form that was an epistolary idiom with no more meaning than the affection implied by the standard English letter open-ing, "Dear. . . ." (For an example from Hellenistic letters, see Pestman 1990: 77.) Peter, however, modifies and expands the greeting to "grace [χάρις, *charis*] to you and may peace [εἰρήνη, *eirēnē*] be multiplied." This greeting employs the noun that had become the distinctively Christian term for summing up "all that man receives by the free and unmerited gift of God" and joins it with the standard Semitic greeting, *šālôm* (peace), thus expressing "the whole inward state that results from enjoyment of divine goodness" (Beare 1970: 77).

Charis and *eirēnē* appear together in all the Pauline greetings (Rom. 1:7; 1 Cor. 1:3; 2 Cor. 1:2; Gal. 1:3; Eph. 1:2; Phil. 1:2; Col. 1:2; 1 Thess. 1:1; 2 Thess. 1:2; Titus 1:4; and Philem. 3) along with *eleos* (mercy) in 1 Tim. 1:2 and 2 Tim. 1:2. Many commentators understand this to be Pauline influence on the author of 1 Peter. However, in not one of these greetings in the Pauline corpus does the verb πληθυνθείη (*plēthyntheiē*, be multiplied) occur; in fact, in all of the Pauline greetings the implied verb is elided. Achtemeier (1996: 89) construes the inclusion of the verb in the greeting of 2 Pet. 1:2; Jude 2; Pol. *Phil.*; and 1 Clement as additional evidence for a later date for 1 Peter. However, as the greeting became a standard in Christian circles, it seems more plausible that the longer form of it with the explicit verb would be the older form and that once the greeting had come into frequent use, the verb might or might not have been included.

Peter's greeting is sometimes taken as a reference to the specific salvation or peace that marks the messianic age (Cranfield 1958: 18). Clowney (1988: 27) considers the greeting not merely a wish, nor even a prayer, but "a declaration of God's blessing to those who are in Christ," which presents in miniature the whole message of Peter's letter, in spite of the verb's optative mood. Hort and those following him point out that the greeting echoes that of Nebuchadnezzar's letter in Dan. 4:37c LXX (Rahlfs ed.) and Theodotion's Dan. 4:1 (Rahlfs) and as such is a prayerful wish that the grace and peace Daniel received in his hostile Diaspora situation might also attend the tribulations of the Asian Christians (Hort 1898: 26–27). However, the occurrence of the greeting in the LXX may actually indicate that too much is made of the greeting in all of these interpretations. Perhaps it was simply the way a Jewish writer opened a letter in Greek.

Nestle (1898–99) argues similarly that Hort and those following him place too much exegetical weight on the greeting, and identifies what is probably the closest parallel to Peter's salutation and greeting. Nestle points out that the letters of Rabban Gamaliel II (b. Sanhedrin 11b) also begin "May your peace be multiplied" (שְׁלָמְכוֹן יִשְׂגֵּא, šĕlāmĕkôn yiśgēʾ), even when the letters merely announce when the tithe would be collected or the imposition of an intercalatory month in the lunar calendar, situations that do not call for an explicit prayer for peace amid tribulation. The comparison with 1 Peter is interesting also for the similarity in the salutation, for Gamaliel's letters are addressed to the "Sons of the Diaspora of Babel," "Sons of the Diaspora of Mede," and "Sons of the Diaspora of Greece," which closely parallels 1 Peter's "foreigners of the Diaspora of Pontus, Galatia, Cappadocia. . . ." This is further evidence that Peter is simply closing his salutation by using the standard form of a Diaspora letter.

Notably, the wish for peace also concludes Peter's letter in 5:14: "Peace to all of you who are in Christ." Other elements in the closing of the letter echo the opening. The concept of the Diaspora is echoed by use of the phrase "in Babylon" in 5:13, where the election motif is also picked up by the adjective συνεκλεκτή (syneklektē, chosen together). Peter's concluding remarks clearly form an inclusio with the themes of his opening salutation and greeting.

Summary

The encouragement that Peter will offer his readers in the body of the letter is founded on the insight in his salutation and greeting that becoming a foreigner with respect to society is a consequence of being chosen to participate in the new covenant in Christ. As Peter's readers face and struggle with the experience of alienation, the only sure basis of their hope is the benefits of their relationship with God in Christ, which Peter begins to list in the immediately following paragraph. The purpose of the Spirit's work in their lives is to bring them into a covenantal relationship with God that has been established by the blood of Jesus Christ, with all of its life-changing implications. Peter begins a letter that is to instruct and motivate Christians in their lifestyle and relationships by reminding them that it is to this purpose they have been chosen by God the Father through the work of the Spirit. His opening thought goes right to the heart of the issue this letter will address.

Additional Notes

1:1. Although all English translations must supply definite articles in this verse, note that there are none in the Greek text of the greeting. As Achtemeier (1996: 79) notes, "Articles tended to be omitted in formulaic language, and hence were often absent from epistolary introductions; these two verses, however, are longer than the normal ancient letter opening. As presently structured, the language has a solemn, even archaic flavor." The typically anarthrous identification of the sender is found in the Pauline Letters as well. Only 2 and 3 John include the article within the syntax of the sender's identification (probably suggesting that the correspondence was not just from "an elder" but from "the elder," whose personal identity would have been known to the recipients; see BDF §252).

1:1. Since both ἐκλεκτοῖς (eklektois, chosen) and παρεπιδήμοις (parepidēmois, foreigners) can be either adjectival or substantive, is Peter writing to the "elect who are sojourning" (taking eklektois as the substantive, as does the NIV and NLT; also Achtemeier 1996: 79)? Or is he writing to the "chosen sojourners" (taking parepidēmois as the substantive, as NASB [1995], NKJV, and NRSV; also Beare 1970: 74)? The adjectival use of parepidēmos to modify another substantive occurs only infrequently in the extrabiblical writers. Of the following occurrences, only one is clearly adjectival (Polybius, Historiae 32.6.4); other defective readings might possibly be an adjective (Athenaeus, Deipnosophistae 5.21.12; 5.25.10; 10.52.27; 12.54.11; 13.42.17; 13.44.3; Diodorus Siculus, Bibliotheca historica 1.4.3; 1.83.8; 4.18.1; 4.27.3; 4.67.4; 9.25.1; 10.6.2; 13.27.3; 19.61.1; 29.32.1; 32.15.3; Plutarch, Timoleon 38.2.3; Eumenes 1.2.2; Pericles 665.B.4; Praecepta gerendae rei publicae 811.B.10; Herodoti malignitate 871.F.6; Polybius, Historiae 4.4.1, 2; 10.26.5; 13.8.3; 22.13.5; 22.20.4; 26.1.3; 27.6.3; 28.19.2; 30.4.10; 32.6.4; 32.6.6). One clear occurrence of parepidēmos as an adjective is found in Polybius (second–third century BC): πᾶσι τοῖς Ἕλλησι τοῖς παρεπιδήμοις (pasi tois Hellēsi tois parepidēmois, for all the visiting Greeks [in Rome]). Such an adjectival use in 1 Pet. 1:1 would render the translation, "to the visiting elect of the Diaspora of. . . ."

However, in 1 Peter adjectives precede the substantive at least twenty-two times compared with following it at least sixteen times, suggesting that eklektois may be modifying parepidēmois. On the other hand, in the three other occurrences of eklektos in 1 Peter (2:4, 6, 9), it follows its substantive, though two of these are probably constrained by the word order of a quotation from the LXX. A few commentators want to take the prepositional phrases of verse 2 as modifying ἀπόστολος (apostolos, apostle) or even the entire thought of verse 1 (e.g., Grudem 1988: 50). Nevertheless, the later thrust of the letter suggests that it is the chosen-ness of the recipients with its alienating consequences that is the focus, not Peter's apostleship or the geographical setting of the recipients.

It is therefore best to take eklektois and parepidēmois as two substantives in apposition: "to the chosen, the foreigners of the Diaspora," where eklektois describes the addressees' relationship to God and parepidēmois denotes their relationship to society.

1:2. Agnew (1983) argues that the preposition eis has a causative sense (because), but his view has not received wide support. If such a sense for this preposition is admitted, its occurrence is relatively rare. Agnew is following Dana and Mantey (1955: 103), who support such a sense of the preposition, using the debatable example of Rom. 4:20. Moreover, Agnew's construal of the sense of the preposition then necessarily implies that the genitive "of Jesus Christ" ('Ἰησοῦ Χριστοῦ, Iēsou Christou) has a subjective sense with respect to "obedience" (ὑπακοήν, hypakoēn). In this understanding, the addressees were chosen *because* of the obedience that Jesus achieved, culminating in his death, referred to euphemistically as the sprinkling of his blood. While it is true that the genitives of the immediately preceding prepositional phrases ("foreknowledge of God" and "sanctification of the Spirit") are subjective genitives, Agnew's construal does not do justice to the use of the phrase "obedience and sprinkling" in the covenant language of the OT.

II. The Opening of the Letter: Reassurance for God's People (1:3–2:10)

In his opening to the body of his letter, Peter unpacks what it means to participate in the new covenant of Christ's blood into which his readers have entered by the Father's choice and the Spirit's consecration (1 Pet. 1:2). Covenant with God was the key concept in ancient Israel's self-understanding. Peter draws continuity between the old Mosaic covenant and the new covenant in Christ's blood as he applies elements of the former covenant to his Christian readers. Peter includes elements of the old covenant in the opening of his letter but reinterprets them in reference to Christ. LaVerdiere (1969: 2910) observes:

> Election, obedience, sprinkling with blood, sanctification by the Spirit, the abiding word of God, a living temple, a new priesthood, a holy nation, the people of God, the very mention of Christians being dispersed as foreigners—all these and other themes recall many elements of the covenant theology . . . of the Old Testament.

The prophetic Scriptures of the OT can serve Peter's readers because they proleptically spoke of the gospel of Jesus Christ, which has now been preached by evangelists sent by the Holy Spirit (1:10–12). The Spirit who came at Pentecost as the consequence of Christ's death, resurrection, and ascension was the same Spirit who through the prophets of the OT predicted the sufferings of the Christ and the glories that would follow. So closely does Peter associate the Spirit's work with Christ that he refers to the Spirit who was present with the prophets as the Spirit *of Christ* (1:10–12).

The call to holiness first issued in the Pentateuch to Israel as God's chosen people is now the call to Christians (1:15), who have been given new birth by the Holy One. They are called to be holy like the One who begot them by the imperishable seed of his living and enduring word.

Like the OT people of God, Peter's readers have also been redeemed by a blood sacrifice but with the all-important difference that the blood is no longer that of animals but the precious blood of the blameless and spotless lamb, Jesus Christ himself. Through Christ, Peter's readers are placing their faith in no other god but the God of Israel (1:21).

The temple that was the centerpiece of the old covenant has been reconceived as a spiritual house into which those who come to Christ are being built as living stones, with the Living Cornerstone being the resurrected Christ himself (2:4–8). Christ has become the touchstone of one's destiny: acceptance or rejection of him will determine one's eternal relationship with God (2:6–7).

And finally, Peter's readers themselves are endowed with the descriptors of ancient Israel: they are the people of God, a chosen race, a royal priesthood, a holy nation, a people for God's special possession (2:9).

Peter ends the opening of the letter with a second reference to God's mercy (2:10), forming an inclusio with 1:3. In 1:3 he attributes to God's abundant mercy the giving of the new birth, and he closes the opening of the letter with the same thought, that his readers once had not received mercy but now, by virtue of their new birth, have received God's mercy (2:10).

The opening of 1 Peter (1:3–2:10) is a summary of how the old covenant has been transformed into the new by the death and resurrection of Jesus Christ. It presents the new life in Christ into which Peter's readers have been born again.

A. Doxology as the Basis for the Christian Life (1:3–12)

First Peter 1:3–12 opens the body of the letter by providing a theological and hermeneutical basis for the Christian life that introduces the major motifs and themes of the letter. In the Greek, these verses constitute one very long sentence that is composed of a series of subordinate clauses modifying the main clause "Blessed be the God and Father of our Lord Jesus Christ." Doxology provides the context for Christians' new life in Christ (1:3–5) because both their experience of suffering grief in trials (1:6–7) and their present and ultimate salvation is the goal not only of their faith but also of the plan of God as revealed to the prophets (1:8–12).

Analyzed rhetorically, verses 3–12 form the *exordium*, which is a persuasive description of the situation that precipitates the letter (Thurén 1995: 90–91; Tite 1997: 52). The *exordium* prepares readers psychologically for the message that follows, making the audience well disposed, attentive, and ready to receive instruction. It is not necessary to see the author of 1 Peter as a classical Greek orator; however, it would not be surprising to find styles and forms culturally familiar to the recipients in a letter that addresses a broad audience. Characteristic of an *exordium*, this section includes no explicit exhortations or commands. Rather, it attempts to create a good atmosphere for Peter's argument by describing the life of his readers in the most ideal terms and allowing that they may already be living accordingly. Thurén (1995: 91) sees this as putting at ease any negative expectations his readers may have, so they can hear him without being defensive, as well as being a form of encouragement to follow his subsequent exhortations by implying that they are already living consistently with them, at least to some extent.

Those to whom Peter writes have been given new birth into a living hope and an inheritance that will be fully realized at the final revelation of Jesus Christ. Until that time, their Christian faith brings them into conflict with the values and priorities of the society in which they live. This conflict causes them to suffer grief in various kinds of trials, not in spite of being Christians but precisely because they are Christians. The fact that they suffer conflict with their society is evidence that their faith in Christ is genuine; otherwise, they would not choose to live in a way that causes suffering.

Whatever suffering they experience for the name of Christ is, however, subordinate to the great joy that results from being spiritually reborn into a living hope through the resurrection of Jesus Christ. Because suffering for the name of Christ is evidence of a genuine faith that will lead to salvation, it is apparent that these Christians are in fact receiving the goal of that faith, the salvation of their souls. The prophets of ancient Israel eagerly desired to know about this salvation as they inquired into the circumstances that would lead to the sufferings and glories of the Messiah, which had been revealed to them through the Spirit of Christ. This fore-witness of Israel's prophets stood as a confirmation for those who would later be called Christians that the executed Jesus was indeed the long-awaited Messiah.

Peter draws his readers into solidarity with the OT people of God by providing in these verses a theological basis for their identity as covenant people chosen by God to participate in the new covenant in Christ. He explains that Israel's prophets ministered their revelation of the suffering and glories of the Messiah not for their own generation alone but for those who would later come to be called Christians. Therefore, Peter will not hesitate to exhort his readers with the teachings and exhortations of the OT writers.

Kendall's (1986) analysis of the literary structure of 1 Peter shows that these introductory statements about the Christian life in terms of the covenant form the foundation for the exhortations found in 1:13–5:11. First, this opening of the letter introduces the terminology and motifs that will later be developed. Second, Peter's claims here serve as the presupposition for the later exhortations. The letter opening also functions to introduce the theological themes of the letter, which Kendall (1986: 117) summarizes to be "saving grace as a movement from present suffering to future glory in the nonbelieving world and as a fellowship of love in the believing community."

1. The Opening Doxology (1:3–5)

With these verses Peter shifts his focus from God's redeeming mercy to the realities of the believer's new life in Christ. The redeeming act of the God and Father of Jesus Christ is described as giving Christians new birth through the resurrection of Christ. It is difficult to imagine a more sweeping concept than a new birth. Just as people receive their ethnic identity, their citizenship, their socioeconomic class, and their innate potentialities from their biological parents, Christians have a new identity and a new citizenship that redefines their relationship with society and transforms their identity and character. W. Barclay (1976: 171) perceives the richness of these verses: "There are few passages in the New Testament where more of the great fundamental Christian ideas come together."

    a. Eulogy (1:3a)
    b. New birth through Christ's resurrection (1:3b)
    c. New life as living hope and new inheritance (1:3c–4)
    d. Heirs guarded by God's power (1:5)

Exegesis and Exposition

³Blessed be the God and Father of our Lord Jesus Christ, who according to his abundant mercy has given us new birth into a living hope through the resurrection of Jesus Christ from the dead, ⁴into an imperishable, unspoilable, unfading inheritance that is kept in heaven for you, ⁵who are guarded by God's power through faith for a salvation ready to be revealed at the end.

a. Eulogy (1:3a)

The eulogy of verse 3 marks a distinct transition from the salutation of the letter, with its focus on the chosen foreigners of Asia Minor, to God as the source of covenant benefits. The predicate nominative construction of verse 3 is formed by the nominative adjective εὐλογητός (*eulogētos*, blessed), an implied verb (the optative of εἰμί, *eimi*, to be), and the nominative articular noun ὁ θεός (*ho theos*, God). The eulogy "Blessed be God . . ." is familiar to the Jewish tradition, found, for instance, in the Eighteen Benedictions (Oesterley 1925: 60–61). Peter may here be using the Jewish form, but he makes it distinctively Christian by identifying God as the God and Father of our Lord Jesus Christ. The centrality of Jesus Christ to Peter's thought is indicated by his mentioning that name four times in the opening three verses of this letter. The Christian is to take Jesus' God as their God, Jesus' Father as their Father. The verbal agreement between this verse and 2 Cor. 1:3 and Eph. 1:3 indicates only that the phrase was standard apostolic language, not that Peter is dependent on Paul here (contra Beare 1970: 81).

Either praise or blame of the audience is found in the *exordium* of classical oration (Aristotle, *Rhetoric* 3.14). Notably, this "*exordium*" offers praise not of the readers but of the God and Father of Jesus Christ.

b. New Birth through Christ's Resurrection (1:3b)

God is further identified in this eulogy as the one who has given new birth according to his abundant mercy. In verse 2, God's foreknowledge issued in the election of the Christians to whom Peter writes. Here Peter identifies a second aspect of God's character—his abundant mercy—that is the basis for the Christian's existence. The Greek word translated "mercy" (ἔλεος, *eleos*) was used in the ancient Greek translations of the parallel passages of Exod. 20:6 and Deut. 5:10 to translate the Hebrew חֶסֶד (*hesed*, gracious mercy), which is a word closely associated with God's covenantal name. When God forbids idolatry in the second commandment, he promises to be a God who shows *hesed* to a thousand generations of those who love him and keep his commandments. God's covenant with Israel miscarried because they violated the second commandment by worshipping the golden calf. Nevertheless, God revealed his glory to Moses by identifying himself as "the LORD, the LORD, the compassionate and gracious God, slow to anger, abounding in love [Heb.: רַב־חֶסֶד, *rab-hesed*; LXX: πολυέλεος, *polyeleos*] and faithfulness" (Exod. 34:6 NIV). Just as in 1 Pet. 1:2, Peter's language here is covenantal, echoing the covenant language of God's attributes.

The Greek word translated "given new birth" is the articular masculine participle of ἀναγεννάω (*anagennaō*), a verb that does not occur in other books of the NT or the Greek OT. It is found only one other place, in 1:23: "For you have been born again [ἀναγεγεννημένοι, *anagegennēmenoi*], not from perishable seed, but from imperishable, through the living and abiding word of God." God is eulogized here not as the great Creator of all but as the One who has chosen to redeem by giving new birth.

At one time it was thought that 1 Peter here borrowed the concept of new birth from the mystery religions, where it was believed that the initiate experienced a new birth as the result of the rites of initiation (Perdelwitz 1911; see Selwyn 1958: 305–9 for a rebuttal). However, the statements about new birth in the mystery religions are considerably later than the NT (Goppelt 1993: 82n16), and birth as the beginning of a new life is too ubiquitous a religious symbol to determine dependent relationships in the history of religions. Therefore, it is best to look to the closest historical source religion, in this case Judaism, for the use of this concept in 1 Peter. As Selwyn points out, although there is no single corresponding word in Aramaic for "new birth," new birth was nevertheless a way of referring to conversion in the rabbinic literature—for instance, "A newly converted proselyte is like a new-born child" (Selwyn 1958: 306). However, given the difficulty of dating the rabbinic material, it is hard to ascertain whether such rabbinic use was contemporary with the NT writers. Selwyn (1958: 306) observes, "Even Rabbinic ideas which meet us first in the second century are more easily assigned to sources within their own consistent and tenacious tradition than to any borrowing from the Gentile world."

Goppelt is perhaps on firmer ground when he looks not to the rabbinic material but to Qumran for the Jewish background of Peter's use of the new-birth concept. He takes 1QH 3.19–23 as indicating that the Essenes understood one's personal entry into their community as acceptance into a new covenant and a new eschatological creation. He traces the concept of new birth in 1 Pet. 1:3 to the "context of motifs emerging from the self-understanding of the Qumran community" (Goppelt 1993: 82–83). This idea was transposed into the Hellenistic milieu by replacing the concept of "new creation" with "new birth," which Goppelt claims was generally more in vogue (although note 2 Cor. 5:17, which was surely intended to be understood in a Hellenistic context).

The most immediate source for the new-birth concept is found in the first-century Christian tradition that originated in the teachings of Jesus himself. Gundry (1974; 1966–67) argues persuasively that 1 Peter includes many allusions to sayings of Jesus, along with a few allusions to the Lord's actions, that according to the Gospels occur in episodes where Peter was either present or had a strong personal interest (see also a rebuttal in Best 1969–70). In this case, Gundry observes that 1 Pet. 1:3, 23, and 2:2 all involve the concept of the re-birth found also in John 3:3, 7, where Jesus declares, "Very truly I tell you, no one can see the kingdom of God without being born again" (TNIV). Given the ample evidence Gundry cites for other allusions, the teachings of Jesus were most likely one of Peter's sources. Schutter (1989: 35) reaches the conclusion that 1 Peter is more dependent on oral Christian sources than written, which is consistent with Gundry's observation.

Peter's conception of new birth includes "entrance into a new order of existence, but combines with it that of divine parentage: men enter the new life as children of its Author" (Hort 1898: 33). Thus, for the author of 1 Peter, God is not Father by virtue of his role as Creator but rather because of his distinctive role in the new birth of those whom he has chosen to be set apart for the new covenant in Christ.

c. New Life as Living Hope and New Inheritance (1:3c–4)

To those he has chosen, has God given new birth into two things, a living hope and an inheritance, or, as some claim, three things—salvation in addition to hope and inheritance (Achtemeier 1996: 94, 97; du Toit 1974: 64)? And what is the relationship between these items? Apposition? Parallel? Sequential? The syntax readily admits of a new birth εἰς ἐλπίδα (*eis elpida*, into hope) and εἰς κληρονομίαν (*eis klēronomian*, into an inheritance). But does the third prepositional phrase, εἰς σωτηρίαν (*eis sōtērian*, into salvation, 1:5), modify ἀναγεννήσας (*anagennēsas*, has given new birth) or φρουρουμένους (*phrouroumenous*, who are guarded, 1:5; construing the voice of the participle as passive with Achtemeier 1996: 97)? In other words, is Peter saying that Christians are given new birth *into* salvation, or that they are being guarded *for* salvation? Both may be theologically true, but what is Peter saying here? Neither discourse analysis nor lexical study provides a clear answer (see the additional note on 1:5). The grammatical construction suggests that each of the three participles, *anagennēsas*, *tetērēmenēn*, and *phrouroumenous*, govern the prepositional phrase that follows, indicating that the new birth (*anagennēsas*) is into only hope (*elpida*) and an inheritance (*klēronomian*; as also Dupont-Roc 1995: 205–6). Peter's eschatological perspective that salvation is yet to be revealed tilts the evidence slightly toward taking *eis sōtērian* as modifying *phrouroumenous*. This means that the chosen are given new birth into two things—hope and an inheritance—but they are also guarded by faith until salvation is fully realized at some future time. This thought answers nicely to the threatening situation being addressed by the letter.

Strengthening this conclusion is the observation that where the noun *sōtēria* is immediately preceded by a preposition in the NT, the preposition *eis* occurs in all twenty-four places. This suggests that *eis* in 1:5 is not resumptive: it does not add "salvation" to the preceding "hope" and "inheritance" but is simply the idiomatic preposition to use with this noun. If so, the new birth as presented by Peter here is "into" only two things, which may in fact form a hendiadys referring to the new life of the new believer as a living hope and a new inheritance. "The new life bestowed by the Father through the Gospel is at once a hope and an inheritance" (Hort 1898: 35).

The hope into which the chosen have been given new birth is described as a "living" (ζῶσαν, *zōsan*) hope, a hope that is alive. This is not a personification that means a "growing" hope (cf. Grudem 1988: 55). Rather, it is in contrast with hope that is dead because it is based on futile things. The apostle Paul describes pagan religion and philosophy in Eph. 2:12 and 1 Thess. 4:13 as without hope. The epidemic of hopelessness in our times is not just a modern phenomenon. This hopelessness echoes in Sophocles' reflections on the fate of Oedipus, that it is best not to be born at all and the second best is to die at birth (*Oedipus* 121[a].15; Poole and Maule 1995: 148). In Greek thought, the despair of this life is followed only by the unending night of death. Catullus writes that though the sun can set and rise again, once our brief light sets, there is but one unending night to be slept through (*Fifth Epigram* 4–6; Poole and Maule 1995: 266–67). The existential despair in this life and the bleak view of afterlife in Greek thought killed any hope one might seek; therefore, hope among pagans was dead. This Greek thought is not unlike the existentialist and materialistic philosophy apparent today. In stark contrast, the Christian's new birth has been achieved through the resurrection of Jesus Christ (1 Pet. 1:3). Christian hope is everliving because Christ, the ground of that hope, is everliving. The present reality of the Christian's life is defined and determined by the reality of the past—the resurrection of Jesus Christ—and is guaranteed into the future because Christ lives forevermore.

If the Christians to whom Peter writes had in fact been expelled from Rome, their personal experience may have induced a feeling of helplessness and hopelessness common to those who experience disruptive events beyond their own control (see "Roman Colonization and the Origin of 1 Peter" in the introduction). Moreover, since wealth and inheritance were most often vested in land in the first-century world, a displacement from one's homeland meant that whatever property one stood to inherit would be of uncertain benefit, if any. (This is not unlike, for instance, the situation faced by Cuban exiles, who must leave property and wealth behind in Cuba when they surreptitiously emigrate to the United States.) Thus, the loss of inheritance and family rights could lead directly to feelings of hopelessness. But even if the Christians to whom Peter writes have not been physically displaced, their new life as Christians affected their social status. It may even have jeopardized their inheritance as members of pagan families, much as some Muslim, Hindu, or Jewish families still today will disinherit a family member who converts to Christianity. Such experiences may understandably result in feelings of hopelessness.

Peter, however, points out that these Christians, who are foreigners with respect to their place of residence, have been given new birth into a new family by the word of God the Father. This new birth has brought to them a new inheritance that cannot be touched by the vicissitudes of time and circumstance. Peter describes their new inheritance with three alpha-privative adjectives: ἄφθαρτον (*aphtharton*, imperishable), ἀμίαντον (*amianton*, unspoilable), ἀμάραντον (*amaranton*, unfading). As Michaels (1988: 21) explains:

> Each of these words in its own way drives home the point that the inheritance of which Peter speaks is an eternal one. . . . In general ἄφθαρτον refers to freedom from death and decay, ἀμίαντον to freedom from un-

cleanness or moral impurity, and ἀμάραντον to freedom from the natural ravages of time.

Or, as Beare (1970: 83–84) so eloquently puts it, "The paronomasia of the three verbals is most effective; the inheritance is untouched by death, unstained by evil, unimpaired by time; it is compounded of immortality, purity, and beauty."

Peter's description of this inheritance brings immediately to mind Jesus' teaching in the Sermon on the Mount:

> Do not store up for yourselves treasures on earth, where moth and rust destroy, and where thieves break in and steal. But store up for yourselves treasures in heaven, where moth and rust do not destroy, and where thieves do not break in and steal. For where your treasure is, there your heart will be also. (Matt. 6:19–21 TNIV)

Gundry (1966–67: 337) considers the threefold description of the inheritance in 1 Pet. 1:4 to be an adaptation of Jesus' teaching about the threefold benefit of treasure in heaven as preserved in Luke 12:33, "Sell your possessions and give to the poor. Provide purses for yourselves that will not wear out, a treasure in heaven that *will never fail*, where *no thief comes near* and *no moth destroys*" (TNIV, emphasis added).

The inheritance of land was the major source for increasing one's wealth, social status, and security (Alston 1998: 218; MacMullen 1974: 101). In light of the role that land played in inheritance in both the Greek and the Semitic worlds, Peter's teaching about the nature of their new inheritance invites a comparison of the new "land" in which they hold inheritance (their share in the kingdom of God) with the land rights of their birth. This comparison might have been especially meaningful to Christians displaced from their homeland (in the Diaspora). Jewish Christians remembered that the land of the old covenant had been ravished, defiled, and defaced successively by the Assyrians, Babylonians, Persians, Ptolemies, Seleucids, and Romans and that the Jews lived in the Diaspora away from the benefits of their inheritance. Grudem (1988: 58) explains:

> The "inheritance" of the New Covenant Christian is thus shown to be far superior to the earthly inheritance of the people of Israel in the land of Canaan. That earthly land was not "kept" for them, but was *taken from them* in exile, and later by Roman occupation. Even while they possessed the land, it produced rewards that *decayed*, rewards whose glory *faded* away. The beauty of the land's holiness before God was repeatedly *defiled* by sin (Num. 35:34; Jer. 2:7; 3:2). (emphasis in original)

Such could never happen to them again in their new home in Christ's kingdom, into which they have been born again. Jewish or Gentile

Christians, if expelled from their place of residence, have experienced life-shaking economic and social upheaval. However, now their new inheritance is secure, for it is even now being kept (perfect participle of τηρέω: τετηρημένην, *tetērēmenēn*) "in heaven" for them, far beyond the reach of the events of this world.

d. Heirs Guarded by God's Power (1:5)

The Christian inheritance exists now and is being kept safe from the vicissitudes of this world, but also the heirs for whom it is being kept are themselves guarded by God's power through faith (1 Pet. 1:4–5). Peter's choice of verbs here suggests that though the heirs may be in peril, nothing less than the power of God himself watches over them. Paradoxically, it is their faith in Christ that has put them in jeopardy with respect to their society, but it is that very faith in Christ that identifies them as legitimate heirs, whom God powerfully protects (Calvin 1963: 233). The word in 1:6 translated "trials" (πειρασμοῖς, *peirasmois*) is the same word found in the Lord's Prayer: "Lead us not into *temptation* [*peirasmon*]" (Matt. 6:13 TNIV). The stated purpose of Peter's letter is to convince his readers to stand firm in the "true grace of God" (5:12). The trials provoked by Christian faith are implicitly a temptation to renounce that faith, at least to the extent that such trials can be avoided. As Perkins (1995: 30) observes, the request in the Lord's Prayer to avoid temptation "reminds us that no Christian seeks the 'testing' of his or her faith. Nor does God set up such trials as an obstacle course or entrance exam. But Christians have known from the beginning that no genuine faith will exist without them." The transformed values by which they live as followers of Christ might well alienate them from nonbelievers, whose lives are ordered by a different set of values, creating conflicts and tensions for the Christians. However, the faith that alienates them from their society is the same faith that provides the resources by which they may endure the alienation. In spite of suffering, the continuing trust they place in the Father of the Lord Jesus Christ marks them as his heirs (cf. 2:23; 4:19).

Christians are guarded by God's power until they are ushered into a salvation (σωτηρίαν, *sōtērian*) that is now ready (at the time Peter writes and henceforth) to be revealed at the "last time" (ἐν καιρῷ ἐσχάτῳ, *en kairō eschatō*). It is now ready because the past events of Jesus' death, resurrection, and ascension have achieved it. In the immediate context, the phrase "the last time" points to a future event, the parousia, or reappearing, of Jesus Christ (1:7). Throughout the letter, Peter anticipates a future time that will be marked by God's judgment of all people and the attainment of glory for the believer in Christ (2:12; 4:7, 17–18; 5:4, 10). Parker (1994: 28), however, argues that such verses, and especially the phrase *en kairō eschatō*, have been misunderstood as a future reference when they should be construed, citing Hort, as "in a season of extremity." Although Parker's argument is not convincing (see Tite 1997: 77), his point is well taken that the eschatological concept in 1 Peter refers to "the significance of the present possession of Christ" and not exclusively to "the wonders of a future glory" (see point 6, "First Peter's Eschatology," under "Major Themes and Theology" in the introduction). The certainty of future salvation animates the hope in which Christians now live, making the eschatological future a present reality. This is a consolatory technique intended to relieve feelings of oppression by so closely interweaving the glories of the future with the present that the present is transformed in the thought-world of Peter's readers (Tite 1997: 77).

The term *sōtēria* (salvation) was used more broadly in first-century Greek-speaking culture than it is among some Christians today, who may limit its reference to one's spiritual state. In the Hellenistic world, *sōtēria* referred to deliverance from any threat—personal, political, or military—and not necessarily by divine intervention. In the NT this noun and its cognate verb σῴζειν (*sōzein*, to save) are used to refer to deliverance from physical danger (e.g., Matt. 8:25), from disease (e.g., 9:21), and from sin (e.g., 1:21). The same word refers to the reward for standing firm in the face of persecution (e.g., Matt. 10:22; 24:13). In 1 Peter, the benefits of the new birth are a present reality, but salvation is yet to be revealed at the end of history. Peter's teaching presents a good corrective to the popular thought that at death Christians go "up" to heaven to receive their full and final reward. Peter presents salvation as fully attained only at the final judgment, at the end of history when Jesus Christ is revealed. Therefore, in Peter's thought *sōtēria* (salvation) refers to the ultimate deliverance that is the final goal of redemptive history and in which believers in Christ will partake. It is a deliverance from this current state of existence as foreigners in a world hostile to God and into a place of existence in which there will be no such dissonance. Christians are sure to attain to this final state of existence because they have been spiritually born into it through the resurrection of Christ. For Peter, *sōtēria* is the coming inheritance, to which they are now fully entitled but do not yet fully possess.

Peter's vision of an eschatological inheritance in which Christians will no longer be foreigners coheres with Jesus' proclamation of the kingdom of God, which was the central theme of his teaching throughout his public ministry from baptism to ascension (Matt. 3:17; Mark 1:15; Luke 4:43; Acts 1:3). The promise of land made to the patriarchs and to David's dynasty became a typological reference to the eschatological inheritance of a place where all hearts are governed by God's gracious rule. The distinctiveness of Peter's Christian eschatology is his identification of the resurrection of Jesus Christ as the means by which new birth into the eschatological kingdom of God is given.

The Christians to whom Peter writes participate in the eschatological kingdom, whose fullness is still future, by allowing their present life of faith in God to be informed and energized by the unseen reality into which they have been reborn. Their self-understanding and resulting conduct are no longer to be shaped primarily by their society and culture, and hence they belong no longer solely to the society and culture in which they reside but to the society and culture of God's kingdom.

Summary

New birth through Christ's resurrection results in personal hope, which redefines one's status both in society (in terms of alienation) and in the kingdom (in terms of a share in eternal inheritance). This message of living hope is addressed to

> those who are at the margins of society, reviled and accused. They know how they appear in society's eyes. They need a larger perspective, which the author provides not in psychological or sociological terms of self-esteem, but by helping them see their privileged place in the context of God's plan for history, a privilege they had not achieved but had been granted by God's grace. (Boring 1999: 65)

Christians in many locales today may not experience social alienation for the name of Christ to the extent experienced by the Christians of first-century Asia Minor or to the extent Christians in third-world or Muslim countries do today. But all Christians need to have their self-understanding transformed by Peter's message of the reality of the living hope into which they have been reborn.

Additional Note

1:5. Has God given new birth into two things, a living hope and an inheritance, or three—salvation in addition to hope and inheritance? Discourse analysis does not clearly indicate whether *eis sōtērian* is governed by *anagennaō* or by *phroureō* (du Toit 1974: 63–64). The verb *anagennaō* does not occur in the NT, apart from 1 Peter, or in the LXX, but γεννάω (*gennaō*, beget) frequently occurs with prepositions. In the Greek Bible, both *gennaō* and *phroureō/phrouroō* twice occur with *eis* following. When complementing *gennaō*, *eis* specifies the state into which the birthing results (e.g., Prov. 11:19; Sir. 41:9). When complementing *phroureō*, as found in Gal. 3:23, *eis* may be specifying one of two relationships. It may specify the temporal point at which the guarding is no longer necessary—"until the faith that was to come would be revealed" (TNIV) or "until faith in Christ was shown to us" (NLT). Or it may specify that which the guarding prevents the experience of—"kept . . . shut up unto the faith that should afterwards be revealed" (KJV) or "kept in custody . . . being shut up to the faith which was later to be revealed" (NASB).[1] Only

---

1. Galatians 3:23 and 1 Pet. 1:5 form an interesting contrast with respect to faith and salvation. In Galatians, "we" were guarded by the law until faith was revealed. In 1 Peter, "we" are guarded by faith until salvation is revealed.

the first of these alternatives makes sense in the context of 1 Pet. 1:5: Christians are guarded by faith until that time when salvation is revealed. (We are hardly guarded by faith to keep us from salvation!) Although it is a difficult call, this thought seems more consistent with the eschatology of 1 Peter than the alternative of taking *anagennēsas* to govern *eis sōtērian*, yielding the sense that the chosen are given new birth into a salvation that has not yet been revealed. The thought that God protects both the inheritance and the heir until deliverance is complete answers nicely to the threatening situation addressed by 1 Peter.

2. Joy and Suffering in the New Life (1:6–9)

The new birth brings Peter's readers great joy, for they have both a living hope for this life and an everlasting inheritance in the life hereafter. However, their identity as Christians also brings them suffering and grief in various kinds of trials. Peter makes the astonishing claim that the suffering they presently experience is a test of faith that will end in praise, glory, and honor when Jesus Christ is revealed. Suffering is a test of the genuineness of their faith in Christ, especially because they have neither seen nor presently see him. Therefore, even their suffering is an opportunity for joy because it confirms their faith and the salvation that will certainly be theirs in the end.

a. Joy transcends trials (1:6, 8b–9)
b. Genuine faith is tested faith (1:7)

Exegesis and Exposition

⁶You rejoice in this, although for a little while you have had to suffer grief in all kinds of trials, ⁷in order that the genuineness of your faith—which is more valuable than gold that perishes even though refined by fire—may be found to result in praise, glory, and honor when Jesus Christ is revealed. ⁸Although you have not seen him, you love him; although you do not see him now, you believe in him. And you rejoice with a glorified joy beyond words, ⁹because you are obtaining the goal of faith, your salvation.

a. Joy Transcends Trials (1:6, 8b–9)

Although verses 3–12 form one long sentence in the Greek, the subordinate phrases in verses 6–9 have structure within themselves. The two occurrences of the verb ἀγαλλιᾶσθε (*agalliasthe*, you rejoice), in verses 6 and 8, form an inclusio, with the present joy of Christians qualified by certain concessions in between:

You rejoice in this
    although you have had to suffer grief
      for a little while now
      in all kinds of trials
      in order that the genuineness of your faith . . . may be
        found . . . ;

> *although* you have not seen him, yet you love him;
> *although* you do not see him now, yet you believe in him.
> You rejoice with a glorified joy beyond words
>   because you are obtaining the goal of faith, your salvation.

With verse 6 Peter shifts the focus from the certainties of future eschatological glory to the more dismal realities of the present. However, the future eschatological perspective is important, for it is meant to determine how Christians are to face life in their present situations. The verse begins with a prepositional phrase and a relative pronoun, ἐν ᾧ ἀγαλλιᾶσθε (*en hō agalliasthe*, in which you [will?] rejoice). Some take the antecedent of the relative pronoun *hō* to be the immediately preceding phrase, ἐν καιρῷ ἐσχάτῳ (*en kairō eschatō*), making the prepositional phrase an adverbial expression of time specifying when they will rejoice, in the "last time" (T. Martin 1992b: 310). This requires taking ἀγαλλιᾶσθε (*agalliasthe*, you will rejoice) as present in form but future in sense (Bigg 1956: 103; T. Martin 1992b: 310–11). Similar syntax in the LXX argues against an adverbial sense for this prepositional phrase, especially in the Psalms, where the verb *agalliasthe* is often found with *en*, which phrase expresses the grounds of the rejoicing, in this case represented by the relative pronoun *hō*. Moreover, as du Toit (1974: 68) observes, a temporal construal provides "a too narrow basis for the reference to the unspeakable joy of the faithful." Although the deliverance of the believer through faith in Christ will produce joy in the end, that joy is nevertheless tasted in this present life.

Taking the relative pronoun *hō* to be masculine singular, a few prefer to understand its antecedent to be either θεός (*theos*, God) or Χριστός (*Christos*, Christ) from verse 3 (Hort 1898: 40). Du Toit (1974: 68) argues that construing the antecedent as *theos* produces "an exceedingly fine structural pattern" from the perspective of discourse analysis and is completely in keeping with the OT expression to "rejoice in the Lord." However, he concurs that there is little difference in sense between this construal and taking the relative pronoun as a neuter singular with reference to the entire preceding thought in verses 3–5, which is the way most interpreters read it (Achtemeier 1996: 99; Best 1971: 77; Beare 1970: 86; Calvin 1963: 234; Grudem 1988: 60; Thurén 1995: 71). Calvin (1963: 234) observes, "*In which* refers to the whole subject of the hope of salvation laid up in heaven" (emphasis original).

The mood of the verb *agalliasthe* is also ambiguous. Its form permits it to be taken as (1) present indicative (you rejoice), (2) present imperative (rejoice, or keep on rejoicing), or (3) present indicative in form with future force (you will rejoice). Du Toit (1974: 70–71) has argued for the imperative mood on the basis of a shift to second person and because, of the nine times the verb occurs in the LXX in the second person, eight are "intended" as imperatives. Recent rhetorical analysis of 1 Peter suggests that an imperative is unlikely to be found in a paraenetic letter's opening section, which states the context in which the letter is to be read and prepares the reader for the imperatives that will indeed follow later (T. Martin 1992b).

Thurén (1990) presents the intriguing idea that this is only the first of several items throughout 1 Peter that are ambiguous on the lexical, syntactical, or ideological levels and that were deliberately expressed in forms that could be taken differently by different readers. So, for those readers who are in fact rejoicing despite their grievous trials, *agalliasthe* can be read as an indicative affirming that "you rejoice." For those readers who are not in fact rejoicing, the construal of the verb as an imperative form, "rejoice," instructs them in the attitude they are to adopt. The verbs ἀγαπᾶτε (*agapate*, you love), πιστεύοντες (*pisteuontes*, believing), and the second occurrence of *agalliasthe* in verse 8 are also grammatically ambiguous in form. Thurén also discusses the ambiguity of the much-debated imperatival participles in 1 Peter from the perspective of this theory (for a discussion of imperatival participles in 1 Peter, see the second additional note on 1:13). He has a point about the different needs of the broad audience that Peter is addressing. But it is hard to see a deliberate strategy at work when the ambiguous forms of the present indicative and imperative are simply a happenstance of the Greek language. What other choice did Peter have?

Taking the antecedent of the relative pronoun *hō* as the whole subject of the hope laid up in heaven coheres well with Peter's flow of thought, for it provides the perspective from which he wants his readers to view their present sufferings. They are to rejoice in the promise of eternal glory into which they have been born again through the resurrection of Jesus Christ, although they are in distressing circumstances and although they have not personally seen Jesus (as the author has?). In other words, the trying circumstances Peter's readers are in would not, humanly speaking, give them any reason to hope in the glorious future that is theirs in Christ. Nor have they had the empirical experience of witnessing Jesus either during his life or in his resurrection glory. They love Jesus even though they did not see him (ἰδόντες, *idontes*, aorist); they believe in Jesus even though they are not now seeing him (ὁρῶντες, *horōntes*, present). They are truly walking by faith, not by sight, and therefore are blessed as Jesus himself promised in John 20:29: "Blessed are those who do not see [me] and believe."[1]

b. Genuine Faith Is Tested Faith (1:7)

However, the joy of knowing one's ultimate eschatological future does not make the distress of one's current circumstances any less real or

---

1. Gundry (1966–67: 337–38) considers this another one of the many sayings of Christ that are reflected in the words of 1 Peter.

disquieting. Peter concedes the reality of his readers' distress yet qualifies it with further thoughts of encouragement. Their suffering is coming "by all kinds of trials," suggesting that there was no one pressing trial or persecution in view. The adjective translated "all kinds" (ποικίλος, *poikilos*, 1:6) in some contexts means "many-colored." The same adjective is found in 4:10, where it refers to the many kinds of expression of the grace of God. The clause "although for a little while you have had to suffer" acknowledges the reality of suffering but qualifies it as being only "for a little while" and suggests the necessity of the suffering by hinting at its purpose. Recognizing that suffering is relatively brief and necessary makes it more bearable. Perhaps of greatest encouragement, Peter explains how the sufferings are purposeful. The purpose clause (ἵνα, *hina*, in order that) has as its subject τὸ δοκίμιον ὑμῶν τῆς πίστεως (*to dokimion hymōn tēs pisteōs*, the genuineness of your faith). The suffering in view proves the genuineness of their faith, which will result in praise, glory, and honor when Jesus is revealed. Thurén's (1995: 100) rhetorical analysis of these verses results in three related conclusions:

1. You rejoice despite suffering, since suffering does not prevent joy.
2. You are willing to suffer in order to glorify God.
3. You are willing to suffer in order to obtain glory.

In subsequent verses (2:9, 12; 4:11) it is God who receives the praise and glory because of the behavior of Christians; the second thought therefore is probably primary in Peter's logic, with the first and third being implied. Their trials are presented explicitly as a testing so that their faithfulness to God in any and all circumstances could be proved to themselves and others to be the genuine type of faith that will result in eternal glory.

Peter does not wish his readers to confuse the testing of their faith with the failure of their faith or to think that their distress implies they have inadequate faith. He uses the imagery of refined gold, the most precious material then known. As precious as gold may be, it nevertheless is perishable even though it has been refined by fire. Although the reference to gold tested by fire may suggest images of horrific persecution, such as experienced by the Christians in Rome under Nero, this is most likely a more specific interpretation than the reference warrants. Fire was a common symbol for affliction, adversity, and judgment in both Jewish and Greek thought quite apart from Nero's actions. Seneca, the most important literary and public figure in Rome in the mid- to late-first century, uses the same metaphor in his proverb *Ignis aurum probat, miseria fortes viros* (Fire tests gold, affliction tests strong men; *Ep., On Providence* 5.10). The metaphorical fire of affliction is found in biblical thought as well, with the fiery image a reference to the Lord trying human souls (e.g., Ps. 66:10; Prov. 17:3; 27:21; Zech. 13:9; Mal.

3:3). Particularly in the prophetic passages, the refining fire of God's testing is preparation for eschatological perfection. Peter's thoughts on suffering as a test of faith stand squarely in the Jewish tradition expressed, for instance, in Sir. 2:1–6, which is perhaps the closest lexical and conceptual parallel:

> My child, when you come to serve the Lord, prepare yourself for testing [πειρασμόν, *peirasmon*].
> Set your heart right and be steadfast, and do not be impetuous in time of calamity.
> Cling to him and do not depart, so that your last days may be prosperous.
> Accept whatever befalls you, and in times of humiliation be patient.
> For gold is tested [δοκιμάζεται, *dokimazetai*] in the fire, and those found acceptable, in the furnace of humiliation.
> Trust [πίστευσον, *pisteuson*] in him, and he will help you; make your ways straight, and hope [ἔλπισον, *elpison*] in him. (NRSV)

Peter's point is that gold, even though it has been smelted through a refining fire that burns up all that is not genuine, will nevertheless perish in the final fiery judgment. Calvin (1963: 235) takes the fire both as a purifying process by which dross (anything that is not of faith) is consumed and as a test of a genuine precious metal.

The faith of Peter's readers is being smelted in the fire of various kinds of trials in this life. But when the most precious things of this world—such as gold—have been destroyed by fire (cf. 2 Pet. 3:10–11), Christian faith that has been proved genuine will be shown to be the most precious of all because it will deliver one from that day of final, fiery destruction when Jesus Christ is revealed (cf. 1 Pet. 1: 5). Therefore, Peter reminds his readers that genuine Christian faith is more valuable than anything the world can offer.

This may explain the purpose of suffering grief in all kinds of trials (1:7–8), but why is suffering "necessary" (1:6)? The first-class conditional of fact joined with the participle of the impersonal verb δεῖ (*dei*, it is necessary) indicates that the suffering Peter has in mind may be an inevitable situation, not merely a possible occurrence. For, by virtue of being chosen to respond in faith to the gospel (1:1–3), one is at the same time necessarily alienated from the priorities and values of unbelieving society, which inevitably results in various types of suffering. Just as physical birth bestows citizenship based on that of one's parent, Christians have been given new birth by the divine Father bestowing on them a new citizenship and inheritance in the kingdom of God. This new identity and allegiance make them to some extent aliens within society. Therefore, those who are intent on serving the Lord must not be surprised by the distress that they experience in many kinds of trials (cf. 4:12). While their faithfulness to God may be why they are not receiving any praise, glory, or honor from their society, that same faithfulness will ultimately result in praise, glory, and honor when all is said and done. Therefore, the very experiences that cause them distress because they are Christians should also cause them joy because they are Christians. They rejoice with a joy that is beyond words and that has been glorified even by the dark circumstances in which they possess it.

3. The Christian's Advantage over the Prophets and Even the Angels (1:10–12)

In the final statement describing his readers' situation, Peter explains their privileged status because of the knowledge of the gospel they have received. He compares their knowledge of God's redemptive work as superior to that of both the prophets and the angels. Comparison with the first group situates Peter's readers as privileged historically, and with the second group, cosmically.

Peter points out that his readers are privileged to be participating in a salvation that Israel's prophets eagerly desired to learn about as they inquired into the circumstances and time of the Messiah's sufferings and subsequent glories. The Spirit of Christ revealed those sufferings and glories to the prophets as a forewitness, allowing the prophet's own generation to live with confidence in the salvation that would one day be achieved. But the prophets' forewitness of the sufferings of the Messiah functions for Peter's readers as a confirmation that the crucified Jesus is indeed the Messiah. Consequently, the unity of the prophetic message of the OT and the Christian gospel is the basis on which Peter will use the teachings and ethics of the OT to exhort and instruct his readers.

In these verses Peter establishes the relevance of the OT for his readers, and he will continue to use the OT throughout his letter both to further explain Jesus and to exhort his readers with its ethical teachings. The hermeneutic that Peter explains in 1 Pet. 1:10–12 allows him to draw his readers' self-understanding into solidarity with the OT people of God, giving them a new heritage now that they have abandoned the empty way of their biological ancestors (1:18), whether Gentile or Jew. They are no longer citizens of diverse nations but have been joined to the one people of God. Therefore, their self-understanding must be reshaped in accordance with this new reality that is of the greatest value.

a. Three exegetical questions (1:10–11)
b. The forewitness of the prophets (1:12a)
c. The angels' interest in the gospel (1:12b)

Exegesis and Exposition

[10]The prophets who prophesied about the grace that has come to you sought out and carefully inquired about this salvation [11]by looking into what circumstances or what the time would be like that the Spirit of Christ in them was revealing by foretelling the sufferings that would come to Messiah and the glories after. [12]It was revealed to the prophets that not for themselves but for you they were ministering [these] things, things now told you through those who preached the gospel to you by the Holy Spirit sent from heaven, things into which angels eagerly desire to look.

a. Three Exegetical Questions (1:10–11)

The prophets sought out and carefully inquired about the salvation that had come to the Christians of Peter's day. By pointing this out, Peter draws a continuity between what had been foretold in the OT and what has been realized in the life of Jesus and preached in the gospel. The Christians to whom Peter writes are not to understand themselves as practitioners of yet another new religion in the world, founded on the person of Jesus of Nazareth. Rather, they are being privileged with the knowledge of the gospel that fulfills God's mysterious plan as revealed to the prophets of the OT and that brings them into continuity with what God has already been doing through ancient Israel. Jesus Christ has already been a part of that work, for it is the "Spirit of Christ" who has revealed the sufferings and glories of the Messiah to the prophets. The knowledge imparted by forewitness to the prophets is now being preached by Christian evangelists as having been historically realized in the life of Jesus. Therefore, Peter views the gospel of Jesus Christ as one with the message of the OT.

This passage raises three interrelated exegetical questions: (1) Are the prophets mentioned OT prophets or charismatic prophets contemporaneous with Peter's readers (e.g., Agabus in Acts 21:10–12)? (2) How should the unusual phrase τὰ εἰς Χριστὸν παθήματα (*ta eis Christon pathēmata*, the sufferings to Christ) be translated and understood? Similarly, (3) how should the phrase εἰς τίνα ἢ ποῖον καιρόν (*eis tina ē poion kairon*, into which or what sort of time) be translated and understood? These phrases are central to Peter's thought: prophets did their seeking and studying specifically by inquiring *eis tina ē poion kairon* the Spirit of Christ was referring when revealing *ta eis Christon pathēmata*.

The latter phrase, *ta eis Christon pathēmata* (and not the prepositional phrase *eis tina ē poion kairon*) is the direct object of the participle προμαρτυρόμενον (*promartyromenon*, witnessing beforehand), a participle that gives the manner or mode of the imperfect indicative verb ἐδήλου (*edēlou*, was revealing). How the syntax of the phrase *ta eis Christon pathēmata* is construed will determine which prophets are in view. As

Warden (1989: 5) observes, "If the phrase alludes to the suffering of Christ, the prophets of the passage are of necessity Old Testament personalities." However, there has been some exegetical debate. Selwyn (1958: 134) sees here "a phrase with a wider reference than to the O.T. prophets only, and [that] embraces the whole prophetic tradition, including the Christian prophets." Warden (1989: 12) corroborates Selwyn's arguments and concludes that "the prophets of 1 Peter 1:10–12 are contemporary prophets among the first readers of the epistle." Both interpreters have understood *ta eis Christon pathēmata* to be sufferings of God's people as they experience the messianic woes leading up to the return of Christ (Selwyn 1958: 136; Warden 1989: 6).

The phrase *ta eis Christon pathēmata* is often translated "the sufferings of Christ" (KJV, NIV, TNIV, NASB) even though the genitive Χριστοῦ (*Christou*, of Christ) is not present. Instead, a prepositional phrase, *eis Christon*, adjectivally modifies the head noun *pathēmata*. By taking *eis* to mean "on behalf of," this syntax has been understood by some interpreters to refer *not* to sufferings experienced by Christ himself but to those experienced by Christians because of Christ. The plural form of *pathēmata* has been taken to refer to the suffering of many, whereas a singular would be expected if it referred to the crucifixion of Christ. (And note that the "glories" that follow are also plural.) The REB translates this phrase in the context of 1 Peter as "sufferings in Christ's cause." Selwyn (1958: 136) renders it "the sufferings of the Christward road," in an apparent attempt to capture the preposition's sense of directional movement.

A second way of construing the *eis* phrase is to take it in the sense of an extension in time with the meaning of "until." BDAG 289 gives Gal. 3:24 as an example of this sense, ὁ νόμος παιδαγωγὸς ἡμῶν γέγονεν εἰς Χριστόν (*ho nomos paidagōgos hēmōn gegonen eis Christon*), which can be translated, "The law was put in charge of us until Christ came" (TNIV). However, the sense of the prepositional phrase in Gal. 3:24 is also disputed, with the NIV and NASB translating that the law was to lead us "to Christ."

Scott (1905) construes a temporal sense of *eis* in 1 Pet. 1:11, arguing that the sufferings are not those of Christ but refer to the messianic woes leading up to the second coming of Christ, woes to be suffered by God's people. Thus understood, the Spirit of Christ has foretold through the prophets the very season of sufferings that the Christians of Asia Minor are experiencing and, furthermore, that their sufferings indicate that the return of Christ is close at hand. This interpretation coheres well with 4:17, in which Peter explains that the sufferings of his readers are in some way a part of the eschatological judgment (see comments on 4:17).

Nevertheless, the sense of this syntax elsewhere in the NT indicates that the phrase *ta eis Christon pathēmata* indeed refers to the sufferings of the Christ, which—as Peter will go on to explain in chapter 2—are also to be experienced by those who follow him. Elsewhere the prepositional phrase with *eis* adjectivally modifies its head noun by specifying the recipients of the verbal action implied by the noun. Perhaps the closest syntactical parallel to 1 Pet. 1:10 is 2 Cor. 1:11, where, in the phrase τὸ εἰς ἡμᾶς χάρισμα (*ta eis hēmas charisma*, the grace to us), the head noun *charisma* implies the verb χαρίζομαι (*charizomai*, show gracious favor) and the prepositional phrase *eis hēmas* expresses the recipients of the implied verbal action. This understanding yields the translation "the gracious favor granted us."

A second close parallel is in 2 Cor. 11:3, with its phrase τῆς ἁπλότητος τῆς εἰς τὸν Χριστόν (*tēs haplotētos tēs eis ton Christon*, the devotion to Christ), where the head noun *haplotētos*, "sincere devotion," implies the verb "to be devoted." The prepositional phrase *eis ton Christon* indicates the recipient of that sincere devotion, Christ. Seven other similar examples of this adjectival use of *eis* can be found (Acts 20:21; 26:6; 1 Cor. 15:10; 16:1; 2 Cor. 8:4; 9:1; Eph. 1:15).

Furthermore, the syntax of *ta eis Christon pathēmata* in 1 Pet. 1:11 is parallel to the syntax in 1:10: τῆς εἰς ὑμᾶς χάριτος (*tēs eis hymas charitos*, the grace to you), translated "the grace that has come to you." The head noun, *charitos*, implies the verb *charizomai* (show gracious favor), where the prepositional phrase *eis hymas* indicates the recipients of the grace, namely, "you." The genitive, "your grace," is not used here, probably to avoid the possibility of it being taken to mean the gracious behavior of the Asian Christians. It would seem that the parallel syntax of two somewhat unusual adjectival expressions in such close proximity should be understood to have a parallel sense. In 1:11 the head noun is *pathēmata* (sufferings), which implies the verb "to suffer." Following the pattern observed, the prepositional phrase *eis Christon* indicates the recipient of the sufferings, Christ.

Moreover, the noun *pathēma* occurs two other times in 1 Peter in reference to Christ (4:13; 5:1), where the genitive τοῦ Χριστοῦ (*tou Christou*, of Christ) is explicitly found in both occurrences. Therefore, both general NT usage and evidence specific to the letter indicate that in 1:11 Peter does indeed have in mind the sufferings that Jesus Christ endured. He chooses a prepositional phrase with εἰς rather than the genitive because of the prophetic perspective of the immediate context. In other words, the prophets in view were speaking long before the sufferings occurred, but they knew that sufferings would come to the Messiah. In the parallel syntax of verse 10, those prophets also foresaw the grace that would come and, in Peter's opinion, had come *eis hymas*, "to you," the Christians to whom Peter writes. Just as the Messiah would be the recipient of sufferings, God's people, among whom the Christians of Asia Minor now find themselves remarkably included, will be the recipients of grace.

The phrase "Spirit of Christ" (πνεῦμα Χριστοῦ, *pneuma Christou*) in verse 11 is somewhat unusual, occurring elsewhere only in Rom. 8:9, "And if anyone does not have the Spirit of Christ [πνεῦμα Χριστοῦ], they do not belong to Christ" (TNIV). Similar expressions are found in Phil. 1:19, where Paul rejoices in the help given by "the Spirit of Jesus Christ" (τοῦ πνεύματος Ἰησοῦ Χριστοῦ, *tou pneumatos Iēsou Christou*). In Acts 16:7, the apostle Paul is prevented from entering Bithynia—one of the very provinces to which Peter now writes—by "the Spirit of Jesus" (τὸ πνεῦμα Ἰησοῦ, *to pneuma Iēsou*). And in Gal. 4:6, Paul writes that God sent "the Spirit of his Son" (τὸ πνεῦμα τοῦ υἱοῦ αὐτοῦ, *to pneuma tou huiou autou*) into our hearts.

In 1 Pet. 1:11 the point seems to be that the Spirit who was the agent of revelation to the prophets of old is the same Spirit of Christ known to the first-century church. The Spirit who had inspired the prophets was the same Spirit who descended on Jesus at his baptism, identifying him as the Messiah who would experience the foretold sufferings and the glories that would follow. Peter thereby shows a continuity of the presence of the Spirit with the prophets and with the Christians, who receive the gospel of God's mercy centered in the suffering and glorification of Jesus Christ.

A second prepositional phrase in 1 Pet. 1:11, εἰς τίνα ἢ ποῖον καιρόν (*eis tina ē poion kairon*, into which or what sort of time) is also a matter of exegetical debate. This phrase, again introduced by the preposition *eis*, is the object of the participle ἐραυνῶντες (*eraunōntes*, look into), meaning that the prophets sought out more information by looking *eis tina ē poion kairon*.

The second component of the prepositional phrase following the conjunction *ē* is translated without debate as "what sort of time" or "what manner of time." The Greek noun *kairos* is used to denote a season of time or appointed time and occurs frequently in the NT to refer to the eschatological season when God's promises will finally be realized, following similar usage of the word in the LXX. The Spirit of Christ was foretelling the sufferings of the Christ and thus, by necessary inference, revealing to the prophets a time when Messiah would suffer. The prophets are curious to know in what season of time such an untoward thing could happen.

The first component of the prepositional phrase, *tina*, has received more discussion among interpreters. The eminent biblical scholar F. F. Bruce (1959: 67) is among the minority of interpreters who take *tina* as a masculine singular accusative interrogative pronoun, translating "what person or time." Best (1971: 81) follows Bruce, arguing that otherwise the two components seem redundant. However, if the two components were different but corresponding, one might expect the conjunction to be καί (*kai*, and)—"they looked into what person *and* what sort of time"—not ἢ (*ē*, or).

Most interpreters construe *tina* as a masculine singular accusative interrogative adjective in grammatical agreement with *kairon* and used somewhat redundantly with *poion* for rhetorical emphasis, rendering the phrase "what time or what sort of time." Michaels (1988: 42) explains the rhetorical effect of this redundancy as perhaps broadening the prophetic inquiry:

> The word order and the choice of conjunctions (ἤ rather than καί) suggests that ποῖον interprets and broadens τίνα. . . . The rhetorical effect of the second component is to make the reference even more general than it starts out to be, "what time (i.e., when) or (at least) what sort of time" will it be when the Messiah suffers. The phrase refers not only to the precise question "when shall these things be?" but several related questions having to do with the future of the world, the signs preceding the end, and the fate of the prophet's own generation.

As Michaels (1988: 42–43) points out, the prophets of the OT times, judging from their writings, were in fact more prone to inquire about *when* their prophetic visions would occur than *who* the Messiah would be. For instance, in Dan. 9:2, Daniel is seeking to understand the times previously prophesied by Jeremiah. In 12:6–13, the prophet asks a heavenly messenger, "*How long* shall it be till the end of these wonders?" (NRSV). He receives the answer "Go your way . . . because the words are shut up and sealed *until the time* of the end" (NIV). Similarly, Ezra asks the Lord, "*How long? When* will these things be [coming to pass]?" (2 Esd. [4 Ezra] 4:33 NRSV). And later he wonders (4:51): "Do you think that I shall live *until those days*?" (NRSV). In Hab. 2:1–4, the prophet inquires of the Lord and is told that "the vision *awaits its time*. . . . If it seems slow, wait for it; it will surely come. . . . The righteous shall live by faith" (all italics added).

Clearly there was great interest among the prophets in *when* their visions of the future would be realized, with specific attention to whether the prophet and his generation would still be alive at the time of fulfillment. Because of this external evidence, most interpreters take both *tina* and *poion* as interrogative adjectives, rendering the phrase "what time or sort of time." On the other hand, Kilpatrick (1986) has shown that in the NT, forms of τίς, τί (*tis, ti,* who? what?), including τίνα (*tina*), are generally and most frequently used not as adjectives but as pronouns.[1] Of the more than one thousand occurrences in the NT, the word occurs less than twenty times as an adjective. Moreover, in all other occurrences in 1 Peter, *tis, ti* function as pronouns. This would seem to tilt the meaning to be that the prophets wanted to know to whom or what sort of time their prophecies pointed. However, even if *tina* here

---

1. Kilpatrick says τίς, τί function as adjectives in Mark 4:30; 8:37; John 18:29; Rom. 6:21; 1 Cor. 15:2; 2 Cor. 6:14, 15, 16 (quotations from OT); 1 Thess. 2:19; 3:9; 4:2; Heb. 7:11; 12:7; Acts 7:49; 10:29; 24:20; Luke 11:11; 14:31; 15:4, 8; 23:22.

is taken as a pronoun in agreement with general NT usage, it need not be understood as masculine singular accusative, referring to *who* the Messiah will be. If *tina* is parsed as a neuter plural accusative interrogative pronoun (what things?), the search of the prophets is not centered on *who* the person of the Messiah would be but on *what circumstances* would lead to his suffering.

b. The Forewitness of the Prophets (1:12a)

Despite the knowledge revealed by the Spirit of Christ to the prophets, they apparently did not enjoy complete satisfaction in their inquiries: they were told only that their work was not for their own times but for a future generation. Peter interprets that future generation to be both the people who witnessed the resurrection of Jesus and the generations to follow.

In a move that splits Christian interpretation of the OT prophets from subsequent Jewish interpretation, Peter identifies what was foreknown by the prophets to be the very things that have now been preached to his readers through those who evangelized them:

In the Past	In the Present
Prophets prophesied these things	that evangelists have now preached to you.
The Spirit revealed future things to the prophets.	Now the Spirit has told you [the same things] through evangelists.
Prophets inquired into the circumstances or time of the Messiah's sufferings and glories.	Angels eagerly desire to look into the Messiah's sufferings and glories.

Compared with the prophets, the generation that saw Jesus had a privileged status that was announced by Jesus himself (Luke 10:23–24 // Matt. 13:16–17): "Blessed are the eyes that see what you see. For I tell you that many prophets and kings wanted to see what you see but did not see it, and to hear what you hear but did not hear it" (TNIV). And again in Matt 11:11, Jesus states, "Truly I tell you, among those born of women there has not risen anyone greater than John the Baptist; yet he who is least in the kingdom of heaven is greater than he" (TNIV). Of all the times to be alive in human history, it is a supreme privilege to be alive in the period of history following the coming of Christ, when the gospel is clearly preached. Through the witness of those who saw and heard Jesus, subsequent generations also see and hear.

Peter, however, does not press the privileged status of his readers. Rather, he builds on the unity of the OT prophetic message with the Christian gospel as an apology for the cross and a foundation for his exhortations that follow. It does not appear that it was primarily Peter's knowledge of the OT prophecies that led him to the Messiah. Rather, it was actually seeing and hearing Jesus. But *after* he recognized Jesus as the Messiah on the basis of Jesus' teachings and miracles, the prophets' forewitness provided a biblical basis that helped Peter later come to grips with the necessary suffering and death of the Messiah, the very concept he had once so resisted as unthinkable (Mark 8:31–33). By witnessing to the sufferings of the Messiah before they happened, the prophets provide a confirming forewitness that a crucified man would indeed be the long-awaited Messiah.

Peter knows his readers also needed to understand what he himself had come to know: that the suffering and death of Jesus Christ was not an untimely accident or tragic mistake but rather a necessity that had long been foretold. After the Christ has suffered, the predictive aspect of prophecy recedes, and the prophecy becomes a confirmation for the benefit of the generation who would see the Messiah suffer, and for the generations to follow them, that they might rightly understand the cross of Jesus. They need to know that the foreseen suffering of the Messiah necessarily preceded the expected glory of the Messiah. Peter extends this concept to develop the idea that as followers of Christ, his readers should therefore not be surprised when they, too, suffer (1 Pet. 4:12). Their sufferings for the name of Christ unite them to the experience and purposes of their Lord.

c. The Angels' Interest in the Gospel (1:12b)

Peter notes the privileged status of his readers by observing that even angels are intently interested in these things. Angels (there is no definite article) eagerly desire to παρακύψαι (parakypsai, to peer into from without). The verb does not require the preposition eis but occurs with it, for instance in John 20:11, where Mary "peers into the empty tomb." In James 1:25 the expression is used to describe the person who "looks intently into the perfect law." Jewish apocalyptic writings frequently speak of the angels as observers of earthly events. For instance, in 1 En. 9.1 the great archangels Michael, Surafel, and Gabriel observe the bloodshed and oppression on the earth. In the NT, Jesus himself claimed that angels in heaven rejoice over one sinner who repents, implying angelic attentiveness to earthly happenings (Luke 15:10).

The direct object of the angels' interest is the neuter plural relative pronoun ἅ (ha, which), referring back to the things (the neuter plural relative pronoun ha earlier in 1 Pet. 1:12) that are being preached to Peter's readers. That pronoun in turn refers back to the αὐτά (auta), "things the prophets ministered" that were for Peter's generation but not their own. The "things now told you through those who preached the gospel to you by the Holy Spirit sent from heaven" are the same "things" that the prophets ministered.[2] Michaels (1988: 48) takes the antecedent

---

2. The author's wording here perhaps suggests that he himself was not the evangelist who brought the gospel to those to whom he now writes (see "Date and Authorship" in the introduction).

of these pronouns to be "the mystery of God's redemptive plan." Selwyn (1958: 138) understands the antecedent to be "the circumstances of the Church and the progress of its redemptive work." However, the things the prophets ministered and into which angels desired to look are specifically the sufferings and glories destined for the Messiah in verse 11 (Achtemeier 1996: 111; Shimada 1981: 146–47). It is specifically the sufferings of Jesus in his crucifixion and the glory of his resurrection that are being preached throughout the Roman world.

There is some debate whether these angels are those who serve God or the fallen angels hostile to God. Peter mentions angels in only one other passage, 3:22, where he states that angels, authorities, and powers are in submission to the resurrected Christ.[3] Boring (1999: 66) construes the verb ἐπιθυμοῦσιν (epithymousin, eagerly desire) to have the negative connotation of "lusting after" and assumes these are the same beings referred to in 3:19–22. However, there is nothing to suggest fallen angels are in view here, nor would that sense sit well in the flow of thought in 1:12. The point is that the sufferings and glories of Christ that have been preached to Peter's readers not only were the subject of the prophets' attention but are even the center of the angels' interest. He shows his readers, who were suffering a loss of status in their society because of Christ, that in fact they were more privileged in the perspective of redemptive history than they could have known—more privileged than either the great prophets of old or the angels above. This provides further motivation for joy even in the midst of suffering. Clearly the gospel message is of great value if it is the focus of attention of the prophets of old and the angels of heaven. Christians should therefore rejoice that they have obtained that precious message.

Summary

Peter concludes that just as the sufferings of Jesus were followed by glories (1:11), those who suffer for the name of Christ will also find glories when Jesus appears. Whatever suffering the Christians of Asia Minor have experienced is to be understood as a part of that redemptive plan foretold long before to the prophets. This is to be a strong word of encouragement to them not to give up on Christ. Peter's understanding of the solidarity of Christ with his followers may explain Peter's use of the plural *pathēmata* and *doxas*—Christ's suffering and his glory extended to his followers.

According to Peter, the revelation of the sufferings and subsequent glories of the Messiah given to the prophets is ultimately intended for the benefit of a later generation. The relationship between the prophets'

---

3. If fallen angels are in view in 3:19 as the beings to whom Christ preaches, they are referred to there with a different word, πνεύμασιν (pneumasin, spirits). See comments on 3:19.

message for that later generation and its meaning for their own time is understood by recognizing that the same Spirit is at work in both. The Spirit of Christ revealed the sufferings of Christ to a particular prophet in a particular generation so that as the prophet addressed the people and issues of his own time, he did so from an eschatological viewpoint that proleptically knew of the suffering and glories of the Messiah before they became historical realities. Because of this forewitness, the prophets could offer to their own generation counsel that presupposed the ultimate triumph of God's redemptive purposes because the prophets had witnessed it, even though they themselves lived in times that would call that confidence into question.

The prophets spoke to God's people who were suffering but who nevertheless were to live as if the eschatological reality of salvation— the cross and resurrection of Jesus—had already occurred. In other words, God's people of the OT time who lived their lives on the basis of the prophets' words, as if eschatological salvation had already been accomplished, were living their lives from the same perspective as Peter's readers and other believers who live on this side of Easter.

Because the prophets forewitnessed the sufferings and glories of Jesus Christ, God's people of that time could live with certainty concerning it. And as Kaiser (1970: 95) observes, the prophets and those of his generation "were ignorant of the same things of which we are ignorant concerning our Lord's second return": the circumstances and the time. Peter's hermeneutic affirms the unity of the work of God in both covenants, which will allow him directly to apply OT exhortations and ethics to his Christian readers of Asia Minor. And this he begins to do in the next paragraph.

B. Be What You Are (1:13–2:3)

Consistent with the pattern found elsewhere in the NT, the author follows the opening statements of his letter, in which he describes the nature of new life in Christ, by exhortation that uses imperative forms. Peter prescribes four actions, each expressed in main clauses containing an aorist imperative form and each qualified by subordinate clauses: (1) set your mind on the grace ahead, (2) be holy in your whole way of life, (3) love one another earnestly, and (4) crave pure spiritual milk. By directly applying OT passages to his readers, the author immediately employs the hermeneutic he just explained in 1:10–12. Allusions to the exodus event, quotations from the Holiness Code of Leviticus and from Isaiah, and echoes of Ps. 34 are woven together to create a new-covenant context for these four exhortations.

1. Be Children of the Father (1:13–21)

After opening his letter with a glorious doxology for the great work of God's mercy in Jesus Christ (1:3–12), Peter turns his attention to describing the appropriate response in the lives of those who have received such grace. Peter's exhortations in this section are based on God's character and the believer's new status in a father-child relationship with God. As the old saying goes, "Like father, like son." The character of Christians is to reflect the character of their divine Father. Their old way of life inherited from their ancestors was useless (1 Pet. 1:18). Their new life was secured with nothing less than the blood of Jesus and is therefore of greater value than things secured even with silver and gold. Peter's readers are called to recognize the value of their new status as God's children and to live out their new relationship to their Father by becoming like him, rather than persisting in the old ways that reflected the character of their sinful ancestors.

a. Set your hope fully on God's grace (1:13)
b. Be holy as God is holy (1:14–16)
c. Live in reverent fear of God, your judge (1:17)
d. The high price of your redemption from your former life (1:18–21)

Exegesis and Exposition

[13]For this reason, fully set your hope on the grace to be brought to you when Jesus Christ is revealed by making your mind ready for action by being self-controlled. [14]As obedient children, do not be conformed as previously to the desires of your ignorance; [15]instead, corresponding to the holiness of the one who called you, you too be holy in [your] whole way of life. [16]For it is written, "Be holy because I am holy." [17]And since you appeal to a Father who impartially judges according to each one's work, conduct yourselves in reverent fear for the time of your sojourn, [18]knowing that not with perishable things, such as silver or gold, have you been redeemed out of the useless way of life you inherited from your ancestors. [19]Rather, [you have been redeemed] by the precious blood of Christ, [blood] like that of a blameless and spotless lamb, [20]who, being foreknown before the foundation of the world, has been made known at the last times for your sake, [21]who through him ⌐trust¬ in God, who raised him from the dead and gave him glory, so that your faith and hope are in God.

a. Set Your Hope Fully on God's Grace (1:13)

Verse 13 forms a transition between the opening of the body of the letter, with its majestic description of what God has done in Christ, and the exhortations of the letter, which are the necessary implications if Peter's readers are to live consistently with who they are in Christ. The author shifts to a series of exhortations by using a strong inferential conjunction, διό (*dio*, for this reason). Clearly this conjunction indicates that verse 13 is not introducing an entirely new theme "but rather implies a pause which accentuates that the argument of the preceding verses is now rounded off and applied to the situation of the readers" (du Toit 1974: 60). However, the verse also clearly introduces the section that begins in verse 14. Because verse 13 is integral both to the section that precedes it and to the one that follows it, it is a hinge or bridge verse that can be discussed separately from, but in reference to, both sections.

The exhortations that follow are being given for the reason that is found in 1:3–12, which is one long sentence in the Greek. The main thought of that sentence is "Blessed be the God and Father of our Lord Jesus Christ," who has given us new birth according to his abundant mercy, into a living hope, through the resurrection of Jesus Christ and into an imperishable, pristine, and unfading inheritance. As Christians, Peter's readers are a new people with a new identity, and they are (1) to set their hope fully on the grace that will come when Jesus Christ is revealed (1:13), (2) to be holy (1:15), (3) to love one another earnestly (1:22), and (4) to crave what nourishes their new life (2:2). As Clowney (1988: 61) puts it, "The imperatives of Christian living always begin with 'therefore.' Peter does not begin to exhort Christian pilgrims until he has celebrated the wonders of God's salvation in Jesus Christ."

Reading τελείως (*teleiōs*, completely) as modifying the verb ἐλπίσατε (*elpisate*), the first of these imperatives is to "fully set your [pl.] hope." *GELNT* assigns this verb to two semantic domains (domains 25.29 and 30.54; see first additional note on 1:13). First, the verb is in the domain of "Hope, Look Forward To," defining its meaning as "to look forward with confidence to that which is good and beneficial." Second, it is in the domain meaning "To Think concerning Future Contingencies," defining it as "to expect, with the implication of some benefit." These two senses are quite close in meaning, and either could be appropriately construed in 1:13. The point is that the hope of which Peter writes is not simply a wish for the future, as the word is most often used in modern English (e.g., "I hope it doesn't rain tomorrow," even though there can be no certainty about atmospheric conditions). Rather, the Greek verb ἐλπίζω (*elpizō*, hope) as used in the NT involves the idea of assurance that what is hoped for will certainly come to pass. This is because future hope in the NT is based on something that has already happened in the past, the resurrection of Jesus Christ.

Peter writes in 1:3 that his readers have been given new birth into a living hope through the resurrection of Jesus Christ from the dead. Because the hope is living, the lives of his readers should manifest a confident expectation that they will receive grace, not wrath, when Jesus Christ is revealed. Beare (1970: 96) reads this as an ingressive aorist (start to hope), implying "the purposeful adoption of a new attitude of mind and heart." Certainly the author would wish any of his readers who have not set their hope on the grace to be revealed in Christ to begin to do so. However, the fact that the addressees have already experienced suffering for the name of Christ suggests that Peter is exhorting them to continue to hope (despite the aorist tense) even though it may at times seem futile. Moreover, they are to set their hope *fully* on this coming grace with an undivided confidence and to place no confidence in the things that society trains us to put our hope in, such as status, education, money, and so on.

Peter therefore orients his readers to a future eschatology of a grace that is fully present but not fully realized in their lives, a grace that is fully guaranteed by the past event of the redeeming death and resurrection of Jesus Christ. Although saving grace is a present reality, the gracious gift of final deliverance awaits a future realization. The inheritance that is currently kept in heaven (1:4) as the full and final salvation (1:9) will be finally and completely theirs when the rule and authority of Jesus Christ that is now hidden becomes universally manifested.

Although there was a time when some interpreters, following Erasmus, took the revelation of Christ here as a reference to one's increasing knowledge of the gospel, defined as Christian doctrine, most commentators today take Calvin's tack in understanding "when he is revealed" to refer to the parousia of Jesus Christ (Achtemeier 1996: 119; W. Barclay 1976: 183; Beare 1970: 96; Best 1971: 85; Calvin 1963: 243–44; Goppelt 1993: 107; Kelly 1969: 66; Michaels 1988: 56). Peter's future-oriented thought contrasts—though it does not conflict—with the apostle Paul's instruction that his readers set their hearts and minds on things above, not upon earthly things (Col. 3:1–4). If both apostles are thinking similarly, Paul is clearly looking toward the parousia of Christ, suggesting that is also in view in Peter's thinking.

It has been thought that the author of 1 Peter commonly uses participles as imperatives (Grudem 1988: 76; Michaels 1988: 51; Moulton 1985: 181; Snyder 1995; Stibbs 1979: 85), but it is not clear that this is how they are being used here. Rather, the two participial phrases, literally, "binding up the loins of your mind" (ἀναζωσάμενοι τὰς ὀσφύας τῆς διανοίας ὑμῶν, *anazōsamenoi tas osphyas tēs dianoias hymōn*) and "being self-controlled" (νήφοντες, *nēphontes*), are probably adverbial (for a discussion of imperatival participles in 1 Peter, see the second additional note on 1:13). The first specifies the mode in which one is to set one's hope fully, by preparing one's mind for action; the second indicates the mode by which one "binds up the loins of one's mind," by being self-controlled. They both acquire an imperative sense by virtue of their relationship to the main verb, *elpisate*, which is in the imperative mood.

The phrase "bind up the loins" is a Semitic idiom that describes the act of tucking up a long robe into a belt, allowing the legs more freedom of movement. The equivalent modern idiom might be "roll up your shirt sleeves" as one prepares for intentional effort. "Girding the loins" may be an allusion to Exod. 12:11, where the LORD instructs his people to prepare for the exodus by eating their final meal in Egypt with their sandals on and their loins girded (cf. Exod. 12:11 LXX: αἱ ὀσφύες ὑμῶν περιεζωσμέναι, *hai osphyes hymōn periezōsmenai*, using a different Greek verb). Peter possibly uses this idiom for being prepared because Jesus also used it in his teaching about being ready for the master to return in Luke 12:35–36, using words of Exod. 12:11 LXX. (This is one of the few places where Gundry and Best are in agreement about 1 Peter's use of Jesus' teaching [Gundry 1966–67; Best 1969–70].) Paul also uses the idiom of girding the loins with truth in Eph. 6:14. Polycarp uses the same phrase in his exhortation to the Philippians, "Binding up your loins, serve God in fear" (Pol. *Phil.* 2.1). Peter's point is that one sets one's hope on future grace, not by idle wishfulness or unfounded optimism, but by a mental resolve to live in such a way as to manifest the "living hope" of the Christian believer. The Christian hope is a reality to be recognized and acted upon now.

But how does one "bind up the loins of one's mind"? The second participle, νήφοντες (*nēphontes*), gives the mode by which the idiom is realized: by being self-controlled. (Note the present tense of the participle, suggesting an ongoing action.) Although the verb can refer to sobriety as the opposite of alcoholic drunkenness, when used in the context of thinking, it refers to "a broader range of soberness or sobriety, namely, restraint and moderation which avoids excess in passion, rashness, or confusion" (*GELNT* domain 88.86), hence self-control. The mind is not to be understood narrowly as denoting only the intellectual life but as that which determines conduct. The avoidance of intoxication is certainly included, especially in any society where those who have no hope often take refuge in drunkenness. Peter wishes his readers to avoid any form of mental or spiritual intoxication that would confuse the reality that Christ has revealed and deflect them from a life steadfastly fixed on the grace of Christ. Self-control of the mind facilitates prayer (1 Pet. 4:7) and an awareness of the devil's ways (5:8).

In other words, Peter instructs his readers to set their hope on the grace that will be theirs when Jesus returns by being fully able to think and act on the basis of their true nature in Christ, despite whatever hostility such a lifestyle might provoke from their society. Peter's readers cannot resolve to make the hard ethical choices he will enjoin on them if they do not have their minds fixed on the final outcome of that resolve. In his next imperative (1:15), Peter will further explain the principle that is to shape their self-controlled living.

b. Be Holy as God Is Holy (1:14–16)

First Peter 1:15 states the second of four imperatives: be holy in your whole way of life. Peter justifies this command on the basis of his readers' relationship with God both as his children (1:17) and as believers in God (1:21). Consistent with Peter's understanding of the OT writings (1:10–12), he directly enjoins upon his readers what God had previously told his chosen people in the book of Leviticus. He presses the point that the new birth given by God the Father (1:3) necessarily implies a decisively altered way of life that is characterized by the new knowledge of God and Christ. Be holy

> as the obedient children of God you now are (1:14a);
>
> by not being conformed to your ignorant desires as previously (1:14b);
>
> in your whole way of life (1:15);
>
> in obedience to the God whose holy character is expressed in the books of Moses, specifically Leviticus (1:16).

What is holiness as Peter enjoins it upon his readers? Their holiness is to correspond (κατά, *kata*) to the holiness of the one who has called them, whom Peter has already identified as God himself (see additional note on 1:15). To be holy means that Christians must conform their thinking and behavior to God's character. The character of God was first revealed through the covenant God made with the people he had chosen for himself. The moral aspect of that covenant was summarized in what we commonly call the Ten Commandments (Exod. 20:1–17; Deut. 5:1–22). Living in right relationship to God demanded obedience to these commandments. By living in covenant with God, ancient Israel would be set apart from the ways of the world. For God's ways are distinct from the ways of a fallen world, and he does not deal with the world on its own terms (e.g., "My thoughts are not your thoughts, nor are your ways my ways" [Isa. 55:8 NRSV]). Therefore, his people are to identify with him by being set apart and by relating to the world on the terms that God prescribes.

God's revelation of his character in the old covenant paled in comparison with the revelation of his character as a living human being in Jesus Christ. Therefore, Peter's command in 1:15 that his Christian readers be holy was a call to live in obedient relationship to Christ that by definition would set them apart from the customs and values of unbelieving, pagan society. The Christian's morality would be defined by, and derived from, the character of God their Father as first revealed in Scripture and then ultimately in the life of Jesus Christ. In these verses, Peter initially defines the call to be holy by specifying the opposite of what he means: "Do not be conformed as previously to the desires of your ignorance" (1:14). In other words, to be holy requires a change in one's way of life from before, when one's behavior was determined by unrestrained impulses to sin, even in ways accepted by society. God's call that has brought Christians to Christ is also a call to deny those sinful impulses and abstain from certain social customs and practices, making one a stranger within one's own society. Verses 14–19 present several contrasts between the former and the current state of Peter's readers:

Formerly	Now
ignorance of God	knowledge of Christ and God
are not God's children/people	are God's children/people
controlled by desires	controlled by obedience to God
futile way of life	holy way of life
affirmed by society	misunderstood and maligned by society

Peter's call to holiness is concerned not only with the religious aspects of one's life but also with one's whole way of life (ἐν πάσῃ ἀναστροφῇ, en pasē anastrophē, 1:15). He is not saying, for instance, that instead of offering sacrifices to Artemis, Christians are now to offer them to God instead. The call is to live differently, not just practice religion differently. The sweeping nature of the transformation is commensurate with the sweeping nature of the new birth and the consequential new identity of the people to whom Peter writes (1:3).

By quoting from Leviticus, Peter immediately applies in verse 16 the principle he has explained in 1:10–12—that the prophets knew they were ministering not to themselves but for "your sake." He claims that his readers must be holy in their whole way of life because God has said to his people "Be holy because I am holy." Peter assumes that the OT writings are authoritative and normative for his Christian readers, regardless of their previous ethnic origin. He makes no distinction between the Jewish and the Gentile Christian in his application, nor does the span of time between Leviticus and his letter mitigate the relevance of God's ancient revelation of himself. By quoting from Leviticus, Peter establishes the principle that the holiness to which the Christian is called in Christ is consistent with God's character as revealed in the ancient covenant with Israel. However, Peter does not enjoin on his Christian readers the specifics of the Levitical religion of ancient Israel. In terms of moral transformation, the goal of both the old and the new covenants is the same—to create a people who morally conform to God's character.

The statement "Be holy because I am holy" is found with slight variations four times in Leviticus (NIV):

- "I am the LORD your God; consecrate yourselves and be holy, because I am holy." (11:44)
- "Speak to the entire assembly of Israel and say to them: 'Be holy because I, the LORD your God, am holy.'" (19:2)
- "Consecrate yourselves and be holy, because I am the LORD your God. Keep my decrees and follow them. I am the LORD, who makes you holy." (20:7–8)
- "You are to be holy to me because I, the LORD, am holy, and I have set you apart from the nations to be my own." (20:26)

First Peter 1:16 quotes Lev. 19:2 LXX exactly. Leviticus prescribes the customs and rituals that the priests of God's covenant will perform, which will set the worship of Yahweh apart from the pagan worship of other nations. Leviticus 11–20, including a portion of what is sometimes referred to as the Holiness Code, gives God's instructions to the entire nation of ancient Israel, not just to its priesthood (11:2; 12:1; 15:2; 17:2; 18:2; 19:2; 20:2). These chapters include regulations concerning clean and unclean food, purification after childbirth, regulations about infectious skin diseases and mildew, bodily discharges, unlawful sexual relationships, and various other laws. Interestingly, Peter does not mandate that his first-century readers in Greco-Roman Asia Minor follow the particular instructions of the Holiness Code. His application of the OT law is direct but differentiated. He quotes Lev. 19:2 to establish the principle that, as Christians, his readers must be set apart from their surrounding culture in a way that is consistent with God as revealed in Jesus Christ. Just as ancient Israel observed customs and morals that set them apart from the ancient Mesopotamian cultures, Peter instructs his readers that they, too, must be set apart from the customs, rituals, and values of their culture in which they once so freely participated. It is this principle of holiness unto God—of being set apart in a relationship with God—that truly defines them as foreigners and resident aliens with respect to their society. Peter presses their new status as holy in 1 Pet. 2:9, where he describes them collectively as "a chosen people, a royal priesthood, a holy nation, a people belonging to God" for the purpose that they may declare the praises of the God who redeems.

Peter's differentiated application of Leviticus is interesting in that it preserves the authority of God's word to ancient Israel as binding on Christians, but it does *not* prescribe the specifics of the Levitical code as the way of life to be followed by his Christian readers. The apostle recognizes continuity of authority and principle between the OT and Christians but also differences in the particulars because his readers live after the resurrection of Jesus Christ and after the coming of the Holy Spirit at Pentecost, as well as in a different time and place than ancient Israel. Christians are no less God's people than was ancient Israel, and no less accountable to God than Israel was, but their holiness is expressed in ways that are appropriate to their own historical moment. Peter's example is instructive for hermeneutics today as Christians seek to submit to the authority of the OT, yet without seeking a priest to examine mildew in the bathroom (cf. Lev. 14:33–57).

The verse immediately following the charge to "be holy" in Lev. 19:2 reads, "Each of you must respect his mother and father" (19:3 NIV). Perhaps it is mere coincidence that Peter's second imperative is also expressed in terms of the father-child relationship. In 1 Pet. 1:15 he begins his second imperative by addressing his readers as "obedient children" (lit., "children of obedience"). Many commentators construe this expression to be synonymous with the Semitic idiom "sons of" and understand it to refer to people characterized by obedience (e.g., Clowney 1988: 65; Selwyn 1958: 140). However, that Hebrew expression is seldom translated in the LXX by the more general word "children" (τέκνα, tekna) as we find in 1:14. Whether or not it is a Semitism, it links the obligation of obedience to the Christians' new relationship with God as Father (cf. 1:3, 17). Because obedience to one's father was what most characterized the father-child relationship in Greco-Roman society, Peter is pointing out that because of their new birth, obedience should also characterize the Christians' relationship with God, and the definition of that obedience is found in God's revelation to ancient Israel.

c. Live in Reverent Fear of God, Your Judge (1:17)

Verses 17–21 form one long sentence in the Greek, which further explains the call to a new life of holiness in light of a fatherly relationship with God. Achtemeier considers it to express "virtually the whole of what he [the author] has to say and indeed virtually the whole of the import of the Christian faith" (Achtemeier 1996: 124). The main thought is, "Live out the time of your sojourn in reverent fear" of God because

1. the God you call upon as Father is nevertheless the impartial Judge of each one's work (i.e., life), including yours;
2. you have been redeemed by the death of Jesus from your former way of life;
3. your faith and hope are the result of God's eternal plan to raise and glorify Christ.

The first-class conditional (or condition of fact) in verse 17, εἰ πατέρα ἐπικαλεῖσθε (ei patera epikaleisthe, if you call on a Father), indicates Peter's understanding that since they have become God's children by virtue of being born again (1:3), they consequently have a new life that is to be lived markedly different from the old one. Along with their new life, Peter wants his readers to recognize that they also have a new responsibility, to live in obedience to God. As has often been said, the indicative of God's grace precedes the imperative of God's commands.

Moreover, the Father they call upon is also their impartial Judge. The intimate relationship between the believer in Christ and God as Father does not give license to the Christian to live as he or she wishes, for God judges morality impartially. As Beare (1970: 100) puts it, "Our knowledge of Him as Father must not dispel our dread of Him as our Judge." The special privilege of calling God "Father" does not excuse the believer from nevertheless being judged by God, because every person will be judged by God according to the same standard. The pagan life that God abhors will be no less abhorred if it is lived by one who professes to be a Christian. The Christian who has been born again of the Father must live in fact as a child of God.

Since the child shares in the character of the father, the Christian life is to conform to God the Father's moral standard. In this intimate relationship, the believer is both informed by Scripture (1:10–12) and empowered by the Spirit (1:2) to live a new way of life that will not invoke God's condemnation in time of judgment. Formerly apart from Christ, Peter's readers had no knowledge of the God who would judge the world. But the very knowledge of Christ that brought them into relationship with God also brings them knowledge of sin and God's wrath upon it. They are therefore to live out the time of their sojourn in fear of God, now that they know he holds the power to judge sin.

d. The High Price of Your Redemption from Your Former Life (1:18–21)

Moreover, the evil that Christ redeemed them from at the highest cost of his own life is nothing other than the evil of their former way of life, which verse 18 describes as the useless way of life inherited from their ancestors (and which 2:9 will describe as "darkness"). Therefore, to continue to live in one's useless former ways is implicitly to deny the value of Christ's death.

The verb translated "redeemed" (λυτρόω, lytroō) and its cognate noun λύτρον (lytron) were used in Greco-Roman culture to refer to the manumission of a slave. The slave would receive his or her freedom after depositing money in the temple of a god or goddess, money which would then be paid via the temple's treasury (minus a commission) to the slave's owner with the thought that the god or goddess was buying the slave (Deissmann 1927: 318–34). The former slave would then be free in the eyes of his former owner and society but would be considered a slave of the god or goddess. The sum of money paid for the redemption was referred to as the τιμή (*timē*, price), and the slave was considered to have been redeemed by the deity.

Peter's thoughts resonate with this custom, for he describes his Christian readers as having been redeemed (ἐλυτρώθητε, *elytrōthēte*), using the passive voice that implies God as the subject. They are free but nevertheless slaves of God (2:16), bought not with a *timē* of silver and gold but, in what seems to be a play on words, with the τιμίῳ (*timiō*, precious, valuable) blood of Jesus Christ (1:19). Although Peter's language might resonate with the Greco-Roman custom of manumission, the idea of redemption by the blood of a lamb is clearly rooted in the OT, most frequently found in Leviticus, Psalms, Exodus, and Isaiah—the very books from which Peter so often quotes.[1]

Redemption is related to the OT context of deliverance from foreign exile, which fits well with Peter's characterization of his readers as foreigners of the Diaspora of Asia Minor. In the LXX the Greek verb λυτρόω (*lytroō*, redeem) most frequently translates the Hebrew verbs גָּאַל (*gāʾal*, redeem) and פָּדָה (*pādâ*, ransom), which are both used to refer to the liberation of God's people from foreign exile. For instance, in Deut. 7:8, the LORD "kept the oath he swore to your forefathers that he brought you out with a mighty hand and redeemed you from the land of slavery, from the power of Pharaoh king of Egypt" (NIV). In Isa. 52:3 the prophet speaks of the release of God's people from Babylon: "For this is what the LORD says: 'You were sold for nothing, and not with money you shall be redeemed'" (*NETS*). When Peter points out that his readers have not been redeemed with silver or gold, he is echoing Isaiah's prophecy, which he will quote extensively in chapter 2. Christ's redemption has delivered them from the bondage of the sin that characterized their former way of life and that continues to be practiced all around them in pagan society.

The thought of manumission is not unique to Greco-Roman culture. It is also found in Ps. 34:22 (33:23 LXX), a psalm that Peter also subsequently alludes to (1 Pet. 2:3) and quotes (3:10–12). The psalmist writes, "The Lord will *redeem* the lives of his slaves; none of those who *hope* in him will go astray" (Ps. 33:23 LXX, emphasis added). These words of the psalm resonate with Peter's emphasis on hope in the immediate context (1 Pet. 1:13, 21). Furthermore, Ps. 34 is a psalm of deliverance and, in its Greek form, specifically deliverance from the hardships of sojourning in exile (παροικιῶν, *paroikiōn*, Ps. 33:5 LXX). This psalm is explicitly appropriate for Peter's readers and connects directly in the immediate context to Peter's command in 1:17 that they live out the time of their sojourn in fear of God. Moreover, Peter alludes to Ps. 34:8 (33:9 LXX), "Taste and see that the Lord is good," as in 1 Pet. 2:3 he writes, "Now

---

1. The verb λυτρόω and cognate noun λύτρον occur at least 26 times in the LXX of Leviticus, 27 times in Psalms, 12 times in Isaiah, and 11 times each in Exodus and Numbers.

II. The Opening of the Letter: Reassurance for God's People
    B. Be What You Are

that you have tasted that the Lord is good." Peter's images of redemption here are apparently a conflation of Isa. 52:3 and Ps. 34 (33 LXX).

The concepts of the exodus from the slavery of Egypt and the exile of Babylon, together with the manumission of a slave, imply a transition from a former way of life to a new state once one has been redeemed. Peter explicitly states this in 1:18: "You have been redeemed *out of the useless way of life you inherited from your ancestors*" (emphasis added). Interestingly, Peter does not connect redemption directly with freedom from sin and guilt, nor does he portray redemption in contrast to the society in which his readers live. Rather, redemption is defined in contrast to the way his readers lived before they came to faith in Christ, a heritage that, though culturally venerated, he describes as "useless" (ματαίας, *mataias*).

Van Unnik's (1969) study shows that the πατροπαράδοτος (*patroparadotos*, ancestral way of life) was esteemed and venerated as the basis of a stable society in both Greek and Jewish culture. First Peter is probably the first Christian writing to use the word in a negative sense for one's way of life before coming to Christ. Peter adds the adjective ματαίας (*mataias*, vain, useless) to describe the quality of that preconversion life. In the LXX this adjective is often used substantivally to describe pagan idols (e.g., 1 Kings 16:2; Hos. 5:11; Jon. 2:9 [2:8 Eng.]; Isa. 44:9; Jer. 2:5). Peter describes the former way of life before the new birth as useless, possibly even idolatrous, no matter how venerated by its indigenous culture. Goppelt (1993: 117) explains the adjective as describing

> what a world of mere appearance erects against reality; what therefore is deceptive, pointless, and senseless. Greek tragedy, like the LXX and the NT, speaks of a form of human conduct that strides senselessly into the void; only the standards of measure differ. . . . According to the NT all are futile who in point of fact deny God, Christians included (I Cor. 15:17; Tit. 3:9; Jas. 1:26). Those who do not draw their life from God lose themselves in their world to unrelatedness, since they understand neither themselves nor those with whom they come in contact in terms of their origin and destiny.

The ancestral way of life, though appearing to offer a venerable reality, is precisely that from which one has been redeemed when given new birth into the only true reality established by the resurrection of Christ. This implied contrast between the futility of a misperceived reality and the true reality now found in Christ parallels the later explicit contrast in 1:22–25 between the transient nature of the glory of human culture and the eternal word of the Lord through which the readers have been reborn.

This description of the readers' life before Christ, especially when combined with Peter's reference to their ignorance before coming to

Christ (1:14), is considered by most commentators to identify Peter's readers as primarily Gentiles. It is argued that the way of Judaism could not be so described, especially by an author who presents himself as one of the Jewish apostles of Christ (e.g., Clowney 1988: 18; Davids 1990: 8; Grudem 1988: 38). Calvin (1963: 245, 247–48), however, is one of the few interpreters who claim that Peter's original readers were indeed Jewish converts. He argues that all knowledge without Christ is profitless and therefore is ignorance. One need only think further of Paul's testimony in Phil. 3:4–9 to hear a Jew describe the heritage passed down to him as "garbage" (useless) compared with "the surpassing worth of knowing Christ Jesus my Lord" (TNIV). Since the "ignorance" in 1 Pet. 1:14 is specifically in the context of the redemption achieved by Christ and because the adjective "useless" in verse 18 generally describes all cultural systems that are not based on the reality of Christ, these verses do not decisively indicate that only Gentiles are in Peter's view. He asks his readers to exchange the heritage handed down by their ancestors—whether Jewish or Gentile—for the heritage of ancient Israel as interpreted through the resurrection of Jesus Christ.

The foreknowledge of Christ's redeeming death (1:19–20) corresponds to God's electing foreknowledge of those who would be redeemed by it (1:2). Thus God knew the complete program of redemption before the foundation of the world. The revelation of this program is for the benefit of those who through the hearing of the gospel would put their faith in God and enter into the living hope of the new birth based on the resurrection of Christ (1:3). The expression φανερωθέντος ἐπ᾽ ἐσχάτου τῶν χρόνων (phanerōthentos ep' eschatou tōn chronōn, has been made known during the last of times, 1:20) is clearly a reference to the past event of Christ's life, death, and resurrection. A different verb, ἀπο-καλύπτω (apokalyptō, reveal), or its cognate noun is used in 1:5, 7, 13; 4:13; and 5:1, where the future revelation of Christ is in view. Moreover, a difference between 1:20 and 1:5 in the prepositional phrase used (ep' eschatou tōn chronōn compared with en kairō eschatō) also suggests that even though the "last of times" was ushered in with the life, death, and resurrection of Jesus, there remains a future point in time (the use of the dative of time, en) when a further, more universal revelation of Jesus Christ will occur.

The result (ὥστε, hōste, so that, 1:21), that Christ has been made known to those who respond in faith to the gospel, is to direct their faith and hope to God, specifically to the God who is the Father of Jesus Christ (1:3), by whose foreknowledge this great plan of redemption was conceived and accomplished (1:2, 18–21). Verse 21 reassures Peter's readers that to have faith and hope in Christ is to have faith and hope in the God of ancient Israel, for God raised Jesus from the dead and glorified him. This thought may be especially reassuring to Jewish Christians, who need to realize that obedience to Christ's demands is not apostasy from the covenant faith of their fathers but fulfillment of it. Peter understands that the prophets of Israel were actually prophesying the sufferings and glories of Jesus the Messiah (1:10–12). He explains the Christian's relationship to God in covenantal terms of holiness (1:14–16). He describes Christ's redemption in terms of a sacrificial lamb. All of this within the opening of the letter shows that Peter views the Christian's trust in God through Christ to be one with the redemptive work that God had begun with his chosen people, ancient Israel.

Additional Notes

1:13. Because there is no consistent pattern in the placement of adverbs in 1 Peter and because τελείως (*teleiōs*, fully) occurs only here in the NT, it is somewhat ambiguous whether this adverb goes with the preceding participle νήφοντες (*nēphontes*, being self-controlled) or the finite verb ἐλπίσατε (*elpisate*, hope). Most translations and interpreters read the adverb with *elpisate*: NASB, NIV, KJV, NRSV; Achtemeier 1996: 117; Blum 1981: 223; Calvin 1963: 243 (who takes it as temporal: hope to the end); Cranfield 1958: 33; Clowney 1988: 61; Davids 1990: 65; J. H. Elliott 2000: 356; Goppelt 1993: 105; Grudem 1988: 76; Kelly 1969: 64; Reicke 1964: 82; Selwyn 1958: 140. A few, including the TNIV, take the adverb with *nēphontes* (Beare 1970: 95; Bigg 1956: 112; Hort 1898: 65; Michaels 1988: 55). Harris (1929) finds the language in either case to be "unnatural" and wishes to emend the text to read τε ἀεί instead of τελείως, yielding "keep wide awake *at all times*" (emphasis original), but he still takes the adverb with *nēphontes*. Although it is not certain with which term the adverb should be read, the sense of the statement and Peter's eschatology throughout suggest that it should be construed with *elpisate*. For Peter, the parousia with its final vindication of Jesus Christ and those who follow him is the only basis for Christian hope in this life, and one's hope should therefore be set fully on this and nothing else.

1:13. Discussions of the existence of the imperatival, or commanding, participle in Hellenistic Greek often cite 1 Peter, where most of the alleged occurrences of such a construction are found (Moulton 1985: 181; Porter 1992: 185–86; Snyder 1995). The imperatival participle occurs in the nominative case, is not connected syntactically to any finite verb form, and is not an elided periphrastic construction. Rather, it stands in an independent clause where a finite verb would be expected. In 1:13 we encounter the first two participles in the letter that have imperatival force, but not in their own right. The first, *anazōsamenoi*, is syntactically subordinated as an attendant circumstance to the main verb, *elpisate*, indicating the mode by which one sets hope fully: by "girding the loins" of the mind. The second participle in 1:13, *nēphontes*, in a similar relationship is subordinate either to the main verb, *elpisate*, or, as the translation above indicates, is a further explication of the participle *anazōsamenoi*, indicating what it means to gird the loins of the mind, specifically to be self-controlled. Current consensus seems to be that there are only four verses in 1 Peter where a true imperatival participle may occur: 2:18; 3:1; 3:7; and 3:9. See further discussion in the additional note on 2:18.

1:15. Κατά (*kata*) here is a marker for a norm of similarity or homogeneity, meaning "in accordance with" or "in conformity to," where the preposition is used "to introduce the norm which governs something." The norm so introduced is often "at the same time the reason, so that *in accordance with* and *because of* are merged" (BDAG 512, italics original).

1:17. The phrase τὸν τῆς παροικίας ὑμῶν χρόνον (*ton tēs paroikias hymōn chronon*, the time of your sojourn) bears striking resemblance to a phrase found in 3 Macc. 7:19, which refers to a time the Alexandrian Jews were uprooted and forcibly brought to Ptolemais by Ptolemy IV

Philopator: τὸν τῆς παροικίας αὐτῶν χρόνον (*ton tēs paroikias autōn chronon*, the time of their sojourn). Although the Jews viewed this deportation as deliverance, it was nevertheless motivated by the desire of the governing authorities in Alexandria to be rid of them (3 Macc. 7:6–8). When the Jews had safely arrived at their destination, "there too in like manner they decided to observe these days as a joyous festival *during the time of their stay*" (NRSV, emphasis added).

1:21. Major textual critics agree that the distinctive use of the adjective πιστούς (*pistous*, faithful) is to be preferred as the original reading over the participle forms πιστεύοντες/-σαντες (*pisteuontes/-santes*, believe). Either form of the participle would have been used by scribes to conform the unusual phrase to more common expressions (Metzger 1994: 617; Beare 1970: 107; Bigg 1956: 121; J. H. Elliott 2000: 378; see Hort's detailed discussion, 1898: 81–84). However, the adjective does not imply the active transitive verb πιστεύω (*pisteuō*, to believe in) but rather the related quality of trust or faithfulness in those who are so described. Nevertheless, the prepositional phrases "through him [Christ]" and "in God" that qualify the sense of *pistous* do imply an active sense. Therefore, the sense "who trust through him in God" is legitimate in the context, regardless of which reading is thought to be original. Beare (1970: 107) explains, "The adjective brings out the thought of faithfulness; through Christ, we are not only brought to have faith in God, but are enabled to show ourselves faithful to Him in all our life. It is this response in conduct that forms the theme of the entire paragraph."

2. Christian Love Means Moral Transformation (1:22–2:3)

Peter continues to draw out the consequential moral and ethical implications for the Christian's life by presenting the third and fourth imperatives of the series that he began in 1:13. He has already exhorted his readers to set their hope fully on God's grace (1:13) and to be holy after the character of their heavenly Father (1:15). He continues his ethical instruction on how Christians are to live in community with each other with the commands to love one another earnestly (1:22) and to grow in Christ by craving pure spiritual milk (2:2). This begins his teaching on how the community of believers, and not society at large, is to be the Christian's primary social context, for their faith in Christ has brought them into the eternal fellowship of God's people. Peter presents earnest love within the Christian community as the hallmark of having been converted. They are to love one another earnestly and to crave the spiritual nourishment that fosters a vital Christian community.

a. The word of God is imperishable seed (1:22–25)
b. Moral transformation is spiritual nourishment (2:1–3)

Exegesis and Exposition

1:22Because your lives are set apart by obedience to the truth for unhypocritical brotherly love, from your [pure] heart love one another earnestly, 23for you have been born again, not from perishable seed, but from imperishable [seed], through the living and abiding word of God. 24For [the Scripture says],

All humankind is as grass,
and all human glory is as the flower of grass.
The grass withers and the flower falls off,
25but the word of the Lord abides forever.

And this [word of the Lord] is the word of gospel that has come to you. 2:1Therefore, putting off all evil and all deceit and hypocrisies and jealousies, and all backbiting, 2as newborn babies crave the pure spiritual milk so that you might grow up by it into salvation, 3since you have tasted that the Lord is good.

a. The Word of God Is Imperishable Seed (1:22–25)

The third major command of the opening of the letter body, following the exhortations to be holy and to fear God, is to love one another earnestly (2:1 further explains what such a love entails). One's covenant relationship with God is never an individual matter. To be chosen by God and set apart by the Spirit for the purpose of participating in the covenant in Christ (1:2) means necessarily coming into relationship with others who are also so chosen. The Christian life cannot be lived authentically in isolation. Peter shifts his exhortation from how to live rightly in relationship with God to how to live rightly with one another in Christian community.

The command to love is qualified by two participial phrases, both probably causal: (1) love one another because your lives have been set apart by obedience to the truth, the very purpose for which is to relate to others as God intended human beings to relate; (2) love one another because you have been reborn with an eternal nature, and love is the essence of that nature. Of course, "love" must be defined biblically. As J. Wilson (2001: 131) notes, "Love is a terribly debased term today, almost beyond rescue as a description of the good news of the kingdom come in Jesus Christ. . . . We must work to recover an understanding and practice of love. . . . Salvation is living in the way of love." The love Peter has in view is neither a warm, fuzzy feeling nor friendships around a coffeepot after worship, though love as Peter defines it may involve both. Rather, it refers to righteous relationships with each other that are based on God's character, which Christian behavior reflects. Peter describes the quality of relationships rightly lived in the Christian community as "love," and he goes on in his letter to reframe the self-understanding of his readers as a community that constitutes a spiritual house in which God is worshipped by acceptable offerings (2:5).

Christians are to love one another because by obeying the truth, by coming to faith in Jesus Christ, they have set themselves apart from the ways of the world and how they used to treat people. The participle ἡγνικότες (hēgnikotes, consecrate, 1:22) is in the perfect tense, indicating that they are now in the state of having been set apart by their previous obedience to the gospel. The verb ἁγνίζω (hagnizō, make holy) is used consistently in the LXX and in the Gospels and Acts to refer to a ceremonial religious ritual in which one intentionally and voluntarily consecrates oneself to God (e.g., Exod. 19:10; Num. 6:3; Josh. 3:5; 1 Chron. 15:12; 2 Chron. 30:17; John 11:55; Acts 21:24, 26; 24:18). The moral nature of this consecration in 1 Pet. 1:22 is implied by the reference that it has come about "by obedience to the truth."

Preisker (1951) and Cross (1954), who were of the school of thought that 1 Peter originated as a baptismal liturgy, interpret the perfect tense of *hēgnikotes* to refer to the religious ritual of water baptism, which they imagined had just occurred between verses 21 and 22. However, there is nothing in the immediate context to suggest that a baptism is under way, and the perfect tense could just as well refer to an event that occurred at any previous time. Certainly part of obedience to the gospel is water baptism, and that sacrament is a declaration that one has been set apart for Christ. But nothing here suggests that this text is part of a baptismal liturgy. Consecration by obedience to the truth in verse 22 refers back to the purpose for which Peter's readers were chosen in 1:1, for obedience and sprinkling of the blood of Jesus Christ, a hendiadys for the covenant established by Christ's blood.

Moreover, although the use of *hēgnikotes* may at first suggest that a religious ritual like baptism is in mind, the writers of the NT epistles use the word to refer to an intentional and voluntary change of heart (e.g., James 4:8; 1 John 3:3). Therefore, Peter is most likely saying that his readers are to love one another because of their previous conversion, which likely has involved water baptism, and that a moral consecration of their character consistent with God's character is what truly sets them apart for God (cf. 1 Pet. 3:21).

This consecration that was accomplished by obedience to the truth was εἰς φιλαδελφίαν ἀνυπόκριτον (*eis philadelphian anypokriton*, for unhypocritical brotherly love, 1:22). The preposition *eis* carries the force of either purpose or result. Given Peter's exhortation to love another, this prepositional phrase probably states the purpose of the new covenant in Christ's blood to restore a chosen humanity to righteous living. Righteous behavior toward others defines love. For Peter, obedience to the truth of the gospel is not merely intellectual assent to doctrine but must result in a transformation of how Christians treat others, because moral transformation is a central purpose of Christ's redemption. Peter further explains the moral specifics of Christian love in 2:1: Be rid of all malice and all deceit, hypocrisy, envy, and slander of every kind.

The command to love earnestly is further qualified by a second causal participle, ἀναγεγεννημένοι (*anagegennēmenoi*, having been reborn, 1:23), which unites the thought of this verse with 1:3, where the verb first occurred. A crucial question arises: How does having been reborn from imperishable seed imply the command to love one another? What is the logic of this claim? The new birth generates spiritual life from imperishable seed (1:23), the word of God.[1] This is contrasted with the quality of life that comes from perishable seed (human procreation), whose glory at its best is like the fragile and temporary flowers of the field. The life of the believer has been generated by the imperishable (ἀφθάρτου, *aphthartou*) divine seed of God's living and enduring word

---

1. First Peter 1:3 states that the new birth comes through the resurrection of Christ. For a theological discussion of the coherence between new life given by the resurrection of Christ (1:3) and also by the word of God (1:23), see Manns 1995.

(the inheritance is similarly incorruptible, ἄφθαρτον, *aphtharton*, 1:4) in contrast to the perishable seed of all flesh. The love commanded in 1:22 is the result of obeying the truth—responding positively to the gospel—and is made possible by the spiritual energy of the new life God has generated by his eternal word. The Christian's decision to obey the truth by coming to faith in Christ is the manifestation of one's rebirth as a child of God (1:3). Peter instructs that love between Christians involves a moral transformation following from the spiritual reality that those reborn from God's seed will have God's character. The exhortations that follow throughout 1 Peter flesh out what Christian love looks like as a defining quality of one's new, eternal life.

The permanence and quality of new life given by God is contrasted with mere mortal life by invoking a quotation from Isaiah. The conjunction διότι (*dioti*, for, 1:24) is used to validate the preceding statement. Peter's logic here is that the new birth given by God to those who enter the new covenant of Christ's blood in faith is conceived from the imperishable seed of God's word, which generates eternal life. To validate this claim, Peter cites Isaiah. Life conceived by mere mortal, perishable seed is perishable, and even the flower of its greatest glory falls off when the plant perishes. Apart from Christ, whatever glory human beings achieve will inevitably perish. But because the word of the Lord abides forever (1:25), as imperishable seed it generates imperishable, or eternal, life. Peter points out that the abiding word of the Lord of which Isaiah speaks is the very word that has been preached to Peter's readers.

The efficacy of the eternal word of the Lord is contrasted with the glory of humanity, a glory impressive in the imperial age of Rome, one of the greatest empires the world has known. Even so, the greatest glories of humanity are quickly fading in comparison with the eternal glories achieved by Christ's suffering (1 Pet. 1:11). If Peter's readers were facing a choice of loyalties, he shows them the even greater majesty of God's powerful word, which creates the eternal reality into which they have been reborn. He appeals to Scripture to teach them that despite circumstances causing their suffering, they are nevertheless participating in the eternal plan of God.

The passage quoted in 1:24–25 is from the LXX of Isa. 40:6–8, which has numerous other connections both to the NT in general and to 1 Peter. It is worth seeing the larger context of the quotation, for Peter echoes Isaiah's thought elsewhere:

A voice of one crying out in the wilderness:
  "Prepare the way of the Lord,
    make straight the paths of our God.
Every valley shall be filled up,
    and every mountain and hill be made low;

> all the crooked ways shall become straight,
>   and the rough place smooth ways.
> Then the glory of the Lord shall appear,
>   and all flesh shall see the salvation of God,
>   because the Lord has spoken."
> A voice of one saying, "Cry out!"
>   And I said, "What shall I cry?"
> *All flesh is grass,*
>   *all the glory of man is like the flower of grass.*
> *The grass has withered, and the flower has fallen,*
>   *but the word of our God remains forever.*
> Go up on a high mountain,
>   you who bring good tidings to Sion [Zion];
> lift up your voice with strength,
>   you who bring good tidings to Ierousalem [Jerusalem],
>   lift it up, do not fear;
> say to the cities of Iouda [Judah],
>   "Here is your God!"
> . . . .
> He will tend his flock like a shepherd,
>   and gather lambs with his arm,
>   and comfort those that are with young.
>   (40:3–9, 11 *NETS*, emphasis added)

Peter identifies the word of God as understood by Isaiah with the word that has been preached to Peter's readers, the gospel of the Lord Jesus Christ. These verses of Isaiah introduce the promises God makes to redeem his people exiled in Babylon "without silver and without price" (Isa. 55:1; cf. 1 Pet. 1:18). These promises were more than historical prophecies for the future of Israel; they were also, perhaps more importantly, eschatological revelations of God's final redemption of humankind. The verses quoted in 1:24–25, declaring that God's word stands forever, are the focal point of Isaiah's prologue to the revelation of God's eschatological redemption of his people and form the basis for the prophet's proclamation that follows (Westermann 1969: 42). This proclamation of hope and deliverance addresses an Israel that in the sixth century BC found itself a discouraged people exiled in the Diaspora and wondering where God's covenant promises now stood. Isaiah 40 introduces encouragement into this dire circumstance with the announcement "Comfort, O comfort my people, says God" (40:1 LXX). As Selwyn (1958: 152) observes,

> Every leading thought here [in Isa. 40] fits in with what our author [of 1 Peter] has been saying. He too is addressing readers who are exiled . . . and oppressed; and he has the same message for them, the contrast between the perishability of all mortal things (cf. φθαρτός in verses 18, 23) and the incorruptibility of the Christian inheritance and hope. . . . The

passage quoted is, therefore, the focal point of a much longer passage which must have been often present in the Apostle's mind.

Modern commentaries on Isa. 40 written without a thought to 1 Peter nevertheless show how apt the message of Isa. 40 is for Peter's first-century Christian readers. Oswalt (1998: 49) writes of Isa. 40:1, "Without question this is the language of the covenant (Exod. 6:7; 19:5; Lev. 26:12; Deut. 26:17–18; etc.). . . . The descendants of Abraham and Jacob need not fear that God will forget his promises to their ancestors." Those new to a covenantal relationship with God in Christ need to hear the same reassurance. Remarkably, Peter does not hesitate to redirect covenant language first addressed to Israel in exile to his first-century Christian readers in Asia Minor.

The promise of Isa. 40:4–5 is for nothing less than a worldwide theophany of Yahweh. Significantly, Mark 1:1–3 (the Gospel tradition-ally associated with Peter) uses Isa. 40 to herald Jesus and identify him as the Messiah:

> The beginning of the good news about Jesus the Messiah,
> as it is written in Isaiah the prophet:
> "I will send my messenger ahead of you,
>   who will prepare your way"—
> "a voice of one calling in the desert,
> 'Prepare the way for the Lord,
>   make straight paths for him.'" (TNIV)

As Smart (1965: 45–46) observes, the way of the Lord prepared is symbolic of all the roads by which exiles are to come from the four corners of the earth. Furthermore, the ingathering of exiles is but one feature of the day in which God will reveal his power and glory to the whole world. The basis of this promised comfort and confidence is given in Isa. 40:5, "because the Lord has spoken." The same enduring word of the Lord spoken through Isaiah to ancient Israel is respoken by Peter to first-century Christians in a letter that is framed by allusion to the Babylonian exile.

Peter fully recognizes that God's message to sixth-century Israel stands as Christ's word to first-century Christians because he recognizes that it is the Spirit of Christ who revealed God's promises to Isaiah. Without any thought of 1 Peter in mind, P. D. Hanson (1995: 13–14) writes of Isaiah's proclamation in words that show the similar historical situations between ancient Israel and Peter's readers: "When one realizes that this speech was addressed to a people that had experienced the loss of nearly all of those structures and institutions which give identity to a community, it assumes a poignancy especially for readers who face their own personal or corporate existence with apprehension or dread."

Given the suffering of alienation experienced by the first-century Christians to whom Peter writes, the use of Isaiah's words to encourage the church takes on even greater poignancy. For, as Westermann (1969: 34) writes of Isaiah's proclamation, it

> is a cry uttered at a time when men were gradually turning away from God, gradually closing their minds to him, and gradually letting their faith grow cold. These are the circumstances which lent urgency to the cry ["Comfort! Comfort my people!"]. Israel must be aroused. A moment, and it may be too late. And the book's opening words [Isa. 40:1–2] attribute the urgency to God himself, who in his cry insists in bringing comfort to his people.

With similar urgency Peter resends the word of the Lord spoken through Isaiah to comfort a people who are being tested and tried, tempted to turn away from God, tempted to let their faith grow cold. He reminds them that the promises God has made to his people endure forever and that *they* are God's people. Speaking of those glorious promises, Smith (1927: xii–xiii) writes, "Isaiah used Israel's history to encourage God's sixth-century people, and the impetus of that marvelous past he uses in order to interpret and proclaim the still more glorious future—the ideal, which God has set before his people, and in the realisation of which their history shall culminate." Like Isaiah, Peter continues to use the marvelous past, which now includes the glorious resurrection of Jesus Christ, to proclaim a still more glorious future to God's covenant people. Isaiah's eschatology for Israel is 1 Peter's eschatology for the Christian church because Peter has recognized Jesus to be the Suffering Servant of Isa. 53, who brings God's redemption (see comments on 2:20–25). That recognition enables Peter to appropriate the words of the prophets in ministry to the church:

> All humankind is as grass,
>   and all human glory is as the flower of grass.
> The grass withers and the flower falls off,
>   but the word of the Lord abides forever. (1:24–25)

How did these words minister comfort to Israel? And how would they minister to the Christians of Asia Minor? As Smart (1965: 43) observes in Isaiah's message, "The power of God is contrasted with the powerlessness of idols, and the nation is called to remember the incomparable nature of the God with whom they have had to do through the centuries." If Peter's readers are Jews by birth, perhaps newly exiled from Rome and scattered in remote places, they need to be reminded of the power of their God, who has sustained his people throughout the centuries, and of the warning against the idolatry that had ensnared their ancestors. If Peter's readers are Gentiles by birth, they need to have their self-understanding transformed as people who, by virtue of their new birth, are now a part of the people to whom God has been faithful for long ages past. God has protected his people throughout the ages, and his covenant with them did not fail while they were in exile. The Christians of Asia Minor, whom Peter frames as also being in exile (1 Pet. 1:1; 5:13), can face the hostility of their society with the assurance that God is powerful to deliver. Thus Achtemeier (1996: 142) observes:

> The contrast between what is transitory and what is permanent embodied in the quotation [of Isa. 40:6–8] would be highly appropriate for a beleaguered community of Christians facing what gave every appearance of being the permanent, even eternal, power and glory of the Roman Empire. In such a situation, the announcement that the glitter, pomp, and power of the Roman culture was as grass when compared to God's eternal word spoken in Jesus Christ, available through the gospel preached to and accepted by the Christians of Asia Minor, would give them courage to hold fast to the latter while rejecting the former. Even the hostility of that overwhelming power becomes more bearable when its ultimately transitory nature is revealed and accepted.

"This too shall pass," Peter says to Christians discouraged by a hostile society. To those who are tempted to renounce the Christian faith under the pressures of persecution, the quotation from Isaiah is a reminder that apart from Christ all will inevitably perish. There is no place to go when one turns away from Christ.

The Christians of Asia Minor also need to be reminded of the power of their God. Though not quoted, the words of Isaiah continue in 40:12–26, reminding them of the great dimensions of their God:

> Who has measured the water with his hand,
>   and heaven with a span,
>   and all the earth with the palm of a hand?
> Who has weighed the mountains with a scale
>   and the forests with a balance?
> Who has known the mind of the Lord,
>   and who has been his counselor to instruct him?
> Or with whom did he consult, and he instructed him?
>   Or who showed him judgment?
>   Or who showed him the way of understanding?
> Moreover all the nations are as nothing,
>   and they have been accounted as nothing.
> It is he who holds the circle of the earth,
>   and those who dwell in it are like grasshoppers;
> who has set up heaven like a vault,
>   and stretched it out like a tent to live in;
> who has appointed rulers to rule for naught,
>   and has made the earth as nothing. (40:12–14, 17, 22–23 *NETS*)

The author of 1 Peter and his readers face the mighty Roman Empire with all the glory of its culture and the might of its army. But for all their glory, the nations of the earth are as nothing. Those who dwell on earth are grasshoppers in comparison with the great God and Father of our Lord Jesus Christ, who measured off the vastness of the universe with the span of his hand and whose word abides forever. And this is the word that has come to you, the apostle says.

Peter understands that the Christians to whom he writes, whether originally Jew or Gentile, are now all the people of Yahweh. Isaiah's prophecy of deliverance from exile is the abiding word that speaks to all generations. Although Christ has been raised, Peter's readers are still suffering. In that sense Christ's deliverance spoken through the prophet Isaiah is yet future, even for Christians today. Peter's letter brings to the church both the promise of God to deliver and the assurance of his power over the nations that would, time and again, come against his people. Because God's final deliverance is still future for the church just as it was also for Israel, all of God's people of both the old and new covenants are joined in anticipation, making the eschatological promises of the OT as relevant today as when they were first announced. Goppelt (1993: 95) asks an intriguing question: "Is salvation for Christians just as much a matter of the future, just as much given as promise, as for Israel?" (see point 6, "First Peter's Eschatology," under "Major Themes and Theology" in the introduction). In Peter's understanding, the answer would appear to be "Yes." Centuries before Jesus was born, the Spirit of Christ spoke through the prophets to God's people before they went into exile. With the same words he speaks to first-century Christians who are portrayed in Peter's letter as exiled in Asia Minor. By implication, the Spirit of Christ speaks to the church of the twenty-first century as directly through Isaiah's words as he has done to first-century believers and to sixth-century Israel. "The word of the Lord abides forever." And this is the word that has come to you.

b. Moral Transformation Is Spiritual Nourishment (2:1–3)

After Peter has explained to his readers that their new life is generated by God's eternal word and is to be characterized by love defined as moral transformation, he continues to unpack the necessity of sustaining the vitality of his readers' new lives in Christ. This passage contains only one imperative: Crave the pure spiritual milk as infants crave their mother's milk. The metaphor of an infant connects Peter's thought here back to the new birth introduced in 1:3. Craving, and therefore presumably partaking, of the pure spiritual milk is to their new lives what milk is to a newborn, the very sustenance of life.

This fourth imperative, to crave pure spiritual milk, is modified by the participial clause "putting off all evil and all deceit and hypocrisies and jealousies, and all backbiting." Peter here specifies how believers are to relate to one another, unpacking what it means to "love one another earnestly" (1:22). The command to crave the milk that Peter has in mind presumes this ethical transformation, which is how earnest love for other believers is to be expressed. In between the two imperatives of 1:22 and 2:2 stands the ground for both: the word of God has given Peter's readers new birth into a reality that will last forever. Moreover, the goal of God's redemptive work is to restore right relationships among people and between people and God. By limiting his instructions to relationships between believers, Peter is not giving license to treat unbelievers with malice but is here focusing on the dynamics of interpersonal relationships within the believing community.

The participle ἀποθέμενοι (apothemenoi, putting off, 2:1) was used to refer to the removal of clothing, but it need not be taken here as an allusion to taking off the garments of baptism, much less as evidence that this text is a baptismal liturgy (Kelly 1969: 83–84). The use of the same verb in Rom. 13:12; Eph. 4:22, 25; Col. 3:8; and James 1:21 indicates that it was used almost idiomatically in the early church to refer to the shedding of behavior that was inconsistent with the Christian life.

The vices listed in 2:1 that must be put off are those that destroy relationships and hence that destroy community. Peter is explaining in this letter how social alienation that the Christian experiences from society is to be remedied by the genuine fellowship found within the community of believers, the nature of which he describes in 2:4–10. Peter's readers have been given new birth as the people of God and therefore are to exhibit an ethical transformation in their relationships that is characteristic of their Father.

The terms found in 2:1 are the standard words found also in the Pauline ethical tradition (e.g., Rom. 13:13; Eph. 4:25–32; Col. 3:8) and the Dead Sea Scrolls (e.g., 1QS 4.9–11; 10.21–23), which describe attitudes and behavior that destroy community. The first word, "evil" (κακία, kakia), is the most general of the words on the list and was the antonym of the word used in the Greek ethical tradition for virtue (ἀρετή, aretē). There is some discussion of the relationship among the words on this list (Achtemeier 1996: 144; Bigg 1956: 125; Beare 1970: 113; Michaels 1988: 85). Peter exhorts his readers to put off all evil and all deceit, and then he specifies the examples of hypocrisies (for instance, claiming to love fellow believers but gossiping about them) and jealousies. Malicious talk (backbiting) can be allowed no place among the people of God. In this way Peter spells out what he means to love one another "earnestly" (1:22) and also shows that such poor attitudes and behavior are incompatible with craving the pure, spiritual milk (2:2).

First Peter 2:2 continues with the metaphor of an infant craving milk and thus plays on the theme of new birth, introduced in 1:3 and further expounded in 1:23–25. Peter is not describing the recent conversion of his readers, for he has already described all believers as reborn children of God, regardless of how long ago their conversion has occurred. He uses the metaphor to instruct them to crave the things of God even as newborn babies crave milk—instinctively, eagerly, incessantly. Although elsewhere in the NT milk is used as a metaphor for teachings suitable for immature Christians (Heb. 5:12) or worldly Christians (1 Cor. 3:1), such a negative connotation is not found here. Rather, Peter sees milk as that which all Christians need in order to nurture their new life in Christ, so that they will "grow up" into salvation, deliverance from God's judgment when the Lord returns.

The metaphor "as newborn babies, crave the pure spiritual milk so that you might grow up by it into salvation" raises two puzzling questions. How should λογικόν (*logikon*), one of the two adjectives modifying γάλα (*gala*, milk), be understood and translated? And to what does the metaphor of milk refer? The answer to either question informs the other. However the metaphor is understood, it must be logically coherent both with the participial phrase "putting off all evil" (with which it is syntactically joined in the Greek) and with the direct allusion to Ps. 33 LXX in 1 Pet. 2:3 ("since you have tasted that the Lord is good").

Modern interpreters almost unanimously understand the referent of the "pure spiritual milk" metaphor to be the word of God, whether in the form of apostolic preaching or inscripturated in the Bible (Achtemeier 1966: 145; W. Barclay 1976: 191; Bigg 1956: 126; Clowney 1988: 78; Cranfield 1958: 45; Davids 1990: 83; Goppelt 1993: 128; Grudem 1988: 95; Kelly 1969: 85; Reicke 1964: 88; Thurén 1995: 123). (On ἄδολον, *adolon*, pure, see discussion below.) They take *logikon gala* to mean "spiritual milk," using various interpretations of the word "spiritual," and then relate that to the word of God, either through the cognate relationship between λόγος (*logos*, word) and *logikos* or by proximity with the immediately preceding context in 1:23–25: "For you have been born again, not from perishable seed, but from imperishable [seed], through the living and abiding word [*logos*] of God. For [the Scripture says], 'All humankind is as grass, and all human glory is as the flowers of grass. The grass withers and the flower falls off, but the word [ῥῆμα, *rhēma*] of the Lord abides forever.' And this [word of the Lord] is the word [*rhēma*] of gospel that has come to you." Therefore, the milk to be craved is understood to be the pure word-milk, that is, God's word untainted by error. Grudem (1988: 95) finds support here for describing the nature of the Bible: "This adjective implies that Scripture is free from impurity or imperfection, that it will not deceive or lead astray its readers, and that it affirms no falsehood." While Grudem's claims about the nature of Scripture are true, this is probably not what Peter had in mind here.

The thought that Scripture is the milk of Christian life has much appeal both in the immediate context of 1 Peter and on general principle. Certainly, Christians should read their Bible, in which is found the revelation of Jesus Christ, and thereby grow in their salvation from new birth to final glory. Nevertheless, even though this interpretation is coherent and almost unanimous among modern interpreters, it comes with problems. In fact, Hort (1898: 100), followed by Beare (1970: 115), baldly states: "The familiar rendering 'milk of the word' is simply impossible" because *logikos* could never be equivalent for τοῦ λόγου (*tou logou*, of the word) despite any etymological similarity. Few modern interpreters would commit this etymological fallacy, and so they take *logikon gala* to mean "spiritual milk" but, on the strength of the immediate context rather than etymology, understand it to refer to the word of God. However, if Peter specifically had the word of God in mind when he wrote *logikon gala*, he surely could have used the epexegetical genitive τὸ γάλα τοῦ λόγου (*to gala tou logou*, the milk of the word) to refer directly back to 1:23 without ambiguity. Instead, Peter chooses a word rarely used in Christian writings, with the same root as *logos* but with a somewhat different meaning; this fact should be a clue that there probably is more to it.

Further considerations must also contribute to the identification of the referent of the milk metaphor. First, the word-milk interpretation lacks metaphorical coherence with the context presumed to inform it. In 1:23–25, the *logos* of God is identified as the seed, or sperm, that regenerates new life in the believer. The gospel preached to the Christians of Asia Minor is understood to be the eternal *rhēma* of the Lord that, according to Peter, was already known to Isaiah (Isa. 40:6–8). While *logos* and *rhēma* are generally synonymous in Greek usage, it appears that Peter takes advantage of the lexical variation the language offers to distinguish the external preaching of the word of God from the internal effect of regeneration in those who believe it. In 1:25 he uses *rhēma* and in 1:23, *logos*.[2] In Peter's thought, the regeneration of new life by God's word is inextricably linked with the external preaching of God's word; nevertheless, the two concepts are distinct. If the distinction between *logos* and *rhēma* is deliberate, Peter's choice of the cognate word *logikos* in 2:2 would align the milk metaphor more closely with the word (*logos*) of God as the regenerating seed in 1:23 (as opposed to the preached *rhēma* in 1:25). But that introduces a metaphorical incoherence between "milk" and "seed," which raises the question of whether the same concept, word of God, should be construed as the referent of both metaphors.

2. Even if this material originated as an early Christian hymn, it is widely acknowledged that the author reworded his source material to the extent that certain reconstruction of his source is not possible. Moreover, he freely rewords his quotations from the LXX, as in 1:24, and so his wording does not appear to be bound by his sources. He would be free to use λόγος or ῥῆμα consistently if he chose to do so.

If Peter intended this abrupt and unaided shift from the word-seed metaphor that regenerates new life to the word-milk metaphor that sustains it, one must conclude something along the lines that the word of God, as both seed and milk, initiates *and* sustains new life in Christ. As Goppelt (1993: 132) puts it, "That those who are born from the word continue to seek the word as a child seeks its mother's milk is not only a life-sustaining obligation; it also corresponds to their actual need."

A second consideration in the exegesis of 2:1–3 is whether the notoriously difficult-to-define word *logikos* should be taken to mean "spiritual" here, as most interpreters do, and, if so, in what sense? Erasmus understood the milk of 2:2 to be "milk not for the body, but for the soul" (quoted by Calvin 1963: 257). Stibbs (1979: 96) calls it "milk for the mind rather than the stomach." Beare (1970: 115), who rejects the consensus view that the milk is the word of God, nevertheless considers "spiritual" as the best English word with which to translate *logikon*: "that which is proper to the Logos, and the life which is mediated through the Logos (διὰ λόγου—1:23); thus it is virtually equivalent to πνευματικός." In response to the thought that *logikos* is synonymous with πνευματικός (*pneumatikos*, spiritual), readers should consider that Peter employs the adjective *pneumatikos* just a few sentences later to describe the "spiritual house" and "spiritual sacrifices" of the believing community (2:5).[3] Because *logikos* is not found elsewhere in the biblical corpus as a stylistic variation of *pneumatikos*, we must at least consider it possible that Peter wishes to distinguish in some way the quality and character of the milk from that of the house and sacrifices he subsequently mentions.

The word *logikos* is found in clearly metaphorical contexts to mean "spiritual," in the sense of nonliteral. Thus, BDAG 598 cites from the fifth-century *Pelagia-Legenden* the clause "The bishop is the shepherd of the *logikōn* sheep of Christ" (τῶν λογικῶν προβάτων τοῦ Χριστοῦ, *tōn logikōn probatōn tou Christou*), along with a phrase from Eusebius (fourth century), and categorizes *logikon* in 1 Pet. 2:2 as another occurrence of this spiritual sense (cf. Kittel, *TDNT* 4:142–43). Grudem (1988: 95) argues that the word of God is the referent of the milk metaphor and also takes *logikon* here to mean "spiritual" in the sense of "figurative": "long for pure figurative (not literal) milk." Although Michaels (1988: 87) rejects the understanding that the milk is the word of God, he also agrees that *logikon* simply clues the reader that "milk" is not to be taken literally: "The purpose of λογικόν is not to interpret and thereby dissolve the metaphor, but simply to underscore the fact that it is a metaphor (i.e., that Peter is speaking not of literal milk but of a more excellent, although undefined, 'spiritual milk')." McCartney (1991: 128–32, following Selwyn 1958: 155) objects that taking *logikon* as simply indicating

---

3. A similar distinction seems to be found in Romans, where λογικός appears once (12:1) and πνευματικός three times (1:11; 7:14; 15:27).

a metaphor here is rather otiose: "The author does not have to tell his readers that they are *metaphorically* infants, or that the seed of 1,23 is a metaphorical seed, or that the tasting of 2,3 is metaphorical tasting. Certainly the fact that 'milk' is a metaphor in this context is no less obvious than that the other terms are metaphors" (emphasis original).

"Rational" or "reasonable" is another sense of *logikos* given by lexicons as its frequent sense in Stoic writings. McCartney (1991: 131–32) makes a compelling case that in the first century some occurrences of *logikos* previously understood as "rational" should be taken as "having to do with verbal communication," on the basis that rationality and verbal articulation were congruent concepts in the ancient world. He concludes that this evidence permits 2:2 to be understood as the "pure milk of the Word" in a context that "seems to expect something more along the lines of 'having to do with the Word' than either 'spiritual' or 'rational'" or that "begs for something like 'having to do with the Word of God" (McCartney 1991: 130, 132). For McCartney, the word-theology so prominent in the preceding verses demands that *logikos* must pertain to verbal communication, which is then taken to be the verbal communication of the word of God previously mentioned in 1:23–25. However, McCartney's conclusion that *logikos* means "pertaining to speech" does not work in Rom. 12:1, the only other NT occurrence of this word. While the sense of the word need not be the same in both of its NT occurrences, the rarity of its use in early Christian writings suggests that the same sense might be intended when it does occur. Furthermore, is 1:23–25 really the most immediate interpretive context?

Although most commentators take 1:23–25 to be the interpretive context of 2:1–3, the referent of the milk metaphor must first be related to its immediate context, 2:1–3: "Therefore, putting off all evil and all deceit and hypocrisies and jealousies, and all backbiting, as newborn babies crave the pure spiritual milk so that you might grow up by it into salvation, since you have tasted that the Lord is good." The imperative translated "crave" (ἐπιποθήσατε, *epipothēsate*, 2:2) is modified by the participial phrase ἀποθέμενοι οὖν πᾶσαν κακίαν (*apothemenoi oun pasan kakian*, 2:1). This participial phrase can be taken as temporal, translated as "after putting off . . . crave" (as T. Martin 1992a: 175), or as an attendant circumstance that gains an imperatival force by the imperative mood of the main verb, translated "put off . . . crave." Furthermore, the sentence begun in verse 2 is completed in verse 3 with another perceptual metaphor of taste in the direct allusion to Ps. 33:9 LXX (Ps. 34:8 MT/Eng.), which psalm is extensively quoted in 1 Pet. 3:10–12. Therefore, Ps. 33 LXX contributes to the interpretive context within which Peter's command to crave milk should be understood, just as his use of Isa. 40:6–8 LXX supports his command in 1 Pet. 1:22, also in the imperative mood, to love one another earnestly.

The consensus of modern interpreters seems to have overlooked Calvin (1963: 256), who found in this metaphor of the pure *logikos* milk a referent more general than the word of God and yet integrally related to it:

> Now that he has taught that the faithful are regenerated by the Word of God, he exhorts them to lead a life *corresponding with their birth*. . . . *Infancy* is here set by Peter over against the old age of the flesh, which leads to corruption; and by the word *milk*, he includes all the feelings of spiritual life. . . . He then compares the vices, in which the old age of the flesh indulges, to strong food, and milk is called that *way of living* which is suitable to innocent nature and simple infancy. (emphasis added)

Calvin's interpretation has the strength of making a strong logical connection between the participial phrase listing the vices and the imperative to crave *logikon* milk. (The Epistle of James makes a similar connection between ethical transformation and the word, *logos*, of new life, using terms that echo phrases also found in 1 Pet. 2:1; 1:23; and 2:2: "Get rid of all moral filth and the evil that is so prevalent and humbly accept the word planted in you, which can save you" [James 1:21 TNIV].) The sense of *logikos* as it is used in the NT, as *GELNT* defines it, is "true to real nature," which fits nicely with Calvin's understanding that those reborn into the family of God need food that corresponds to the reality of their new life. The Stoics could use the word *logikos* to mean "rational" or "reasonable" in the sense of being true to ultimate reality, which in Stoic thought was ordered by the divine rationality of the *Logos*. Although rejecting Stoic theology, Peter (and probably Paul) plundered the Egyptians, so to speak, by using the same word to describe what is true to the ultimate reality of the new creation that the resurrection of Jesus Christ had established. Paul tells Christians in Rom. 12:1 that presenting their bodies as living sacrifices is their *logikos* worship (worship that is true to the new reality in which they now exist).[4] Peter writes that life in this new reality requires sustenance that is true to its nature. The apostles knew that the reality into which Christians were reborn is defined not by the *Logos* of the Stoics but by the eternal *Logos* of God. Therefore, the verbal revelation of God preached by Isaiah and the prophets and by apostolic tradition and now inscripturated in the Bible articulates the moral reality to which God's people must conform.

The *logikon* milk of 1 Pet. 2:2 is further described by a second adjective, ἄδολον (*adolon*, pure, when used of food to mean "unadulterated" or "uncontaminated"). Those taking the referent of the milk metaphor to be the word of God in the form of either Scripture or apostolic teaching also take this adjective to mean truth unmixed with false doctrine or inerrant (e.g., Clowney 1988: 79 and Grudem 1988: 95, respectively).

---

4. And so Moo (1996: 748) translates Rom. 12:1 as "your true worship."

However, if *logikon* is allowed more generally to mean sustenance that is true to the new life in Christ, then, as Hort (1898: 101) points out, it is

unlikely that St Peter means to contrast ἄδολον γάλα with other milk which *is* adulterated. He is thinking only of the child at its mother's breast, and to him milk is, as such, *the* kind of food which by the nature of the case cannot be adulterated. This, he implies, is the characteristic of the spiritual sustenance which proceeds directly from God Himself. (emphasis original)

Hort therefore takes the milk metaphor to refer to divine grace on which all reborn believers must depend to sustain life in Christ.

Michaels (1988: 89), who like Hort rejects the interpretation that the word of God is the referent of "milk," calls it doubtful "that the full significance of 'pure spiritual milk' for Peter can be summed up in just one word or concept." He writes, "In light of 1:25 there can be no doubt that the medium by which the milk is received is the proclaimed message of the gospel, but the milk itself is more appropriately interpreted as the sustaining life of God given in mercy to his children" (Michaels 1988: 89). Therefore, while it is not incorrect to direct Christians to the word of God in Scripture for spiritual sustenance throughout life, it is unlikely that Peter means to limit the milk metaphor exclusively to the written word of God. This would be especially true at a time before the gospel of Jesus Christ is fully and formally inscripturated in the NT.

This broader interpretation of the milk metaphor is confirmed when the contribution of Ps. 33 LXX (34 Eng.) to the interpretive context is considered. The bold perceptual metaphor of taste in 2:3, "since you have tasted that the Lord is good," is a more immediate exegetical control on how the milk metaphor is intended than the more distant 1:22–25. The predicate adjective, χρηστός (*chrēstos*, good), is found frequently in the LXX of Psalms in reference to God (Ps. 24:8 [25:8 Eng.]; 33:9 [34:8]; 85:5 [86:5]; 99:5 [100:5]; 105:1 [106:1]; 106:1 [107:1]; 118:68 [119:68]; 135:1 [136:1]; 144:9 [145:9]), to God's name (Ps. 51:11 [52:9]), to God's mercy (Ps. 68:17 [69:16]; 108:21 [109:21]), and to God's law (Ps. 118:39 [119:39]). First Peter 2:3 is itself a direct allusion to Ps. 33:9 LXX (34:8 MT/Eng.) as adapted for Peter's new historical moment. Interpreters through the ages have noted the possible wordplay between χρηστός (*chrēstos*, good) and Χριστός (*Christos*, Christ) in 1 Pet. 2:3. The difference between "the Lord is good" and "the Lord is Christ" is but one vowel.[5]

Psalm 33 LXX in its entirety is in Peter's mind as he writes, for he later quotes it more extensively in 3:10–12 as the grounds for his exhortations. Moreover, the language and thoughts throughout 1 Pet. 1–3 echo the

5. Which has generated a multitude of variants reading Χριστός in the Greek manuscripts.

language of Ps. 33 LXX in several places. Peter has already explained in 1:10–12 that Christ is the one who spoke through the prophets (in this case the psalmist), whose words serve the Christians of the apostle's own generation. In 2:3 is the second example of Peter bringing the words of the prophets to the ears of his readers as if the prophets were directly addressing the specific situation of the Asian Christians (the first example being the quotation of Isa. 40:6–8 in 1:24–25).

The superscription of Ps. 33 LXX indicates that the psalm is "of David," when he feigned madness before Abimelech and was released. In the Hebrew it is an acrostic psalm of thanksgiving for deliverance from affliction. Although written centuries before 1 Peter, its words of encouragement are uncannily appropriate for the historical situation faced by the first-century Christians of Asia Minor, whom Peter instructs to bear up through suffering by being faithful to the Lord, who will deliver them.

When the Hebrew text of Ps. 34 is compared to its Greek translation in Ps. 33 LXX, there are no major omissions or additions, but there are some rephrasings that contextualize the psalm specifically for the Diaspora setting. For instance, the Hebrew of Ps. 34:5 reads that the psalmist sought the Lord and the Lord delivered "from all my fears" (וּמִכָּל־מְגוּרוֹתַי, *ûmikkol-mĕgûrôtay*). The Greek version reflects a different pointing, reading מָגוֹר (*māgôr*, sojourning, a participle of גּוּר, *gûr*) and thus is translated by τῶν παροικιῶν (*tōn paroikiōn*, sojournings), a cognate of the Greek word that Peter uses to address his readers in 2:11 (παροίκους, *paroikous*, resident aliens). While deliverance in the Hebrew text is from "fears," in the LXX it is from "sojournings." The LXX translator(s) understood David to have been delivered from the afflictions he experienced while a resident alien among the Philistines, sojourning away from "home" and outside his place of safety. It is impossible to tell if the translator understood the consonantal text to mean "fear" and deliberately created a pun by repointing it to contextualize it for his Diaspora setting or whether that setting so colored his thought that "sojourning" was the only reading that occurred to him. In either case, the LXX rendering is congenial to Peter's later use as he framed his letter in Diaspora language (1 Pet. 1:1; 5:13) and claimed deliverance for his readers from the afflictions of their sojourn in a hostile place, just as David had previously experienced.

When Peter alludes to Ps. 33:9 LXX (34:8 MT/Eng.) in 1 Pet. 2:3, he changes the mood of the verb from the imperative mood (γεύσασθε, *geusasthe*, you [pl.] taste) to the indicative (ἐγεύσασθε, *egeusasthe*, you have tasted), and he omits the second verb καὶ ἴδετε (*kai idete*, and see). His omission of the second verb is probably governed by his use of the milk metaphor in verse 2, since the verb "see" does not have metaphorical coherence with "milk" and is unnecessary for his point. The change of verbal form from imperative to indicative reflects his understanding that his readers have already tasted the goodness of the Lord. The first-class conditional clause (εἰ, *ei*, if, 2:3) implies a condition taken as fact for the point the author is making and is equivalent to "since you have tasted that the Lord is good." The logic of verses 2 and 3, then, is "since you have tasted that the Lord is good, crave . . . ," which makes the implied referent of the milk metaphor their experience of the Lord himself. For the Christian, "there can be no food beyond Christ" (Best 1971: 97). Selwyn (1958: 154) takes the milk to be "the divinely-given nourishment supplied by the Gospel." Hort (1898: 101–2) describes the milk as "a Divine grace or spirit coming directly from above."

Kelly (1969: 86) suggests that the power of the perceptual metaphor is best served by translating, "since you have tasted that the Lord is delicious." Of all the sensory metaphors, tasting is the most intimate and the only one that involves ingestion. Seeing God, hearing God, even touching God, does not carry the powerful connotations that "tasting" implies—making the experience of God internal to oneself. (For a discussion of the idea that God is not a subject to be studied but a banquet to be enjoyed, see Stevick 1988: 707–17.)

This interpretation—that the milk in view is not specifically limited to the word of God—is supported by a further look at how the perceptual metaphor of taste functions in Ps. 33:9 LXX. Peter quotes only the first colon of two: "O taste and see that the Lord is good; / Happy is the one who *hopes* in him" (emphasis added; cf. Heb.: who takes refuge in him). The tasting of the Lord's goodness is related to putting hope in him, which in the context of Ps. 33 LXX is a hope for deliverance from shame (33:6 [34:5 MT/Eng.]), affliction (33:7 [34:6]), and want (33:10–11 [34:9–10]). These were the very things being experienced by the Asian Christians because of their profession of faith in Christ. In this situation, Peter tells them in 1 Pet. 1:13 to set their hope fully on God's grace in Christ. Thus the LXX quotation in 1 Pet. 2:3 forms a conceptual inclusio with Peter's exhortation in 1:13 (see comments on 3:8–12 for a more extensive analysis of Ps. 33 LXX in 1 Peter).

Given that Ps. 33 LXX is part of the immediate context, what does it reveal that may help with the exegesis of 1 Pet. 2:1–3? First, the theme of the word of God is not mentioned even once in Ps. 33 LXX, in contrast to the previous quotation of Isa. 40, where the word of the Lord is a major thought in that OT passage. Had Peter been quoting the psalmist in order to clarify and reinforce the identification of the word of God as the referent of the milk metaphor, he could have chosen a quotation that had metaphorical coherence with the perceptual metaphor of taste. For instance, he could have quoted Ps. 119:103, "How sweet are your words to my taste, sweeter than honey to my mouth!" (NRSV). Peter relates the concepts of both Isa. 40:6–8 and Ps. 33:9 LXX (34:8) to his readers, and they are two different concepts. Hence, it is likely that his thought has moved on beyond his concern with the word of the Lord as the seed of new life in 1 Pet. 1:23–25 to the sustenance of that new life amid times of trouble in 2:1–3.

The word preached to Peter's readers mediated their experience of God (1:25) and gave them their initial taste of the Lord. But when Peter exhorts them to crave spiritual milk, he is not telling them to crave the word of God, as if commanding them to listen to more sermons or to read more Scripture, as good and even necessary as those activities may be. He is saying that God in Christ alone both conceives and sustains the life of the new birth. They are to crave the Lord God for spiritual nourishment. They have tasted the goodness of the Lord in their conversion, but there is more to be had. The more-of-the-Lord-to-be-had by Peter's readers involves putting off all evil and all deceit and hypocrisies and jealousies, and all backbiting (2:1). Refusal to do so would stunt their growth in the new life.

Second, this interpretation allows the participle in 2:1, ἀποθέμενοι (apothemenoi, putting off), to be the mode in which craving for the pure milk is expressed. The participial phrase claims an imperatival force by virtue of its subordination to the imperative form ἐπιποθήσατε (epipothēsate, crave) in 2:2. Peter's readers are to crave the Lord by adopting attitudes and behaviors that will sustain the new life they have begun by faith in Christ. This ethical exhortation is consistent with the content of Ps. 33 LXX, where those who seek the Lord for deliverance must stop speaking deceit and evil (33:14 [34:13]) and must turn away from evil and pursue peace (33:15 [34:14]). Thus it is ethical transformation that qualifies them to be the people whom the Lord will deliver.

In light of the contribution Ps. 33 LXX makes to Peter's thought, reading *logikon* as if it means pertaining to the word is too narrow and can be discarded, but without denying the role of inscripturated verbal revelation in the life of the Christian or the relationship of 2:1–3 to 1:22–25. Peter has both explained in 1:10–12 and amply demonstrated by his use of Isa. 40 LXX in chapter 1 and of Ps. 33 LXX here that the written Scriptures are vitally relevant to the new life of his Christian readers. However, *logikos* milk means not the word-milk but the milk that is true to the nature of the new eschatological reality established by the resurrection of Jesus Christ and into which Peter's readers have been reborn (1:3). This understanding of *logikos* also works well in Rom. 12:1, where Paul instructs Christians to *logikos* worship—worship that corresponds to the new eschatological reality in which they are living in Christ by ethical and moral transformation in contrast to their former ways of worship.

Peter joins theology to ethics in 1 Pet. 2:1–3, forming a transition between his teaching on the eternal, imperishable seed that has made his readers children of God (1:22–25) and his subsequent teaching in 2:9–11 on the nature of God's people, which they have become. Christians crave the Lord by shedding destructive vices so that they "might grow up into salvation" (2:2). Michaels (1988: 91) puts it well when he writes that for Peter, "Salvation is seen not as a last-minute rescue operation from the outside but as the fitting consummation of a process already at work in and among Christian believers." Those who live like hell cannot expect to arrive in heaven.

Therefore, Peter merges the perceptual metaphor of Ps. 33 LXX ("taste and see that the Lord is good") with his concept of the new birth to yield the metaphor of milk as that which is tasted and craved by the newly born. In light of Peter's understanding of the resurrection of Jesus Christ, the thought-world of the Greek psalm is sufficient to explain the milk metaphor, eliminating any need to find influence from the mystery religions (contra Perdelwitz [1911], who even denies that Peter employs a quotation from the Psalms here). Given the fact that milk is a potent symbol of sustenance, it is not surprising that it may have been used in the rituals of many religions. However, Goppelt (1993: 130) has shown that "in no way has the terminology of Gnosticism or of the mystery religions been appropriated" here by Peter (also Selwyn 1958: 305–9). First Peter 2:1–3 may explain how the later second-century use of milk in some Christian baptisms arose (Selwyn 1958: 308), but that subsequent use does not imply that this text was written as liturgy for that purpose, nor does it suggest a second-century date for the book.

The widespread consensus among modern interpreters that the pure spiritual milk of 2:2 is the word of God may seem too strong to question, much less abandon. However, going back at least as far as Calvin, a few dissenters have seen in the metaphor a wider view of God's life-sustaining grace in Christ (Calvin 1963: 257; Hort 1898: 100; Selwyn 1958: 154; Beare 1970: 115; Michaels 1988: 87). This wider view is appropriate to Peter's goal of redefining the readers' self-identity in light of the new reality into which they have come through the new birth. Hearing or reading the word of God is a vital part of this new life, but Christians have not truly ingested God's life-transforming grace until they have put off attitudes and behaviors that are inconsistent with the new life, thereby instinctively, eagerly, and incessantly craving the grace of God.

C. The Identity of God's People (2:4–10)

First Peter 2:4–10 forms the final unit of the opening of the letter. Peter here brings to a stunning climax his description of who his Christian readers are because of who Christ is. There is probably no more sweeping concept for a new identity than the concept of rebirth that Peter introduced in 1:3. His readers have been born again through the resurrection of Jesus Christ from the dead, giving them a new relationship with God the Father as well as a new inheritance and a living hope that will result in their deliverance from God's wrath on the day of judgment. In 2:4–10 he completes the instruction about their new identity by describing to them the nature of the community into which they have been born again. Here Peter emphasizes the community of believers, not in terms of their relationship to one another (having already done that in 1:13–2:2), but in terms of that community's relationship to God, to redemptive history, and to those outside the community.

Consistent with his view that the OT prophets serve Christians, to whom God's grace has come, Peter continues to draw heavily on the OT by quoting or alluding to six LXX passages: Ps. 117:22 (118:22 Eng.); Exod. 19:5–6; Isa. 8:14; 28:16; 43:20–21; and Hos. 2:25 (2:23 Eng.). Though heavily indebted to the Scriptures and interpretive traditions of Judaism, Peter nevertheless creatively transposes them in light of the new reality inaugurated by Christ's resurrection. His use of the OT here is not simply rhetorical ornamentation; each reference contributes to the flow of his argument. The close relationship between Christ and his believers is affirmed not only by the Living Stone/living stones correspondence but also by the structure of Peter's thought, which alternates between Christ and those who respond to (or reject) him:

    2:4a   Christ as Living Stone
    2:4b   believers as living stones

    2:5   believers as spiritual house
    2:6a   Christ as cornerstone of the house

    2:6b   believers never to be shamed
    2:7a   the Cornerstone is honor to believers

2:7b–8a the downfall of those who reject the Living Stone

2:8b stumbling as the destiny of unbelievers

2:9 the new identity of believers: a chosen race, a royal priest-hood, a holy nation, a special possession of God

2:10 believers receive God's mercy and are his people (with the implication that unbelievers do not and are not)

Peter therefore transposes the traditional interpretation of the Jewish Scriptures. He shows that it is response to the gospel promises fulfilled in Jesus Christ, and not genetic descent, that is the divide between those who are the people of God and those who are not, between those who receive God's mercy and those who do not.

1. A Spiritual House and a Holy Priesthood (2:4–8)

After describing the new birth and the ethical transformation necessary for spiritual nourishment of the new life, Peter describes both the Lord Jesus Christ and Christian believers as living stones built into a spiritual "house" in which Christ is the all-important cornerstone. The fact that Peter, whose nickname means "rock," does not give himself any special place in this spiritual house is revealing and suggests that the author was not writing under the later Catholic doctrine of Peter's primacy, upon which the apostolic succession of the papacy was based (Stanford 1945). Peter uses the traditional Jewish understanding of the stone metaphor, but applies it to Jesus Christ, as Jesus himself had. He finds in the stone imagery an expression of both the rejection and exaltation of Jesus Christ, a soteriology based upon divine election, an ecclesiastical mandate for believers, and a basis for judgment of those who reject the Stone. Christian believers who form the spiritual house were once not a people, but now they are God's people. They are chosen and precious to God, for they have received his mercy and love.

Peter presents Jesus Christ as the foundation of God's redemptive work. Two building projects are implied in the image Peter presents: the spiritual house in which Christ is the cornerstone, and the project of those "builders" who reject Christ. He presents the destiny of people based solely on whether they respond to Christ in faith. By doing so, they are built into God's spiritual house. Rejection of the gospel is pictured as stumbling over Christ the Living Stone and falling by the way. In these verses Peter presents an eloquent interweaving of Christology and soteriology that describes the experience of Christ and of Christian believers by quoting several passages from the OT.

    a. The Living Stone and the living stones (2:4–5)
    b. The Stone placed in Zion (2:6)
    c. Jesus—honored cornerstone or stone of stumbling? (2:7–8)

Exegesis and Exposition

[4]As you come to him, the Living Stone who was rejected by human beings but chosen [and] precious to God, [5]you yourselves as living stones are being built

[into] a spiritual house to be a holy priesthood, to offer up spiritual sacrifices acceptable to God through Jesus Christ. [6]For it says in Scripture:

> Behold! I place in Zion a chosen, honored cornerstone
> and the one who trusts in him will never be put to shame.

[7]Therefore, the honor is to you who believe; but to those who do not,

> The stone the builders rejected,
> this has become the cornerstone,

[8]and

> A stone causing stumbling,
> and a rock that is an occasion to sin.

They stumble because they are disobeying the word, to which also they were appointed.

a. The Living Stone and the Living Stones (2:4–5)

The transition from Ps. 33 LXX (Ps. 34 Eng.) to a complex of six more OT passages is triggered by the thought of Ps. 33:5–6 LXX (34:4–5 Eng.) that the Lord is to be not only tasted ("Taste and see that the Lord is good") but also sought:

> I *sought* the Lord, and he hearkened to me,
> and delivered me from all my sojournings.
> *Come to him*, and be enlightened;
> and your faces *shall never be put to shame*. (Ps. 33:5–6 *NETS*, emphasis added)

Peter considers the tasting already to have occurred in the lives of his readers when they experienced the Lord in and after their conversion (1 Pet. 2:3). He now applies the idea of seeking and coming to the Lord as suggested by Ps. 33:5–6 LXX, saying that it is realized in the lives of his readers as they come to Jesus Christ and are built as living stones into God's grand building project of redemption. For Peter, the exhortation of Ps. 33:5 LXX to "come to God" is achieved through coming to Jesus Christ through faith.

    The shift from the metaphor of Christians as infants earnestly desiring milk to Christians as building stones has seemed incongruous to interpreters who attempt to explain it. Beare (1970: 121) makes the unlikely suggestion that the shift in metaphor is an allusion to the many-breasted statue of Artemis at Ephesus in Asia Minor, a dead stone that was incapable of nourishing her devotees in contrast to the true spiritual milk that Christ provides. He notes, however, that the stone in 1 Pet. 2:4 is a building stone and not an idol. Using a different sense of "house" as dynasty, Hillyer (1969a: 126) argues, contra Beare, that the metaphorical shift is perfectly natural in Hebraic thought, where "to be built is to become a house; to become a house is to obtain children." Hillyer's thought is apt within the overall thought of 2:4–10, for the allusion to Exod. 19:5–6 in 1 Pet. 2:9 consists of words from God to the "house [οἶκος, oikos] of Jacob" when he forms them into his covenant nation (Exod. 19:3 LXX).

Peter describes the Lord Jesus Christ, to whom his readers come, as the Living Stone and thereby introduces a dominant image in this passage that has both christological and ecclesiastical significance. The Living Stone was rejected as worthless by "the builders" but was chosen and precious to God. The imagery implies two building projects, one constructed by human builders, the other by God. The human builders examine Christ and find him unfit for building upon. Peter's readers can no doubt relate to the experience of rejection, since they too were being rejected by their society as unfit. Here Peter reintroduces the theme of election (cf. 1 Pet. 1:1–2) and associates the rejection of the Living Stone with the rejection of those who come to him. The parity of Jesus' experience with the experience of Peter's readers is a conceptual structure throughout the book. Moreover, this passage also introduces the soteriological concept that one's response to the Living Stone—rejecting him or coming to him—determines one's relationship to God and, consequently, one's destiny.

Peter identifies Jesus Christ as the rejected stone also in his speech in Acts 4:11–12 and relates response to this stone with salvation. The apostle preaches that Jesus is "'the stone you builders rejected, which has become the cornerstone.' Salvation is found in no one else, for there is no other name given under heaven by which we must be saved" (TNIV). Peter's source for this stone imagery was likely the teachings of Jesus himself, for in all three Synoptic Gospels Jesus prophetically identifies himself with the rejected stone (Mark 12:10–11; Matt. 21:42–44; Luke 20:17–18). In fact, all seven NT passages that quote the OT stone passages unanimously identify the stone as Jesus (in addition to these cited in the Synoptics and Acts, see Rom. 9:32–33; Eph. 2:20–22; and, of course, 1 Pet. 2:4–8).[1] It is highly unlikely that all seven occurrences of the stone imagery in the NT can be accounted for by literary interdependence; therefore, the unanimous voice of the NT on this issue likely represents a common, well-established Christian tradition that most likely went back to Jesus himself. This does not necessarily mean that a written source of stone *testimonia* existed (Achtemeier 1996: 150–51; Best 1969:

1. For a comparison between Peter and Paul in the use of the stone passages, see Oss 1989.

270), for the common association of these three OT stone passages could have been reinforced by oral tradition (Goppelt 1993: 144). Moreover, a well-developed interpretive tradition apparently already existed in Jewish writings that identified the stone with the Messiah. All that remained for the NT writers was to identify Jesus as the Messiah.

The stone image is found in three OT passages (Ps. 118:22–23; Isa. 8:14–15; 28:16), and all three of them are quoted in 1 Pet. 2:6–8. When Jesus applied the rejected stone of Ps. 118:22 to himself, he was probably drawing on the well-established tradition in Judaism that identified the stone with the Messiah. In Isa. 8:14–15, the LORD Almighty is a sanctuary, but he will also be for both houses of Israel "a stone that causes men to stumble and a rock that makes them fall" (NIV). The stone image occurs again in Isa. 28:16 to refer to the object the LORD places in Zion, "So this is what the Sovereign LORD says: 'See, I lay a stone in Zion, a tested stone, a precious cornerstone for a sure foundation; the one who trusts will never be dismayed'" (NIV). In pre-Christian interpretation, the stone image of these three passages came to be understood as messianic. For instance, the LXX of Isa. 28:16–17a (probably second century BC) reads (in English translation):

> Therefore thus says the Lord,
> See, I will lay for the foundations of Sion [Zion]
>   a precious, choice stone,
> a highly valued cornerstone for its foundations,
>   and the one who believes *in him* will not be put to shame.
> And I will turn judgment into hope. (*NETS*, emphasis added)

This Greek version of the passage includes some interesting features that differ somewhat from the Hebrew text. The Greek translator apparently added the prepositional phrase ἐπ᾽ αὐτῷ (*ep' autō*, in him): "Whoever believes *in him* will not be put to shame."[2] The masculine singular pronoun in the added prepositional phrase agrees grammatically with λίθος (*lithos*, stone). However, in collocation with the verb *pisteuō*, the pronoun can also be taken as personal (as the *NETS* translator apparently took it) and possibly as a reference to the Messiah expected to come. Targum Jonathan of Isa. 28:16 understands the stone image of the Hebrew Scripture to be referring to a mighty king. If de Waard (1965: 54) is correct that the Qumran material 1QS 8.8 depends on this Targum, then a messianic reading of Isa. 28:16 existed well before its christological use. Therefore, when Peter describes the Lord to whom his readers are coming as the Living Stone, it is likely a metaphor that

---

2. The Göttingen critical edition considers this the original Greek reading, and it lists no contending variants, as might be expected if the Isaiah verse had been "corrected" by Christian scribes to harmonize with the NT quotations of this passage, all of which include the prepositional phrase (1 Pet. 2:4; Rom. 9:33; 10:11).

would have been understood—at least by Jewish readers—as the resurrected Messiah. The Greek version of Isa. 28:16 also uses the future tense ("I will lay") to refer to God's action. And Isa. 28:17a LXX states a different thought than its corresponding Hebrew text by speaking of hope instead of judgment ("I will turn judgment into hope"), an important motif also picked up in 1 Peter.

Peter's use of the stone passages introduces the theme of Christ's rejection by his contemporaries in spite of his being chosen by God and honored by him. Christ's appointment was first mentioned in 1 Pet. 1:20, where a temporal contrast is made: although he was only relatively recently revealed in these last days, he was nevertheless foreknown (προεγνωσμένου, *proegnōsmenou*) by God before the foundation of the world to be the lamb of redemption without blemish or defect (1:19–20). Here in 2:4, Peter points out that a necessary corollary of Christ's appointment by God was his rejection by the people, which directly led to his redemptive death.

Peter has already addressed his readers as similarly chosen by the foreknowledge (πρόγνωσιν, *prognōsin*, 1:1–2) of God and will now begin to explain that the living stones will suffer as the Living Stone has suffered, not in spite of being chosen by God but *because* they are chosen by God. The experience and destiny of those who come to Christ are bound up with the experience and destiny of Christ himself. While the short-term picture may look bleak because of unjust suffering, the long-term has been made secure by Christ's resurrection, in which Peter's readers will also share. When Peter describes those who come to Jesus Christ also as "living stones," he is implying that their nature derives from the nature of the resurrected Christ. Therefore, the Christians' understanding of their situation is to be shaped by all that Christ has experienced, most important, by Christ's victory over suffering and death.

The parallel between the Living Stone and the living stones implies much about the relationship between Jesus Christ and the life of the Christian, and one wishes Peter had more fully developed the thought (McKelvey 1969). The Christian community is portrayed as a temple, implying that now it—not a literal stone building—is the place of God's earthly dwelling by the Holy Spirit, a place of true worship and of acceptable sacrifice. This is a theocentric image, relating the Christian church to God, unlike the Pauline images of bride and body, which relate the church to Christ. The offerings made in the new temple are acceptable to God through Christ (2:5) but are nevertheless offerings made to God. In Peter's imagery, Christ is included in the spiritual temple alongside believers, but as the foundational, first, and preeminent stone in the new temple, a stone that holds a unique place. Christ is the foundation stone of this new temple; apart from him the new temple would not exist.

The placement of the Living Stone with living stones in the temple implies the close relationship of Christ with believers and their common nature as human beings. The Cornerstone is called "living" by virtue of his resurrection; the same resurrection life enlivens the stones that come to him and take their place in the new temple. The image of the living stones of the new temple also has implications for the conception of the Christian's relationship to other believers. Notably, these living stones are not lying about in idle isolation or disorder in Peter's description. They are not heaped in a pile or scattered across a field. Christians are not individually temples of God in the image that Peter presents. They are each put in place in a spiritual house for the purpose of being a holy priesthood that offers acceptable sacrifices to God.

The image of living stones being built into a spiritual house whose cornerstone is Christ also speaks of the unity, significance, and purpose of all believers, concepts essential for Christian self-understanding. The primary attribute of a temple in first-century thought was its holiness. Just as God's presence sanctified the temple of Jerusalem, the Holy Spirit sanctifies the Christian community, setting it apart as God's own. The unity of the temple is derived from God's presence, the one Cornerstone, and a unity of purpose. There is one single temple into which all believers are built. The Christian church is not primarily a social organization but the new temple where the transformed lives of believers are offered as sacrifice to the glory of God. The imagery of the living stones being built into a single unit implies that the significance and purpose of the individual Christian cannot be realized apart from community with other believers. Coming to Christ means coming into relationship with others, not only in one's own generation but also by being united with believers of every generation, who likewise have been built into God's grand building project. The structure will be completed only when the scaffolding of human history comes down and the kingdom of Christ is revealed in all its glory.

Even if Peter's readers find themselves alienated from their society and suffering a loss of status, Peter assures them that they have become part of a much grander and everlasting community. It is by the values and convictions of this new community that they must now understand themselves, not as self-centered individuals, but as each taking his or her place in the spiritual house. W. Barclay (1976: 195–96) recounts a story that conveys a similar concept about a Spartan king boasting to a visiting monarch about the walls of Sparta. As the visiting king looked around, he could see no walled city and asked, "Where are the renowned walls of Sparta?" The Spartan king pointed to his army and replied, "These are the walls of Sparta, every man a brick." Although the image in 1 Peter is of a building and not a wall of defense, the idea remains that each living stone has a role to play for the integrity and well-being of the whole. God's true house is "spiritual" in the sense that it is constituted by the lives of those who come to Christ.

The term *oikos* used in 2:5 can also refer to a dynasty (a powerful family or line of rulers joined by kinship) as well as to a building where a deity is believed to dwell (a temple). J. H. Elliott (2000: 412) argues that because in 2:5 the phrase "spiritual house" (οἶκος πνευματικός, *oikos pneumatikos*) is nominative singular, it cannot be the object of the verb οἰκοδομεῖσθε (*oikodomeisthe*, you are being built). He construes *oikos* to mean a household, or family, rather than a building, and suggests taking *oikos pneumatikos* as a separate clause, translated "you are a house(hold)" (J. H. Elliott 2000: 412; also T. Martin 1992a). In support of Elliott, 2:9 alludes to Exod. 19:5–6 LXX, where God is addressing the "house of Jacob" and clearly refers to Jacob's descendants. The only other occurrence of *oikos* in 1 Peter is in 4:17 and involves the same ambiguity, even though it is often translated as the "family of God." Nevertheless, the references to both building stones and a cornerstone in 2:4, 6 make it difficult to avoid seeing a structure as the primary image (as also Achtemeier 1996: 159; Best 1969: 280; McKelvey 1969: 128; Schlatter 1999: 58; Seland 1995: 119). The two nominative phrases are in apposition: "You . . . are being built . . . [you are] a spiritual house." The sense is "you are being built into a spiritual house."

On the other hand, if Peter meant to refer unambiguously to a holy building, he could have used either ναός (*naos*) or ἱερόν (*hieron*), words that can refer only to a religious building. The double meaning of *oikos* suggests a metonymy that allows an easy shift from the temple image to the community it houses, "a holy priesthood" (2:9) and "the people of God" (2:10). The same double meaning is in view in 4:17. A similar use of temple imagery with reference to the community is found in the Qumran materials (Gärtner 1965: 72–79; Snodgrass 1977–78: 101–2). John's Revelation presents a similar fluidity in the image of New Jerusalem being both a city and a people (Rev. 21:2).

Peter modifies both *oikos* and θυσίας (*thysias*, sacrifices) in 2:5 with the adjective *pneumatikos* (spiritual). In the symbolic world of these verses, the holy priesthood offers up "spiritual" sacrifices in the "spiritual" house (temple). In other words, it is among Christian believers that spiritual sacrifices acceptable to God will be offered (not the physical, animal sacrifices of Judaism or paganism). The specific nature of these sacrifices has been debated. They have been variously specified as the evangelization of the world (J. H. Elliott 1981: 197; Achtemeier 1996: 158), the "praise of God and a holy, righteous, and honorable way of life" (J. H. Elliott 2000: 423), the Eucharist (Selwyn 1958: 162–63; 294–98), the response of the human spirit to the Holy Spirit (Beare 1970: 123), the "dedication of the entire person to God" (Goppelt 1993: 142), and self-surrender (Hort 1898: 113). Even though 2:9 states that the "royal priesthood" is to declare the praises of God, that declaration is not to be by mere verbal expressions but also by living good lives among the pagans (2:12). As Michaels (1988: 101) observes, the adjective "holy" recalls the use of that same word in 1:15–16, "where holiness is to find its realization in daily 'conduct.'" Therefore, the spiritual sacrifices in view may be understood as all behavior that flows from a transformation of the human spirit by the sanctifying work of the Holy Spirit (1:2). "The whole of life is the offering up of sacrifice" (McKelvey 1969: 130). Such a spiritualization of sacrifice is not unique to Christianity; it is found also at Qumran and in the Psalms and Prophets (Gärtner 1965: 84).

b. The Stone Placed in Zion (2:6)

Peter's concept of the construction of a spiritual house built on the cornerstone of Jesus Christ is validated in verse 6 by citing Isaiah's prophecy of the chosen stone placed in Zion (Isa. 28:16). Although some wish to conjecture that the anarthrous *graphē* here refers to writings other than the canonical OT—such as a collection of messianic texts or other readings—the quotation is clearly from Isaiah, a source that would have been recognized as Scripture. The word is anarthrous probably because Peter is about to quote passages from more than one book of the OT, and thus from "Scripture."

Peter understood that the Spirit of Christ revealed to Isaiah both the sufferings of Christ and the glories that would follow as an encouragement to Peter's Christian readers (1:10–12), regardless of whatever meaning they would have had to Isaiah's own generation. Therefore, Peter offers the words of Isaiah as confirmation of what his readers are now experiencing as believers in Christ. When God announced through Isaiah that he would lay a cornerstone as a sure foundation in Zion, he was announcing the building project of which Peter speaks in 2:5. The apostle Peter announces Jesus Christ to be the Living Cornerstone of that project. Because of the apostle's understanding of the relationship between Christ and believers, he simply extends the imagery to include those coming to Christ as taking their place in the grand building project that God had announced through Isaiah. There is not even a hint that Peter thought of himself as being a special or foundational stone in the church, even though Jesus had given him the nickname that means "rock." His silence here, where such a suggestion would be most natural, lends support to the understanding that the "rock" of Matt. 16:18, on which Christ will build the church, is the confession of Jesus being the Christ, not Peter himself (see also Stanford 1945: 15; France 1998: 30).

But because of their faith in Christ, Peter's readers are experiencing rejection by unbelievers that results in various trials and hardships. Peter explains that their misfortunes are not a sign that God is rejecting them but are the very opposite: the various ways they are being rejected correspond to the rejection the Living Cornerstone has experienced and confirm their election as living stones in God's building program. With

God's promise through Isaiah, Peter reassures them that the one who trusts in Christ, the chosen cornerstone, will never be put to shame.

c. Jesus—Honored Cornerstone or Stone of Stumbling? (2:7–8)

Picking up the adjective ἔντιμον (*entimon*, honored), which describes the chosen cornerstone in 1 Pet. 2:6, Peter consoles his readers by pointing out that the honor (ἡ τιμή, *hē timē*, 2:7) is to those who believe (as also Achtemeier 1996: 160; Beare 1970: 124; de Silva 2000: 40; Goppelt 1993: 145; Marshall 1991: 72; McKnight 1996: 109; Michaels 1988: 104; Reicke 1964: 92). As Beare (1970: 124) notes, Peter apparently takes his cue from the phrase of Isa. 28:16 LXX that those who trust in the Stone placed in Zion will never be put to shame, which he reads as a litotes strongly affirming the opposite of shame.[3] And so Peter understands the promise of Isa. 28:16 LXX to mean that those who trust in the Stone placed in Zion are in fact honored. The honor (the noun is articular, *hē timē*) of believers is a share in the honor that God has bestowed on Christ, with whom they are united in the spiritual house (Beare 1970: 124).

The terms of shame and honor form a contrast in 1 Peter that frames the social situation for Peter's original readers (B. Campbell 1998). As a primary value in first-century culture, honor "concerned the positive social standing, reputation, and status rating of individuals and groups in the opinion of others and of God. 'Shame' . . . entailed sensitivity regarding loss of honor or the actual loss of honor" (J. H. Elliott 2000: 427). In the first-century Roman society of Asia Minor, did conversion to Christ raise or lower one's social status? Did it bring honor or shame to oneself and one's family? Apparently Peter's readers were receiving

> a barrage of verbal abuse designed to demean, discredit, and shame the believers as social and moral deviants endangering the common good. This procedure of public shaming was employed as a means of social control with the aim of pressuring the minority community to conform to conventional values and standards of conduct. (J. H. Elliott 2000: 117)

Such sustained social pressure resulted in undeserved suffering that could lead to despair and eventually even renunciation of the Christian faith. And so Peter reminds his readers of Isaiah's promise that whoever trusts in the Cornerstone placed in Zion will, in fact, never be shamed, and thereby reverses the basis of honor and shame in their self-understanding. Those who trust in the Living Cornerstone that God has placed in Zion will never be put to shame, but those who reject Christ will suffer shameful judgment by God himself, the one who ultimately arbitrates

---

3. Litotes is a literary device in which the negative conveys a strong affirmation of its opposite (cf. Acts 12:18, which mentions "no small commotion" when describing what was a very great commotion).

honor and shame. Therefore, despite the shameful treatment they receive from society, Peter encourages his readers that they, not their accusers, are the ones who receive the true honor by believing in Christ.

Peter's use of the stone passages reaches far beyond the sociological dimension; he uses this imagery to teach that Jesus is the touchstone of one's ultimate destiny. The apostle reflects on the soteriological dimension of the stone imagery by quoting Ps. 117:22 LXX (118:22 Eng.), the passage that Jesus applied to himself to predict his own rejection (Mark 12:10; Matt. 21:42; Luke 20:17). To this quotation Peter adds an allusion to Isa. 8:14 LXX, making this passage the most complete collection of NT references to the stone passages of the OT.

Like Ps. 33 LXX (34 Eng.), quoted in 1 Pet. 2:3, Ps. 117 LXX (118 Eng.) is a psalm of deliverance. It was one of the psalms sung by the Levites during Passover, when the lambs were slaughtered:

> In my distress I called on the Lord, and he hearkened to me. . . .
>> I will acknowledge you because you hearkened to me
>> and became my salvation.
> The stone the builders rejected,
>> this one became the chief cornerstone.
> This was the Lord's doing;
>> and it is marvelous in our eyes.
> This is the day that the Lord has made;
>> let us rejoice and be glad on it.
> Ah Lord, do save us!
>> Ah Lord, do give us success! (Ps. 117:5, 21–25 *NETS*)

In Ps. 117 LXX the rejected stone has become the chief cornerstone of God's building program. (Although the Greek words referring to the cornerstone in 1 Pet. 2:6 and 2:7 are different expressions, both probably refer to the same architectural feature. See additional note on 2:7.) Even in the psalm, the chief cornerstone rejected by "the builders" is closely associated with salvation, implying that to reject the stone is to jeopardize one's salvation. Alluding to the later Greek versions of Isa. 8:14, Peter further describes the stone in relation to those who reject it as a stone of stumbling (προσκόμματος, *proskommatos*) and a rock of temptation to sin (σκανδάλου, *skandalou*, 2:8).[4] Ironically, Peter himself (the rock) was accused by Jesus of being a *skandalon* when Peter rebuked Jesus and attempted to deflect him from his predicted road to rejection and death (Matt. 16:23). Peter had become an occasion for Jesus to sin, a temptation that Jesus vigorously overcame by his sharp rebuke of Peter's thought. Here in 1 Pet. 2:8 Peter claims that Christ the cornerstone presents an opportunity either for trust or for rejection.

---

4. In the latter phrase, Peter follows not Isa. 8:14 LXX but a reading found also in the later Greek versions of Aquila, Symmachus, and Theodotion, as does Paul in Rom. 9:33.

Moreover, rejection of Christ is not an amoral decision; it is itself an instance of sin. This is a message that our religiously pluralistic society today finds just as offensive as did first-century polytheistic society. To reject Christ *is* to stumble and sin. Peter quotes only the portion of Isa. 8 that refers to those who reject and stumble, but that passage also refers to the rock as a refuge for those who trust (Isa. 8:13–14 LXX): "Sanctify the Lord himself; and he himself will be your fear. If you trust in him, he will become your sanctuary, and you will not encounter him as a stumbling caused by a stone, nor as a fall caused by a rock" (*NETS*). Isaiah is speaking of those who *do* trust in the Lord. Peter uses the prophet's words to reflect on those who do not. By implication, those who have not trusted in the Lord have not "sanctified" him, and therefore they have indeed encountered him as a stone and rock over which they have fallen.

As Marshall (1991: 73) summarizes, the quotation of Isa. 28:16 LXX and Ps. 117:22 LXX (118:22 Eng.) functions in Peter's argument first to explain that the unbelief of those who reject Christ was already predicted in the OT prophecies; therefore, the rejection of Christ by friends and neighbors should not cause Christians surprise or doubt in their own faith. Second, Peter has clearly presented Jesus Christ as the only means of salvation, by which all will be judged. When people reject him, they do it to their own peril.

One can see in the NT use of the stone passages a broadening in the identification of the rejecters. In the Gospels and Acts (Matt. 21:42; Mark 12:10; Luke 20:17; Acts 4:11), the rejecters are the leaders of first-century Jerusalem, and the stone is identified as Jesus. In Rom. 9:32–33, where Paul conflates Isa. 8:14 and 28:16, those who reject Christ the cornerstone are the people of Israel as a nation. Here in 1 Pet. 2:8, the rejecters are any and all people, whether Jew or Gentile, who reject Christ.

They reject Christ by "disobeying the word" (2:8). The subsequent use of "disobey the word" in 3:1 and "disobey the good news of God" in 4:17 suggests that "the word" in 2:8 should be similarly understood as a rejection of the gospel message.

Therefore, Peter has the broadest understanding of the builders who reject the stone in relation to Christ. As Beare (1970: 125) explains, "Christ is now seen as the key to all human destiny and the touchstone of all endeavour; faith in Him leads to honour, unbelief to disaster. . . . 'The builders' now is taken to mean all who attempt to build human society or their own lives." With this use of the stone passages, Peter eliminates all neutral ground. The rejection of Christ does not make him go away but in fact has ultimate consequences. One either trusts in the Living Cornerstone or rejects him. As Goppelt (1993: 144, 146) has eloquently put it,

Christ is laid across the path of humanity on its course into the future. In the encounter with him each person is changed: one for salvation, another for destruction. . . . One cannot simply step over Jesus to go on about the daily routine and pass him by to build a future. Whoever encounters him is inescapably changed through the encounter: Either one sees and becomes "a living stone," or one stumbles as a blind person over Christ and comes to ruin, falling short, i.e., of one's Creator and Redeemer and thereby of one's destiny.

According to the apostle Peter, those who stumble by disobeying the word were "appointed" (ἐτέθησαν, etethēsan) to do so. This passing comment, on which Peter does not elaborate, brings readers up short and raises thorny exegetical and theological issues. Commentators are divided on how to understand the appointment of the disobedient. Does God, if we take the verb as a divine passive, appoint those who reject the gospel message both to disobey and to stumble? Or does the appointment to stumble follow someone's own choosing to disobey? This is an exegetical crux that cannot help but be influenced by one's theology, for the antecedent of the relative pronoun in the prepositional phrase εἰς ὅ (eis ho, to which) has been argued both ways. Some take it to mean that stumbling is inevitable once the word has been disobeyed but that God does not appoint people to the disobedience itself (J. H. Elliott 2000: 433–34; Hillyer 1992: 64). France (1998: 34) argues that it means "not that certain people were destined not to believe, but that God's decree is that those who do not believe will stumble and fall" (as also J. H. Elliott 2000: 434). Others argue that the appointment is to disbelief, which then necessarily results in stumbling (Achtemeier 1996: 162–63; Beare 1970: 126; Best 1971: 106; Calvin 1963: 264–65; Clark 1972: 85–86; Grudem 1988: 107–8; Horrell 1998: 42–43; Kelly 1969: 94).

Michaels (1988: 107) understands the appointment of Christ as stone and the appointment of unbelievers to stumbling not as two distinct appointings but as one divine appointment with a twofold result. This thought is supported by the use of the same verb (τίθημι, tithēmi, place, appoint) to refer both to the stone God has placed in Zion (2:6) and to the appointment of those who disbelieve and stumble (2:8). When God appointed Jesus Christ as the atoning sacrifice, to be the stone placed in Zion, by that act God also necessarily appointed two consequential outcomes with respect to acceptance or rejection of Christ. There would be those who receive the message of the gospel, described in 1 Peter as those "chosen" (eklektos) by God's foreknowledge (1 Pet. 1:1–2). There would also be those who would not believe, whose opportunity for disbelief was set [tithēmi] with the setting [tithēmi] of the Stone in Zion. Therefore, the doctrine of election can be argued from 1 Peter, but the corollary of reprobation is not addressed in these verses (as also Prigent 1992).

Hort (1898: 123) argues that the builders appointed to stumble by disbelief should be interpreted in the context of Rom. 9–11 and taken as a reference only to the Jews at the time of Jesus, whose rejection of the Word led to the atonement of the cross (as also Beare 1970: 126; Reicke 1964: 92). But since 1 Peter is not directly dependent on Romans, it is difficult to justify using Romans as the context in which to read 1 Peter. Moreover, Peter makes no reference to the Jews in his letter, and his use of the quotation seems to be a broader reference to all who disobey and reject the gospel, especially the people of Asia Minor, with whom his readers are familiar. Hort (1898: 123) observes that the purpose of Paul's argument in Romans is "to draw the utmost range of human perverseness within the mysterious folds of God's will, so that nothing should be left outside, that God's will may be seen at last in the far future accomplishing its purpose of good." That observation is also helpful here, where Peter's intent is clearly similar.

It is impossible to escape the force of Peter's teaching that God has sovereignly determined both the destiny of those who come to Christ and of those who disobey his word and reject his gospel. As McKnight (1996: 109) summarizes, "God's act of appointing Jesus as the living Stone has become both honor for believers and judgment for unbelievers; this was God's design, and everything happens according to his will." Rejection of Christ does not excuse one from the purview of God; rather, it confirms that one has not (yet) been born again into the living hope of which Peter speaks. This is not to say that Peter teaches that those in disobedience to the word at one point in time are forever excluded from the hope of salvation. To the contrary, he admonishes his readers to live in such a way as to persuade unbelievers to accept the gospel of Christ (e.g., 2:12; 3:1). However, ultimate destiny rests on whether one eventually accepts God's mercy as extended in Christ. Those who persist in their rejection of the gospel of Jesus Christ will inevitably find themselves shamed by the ultimate judgment of God.

Additional Notes

2:5. The form of the verb *oikodomeisthe* could be either indicative (Achtemeier 1996: 155; Davids 1990: 87; J. H. Elliott 2000: 413; Hort 1898: 109; Michaels 1988: 100; Seland 1995: 101) or imperative (Bigg 1956: 128; Goppelt 1993: 139–40; T. Martin 1992a: 180–81; Perkins 1995: 43). Thurén (1990: 21) cites this as another example of purposeful ambiguity in 1 Peter that functions as either descriptive or a command, addressing the situation of a diverse audience. But the imperative sense, "Let yourselves be built," does not seem as apt in the immediate context, which correlates "coming to Christ" in 2:4 with "being built into a spiritual house" in 2:5, because coming to Christ is a reference to the conversion already experienced by Peter's readers. An imperative here would suggest that Peter is exhorting his readers to come to Christ, an evangelistic thrust not evident elsewhere in the letter. Therefore, it seems more apt that the verb of 2:5 is indicative, describing the relationship with one another into which his readers have already come.

2:7. Although it is clear that the Living Stone is the foundational and unifying element of the spiritual house, two different terms are used to refer to it (in 2:6, ἀκρογωνιαῖον, *akrogōniaion*; in 2:7, κεφαλὴν γωνίας, *kephalēn gōnias*). Moreover, the precise architectural referents of these terms is unclear. Although Jeremias has argued that contemporaneous Greek texts use *akrogōniaion* to refer to a capstone located high up and not at ground level (Jeremias, *TDNT* 1:792), the LXX of Isa. 28:16 puts *akrogōniaion* in relation to the foundation (εἰς τὰ θεμέλια, *eis ta themelia*), suggesting a ground-level location. The expression *kephalēn gōnias*, literally translated "head of the corner," seems to involve similar uncertainty (McKelvey 1969: 199). But Peter is not reaching for architectural precision here; he simply quotes the terms already found in his two source LXX texts, Isa. 28:16 and Ps. 117:22 (118:22 Eng.). Moreover, his further comment that this is a stone over which people will stumble implies that the terms function in his imagery at ground level, regardless of the architectural position of the referent in the original source text. Because the English word "cornerstone" usually refers to a foundational stone at ground level, it is the most appropriate translation of both terms in this particular instance. For an extensive discussion of the issue, see McKelvey 1969: 195–204.

2. Now You Are the People of God (2:9–10)

After reflecting on the shame that those who reject Christ must bear, Peter now turns his thought back to his readers who have believed in Christ. "But you," he says to his readers, are not among those who have been appointed to stumble because you have obeyed the word. Obeying the word by putting faith in Christ gives Peter's readers a share in Christ's honor, described here with four phrases echoing Isa. 43:20–21 and Exod. 19:6: (1) a chosen race, (2) a royal priesthood, (3) a holy nation, (4) a people for God's special possession. Here again, Peter unabashedly applies terms to his Christian readers that were used previously only to describe God's chosen nation of ancient Israel.

a. You are a chosen race (2:9a)
b. You are a royal priesthood (2:9b)
c. You are a holy nation (2:9c)
d. You are a people for God's special possession (2:9d)
e. You are a people who have received God's mercy (2:10)

Exegesis and Exposition

[9]But you are a chosen race, a royal priesthood, a holy nation, a people for [God's] special possession, so that you may proclaim the mighty acts of the one who has called you out of darkness [and] into his marvelous light. [10]You were once not a people, but now you are the people of God; you had not received mercy, but now you have received mercy.

a. You Are a Chosen Race (2:9a)

The phrase "a chosen race" (γένος ἐκλεκτόν, *genos eklekton*) echoes Isa. 43:3, which announces that God himself is Israel's only savior, who will deliver his people from their exile in Babylon. Peter frames his letter in the motif of the historic Babylonian exile in order to identify his readers with the OT promises of deliverance. In Isa. 43:20–21 God declares he will provide water in the desert to give drink to "my people, my chosen, the people I formed for myself that they may proclaim my praise." The LXX of Isa. 43:20 includes the phrase "my chosen race" (*to genos mou to eklekton*), which is echoed in the words of 1 Pet. 2:9, "you are a chosen race" (*genos eklekton*). The term *genos* refers to people descended from a common lineage, in the case of Isa. 43 the descendants of Abraham. Isaiah 43:21 states the purpose for which this race has been chosen: that they may proclaim God's praises. Peter directly applies the same mandate to his Christian readers of first-century Asia Minor: "that you may proclaim the mighty acts of the one who has called you out of darkness into his marvelous light" (2:9). As Peter later teaches, this declaration of praise is not simply verbal but a life lived righteously.

In biblical theology, Israel's deliverance from exile in Babylon is the typological forerunner of the greater deliverance achieved by Jesus Christ, deliverance of God's people out of darkness into light. Peter here makes the radical claim that those who believe in Jesus Christ—whether Jew, Gentile, Greek, Roman, Cappadocian, Bithynian, or whatever—though from many races, constitute a new race of those who have been born again into the living hope through the resurrection of Jesus Christ. Here is the foundational cure for the evils of racism in human society.

The understanding of Christians that they formed a new race among humanity was precisely one of the points for which they were criticized and persecuted by first-century pagan society. The Roman writer Suetonius refers to Christians as a separate class: "Punishment was inflicted on the Christians [*Christiani*], a class [*genus*] of men given to a new and mischievous superstition (*Nero* 16; Rolfe 1939). This perception, as Colwell (1939: 58; also Frend 1967) observes, led to practices and attitudes—whether justified or not—that alienated Christians from the people of the empire. From the conception of Christians as a distinct race came the accusation that believers in Christ were "haters of mankind." The very goals of Peter's letter—that believers form internal bonds within the Christian community and repudiate certain attitudes and practices of their society—also gave rise to the charge that Christians were antisocial. (However, see comments on 2:11–17.) Christians were perceived to repudiate pleasures (e.g., the theater, the races, the gladiatorial combats), break home and family ties, ruin business, abandon pagan religious ritual, and avoid civic duties (Colwell 1939: 61; Frend 1967). This very concept of the new race caused much of the popular opposition to Christianity in the first few centuries. But as Colwell (1939: 71) observes, "It was also the victory that overcame the world," as Christians lived as members of a new race and paradoxically won over the masses.

Peter further describes his readers as "a royal priesthood, a holy nation, a people for God's special possession," language taken directly from Exod. 19:5–6 LXX: "Now if by hearing you listen to my voice and keep my covenant, you shall be to me *a people special* above all nations. For the earth is mine. And you shall be for me *a royal priesthood* and *a holy nation*. These are the words you shall say to the sons of Israel" (*NETS*, emphasis added). Reaching further back into Israel's history to the time of the exodus from Egypt, Peter draws from the language of the covenant that constituted Israel as God's chosen nation. The exodus, being also a deliverance from the oppression of Egypt, is used throughout the NT as a type of what God has done in Christ. In Exod. 19, Moses is addressing those whom he has led to Mount Sinai, who will soon become God's holy nation on the basis of a covenant. By keeping the terms of the covenant, Israel would maintain her status as a royal priesthood and a holy nation. Although Aaron and his sons played a special priestly role within the covenant people, the royal priesthood of the holy nation in Exod. 19 is in relation to the rest of the earth. Just as Aaron and his sons mediate between Israel and God, the entire nation of Israel was to play a mediating role between God and the nations.

b. You Are a Royal Priesthood (2:9b)

"You are a royal priesthood," Peter writes, applying the identification to the people of the new covenant in Christ, who are now ordained with the role of a royal priesthood mediating God in Christ to the nations. The identity of Christian believers as collectively constituting a priesthood is the controlling image from 1 Pet. 2:4–5. By offering spiritual sacrifices that are "coextensive with the lives of the faithful," the church "brings the kingdom of God into being here below" (Congar 1962: 178–79). Its faithful consecration to God, the King of the universe, therefore makes its priesthood a royal service. Whether taken as two substantives (kingdom and priesthood; cf. J. H. Elliott 2000: 437; Best 1969: 291) or as an adjective and a substantive (royal priesthood), 1 Peter is the only epistle to give this magnificent title to the Christian community, indicating "the collective pedigree and role of the people of God as being royal and priestly" (Hill 1982: 45–46).

The Reformation doctrine of the "priesthood of all believers" has sometimes been understood to endow every believer with the rights and authority of the ordained clergy. Such an interpretation arose at a time when the ordained clergy were abusing their spiritual authority in various ways. Luther writes, "Let everyone, therefore, who knows himself to be a Christian, be assured of this, that we are all equally priests [*sacerdotes*], that is to say, we have the same power in respect to the Word and the sacraments" (Wentz 1959: 116). Since Luther's time, this interpretation of 1 Pet. 2:5, 9 has at times been used to bring the Christian laity into sharp tension with the ordained clergy. Moreover, it is often taken to mean the individual believer has a spiritual authority equal to that of the ordained priest or minister. But this is probably a misuse of Luther's thought, for he immediately continues, "However, no one may make use of this power except by the consent of the community or by the call of a superior" (Wentz 1959: 116).

Whether or not Luther's interpretation has been rightly understood and applied throughout history, Peter's thought here is not in the context of spiritual authority, nor is it focused on the qualities of the individual believer.[1] It is not the concept of clerical authority but rather the theme of obedience and holiness that Peter has in view, concepts that were also present in the original context of Exod. 19. An ancient priesthood was to be sanctified and set apart from the people at large for their ministry to the deity, to whom they had special access. Accordingly, the entire nation of ancient Israel was to be set apart from the nations of the world to serve God through obedience to the covenant with him, which obedience constituted Israel's holiness. Peter now declares similarly that collectively Christian believers are to perform that same function with respect to the nations among which they are scattered. By obedience to the new covenant in Christ's blood (1 Pet. 1:2), they are to be sanctified and set apart from the peoples of the world. The modifier "royal" is apt, for Christians know God as their King, to whom they now owe allegiance. The kingdom of God is composed of believers who must think of themselves as holy with respect to the world, set apart for purity and a purpose demanded by God. This is the priesthood that serves the King of the universe.

Peter also does not have in view the relation between this royal priesthood and the special offices of the ministry that have developed. However, as France (1998: 38) observes, in Exod. 19:6 "the original constitution of the whole nation as a 'priesthood' . . . did not preclude the subsequent establishment of a more restricted priesthood of the sons of Aaron, in which the priesthood of the whole people was more specifically focused."

c. You Are a Holy Nation (2:9c)

"You are a holy nation," Peter continues, building on the new-covenant theme and suggesting the thought that the true social context of his readers was not first-century Greco-Roman culture but the new nation constituted by believers in Christ (centered in the kingdom of God). God established the covenant at Sinai, which formed ancient Israel as a holy nation on the blood of a sacrifice (Exod. 24). God established the new covenant in Christ by the sacrifice symbolized when Jesus at the Last Supper lifted the cup and said, "This is my blood of the covenant, which is poured out for many" (Mark 14:24 TNIV).

The designation of believers as a holy nation reinforces the concept of obedience and sanctification, with each of the four descriptors mutually interpreting the others. It refers not so much to their moral status but to their calling as a people set apart for God, and therefore a calling to moral quality. Ancient Israel's holiness as a nation derived from the holy King of the universe, who had cut a covenant with them, binding them to himself as his chosen nation and special possession. The words

---

1. For an interesting analysis of Luther's interpretation and his influence on the semantic value of the English word "priest," see Erling 1999.

"chosen," "royal," and "holy" are adjectives that describe collectively the nature of the relationship of Christian believers to the Father of the Lord Jesus Christ.

Just as the understanding of Christians as forming a new race brought potential alienation from popular society, the potential conflict of loyalties brought charges of treason and poor citizenship upon Christians of the Roman Empire. Jesus' instruction to "Give back to Caesar what is Caesar's and to God what is God's" (Mark 12:17 TNIV) presents the issue of deciding which is which. First-century Christians were often persecuted and executed not because they worshipped Jesus—in a polytheistic society, what is one more god?—but because of the higher claim of the gospel that only in Christ is the One, True God to be worshipped. Because the prosperity and welfare of the empire were believed to depend on religious forces, the Christian's exclusive allegiance to Jesus as God was naturally viewed as detrimental to the rest of society. From that perspective, Christians were bad citizens of the empire, and this made them subject to accusations of treason. The self-understanding of the early church as a holy nation is attested by the force brought against them by the Roman state. As Merrill (1924: 68) points out, "There finally came a time when it [the Roman Empire] must either fight or tamely acknowledge a super-power within its own borders."

Under the modern ideology that separates church and state, it is perhaps easier today to separate what belongs to Caesar from what belongs to God. But to the extent that government formulates policy directly bearing on moral and ethical issues (e.g., abortion, war, the place of religious faith in the public forum), Christians still have to face the problems raised by holding dual citizenship—in the country of their residence and in the holy nation of God.

d. You Are a People for God's Special Possession (2:9d)

The fourth descriptor, "a people for [God's] special possession," is an allusion to both Exod. 19:5 and Isa. 43:20–21, where God refers to his holy nation in the context of the exodus and later in the Babylonian exile, respectively, as the people out of all the peoples of the world that God claims for himself. Although the whole earth and everything in it belongs to God (Exod. 19:5), the ancient nation of Israel was to be God's special possession. In Exod. 19:5–6 the order reads, "You shall be to me a special possession. . . . You shall be to me a royal priesthood and a holy nation." "Special possession" is further defined there by "royal priesthood" and "holy nation." In 1 Pet. 2:9 the same point is made with different syntax and a shift in verb tense: "You are . . . a royal priesthood, a holy nation, a people for [*eis*] [God's] special possession." Michaels (1988: 109) observes Peter's future-oriented use of *eis* in various eschatological expressions and translates the phrase as "a people destined for vindication." Whatever eschatological connotations the phrase may hold, the holy and priestly character that people of the covenant of Christ collectively exemplify defines what it means for them to be God's special possession in a way that the rest of humanity is not.

When God's people were delivered from Babylonian exile, they were to declare τὰς ἀρετάς (*tas aretas*, the mighty acts, praises) of God (Isa. 43:20–21 LXX). The raison d'être of God's "chosen race, royal priesthood, holy nation" is to constitute a special people who make known what God has done, displaying his power, grace, and mercy. Peter calls his readers to that purpose as well in 1 Pet. 2:9: "so that you might proclaim the mighty acts of the one who has called you out of darkness and into his marvelous light." The word *aretē* was used to refer to the excellent character of one who is worthy of praise, as expressed, for instance, by acts of civic beneficence. Greek moral philosophers use *aretē* in discussing virtues of character that Greek society highly esteemed. In the religious context, the word referred to manifestations of divine power, which is the likely sense it carries in Isa. 43:21 LXX. The deliverance of the Jews from Babylonian exile through the pagan king Cyrus was itself an expression of God's power and beneficence toward his people, thus revealing his character and resulting in his praise. Therefore, in 1 Peter *aretas* can be understood either as praises or God's mighty acts that are the basis of that praise, though under the influence of Isa. 43 perhaps the latter is more in view.

e. You Are a People Who Have Received God's Mercy (2:10)

Peter's final description of his readers in 2:10 alludes to Hos. 2:23 (2:25 LXX), implying that Peter's readers are, amazingly, a fulfillment of that ancient prophecy: "You were once not a people, but now you are the people of God; you had not received mercy, but now you have received mercy." In Hos. 2 the Lord speaks of a time when his royal priesthood and holy nation would be restored after the people's egregious failure to keep the covenant with him, which had constituted them as his royal priesthood and holy nation. In running after other gods and indulging in pagan practices, Israel had broken covenant with Yahweh. The nation was no longer his special possession in that it had forsaken its role as a royal priesthood and a holy nation. Consequently, God no longer had a people who were functioning as his special possession. Because his people acted like the pagans of the surrounding nations, they were to be sent into exile, scattered among them.

But God spoke through the prophet Hosea, promising a future restoration, a time when by unmerited love and mercy God would again constitute a people for his special possession, who would declare the mighty act of God that brought them into existence. "I will show mercy to the unloved, and I will say to those who are not my people, 'You are my people,' and they will say, 'You are the Lord my God'" (Hos. 2:25 LXX). Peter's final statement about the identity of his Christian readers implies that their conversion to Christ is the fulfillment of that promised restoration. Amazingly, God's love and mercy were not limited to the people of Israel and Judah. God's chosen race was no longer limited to the descendants of Abraham, Isaac, and Jacob. Isaiah and Hosea had spoken of a reconstitution of God's exiled people, traditionally interpreted to mean the regathering of Judah and Israel from their far-flung places of exile. But Peter addresses his Christian readers as people of the Diaspora (1 Pet. 1:1) and sends greeting from those in "Babylon," the symbolic capital of exile (5:13). God's regathered royal priesthood and holy nation—his newly chosen race, according to Peter—would be those who had been reborn as the children, not of Abraham, but of God the Father himself through the resurrection of Jesus Christ. The Christian community declares by its existence, by its liturgy and worship, by the daily lives of its members the mighty deed of Christ's resurrection, which reveals the praiseworthy character of God.

Summary

First Peter 2:1–10 describes Peter's Christian readers in terms intended to make them realize the distinctive honor that is theirs as believers in Jesus Christ. These verses advance the argument of 1:13–25 in preparation for Peter's explicit exhortations to follow (Thurén 1995: 129–30). He has pointed out that because of the new life and status that God in his mercy has granted them, they are to live in obedience to God's will. In 2:1 their former way of life is condemned as not just empty (1:18) but, what's more, as evil (2:1). The end of those who persist in that way is disastrous (2:8). Though they may be scattered across the vastness of Asia Minor, in truth they have been built into one spiritual house (2:4–5). As living stones in that house, they share the honor of the Living Stone the builders rejected (2:6–7). The unity, significance, and purpose of the Christian community is presented and then underscored by endowing it with the descriptions once used of God's ancient holy people, Israel. Peter's readers are to understand themselves in these terms, regardless of how their society labels them. With this exposition of their new identity in Christ, Peter is now ready to instruct his readers in how to discharge their role as a people chosen for God's own possession in relationship to the world in which they live.

III. As God's People, Live Godly Lives (2:11–4:11)

The discourse unit from 2:11 through 4:11 forms the middle of the letter body and as such is the heart of 1 Peter's teaching. Having explained to his readers their identity as God's people, Peter now addresses the matter of pressing concern and begins to instruct them on how as God's people to live in right relationship with unbelievers in a pagan society. As our own modern society becomes more religiously diversified, Peter's instructions ring true and clear for believers today, who must first understand who they are in Christ as they attempt to live rightly in an increasingly un-Christian world.

Peter advises his readers to engage their society as resident aliens and foreigners. Whether this description is based on their actual historical and sociological situation or whether it is a purely spiritual metaphor describing the believer's relationship to the world, Peter is calling his readers to recognize that they are living in an alien place that has different values and practices than those appropriate for the people of God's holy nation. To live rightly in such a place, the apostle gives his readers two major principles of engagement: (1) their allegiance to God in Christ does not exempt them from submitting to pagan authority, and (2) they must maintain their identity as God's holy people and consequently be prepared, if necessary, to suffer unjustly and without retaliation for holding to their convictions and values as followers of Jesus Christ.

Depending on their temperament and situation, it is easy to imagine that some of Peter's readers might naturally wish to resist either verbally or physically those who are unjustly maligning and grieving the Christian community. Others may be adopting a more passive stance of privatizing their Christian faith and publicly assimilating to their culture—becoming closet Christians, so to speak. Because Peter's letter is addressed to such a large geographical area, the nature and extent of persecution no doubt varied from place to place. Peter's exhortation effectively corrects both theoretical tendencies, resisting and privatizing (Thurén 1995: 86–87). Because this controversial issue is at the heart of the letter, Peter musters a profoundly theological argument to support his teaching, the example of Jesus Christ himself.

A. Commendable Social Behavior as God's People (2:11–3:7)

First Peter 2:11 marks Peter's transition to the heart of his argument and introduces his main concern: that Christians live rightly among the Gentiles. Regardless of where Peter's readers find themselves scattered, they are to live as faithful witnesses to the truth of Christ's gospel in a way that does not unnecessarily offend the expectations of their society. Peter conceptualizes the relationship of Christians to society as that of visiting strangers or resident aliens, those who appreciate, respect, and value their host land but nevertheless maintain their own distinct identity within it.

1. Lifestyle Evangelism (2:11–12)

Peter instructs his Christian readers that they are to live appropriately within pagan society as those who are in many respects but visitors. The visitor mind-set is intended to motivate them to maintain a way of living that would be recognized as good by their Gentile neighbors who speak against this foreign sect of Christians as evildoers. According to Peter, the visitors' goal should be to live in such a way as to quiet the negative stereotypes associated with this foreign religion, Christianity. This is to be accomplished by being people who do not indulge in self-destructive behavior and whose lifestyles can be recognized as good even by their pagan neighbors. In this form of lifestyle evangelism, Peter expects that instead of speaking evil against Christians, these Gentiles will be among those who ultimately glorify God.

Exegesis and Exposition

[11]Dear friends, I urge [you] as resident aliens and visiting foreigners to abstain from carnal desires that war against the soul, [12]and maintain a good way of life among the Gentiles, in order that although they speak against you as evildoers, because they recognize [your way of life from] your good works, they will glorify God on the day of [his] visitation.

Peter begins the exhortations of his letter by addressing his readers as "dear friends" (ἀγαπητοί, *agapētoi*), before he begins his difficult instructions about how they are to live in relationship to unbelievers within their society. Though they may be estranged from their neighbors because of their faith in Christ, he reminds them that they have his apostolic affection.

The verb παρακαλῶ (*parakalō*, I exhort) introduces Peter's central concern and marks these verses as a transition to the body of the letter, in which Peter exhorts Christians to live in right relationship with their society. His opening exhortation is twofold, stated first in the negative ("abstain from carnal desires") and then in the positive ("maintain a good way of life"; see additional note on 2:12). This good way of life contrasts with the previously mentioned "useless way of life" in which Peter's readers once lived (1:18).

They are to receive the apostle's exhortation as "resident aliens and visiting foreigners" (παροίκους καὶ παρεπιδήμους, *paroikous kai parepidēmous*), the former term being first introduced in 1:17 and the latter in 1:1. This phrase is found in Gen. 23:4 LXX, where Abraham describes himself to the Hittites: "I am a resident alien [*paroikos*] and a visiting stranger [*parepidēmos*] among you. Therefore, sell me property for a burial site." Peter's readers need to reorient their self-understanding with respect to the society in which they live. The terms Peter uses to describe them basically mean that as Christians they are citizens first of God's holy nation and therefore not primarily citizens (i.e., aliens and foreigners) of the society in which they live, to whatever extent the two conflict. With the allusion to Abraham, he reminds his readers that they stand in a long tradition of people who were chosen by God and called to be aliens and strangers in the places where they lived. Estrangement from, and rejection by, their society are therefore no indication of alienation from God or a weakness of Christian faith. To the contrary, the story of redemption tells of God forming his chosen people by calling Abraham to become a resident alien and foreigner in a strange land. The thrust of the description is not to suggest that Christians are away from their true home in heaven, as the NIV reading of 1 Pet. 1:1 suggests. Although that thought is found elsewhere in the NT (Heb. 13:14), the terms as used here define a horizontal relationship with respect to society, not a vertical one with respect to God. The description of resident aliens and foreigners draws Peter's readers into continuity with the nation of Israel, who began their history as aliens in Egypt and lived much of their history as resident aliens and foreigners in exile.

The subordinating conjunction ὡς (*hōs*, as) is characteristic of the style of 1 Peter, occurring twenty-seven times throughout the letter. Both its causal and comparative senses are found in his letter. A causal sense appears in 2:13: "Be subject . . . to the emperor as [i.e., because he is] the supreme authority." The comparative sense is represented by 1:19: "the precious blood of Christ as of [i.e., who is like] a blameless and spotless lamb." The exegete has to decide which sense is intended in a given occurrence. Some of the figurative (comparative) images introduced by *hōs* are obvious, such as the phrase "as newborn babies" (2:2) or "as living stones" (2:5). The instance here in 2:11 cannot be so easily decided. J. H. Elliott (2000: 457) argues that the *paroikoi kai parepidēmoi* refer to an actual social class in Asia Minor. Hence, he construes the *hōs* here as evidence that "the addressees are not simply compared to aliens and strangers but are actually identified as such," with the sense "as the resident aliens and strangers that you actually are." But those who understand Peter to be describing the pilgrimage of the Christian in this life toward the heavenly homeland take the *hōs* here in its comparative sense as indicating the presence of this metaphor (Achtemeier 1989: 223–24). The theory that Peter is addressing people who had actually been displaced from elsewhere may explain the disagreement of interpreters. In the original context of the letter, the *hōs* may have functioned primarily as causal to the original readers, though not without figurative overtones (*"because* you are resident aliens and foreigners"). Once Peter's letter began to circulate in other areas among people who did not share the experience of Peter's original readers, the comparative sense was construed (*"as* resident aliens and foreigners").

If Peter's readers are actually in some sense aliens and foreigners to their social reference group, the causal *hōs* here would imply the figurative connotation necessary for Peter's point, making its metaphorical aspect applicable to a broader audience. In fact, it is exactly in this verse that Peter begins to describe the demands of the Christian life. Whether or not Peter's original readers are actual resident aliens and strangers in Asia Minor, Peter instructs them to recognize that their foreignness in society is a consequence of their faith in Christ—which is poignant if they have in fact been deported from Rome because of the disturbance over *Chrestus* (see "Roman Colonization and the Origin of 1 Peter" in the introduction). Because all Christians are citizens of God's holy nation, they are to understand themselves as resident aliens and foreigners wherever they may be residing. Once the letter was circulating away from its original historical destination, the figurative or spiritual sense naturally emerged as the predominant understanding.

The force of the comparison derives from the observation that foreigners in the ancient world, whether in residence or just passing through, did not fully participate in the customs and practices of the host culture. Foreigners had neither the privileges nor the responsibilities of citizens. Their foreignness was observable in ways that preserved their own identity. Foreigners abstained sometimes by their own volition, sometimes because they were not legally entitled to participate in the customs of the host society. Both forms of abstinence were well known to Jewish people living in the Diaspora, the framework in which Peter invites his readers to understand themselves. Achtemeier (1996: 174) observes, "It was precisely the precarious legal status of foreigners that provided the closest analogy to the kind of treatment Christians could expect from the hostile culture in which they lived." The moral estrangement Christians experienced in their society was a consequence of not sharing society's values and customs. As a citizen of God's holy nation, the Christian was therefore an alien and foreigner in pagan society, wherever that might have been.

As resident aliens and foreigners, Peter's readers are instructed to abstain from carnal desires, maintaining (ἔχοντες, *echontes*) "a good way of life" (τὴν ἀναστροφὴν καλήν, *tēn anastrophēn kalēn*, 1:12) among the Gentiles. The word ἔθνεσιν (*ethnesin*) can be translated either "Gentiles," emphasizing the ethnic identity of all who are not of God's nation, or "nations," acknowledging the geopolitical entities of the Gentiles. Both Peter and Paul, following Jewish thought, use the designation ἔθνη (*ethnē*) to refer to those outside the community of Christian faith. Peter sees Christians as God's nation among the nations and is concerned with how the Gentiles perceive Christian behavior.

The recurrence of the cognate noun *anastrophē* in 2:12 forms a parallel contrast with "live in reverent fear" (ἐν φόβῳ ἀναστράφητε, *en phobō anastraphēte*) with 1:17. In 1:17 the Christian is to be aware of being observed by God, and the believer's lifestyle is to be lived in reverent fear of God. But God is not the only one watching. Being observed also by unbelievers, that same Christian lifestyle should, to whatever extent possible, be characterized by a way of life that even pagans could recognize as good. In the first century, much Greek moral philosophy renounced a life dominated by the desires of the flesh, even as do those of higher ideals in our own modern society. But also as in our own society, such ideals are more honored in the breach than in the observance.

When Peter tells his readers they must abstain (ἀπέχω, *apechō*, 1:11) from carnal desires, his teaching would be consistent with principles of wise living that even pagans would recognize. However, Peter's basis for the exhortation is distinctively Christian. The verb *apechō* is used elsewhere in ethical exhortation (e.g., Acts 15:29; 1 Thess. 4:3; 1 Tim. 4:3) to refer to abstinence from pagan indulgences that fuel carnal desires within the believer and thus are antithetical to new life in Christ. The carnal desires Peter has in view may include, but are not limited to, sexual sin; the noun (ἐπιθυμιῶν, *epithymiōn*, 1:11) is used elsewhere to refer to any uncurbed human impulse. As far back as Plato (e.g., *Phaedo* 82.C; 83.B; *Laws* 8.835E), the collocation of this verb and noun is found in the Greek ethical tradition, which shares with Jewish tradition condemnation of unrestrained indulgence (e.g., Isa. 54:14 LXX; Jer. 7:10; Philo, *Virt.* 163; Did. 1.4). The "soul" that is the target of spiritual warfare is not to be understood as referring to the incorporeal part of the human being in distinction from the body but the whole self in its new identity in Christ. In addition to the usual list of carnal desires, one could also perhaps add the carnal desire to be accepted by society, which motivates ungodly behavior that is nevertheless socially acceptable.

Self-control that enables one to abstain from carnal passions was highly valued by Greek moral philosophers and would have been recognized as virtuous behavior by all. Peter expects that his readers can live in a way that will be recognized as good even by the standards of unbelieving pagans, which "presupposes overlap between Christian and non-Christian constellations of values" (Volf 1994: 25). The implication of this overlap is that Peter does not seem to be thinking in binary categories that characterize society as evil and the Christian community as good. The apostle does not condemn all of the values and customs of first-century culture and society or advise complete withdrawal from it. "The epistle shows remarkable and refreshing sensibility for the complexity of social realities, bursting a black and white way of thinking" (Volf 1994: 27). Peter recognizes that non-Christian values of his culture overlap in some ways with those of the Christian faith. This suggests that for Peter there is "no one single proper way for Christians to relate to a given culture as a whole" (Volf 1994: 27). Instead, Peter challenges his readers to live by Christian values and, when they conflict with those of society, to be willing to endure graciously the grief and alienation that will inevitably result.

First-century Greco-Roman society marginalized Christians simply because they were known to be different. The Roman writer Suetonius considered Christianity to be a mischievous superstition (*Nero* 16). Tacitus similarly described Christianity as a dangerous superstition and Christians as a race detested for their evil practices (*Annals* 44). It would be a natural human desire to feel anger under such circumstances and to retaliate. Peter's exhortation is to continue to conduct oneself in a manner that the pagans would consider virtuous even by their own standards, in order that their accusations might be shown to be what they are, malicious and unjust slander. The challenge Peter presents to the thoughtful Christian is to live by the good values of society that are consistent with Christian values and to reject those that are not, thereby maintaining one's distinctive Christian identity.

One trait of human nature seems to be that people watch strangers more closely. If Peter's original readers were in fact displaced people, they likely attracted more scrutiny from the indigenous population. Therefore, as Christians they must be especially mindful of how their behavior would be evaluated by the norms of that society. Peter continues to explain that out of fear of God and the desire to serve him, Christians are to be submissive, law-abiding citizens as far as possible (2:13–17). The "good deeds" that were familiar to the Hellenistic ethical tradition are now to be done from the transformed motivation of their relationship to God in Christ. Peter's point reflects Jesus' teaching in Matt. 5:16: "Let your light shine before others, that they may see your good deeds and praise your Father in heaven" (TNIV). It also has points of contact with James 3:13: "Who is wise and understanding among you? Let them show it by their good life, by deeds done in the humility that comes from wisdom" (TNIV). A major concern of Peter is how the newly formed Christian religion will be perceived and evaluated by the norms and ideals of Greco-Roman society. Therefore, "Christians who could show that their religion had enabled them to achieve this status [self-control over the passions] could use their conduct to make a claim for its truth" (Perkins 1995: 47).

According to Peter, a significant outcome of proper Christian behavior with respect to society will be the Gentiles glorifying God "on the day of [his] visitation" (1 Pet. 2:12). Peter goes on to explain how Christians are to live in their interactions and relationships with officials, masters, husbands, and wives (2:13–3:7). He does not advise a withdrawal from, or rebellion against, the roles of society but rather that Christians conduct themselves properly within those relationships. The good reputation Christians are to strive for among non-Christians is an emphasis from the earliest days of the church (e.g., 1 Thess. 4:11–12; 1 Cor. 10:32; Col. 4:5; 1 Tim. 3:7). In Jewish thought, the honor or dishonor of God was determined by how outsiders viewed the deeds of his people (Daube 1956: 338), and this seems to be along the lines of Peter's thought here.

The phrase "the day of visitation" (ἡμέρᾳ ἐπισκοπῆς, hēmera episkopēs) is paralleled elsewhere in the NT only in Luke 19:44, "time of your visitation," referring to the incarnation of God in Christ. Here in 1 Pet. 2:12 the phrase probably refers to the return of Christ, when God again "visits" the earth as he did in the incarnation. In the LXX God's "visitation" is used to refer to God's intervention either with grace for his people (e.g., Gen. 50:24–25; Exod. 3:16) or with wrath on the unrepentant (e.g., Isa. 23:17; Jer. 6:15). The phrase "the day of visitation" occurs in Isa. 10:3 LXX to refer to a day of disaster under divine judgment. Some interpreters, however, understand the day of visitation in 1 Peter to be the time when God intervenes in the unbeliever's life with the offer of salvation (Beare 1970: 164; Calvin 1963: 268; J. H. Elliott 2000: 47; Reicke 1964: 94; Selwyn 1958: 171). Contra this understanding, it should be noted that generally the visitation of God referred to elsewhere in Scripture is of a corporate, not individual, nature and that 1 Peter (1:5, 7, 13; 4:7, 13, 17; 5:1) often mentions the coming day of judgment (Achtemeier 1996: 178; Michaels 1988: 118). Furthermore, 1 Peter throughout is heavily dependent on Isaiah. The day of visitation should probably be understood as a reference to the future final judgment, by which time Peter hopes that unbelievers who have observed the good works of the Christians they have slandered will have come to faith in Christ. The future visitation of God in Christ will be a day of blessing for God's holy nation (cf. 1:5–7) but a day of judgment and condemnation for the "nations" who are not God's people. The witness of a sustained good lifestyle by Christians who are being maligned by their society will be a testimony on the final day of judgment, which will vindicate the Christian's faith. Those who reject the gospel will be condemned by their own harsh judgment of Christians, who refused to indulge in the values and practices of an ungodly society.

Summary

First Peter 2:11–12 introduces the body of the letter, which extends through 4:11. After describing the Christian's new identity in 2:3–10, Peter begins to explain how that identity is threatened and compromised. He introduces the concept of spiritual warfare, where human desires war against new life in Christ. Living as a Christian first requires the resolve to abstain from those inner desires stimulated and validated by ungodly social values, which do violence to the Christian's relationship with God. In addition to the bodily passions, these un-specified desires may include the desire to be accepted by society more than to please God, to rebel against social norms unnecessarily, and to participate in social customs and practices that are abhorrent in God's sight. A primary purpose of a self-controlled life is its evangelistic value for attesting to the truth of the Christian gospel. The winsome way of life of Peter's readers even in the midst of a difficult social situation is hoped to be the witness that would bring unbelievers into the Christian community so that they too might glorify God on the coming day of judgment.

Additional Note

2:12. The participle translated "maintain," ἔχοντες (*echontes*, lit., having) can be construed as a participle of means, "abstain . . . by maintaining" (Achtemeier 1996: 177), or as an attendant circumstance with imperative force by coordination with the mood of the main verb: "abstain . . . and maintain" (J. H. Elliott 2000: 465). The point is well taken that one generally abstains from carnal desires *by* maintaining a good way of life. However, given that some Gentiles might in fact consider the indulgence of carnal desires to be a good way of life, it is probably better to see them as two parallel but often coordinating ideas: "abstain from carnal desires and maintain a good way of life."

2. Submit Even to Pagan Authority (2:13–17)

Peter here begins to specify how citizens of God's holy nation are to relate to the sociopolitical authority of the world in which they live. It may be tempting for Christian believers, especially in pagan societies, to construe their loyalty to Christ as a license for rebellion against the ungodly authorities that govern them. In Peter's view, Christians must be subject to even pagan authorities, even those as ungodly as the Roman emperor, who, at the time Peter wrote, was probably Claudius or Nero. Not only must Christians be subordinate to secular authorities, but they must also "do good" (2:14; ἀγαθοποιέω, *agathopoieō*), for by doing so they will silence slander against Christians, as is God's will.

Exegesis and Exposition

[13]Be subject to every human institution because of the Lord, whether to the emperor because he is the supreme authority [14]or to the governors because they are sent by him to punish those who do evil but to commend those who do good. [15]For it is the will of God that by doing good [you] silence the ignorant talk of foolish people. [16][Live] as free people, but not as using freedom as a cloak for evil—[living] rather as slaves of God. [17]Respect all people; love fellow believers; fear God; honor the emperor.

Subjection to secular human authority is defined in 2:13–15 as part of God's will that his people "do good" in order to silence ignorant slander. Various ideas have been offered as to what "doing good" might involve in first-century society and how that principle might be applied to Christian responsibility at other times and places, especially our own. Reicke (1964: 95–96) suggested that Peter means nothing more than that Christians must be good, law-abiding citizens. He points to organized labor actions of the first century as an example of "subversive activity against society" in which Christians should not have participated (Reicke 1964: 96). Reicke has been criticized on the grounds that his understanding of Peter's ethic results in a social quiescence and maintenance of the status quo that may be inappropriate in certain situations (Sleeper 1968). Sleeper (1968: 284) raises the issues of Christian responsibility toward evil regimes and criticizes Reicke for giving the impression that "a program of non-resistance and an avoidance of 'social aggressiveness'" is an adequate Christian ethic today." He points to the eschatological perspective that provides encouragement to Christians to witness to their world, but he admits that 1 Peter does not give us answers at the level of strategy in "concrete sociological and political terms for our own situation" (Sleeper 1968: 280, 286).

Van Unnik (1954–55: 99), writing a decade before Reicke, points out that "good works" must mean more than simply obeying the laws of the land, "for people obeying the law are not distinguished in a particular way [by the authorities], their conformity being taken for granted." Here in 2:14 Peter suggests that the governors recognize "those who do good" (noun). Following that train of thought, Winter (1988) suggests that the issue here is the Christian as public benefactor, who is honored publicly by the governing authorities for undertaking good works that benefit the city. According to Winter, Peter encourages his Christian readers not to reject or neglect that great civic tradition. If Winter is correct, Peter's original readers must have had both the resources and the standing to do so. This view is congenial to the theory that Peter's readers were among colonists sent from Rome to build up the Roman way of life in cities in Asia Minor (see "Roman Colonization and the Origin of 1 Peter" in the introduction). It would argue against J. H. Elliott's theory that the original readers were from the poorest and most marginalized masses (1981).

Winter's epigraphic evidence establishes the practice of publicly honoring benefactors of the city, but his claim that *agathopoieō* refers specifically to acts of public benefaction is not convincing (cf. Danker 1982, who does not list the cognate verb among those used specifically to refer to benefaction). In 2:15 the noun stands in opposition to the general term "evildoer" (κακοποιῶν, *kakopoiōn*), which has no corresponding place in the semantic domain of public benefaction, suggesting a more general sense for both terms.

Moreover, the verb *agathopoieō* occurs three times in the letter, in reference to slaves, wives, and then generally to all Christians (2:20; 3:6, 17). Peter is apparently applying the general principle of "doing good" in 2:14–15 to the specific cases of slaves and wives in 2:18–3:6. Since slaves and wives were typically not in a position to be public benefactors, it is probably best to construe this verb and its cognate noun to mean good works beyond that normally expected in a given situation, which could be noted by the authorities, by the master, or by the husband. The same verb, *agathopoieō*, is found on the lips of Jesus in Luke 6:35, where he instructs his followers to "do good" even to their enemies. In both Luke and 1 Peter, the deeds encouraged do not seem to be merely private acts of Christian piety but deeds that would also be generally acknowledged by society as good. As seen in 2:12, this further implies that Peter recognizes some common definition of "good" between that society and Christian ethics. As Winter (1988: 93) rightly argues, how could the authorities in Asia Minor observe the good works of their Christian citizens if the word refers only to good morals that are privately expressed? Certainly works of public benefaction cannot be excluded from Peter's idea of "doing good" within the civic sphere for those Christians who have the resources and standing to do so. This thought fits quite well with the Diaspora motif in which the letter is framed, for it follows Jeremiah's instructions: "Seek the welfare of the city where I have sent you into exile, and pray to the LORD on its behalf; for in its welfare you will have welfare" (Jer. 29:7 NASB).

Peter's exhortation here is prefaced by a claim to divine authority. It is God's will (not simply Peter's) that Christians do good even in pagan societies, for by such behavior they will silence the slander about Christianity, and all the more so if they are publicly recognized by the authorities for good works that benefit their city. It is difficult to square this teaching with any worldview that recommends strict separatism from society and withdrawal from civic responsibility as a legitimate Christian lifestyle.

Peter's instructions are firmly positive toward the Roman emperor and provincial governors.[1] He seems to assume that if Christians live as good citizens, the ruling authorities will look with favor upon them—or at least not trouble them. His assumption must be considered in the attempt to date this letter. It is difficult to imagine such an irenic exhortation being issued during the time of Nero's horrific persecution of the church in Rome or anytime after Christians began being martyred by state-sponsored persecution—especially in comparison with the attitude toward Rome presented in the later book of Revelation. The relatively optimistic outlook reflected here comports better with the earlier decades of the church, toward the end of the reign of Claudius or the very beginning of Nero's. At that time Christians were socially and perhaps professionally ostracized in various ways, but they had not yet suffered state-sponsored persecution as a matter of policy. As long as the church enjoyed some protection from the state's suspicion of new religions by virtue of its association with Judaism, Peter appears to be hopeful that it could maintain a measure of good relations with the state, at least to the extent Judaism did.

Peter's exhortation that his readers must be subject to "every human institution because of the Lord" (2:13) is not to be taken as an invitation to slavery. On the contrary, Peter declares his readers to be free people (2:16). They were free to choose to be slaves of God. On the nature of Christian freedom, Selwyn (1958: 174) comments: "The connection

---

1. Although during the Hellenistic period the regional rulers of Asia Minor were called "kings," during the Roman period that title was transferred to the Roman emperor, and a local provincial ruler was referred to as ἡγεμών (*hēgemōn*, governor). See Deissmann 1927: 362.

of freedom with virtue was well established in antiquity. . . . Christian freedom rests not on escape from service but on a change of master." Being free from sin, they are therefore free to choose to live in a way that honors the God whom they serve before the eyes of a pagan society to whom they have no similar obligation. The Christian life "is a free servitude, and a serving freedom" (Calvin 1963: 272). Throughout his teaching, Peter affirms that Christians have been set free from their former way of life so that they can become slaves of God and live in obedience to him rather than as they once did. Peter will soon introduce Jesus Christ, the Suffering Servant (i.e., slave) of God (2:21), as the supreme example they are called to follow.

The question arises how the four imperatives in 2:17 are related. The first of the four is in the aorist tense with the following three in the present; the first and fourth are forms of the same verb, τιμάω (timaō, honor). Would this change in tense suggest that the last three elaborate on what it means to "respect everyone," as suggested by the syntax of the NIV? However, because it does not seem apt to include God in the reference "everyone," some interpreters see no significance to the variation in tense (e.g., TNIV). Various pairings of the four imperatives in verse 17 have been suggested. Bammel (1964–65: 280) proposes an a-b-b'-a' structure by pairing the first and last imperatives because they are forms of the same verb. Achtemeier (1996: 187) observes that the first and last refer to secular concerns, the middle two to Christian. It should also be noted that the first two imperatives are directed at the two social groups in tension (society versus the Christian community) and the last two at the two authorities in tension (allegiance to God versus the emperor), which may suggest an a-a'-b-b' organization. All people are to receive due respect, but fellow believers are to be loved. God is to be feared; the emperor, honored.

Snyder (1991) defends the understanding that the first of the four is a general command that should be understood not as honor to all people but as honor to all whom honor is due: the Christian brotherhood, God, and the emperor. This interpretation avoids the problem of God being included in the phrase "respect everyone." Furthermore, this construal avoids the tension of an apparent discrepancy between this verse, which limits love to fellow Christians, and Jesus' command that Christians must love all their neighbors, even their enemies (Best 1986). Moreover, Snyder (1991) points out that the first of the three present imperatives echoes Peter's prior teaching to live out one's life in fear of God (1:17) and to love fellow believers (1:22), relating those exhortations to the present discussion. More likely, the statement is a comprehensive reference to all contexts in which a Christian lives: social, ecclesial, spiritual, and political. While the syntax and precise structure of 2:17 are difficult to decide, the thrust of the exhortation is clear: Christians must live well by giving each type of relationship its due.

These general instructions about Christian relationships form the immediate context of the specific instructions to servants, wives, and husbands that follow. In fact, the verbs translated "submit" (2:18; 3:1) and "live with" (3:7) are all participles, the first two being forms of the same verb found here in 2:13, ὑποτάσσω (hypotassō). Spencer (2000) concludes that the instructions to the household that follow are syntactically connected to these four directives enjoined on all believers, further specifying the command to be subject to all human authorities (2:13). Proper household relationships "are one type of submission to one human creation, ancient marriage" (Spencer 2000: 111). Although the syntactic connection may be debated, certainly the instructions for relationships within the household must be read within the larger social context of the church, one's relationship to God, and pressing sociopolitical considerations.

3. Christ's Example in Society's Most Basic Unit (2:18–3:7)

Peter further focuses his exhortations concerning the nature of Christian relationships that bring glory to God and form a winsome witness to unbelieving society. Because the household was understood in Greco-Roman moral philosophy to be the foundational unit of civilization, the influence of suspect religions on the family was closely observed. Peter is especially concerned that the freedom of the gospel be expressed in the Christian household in such a way as not to provoke unnecessary accusations against Christianity. At the same time, Peter understands that the gospel of Jesus Christ is subversive to the Greco-Roman social order. The cornerstone of Peter's teaching is the example of Jesus Christ, whose undeserved suffering for the benefit of others and the fulfillment of God's redemptive plan is to be the paradigm for all Christian relationships.

a. The Slave as the Paradigm for Believers (2:18–25)

Peter points to the slave, who was most vulnerable in Greco-Roman society, as a paradigm for the Christian believer who follows Jesus Christ. Because of their Christian commitment, Peter's readers may have been facing a loss of status and empowerment in their society. The slave had the lowest social status and least power and so is a fitting role model for this situation. Moreover, regardless of their social standing, as Christians they are to live as slaves to God, obeying him in every aspect of life (2:16). Peter recognizes that Jesus Christ, God's very Son, was the Suffering Servant (i.e., slave) of Isa. 53, who submitted to unjust suffering in order to serve God's plan of redemption. His suffering provides the example that all Christians are to follow. Therefore, Peter begins to address the issue of commendable behavior in society's most basic unit, the household, by first addressing the Christian household slave before turning to the Christian wife and finally to the Christian husband as head of the household.

   i. The role of "household codes" in Greco-Roman culture (2:18–20)
   ii. Christ dignifies the lowly (2:21a)
   iii. Peter's Christology and the Christian's calling to unjust suffering (2:21b–25)

Exegesis and Exposition

[18]Servants, be subject with all respect to your masters, not only to those who are good and considerate, but also to those who are harsh. [19]For this is grace, if because of a consciousness of God someone bears grief, suffering unjustly. [20]For what credit is it if because you have sinned you are beaten and endure it? Rather, if because of doing good you suffer and endure it, this is grace before God. [21]For to this you were called, because Christ also ⌜suffered⌝ on your behalf, leaving you an example in order that you might follow in the footsteps of him

> [22]who did not commit sin, neither was deceit found in his mouth;
> [23]who when reviled did not retaliate, when he suffered he did not make threats, but instead trusted the One who judges justly;

[24]who himself bore our sins in his body upon the tree, so that having no part in sins we might live in righteousness; by whose wounds you are healed.
[25]For you were like wandering sheep, but now you have returned to the Shepherd and Overseer of your souls.

i. The Role of "Household Codes" in Greco-Roman Culture (2:18–20)

In this passage the heart of Peter's Christology provides the foundational principle for living rightly in society's most common and mundane structure, the household. The juxtaposition of these two seemingly disparate topics is better understood when the importance of household relationships within Greco-Roman society is appreciated. For centuries the Greek moral philosophers wrote about proper relationships within the household, slaves to masters, wives to husbands, and children to parents. Instructions with important points of contact with the NT, "household codes" can be found in Plato's *Republic* (384–370 BC), Xenophon's *Oeconomicus* (ca. 430–355 BC), Aristotle's *Oeconomica* (384–322 BC), Plutarch's *Advice to Bride and Groom* (AD ca. 46–120), Seneca's *Moral Epistles* (ca. 4 BC?–AD 65), and Dio Chrysostom's *On Household Management* (AD 40–ca. 112). (For a comparison of these Greek writers to 1 Peter, see Balch 1981.) Although these writers had different views on slaves and women, all shared a common belief that order in the household, which they believed to be divinely ordained, was the constituent basis for a strong, orderly, and prosperous society.

Modern scholarship has held differing views of the origin and purpose of the NT household codes (Balch, *ABD* 3:318–20; Fitzgerald, *ABD* 3:80–81). Household codes do not appear in the OT or in Jewish writings until Judaism engages the Greek worldview (e.g., Philo and Josephus). The copious writings concerning household management and their prominent place in the Greco-Roman culture suggest that no religion or philosophy entering that moral world could ignore addressing the same topic. Peter and Paul, whose theology and ethics are deeply rooted in the tradition of the OT, nevertheless include household codes in their letters to audiences whose worldview probably would have been influenced by the Greek moral writings. Even though both apostles address the topic of order in the household, neither simply affirms Greco-Roman expectations.

The function of the household codes in the NT ethical instruction is also debated (Balch, *ABD* 3:318–20; Fitzgerald, *ABD* 3:80–81). Some argue that they represent a legalistic response to social unrest in the church caused by egalitarian movements among women and slaves (Crouch 1972). J. H. Elliott (2000) argues that the household code functions to bring to the church a cohesive identity that would be consistent with its missionary goals. Balch (1981) contends that the codes function apologetically in response to social criticism of the effect of Christianity on the household and therefore on the social order. These various views are not necessarily mutually exclusive. Moreover, Peter and Paul may not have had precisely the same reason in mind for including the household code in their writings. Both apostles do teach that new life in Christ is to be lived out within existing social structures. However, the function of the code in Col. 3:18–4:1 seems directed to correcting false teaching. Peter's use of the code functions apologetically in its immediate context (cf. 1 Pet. 2:12; 3:15). While addressing the topic of household management and using a form similar to the Greek moral writers, Peter puts household relationships on an entirely new footing that subverts the moral code as previously taught by the Greek philosophers.

In reference to the precepts given to parents, children, and brothers in Greco-Roman thought, Seneca (*Ep.* 95) writes: "No one will do his duty as he ought, unless he has some principle to which he may refer his conduct. We must set before our eyes the goal of the Supreme Good, towards which we may strive and to which all our acts and words may have reference—just as sailors must guide their course according to a certain star" (Gummere 1943: 87). Seneca further observes that humankind cannot make progress until it "has conceived a right idea of God." First Peter agrees that there is a right idea of God, which must guide all of life, but goes further by claiming that the right idea of God is to be found in Jesus Christ (1:3). It is not the philosophy of great thinkers but the new birth through Christ's resurrection that is needed as the basis of ethics. The "certain star" to which all our acts and words as Christians must have reference is not the Supreme Good of Greek philosophy but the Supreme God revealed in Jesus Christ. Thus, Christian slaves, wives, and husbands are to conduct themselves within the social expectations of their day as transformed by Peter's instructions because of their new relationship to God in Christ.

Because of the pervasive and sustained interest in proper household relationships as foundational to the empire's well-being, it is not surprising that when both great apostles, Peter and Paul, write to destinations holding a Greco-Roman worldview, they give instructions on how Christians who have realigned their sociopolitical loyalties with the kingdom of God are nevertheless to live responsibly in society. The same slave-master, wife-husband, child-parent pairs found in the NT *Haustafeln*, or "household codes,"[1] are found throughout the Greek philosophers, but with significant differences between the NT and the Greek writers. The similarity in form indicates that the NT writers are deliberately

---

1. This German word has come to be an almost technical term for referring to this form of teaching. It originated with Luther's German translation of the Bible, where Eph. 5:21–6:9 and Col. 3:18–4:1 were headed by the singular, *Haustafel*, literally, "household table."

engaging this aspect of Greco-Roman culture. The differences between the NT and the Greek philosophers on this topic demonstrate that the apostles' view on this topic has been formed by the religious convictions of the OT and not by the Greek thought they are engaging.

The very name "household codes" obscures the original function of the teaching as instructions on how to fulfill one's sociopolitical duty within greater society as a slave, a wife, or a husband. Plato taught that each person in the household has a place under the man's authority. The child, the woman, and the slave are each to submit in different ways to the man's authority and are not to aspire to the roles of another (*Republic* 4.433A, C–D). The acceptance of one's station is fundamental to right household management, which "demands in the first place familiarity with the sphere of one's actions"—in other words, behaving in the manner appropriate to one's own role (Aristotle, *Oeconomica* 2.1.1). Goppelt's (1993: 162–79) suggestion that these be understood as "station codes" is more accurate to their function, since Greek moral philosophy understood each person's position in life to be divinely mandated, and the wise person faithfully performed the duties of his or her station.

Because of the importance of household relationships for social stability, religions introduced into the empire by foreigners were judged in large part by whether or not they complied with the expectations for household relationships. One of the apologetic tasks for a religious group was to show compliance with the important elements of social order, as Josephus does for Judaism (*Ag. Ap.* 2.158, 193, 220, 225, 235, 293). In contrast to Judaism, the Egyptian Isis cult was viewed as a threat to the Roman way of life because it permitted a woman authority over her husband (Balch 1988: 29). Therefore, the "household codes" of the NT had important apologetic value as the newly formed religion of Christianity took root in Greco-Roman society. This no doubt was a concern of the apostle Paul, since he teaches on proper roles for men and women in church order in the city of Ephesus (1 Tim. 2:1–3:13).

Since slavery is not an accepted part of Western society today, modern preaching of 1 Pet. 2:18–3:7 (as well as Eph. 5:21–6:9 and Col. 3:18–4:1) has primarily focused on the instructions addressed to wives and husbands as a type of marriage manual, obscuring its original sociopolitical message and function. Even more distorting is the disproportional attention usually lavished on the instructions to wives. The modern concept of the privatization of whatever goes on within the home further distorts our understanding of this passage as well, for in the first century behavior within the home was perceived very much as society's business. As Balch (1981: 26) observes, "The household relationship which we normally consider private, individual matters are here [in Greek thought] part of a social-political philosophic ethic." The latent sociopolitical function of household relationships within the teaching of 1 Peter must be retrieved if the apostle's teaching is to be more fully understood and appreciated.

Peter's emphatic opening description of Christians as those who have been born again into a new life with new allegiances and the further description of Christians as a people set apart as God's own possession and as a kingdom of priests make it necessary for Peter to explain how the new life in Christ is to operate within the most basic social unit, the household. The apostle Peter informs Christians of their duties in a way that affirms part of the Greco-Roman social order while subtly rejecting those premises that are not compatible with the gospel. Peter is concerned that Christians not use their moral freedom in a way that brings condemnation on the infant church for subverting social order. At the same time, the moral freedom that Christians have been given in Christ transforms their understanding of themselves in ways unparalleled in the Greek moral philosophy of their time.

Slaves (2:18) and wives (3:1) are both exhorted using forms of the same verb, ὑποτάσσω (hypotassō, be subject to). Slaves and wives also shared some common social expectations in first-century Greco-Roman culture in distinction from those expected of the male head of household. Therefore, some discussion of the historical background common to both is necessary in order to understand 2:18–25 and 3:1–6 in their original historical setting.

One of the debates of NT scholarship is whether the NT writers were more influenced by Jewish backgrounds or by the Greco-Roman. The either/or polarity sometimes implied by the discussions is misleading because both backgrounds are important in virtually every book. In explaining the significance of Jesus Christ, Peter and other writers of the NT are drawing from the wellspring of Judaism and its religious heritage. The very Jewish nature of Peter's epistle demonstrates that its author's thought is steeped in the traditions and writings of the OT. However, the audiences to which 1 Peter and other NT writings are addressed, whether they were primarily Jewish Christian or Gentile Christian, lived in societies that were shaped by the Greco-Roman worldview. Therefore, it is particularly fitting, when the apostles instruct their readers on how to live as Christians within such a society, that they engage the thought-world of the Greco-Roman writers whose ideas shaped the values and expectations of that society. This is not to say that the NT writers were unduly influenced by pagan thought or to blur the distinction between the Judeo-Christian worldview and that of the Roman Empire. Therefore, those who feel compelled to defend exclusively or primarily a Jewish background and reject the part that Greco-Roman backgrounds play in the household codes miss the nuanced sensitivities of the NT writers.

There is some debate whether the form of the Greek words for "slaves" (οἱ οἰκέται, hoi oiketai) in 2:18 and wives (γυναῖκες, gynaikes) in 3:1 should be taken as vocative (the case of direct address) or as nomina-

3. Christ's Example in Society's Most Basic Unit
a. The Slave as the Paradigm for Believers
1 Peter 2:18–25

tive. Nominative forms are found most frequently in the Greek moral philosophers, who refer to slaves and wives as classes of people but in general do not directly address them. The context and structure of the 1 Peter passage suggests that here these words are vocatives. Unlike the Greek writers, Peter directly addresses both slaves and wives, assuming that both have a moral responsibility for their own behavior that exceeds social expectations of that day.

Although instructions are often given about master-slave relationships in the Greek writings, slaves were not directly addressed as free moral agents as we find in the NT (Balch 1988: 33). Aristotle, for instance, describes slaves as human chattel of two kinds: those in positions of trust and brute laborers (*Oeconomica* 1.5.1–2; cf. Seneca, *Ep.* 47). While wives do not have the full social and legal status of their husbands, they are not thought of as human chattel (contra popular belief) in Greek moral philosophy. In fact, within the walls of the home, wives enjoyed a large degree of authority over slaves, children, and property. In *Advice* §33, Plutarch (AD 46?–120) explains that a man ought to exercise control over a woman "not as the owner has control of a piece of property, but, as the soul controls the body, by entering into her feelings and being knit to her through goodwill. . . . It is possible to govern a wife, and at the same time to delight and gratify her" (Babbitt 1971: 323).[2]

In the Greek writings, wives, like slaves, receive instruction through their husbands because both slave and wife are thought to be deficient, though not in the same way.[3] Aristotle understands the slave to be incapable of deliberative thinking, while the wife has the capability but not the commensurate authority (Balch 1981: 34–35). Thus, it is proper to direct all instruction through the man, who has both the capability and authority to reason fully. Moreover, the instruction of the wife should be the object of the husband's unstinting care (Aristotle, *Oeconomica* 3.2). While some modern interpreters consider the NT household codes to be hopelessly chauvinistic, they fail to read the codes against their contemporary literature, which shows that the NT writers actually subverted cultural expectations by elevating the slave and the wife with unparalleled dignity.

The second distinctive difference between Greek writings and Peter's instructions to Christian slaves and wives is that he rejects the cultural expectation that a slave must worship his or her master's god and a wife must worship her husband's. As Oborn (1939: 135) observes, every well-to-do Roman family had slaves, in some cases in large numbers.

2. However, in an argument against adultery, Epictetus (*Discourses* 2.4.1–8) does refer to women as property: "What then, you say: are not women common property? I agree, and the little pig is the common property of the invited guests; but when portions have been assigned . . . it is wrong to take another man's portion" (Oldfather 1926: 235–37).

3. See Xenophon, *Oeconomicus* 7–10: when Socrates is concerned about a woman's views, he questions her husband about how he has instructed his wife.

It is estimated that almost one-quarter of the empire's population were slaves, so their role was significant to socioeconomic stability. The slave's loyalty to the master's gods assured economic stability. In particular, any religion that advocated equality of any kind between slaves and masters would be met with swift and certain opposition. Wives were similarly expected to follow the husband's religion. In *Advice* 140.19, Plutarch instructs:

> A wife ought not to make friends of her own, but to enjoy her husband's friends in common with him. The gods are the first and most important friends. Wherefore it is becoming for a wife to worship and to know only the gods that her husband believes in, and to shut the front door tight upon all queer rituals and outlandish superstitions. (Babbitt 1971: 311)

If Plutarch's view represents that of first-century Greco-Roman society, a pagan woman who becomes a Christian could appear rebellious for not worshipping her husband's gods, as well as for making friends in the Christian community who were not her husband's friends. First-century social expectations of the wife were quite different from those of our own society, where both husband and wife may have friendships apart from the other and be of different religions without provoking accusations of perverting the social order. This large difference in social expectations suggests that we must be thoughtful about how these biblical instructions are to be observed by Christians today.

Furthermore, the expectation that a wife would worship her husband's gods also raised a problem for the first-century husband who had converted to Christianity. He may have faced the problem of a wife who, though formally expected to follow his new faith, in reality resented being socially demeaned by her husband's association with this strange, new religion. Her rebellion against Christianity might in turn diminish her husband's status in society's eyes because the man was responsible for order in his own household regardless of his religion. What was a man in such a position to do so that he could fulfill his duty as the head of the household while respecting the reality in which he lived? Peter saves his final household instructions for married men (3:7).

In the first century, any religion that did not uphold the proper order between men and their slaves and between husbands and their wives was severely criticized. In fact, foreigners were evaluated and welcomed into society to the extent to which their household patterns were compatible with those of the Greek moral philosophers (Balch 1981). Christianity was not the only religion to come under such scrutiny, but its worldview was certainly suspect. In these verses Peter affirms the sociopolitical order, on the one hand, while simultaneously reworking it on Christian principles so that Christian households become a direct expression of eschatological self-understanding lived out in society (Goppelt 1993: 173).

As Volf (1994: 22) observes, "The household codes in 1 Peter are in fact an example of differentiated acceptance and rejection of the surrounding culture." Balch (1988: 36) refers to them as "selective acculturation." The basis for Peter's reworking of social expectations is the example of Jesus Christ as the Suffering Servant of God, in whose footsteps all Christians—including slaves, wives, and husbands—are to follow.

ii. Christ Dignifies the Lowly (2:21a)

Peter's readers may have been feeling a loss of empowerment and status because of their Christian convictions and the various social misperceptions of what those convictions meant for the social order. As Christians who are to "be subject to every human institution because of the Lord" (2:13), slaves and wives are to be subject to their masters and husbands. Slaves, the lowest social class in Greco-Roman society, have to submit to even unjust masters, and they therefore are here paradigmatic for the status of all Christians (as also Achtemeier 1993: 177; 1996: 195; B. Campbell 1998: 143; J. H. Elliott 1981: 207). Regardless of one's social status, Christians are to consider themselves to be slaves to God, and so the actual slave who is obedient to his master exemplifies that role for the entire Christian community.

But this is not the only reason Peter addresses slaves, and addresses them first at that. Peter here makes the point that God sent his Son as one who would seemingly have so little sociopolitical power that he would end up dying a slave's death by crucifixion. In this passage, Peter identifies Jesus as the Suffering Servant of Isaiah 53, providing us the only NT passage that does so this explicitly and extensively. Peter bases his instructions for *all* Christian members of society on the example of Christ's lowly position in human society, but he first addresses the lowliest—the slave, who by definition is being treated unjustly. The role of the slave in Roman society images the role of Jesus Christ, who was a suffering slave obedient to God but treated unjustly in the world. Therefore, Peter addresses slaves first for the purpose of motivating ethical behavior by Christology, not because they are particularly numerous in the church (though that may well have been true). This intent also explains why he does not address their powerful masters at all. Peter also does not address the parent-child relationship at all because he is primarily interested in instructing the least powerful adults of society on how they should conduct themselves as Christians. The unique nature of Peter's purpose also explains why his sequence and content are different from similar passages in Eph. 5:21–33 and Col. 3:18–22 and calls into question whether the *Haustafeln* provide any relevant evidence of literary dependence between Peter and Paul.

The apostle Peter elevates the dignity and self-understanding of the least empowered people of that time, the slave first and then the wife.

The Son of God has dignified even the lowliest in society by becoming like them in his incarnation. Wives, being next to slaves in the hierarchy of social power and status, are addressed next. Christian husbands, whose social status and power have probably also been compromised in some way because of the gospel, are addressed not only last but also with the fewest words. Peter points to Jesus Christ as the true model for how to live a significant, dignified life of freedom even in the midst of the most oppressive situation.

Peter addresses household slaves by using the more specific word οἰκέται (*oiketai*, household servants) rather than the more general δοῦλοι (*douloi*, slaves) simply because he is concerned specifically with the household unit. Even though household servants fared better than field slaves, both were the property of others and subject to harsh treatment at their master's whims. In 2:16 Peter has just referred to all Christians as slaves (*douloi*) of God, introducing this concept as a way Christians are to understand themselves. The word also connects to Peter's Christology, for Isa. 53:11 LXX refers to the suffering of the servant (παῖς, *pais*, 52:13 LXX) by using a participle of the cognate verb δουλεύω (*douleuō*, serve as a slave). The indirect nature of the associations between Isa. 53 and the passion of Jesus in Mark's Gospel is what might be expected if mediated by Peter, the only NT writer who explicitly identifies Jesus with the Suffering Servant (see Watts: 1998).

Christian slaves may have wondered, or perhaps even wishfully hoped, that their new birth into a living hope would relieve them from the oppressive social expectations of their station. Peter affirms that they are now indeed free people but also that this freedom does not entitle them to rebel against their masters, whether those masters be good and considerate or harsh. Apparently harsh treatment of slaves was socially acceptable and perhaps even expected by the Romans. Seneca, a Roman Stoic philosopher writing about the same time the books of the NT were being composed, criticizes those in power for being "excessively haughty, cruel, and insulting" toward their slaves, whom they should instead view as fully human and to be treated as friends (*Ep.* 47.12).

Even in such a harsh situation, the Christian slave is to submit to the master's authority and to bear up under unjust treatment because of a consciousness of God. The fact that Peter describes such suffering as "unjust" (ἀδίκως, *adikōs*) also implies an unprecedented status for the slave, to whom, according to Aristotle, no true injustice can be done (Balch 1984: 164; Volf 1994: 23).

Because the slave functions rhetorically as the paradigm for all believers, this specific exhortation to bear unjust treatment moves Peter's argument to its most controversial level as he addresses the heart of the problem faced by his readers. The issue of accepting unjust suffering would trigger a range of responses, as even classroom discussion of this passage demonstrates today. Peter both accommodates and subverts the existing social structures. Neither he nor any other NT writer mounts a frontal attack on the social structures of the time, such as slavery. But as Volf (1994: 23) observes:

> The call to follow the crucified Messiah was, in the long run, much more effective in changing the unjust political, economic, and familial structures than direct exhortations to revolutionize them would ever have been. For an allegiance to the crucified Messiah—indeed, worship of a crucified God—is an eminently political act that subverts a politics of dominion at its very core.

As Christians live out their calling in obedience to God even within unjust social structures, they are subverting the status quo and opening a new way of thinking.

Peter's instruction is consistent with the Hellenistic concept that it is morally better to suffer as not guilty than as guilty. But one of the ideals of Christianity is to right injustice, which seems to argue against the Christian community simply accepting unjust treatment of its members. However, when facing the enormity of the first-century Greco-Roman establishment, none of the NT writers holds out much hope for changing the ways of the world. Instead, they exhort the transformation of Christ's people, making the holy nation a colony in this fallen world. Because Peter's readers presumably want God in Christ to be glorified, they are asked to submit even to unjust suffering because, as Christ himself has demonstrated, this is the way to break the world's ways and perhaps one day bring unbelievers to praise and glorify God themselves.

The participle ὑποτασσόμενοι (*hypotassomenoi*, submit) in 1 Pet. 2:18 is the first of four participles in this section that could be labeled imperatival, for it is in the nominative case and not syntactically subordinated to a finite verb (see additional note on 2:18). It could, however, be thought of as the explicit component of a periphrastic expression in which the verb "be" (*eimi* or *ginomai*) is implied. The middle voice of the participle in conjunction with an implied imperatival form of *eimi* or *ginomai* yields "be subject." This is probably the preferable construal here as well as in 3:1.

The command to submit is qualified by the adverbial prepositional phrase "in all fear" (ἐν παντὶ φόβῳ, *en panti phobō*), which is repeated in the instructions to both wives (3:1) and husbands (3:7) by the adverb ὁμοίως (*homoiōs*, in the same way). This reference to fear echoes the exhortation of 1:17 that fear of God is to be the Christian's motivation. Peter therefore understands all Christian members of the household, regardless of their station, to be joined by the common motivation based on their relationship with God.

Aristotle (*Oeconomica* 3.3) defines a distinction between the two kinds of fear recognized by the Greek word φόβος (*phobos*):

The fear which virtuous and honorable sons feel towards their fathers, and loyal citizens towards right-minded rulers, has for its companions reverence and modesty; but the other kind, felt by slaves for masters and by subjects for despots who treat them with injustice and wrong, is associated with hostility and hatred.

This distinction was also known to Hellenistic Judaism (Daube 1956: 130). The Greek word *phobos* is used frequently in the LXX to refer to a reverent stance toward God that motivates right behavior (e.g., Gen. 31:42, 53; Exod. 20:20; Neh. 5:9; Prov. 1:7, 29; 8:13; 9:10; 19:23; 23:17). Proverbs 1:29 is particularly instructive because it refers to the "fear of the LORD" as something that may be chosen rather than an emotion that is simply evoked: "Since they hated knowledge and did not *choose* to fear the LORD . . ." (NIV, emphasis added).

Although both slaves and wives may indeed be terrified of what their master and husband might do to them, the sense of "reverence" is intended here (also applied to the instructions to husbands through the adverb *homoiōs*, "in the same way," 1 Pet. 3:7). Rather than cowering in terror before harsh masters and tyrannical husbands, Christians are to conduct themselves "with all godly reverence" (Achtemeier 1996: 189), "with all due reverence [to God]" (Davids 1990: 105), "with all reverence" (J. H. Elliott 2000: 511), "with deep reverence" (Michaels 1988: 133). They are to choose to fear God by behaving in their relationships in a manner that expresses obedience to him.

However, the other side of the reverence in view is to recognize that the God they revere is also the God who judges impartially (1:17). The station code expounds on 1:17 by setting out how the fear of God's impartial judgment motivates one's demeanor in life's most basic relationships. To submit "in all fear" (2:18, a literal reading of the Greek) means that one's reverence for God translates into "respect" for both good and harsh masters and, in 3:2, respect for unbelieving husbands, while recognizing that God will judge the behavior of the harsh master and unbelieving husband (Sylva 1983: 147). But God will also judge the Christian's disobedience. In 3:7 married men are to live with their women "in the same way" that slaves and wives are to submit, with fear of the One who judges them. Therefore, Christian slaves, wives, and husbands are to conduct themselves respectfully within the social expectations of their day—as modified by Peter's instructions—because of the reverence for God their new life in Christ demands.

The direct transformation of society's structures, even those that are patently unjust, does not seem to be the goal of the NT writers. Rather, it is the transformation of the believer regardless of one's situation that is the primary concern. In fact, Peter seems intent on making sure that Christians do not directly confront the status quo even while he subverts it. The implied assumptions of Peter's teaching (e.g., directly addressing slaves and wives as heirs of the grace of God in Christ who have moral authority over their own lives equal to that of free men), if followed to their logical extent by a society committed to such teaching, will indeed restructure that society.

But Peter is not optimistic about reforming the world. In fact, he assumes that injustice will reign until the Lord's return and that to bear up under unjust suffering without sinning is in fact the calling of every believer regardless of social status. Peter is clear that he is not speaking of suffering caused by one's own misbehavior (2:20; 4:15). But when Christians suffer unjustly and do not sin in response, this is χάρις (*charis*, grace, 2:19) before God. Many commentators understand this phrase in 2:19–20 to mean that God looks with favor (grace) upon a righteous response to unjust suffering (Achtemeier 1996: 189; Davids 1990: 105; J. H. Elliott 2000: 511). The TNIV translates the phrase as "is commendable before God" (2:20). Goppelt (1993: 200) explains how the word *charis*, widely used in secular Greek literature, became a technical theological term in Paul for "God's bestowal of himself through Jesus' work of redemption, the bestowal that bears and shapes the destiny of the person who gives himself or herself over to it." While it may not be assumed that one NT writer uses a term in exactly the same sense as another, Peter does use the word *charis* in 5:12 to sum up the entire content of the letter: "This is the true grace of God." Goppelt (1993: 200) explains: "The author wants to assure the readers that the existence into which they have been placed through Christ is truly grace. Even proper conduct in one's station in this world and especially the suffering connected with it are indeed, grace." Responding righteously to unjust suffering is commendable in God's sight, but *charis* in this context also implies that God's special favor rests upon the righteous sufferer of injustice, further enabling that one to behave in a manner that is commendable by God. Peter makes this point more explicitly in 4:14: "If you are vilified because of the name of Christ, you are blessed, for the Spirit of glory and of God rests on you."

iii. Peter's Christology and the Christian's Calling to Unjust Suffering (2:21b–25)

The presence of a passage about Christ's suffering in 2:21b–25 is unexpected in a discussion about slaves, wives, and husbands. The concept of suffering does not appear in pagan household codes and is unique to Peter's purposes (Thompson 1966: 73). Peter claims that slaves, and by extension all Christians (3:9), are called both to suffer unjustly and to continue to do right as they follow the example of Jesus Christ in his passion. Although this call is embedded in instructions addressed to slaves, Peter has previously referred to all Christians as slaves of God (2:16) and restates the principle explicitly for all his readers in 3:9. First

Peter 2:21–25 forms the heart of 1 Peter's Christology, joining ethics to theology in a profoundly convincing way. Ironically, the suffering of Christ has become central to the Christology of the apostle who most strongly objected to Jesus' prediction of his death (Matt. 16:21–23; Mark 8:31–33).

The suffering to which slaves, and by extension all Christians, are called is not suffering caused by the human condition, such as illness, aging, and death. Nor is it suffering that is the consequence of one's own sin and poor judgment. Peter's call is to suffer unjustly, to suffer even though one has done nothing to provoke or deserve it, simply because one is a Christian. The challenge of the call does not stop there; Peter further exhorts the Christian to keep on doing good even when unjust suffering continues to be the result.

The identity of Jesus Christ as the Suffering Servant poignantly yet enigmatically portrayed in Isaiah 53 is well known in Christian tradition.[4] What may be more surprising is that the church owes this insight to the apostle Peter alone, for it is only here in the NT that Christ's passion is discussed in terms of Isaiah's prophecy of the Suffering Servant. There are six direct quotations of Isa. 53 in the NT (Matt. 8:17; Luke 22:37; John 12:38; Acts 8:32–33; Rom. 10:16; 15:21), but surprisingly only two of them are used in reference to Jesus. The other four quotations of Isa. 53 in the NT apply elements of that vision to aspects of Christian missions and evangelism but not to the person of Christ himself. John 12:38 quotes Isa. 53:1, "Lord, who has believed our message?" as the prophecy fulfilled when the Jews still would not believe in Jesus after seeing his many signs. In Matthew's Gospel (8:17), Jesus' miracles of healing are said to be the fulfillment of Isa. 53:4, "He took up our infirmities and carried our diseases"—quite a different understanding than the vicarious bearing of our infirmities and diseases on the cross that Peter presents. In Luke 22:37 Jesus quotes Isa. 53:12, "He was numbered with the transgressors," as justification for his order that his disciples sell their cloak and buy a sword.

Paul uses the Isaiah passage not in reference to Jesus at all but as a prophetic prediction of his own ministry. He quotes Isa. 52:15 in Rom. 15:21, "Those who were not told about him will see," as a prophetic justification of his own mission to the Gentiles. Paul takes Isa. 53 to mean that although God sent him, his apostolic message would be rejected, and in Rom. 10:15–16, he quotes both Isa. 52:7, "How beautiful are the feet of those who bring good news!" and Isa. 53:1, "Lord, who has believed our message?"

Other than 1 Peter 2:21–25, the closest christological use of Isa. 53 is found in Acts 8:35, where the eunuch is reading from that prophecy

---

4. The Isaiah passage actually runs from 52:13 to 53:12, but for convenience will here be referred to simply as Isa. 53.

and Philip begins there to tell the eunuch the good news about Jesus, but there is no actual exposition in that passage of the specific elements of Isa. 53 as they relate to Jesus. We are thus indebted to the apostle Peter alone for his distinctive christological use of the Suffering Servant passage to interpret the significance of the suffering and death of Jesus. The Suffering Servant Christology may have even originated with Peter, possibly based on Jesus' teaching. Of the five NT verses referring to Jesus as the servant (παῖς, *pais*) of God, two occur in a speech attributed to Peter (Acts 3:13, 26) and two in a prayer of the early Jerusalem church when Peter is in leadership (Acts 4:27, 30). (The fifth passage is Matt. 12:18, which quotes Isa. 42:1–4 in reference to the healings Jesus performed.)

Luke's passing reference to the identification of Jesus and the Suffering Servant suggests that the identification was already well established in Christian tradition by the time Luke is writing, perhaps as early as AD 60–62. Therefore, if 1 Peter is the source of this tradition, the epistle would have to be dated in the 50s or earlier. It is debated whether Jesus himself used the Suffering Servant passage of Isa. 53 to explain his ministry (Hooker 1998). But even those who deny that Jesus saw himself in these terms admit that the identification of Jesus with the Suffering Servant of Isaiah must have emerged in the very early church (e.g., Hillyer 1969b: 144).

On the other hand, if 1 Peter is drawing on a preexisting Christ-hymn that would have also been available to Luke, the absence of this material in its hymnic form in the earlier writings of the NT is somewhat surprising. Most interpreters today have backed away from the claim that this passage was a preexisting hymn that Peter adapted for his purposes. The tradition began with Windisch (1930), was taken up by Bultmann in 1947 (cited by J. H. Elliott 2000: 548n156), and was the consensus opinion until the 1980s, when the work of Best (1971), Osborne (1983), and Michaels (1988) offered better explanations. J. H. Elliott (1985), for instance, once espoused this theory but has retracted it in his most recent work (2000: 548–50). Three observations on 1 Pet. 2:21–25 were once offered to show that it was from a preexisting hymn: (1) the shift from second person to third person and back, (2) the repeated use of the relative pronoun ὅς (*hos*, who), and (3) the shift from material addressed to slaves to christological material relevant to all readers. As Achtemeier (1993: 178) counters, (1) the shift in person would be expected from the use of any source, including a direct use of Isa. 53 LXX; (2) the relative pronoun *hos* is used repeatedly throughout the epistle in places that are clearly not hymnic; and (3) even the material explicitly addressed to slaves is in fact implicitly addressed to the entire community, because the slave, as the least empowered member of society, was to be the paradigm for all believers. The direct use of Isa. 53 LXX provides sufficient explanation of the source material.

As the heart of 1 Peter's Christology, 2:21–25 is worth lingering over. In a notably creative use of OT material, elements of Christ's passion are interwoven with phrases and allusions from Isa. 53 LXX that interpret aspects of his trial and suffering. As Hooker (1998: 93) notes, Peter does not use Isa. 53 as a proof text, but his use of this material has moved beyond a "simple appeal to 'what is written' to the explanation of its *significance*" (emphasis original). This translation of 1 Pet. 2:21–25 highlights the extensive and creative use of Isa. 53 LXX by showing quotations of it in boldface and allusions to it in italics:

2:20b	Rather, if because of doing good you suffer and endure it, this is grace before God.
2:21	For to this you were called, because Christ also suffered on your behalf, leaving you an example in order that you might follow in his footsteps.
2:22	[He,] who **did not commit sin, neither was deceit found in his mouth** [Isa. 53:9];
2:23	[He,] who when reviled *did not retaliate*, when he suffered *he did not make threats* [Isa. 53:7c–d], but instead *trusted* [Isa. 53:6c, 12] *the one who judges justly* [Isa 53:8a];
2:24	[He,] who **himself bore our sins** [Isa. 53:4a, 12] in his body upon the tree, so that being separated from sins we might live to righteousness; [He,] **by whose wounds you are healed** [Isa. 53:5d].
2:25	For **you were like wandering sheep** [Isa. 53:6a], but now you have returned to the Shepherd and Overseer of your souls.

As Achtemeier (1993: 180) observes, Peter uses the language of Isa. 53, but the order of 1 Pet. 2:22–25 follows the sequence of events in the passion of Jesus, with 2:22 and 2:23 alluding to the trial, and verse 24 to the crucifixion. Goppelt (1993: 211) also points out that this passage reflects three fundamental aspects of the passion narrative as described in Mark's Gospel:

1. Verbal abuse refers to slander by the Sanhedrin (Mark 14:65), ridicule by the Roman guards (Mark 15:12–20), and derision by the crucified thief (Mark 15:29–32).
2. Jesus accepts injustice without retaliating; in fact, he accepts it in silence (Mark 14:61; 15:5). His silence can be compared with the loud threats made by previous Jewish martyrs in 2 Macc. 7:17, 19, 31, 35, and 4 Macc. 10:1–3.
3. Jesus entrusted judgment to God, thereby leaving the preservation of justice to God the Father alone (Mark 14:62).

The resurrection of Jesus Christ was not only a historical event but also a hermeneutical event that allowed new understandings of the OT. Reciprocally, the significance of Jesus' death and resurrection is interpreted through the OT, possibly with the aid of insight imparted to

Peter by Jesus before his death. Peter does not start with Isa. 53; rather, he begins with the fact of Jesus' suffering and death and searches the OT to understand its significance (cf. Luke 24:25–27, 44–48). First Peter 2:21–25 is a remembrance of Jesus' suffering, explained and interpreted by the prophecy provided by Isaiah that allowed Peter to make sense of the sufferings of the Christ. But Jesus' suffering also allowed the apostle to make new sense of Isa. 53. As Peter has already explained in 1:10–12, it was the Spirit of Christ who revealed to Isaiah and other prophets the sufferings of Christ and the glories that would follow, and this was done as a ministry for the generations who would look back on the Messiah's death and need an explanation of its meaning. Because Jesus suffered a death reserved for slaves under Roman law, his identity as Isaiah's Suffering Servant (slave) is corroborated. Furthermore, this mode of death, which the Romans reserved for slaves and others lacking Roman citizenship, strengthens the identification between the plight of the "servants" Peter addresses in 2:18 and the Suffering Servant.

Peter presents the unjust suffering of slaves as the calling of all Christians because Jesus was called to suffer unjustly, he "who suffered for you, leaving you an example, that you should follow in his footsteps" (2:21). This is powerful imagery. The Greek word translated "example" (ὑπογραμμόν, *hypogrammon*) was used to refer to a pattern of letters of the alphabet over which children learning to write would trace (Achtemeier 1996: 199). It suggests the closest of copies. English words such as "example," "model," or "pattern" are too weak, for Jesus' suffering is not simply *an* example or pattern or model, as if one of many; he is *the* paradigm by which Christians write large the letters of his gospel in their lives. If Christians are to live as servants of God (2:16), the essence of that identity is a willingness to suffer unjustly as Jesus did, exemplifying in suffering the same attitude and behavior he did. Jesus Christ left us this pattern over which we are to trace out our lives, in order that we might follow in his footsteps. This is a strong image associating the Christian's life with the life of Christ. For one cannot step into the footsteps of Jesus and head off in any other direction than the direction he took, and his footsteps lead to the cross, through the grave, and onward to glory.

The christological paraenesis that follows therefore presumes unjust suffering in the life of the Christian and outlines with what attitude and behavior the Christian is to suffer, thereby following in the footsteps of Jesus. Peter later writes that by following his footsteps, he "leads you to God" (3:18). This imagery of footsteps has likely contributed to the adoption of the Greek verb ἀκολουθέω (*akoloutheō*, follow) to refer to Christian discipleship (e.g, Matt. 4:20; 8:23; 10:38; Mark 8:34; Luke 5:27; 9:23; John 1:43; 8:12; 10:27; 12:26). Jesus himself used *akoloutheō* frequently to summon and lead his earliest disciples, including Peter.

Peter's Christology is here at the same time paraenetic and pastoral. As Matera (1999: 184) describes it:

> The Christology of 1 Peter is a Christology of suffering. . . . By focusing on the sufferings of Christ, 1 Peter shows the intimate relationship between Christology and the Christian life: the *past* suffering of Christ is the *present* condition of believers, while the *present* glory of Christ is the *future* glory of those who follow in the steps of the suffering Christ. While the Christology of 1 Peter may not be the most developed of the New Testament, it is among the most pastorally sensitive. (emphasis original)

What would it have meant specifically for Peter's first-century readers to follow in Christ's footsteps within their sociopolitical situation? The four relative clauses of 2:21–25 portraying Christ's suffering present the model:

1. Christ, who did not commit sin . . . ;
2. Christ, who did not retaliate . . . ;
3. Christ, who bore our sins . . . ;
4. Christ, by whose wounds you are healed.

First, Jesus Christ "did not commit sin, neither was deceit found in his mouth." Since this is a direct quote from the OT, Hebrew parallelism may suggest that the second phrase is a more specific restatement of the first, indicating that Jesus did not sin by lies and deception. Second, when Christ was reviled he "did not retaliate, when he suffered he did not make threats, but instead trusted the One who judges justly." When his adversaries hurled their insults at Jesus, "he did not retaliate"; when Jesus suffered, "he made no threats in return."

There are many different statements made in Isa. 53 about the Suffering Servant, but Peter emphasizes the verbal aspect of the Servant's behavior as lived out by Jesus. Jesus' speech was not deceptive; he did not revile (speak abusively), and he did not threaten. Peter's readers were on the receiving end of abusive speech, ignorant talk, and the like (2:15; 3:9, 16; 4:14). Perhaps Peter begins to describe the Suffering Servant as a model for Christian behavior with these particular phrases because, when people are treated unjustly, it is most tempting to respond by stretching the truth, putting our opponents in a bad light, speaking abusively of others, or making threats. Following in Jesus' footsteps through this trying situation means not responding in kind to the accusers or using deceit, slander, or threats. Peter says as much in 3:9: "Do not repay . . . insult for insult." He advises that in some situations, silence is the best response, as any other response will be turned against them. It is, however, the silence not of passive resignation but of patient confidence (Hill 1982: 55).

After giving the example of what Jesus did not do, Peter reminds his readers of what Jesus did do. Instead of sinning under the pressure of unjust suffering, Jesus continued to trust God. Peter later exhorts his readers to do likewise in 4:19: "So then, let even those who suffer according to the will of God entrust themselves to the faithful Creator by doing good." This is ironic because Christians are to keep on doing good even though the conflict they suffer is being generated because society questions whether a life motivated by faith in Christ is "good." But rather than yield to their adversaries' judgment, Peter's readers are to trust God, who judges justly.

The idea that misfortune indicates divine displeasure was perhaps more prevalent in the ancient world than it is today. Peter reminds his readers that Jesus' unjust suffering did not mean that God had abandoned him; to the contrary, unjust suffering was God's mysterious way to accomplish the redemption of humanity. Jesus' trust was well placed, despite the circumstances that ended in his death. Peter encourages his readers to recognize that their unjust suffering does not mean that the gospel is untrue or that God is displeased with them. To suffer for following Christ is to share the nature of Jesus' suffering in that it is undeserved. It is caused by the world's hostility to Christian allegiance to God, but it will nevertheless accomplish God's purposes.

In 2:24 Peter continues to explain the significance of Jesus' undeserved capital punishment by conflating a phrase from Isa. 53:12 LXX, "He himself bore" (αὐτὸς . . . ἀνήνεγκεν, autos . . . anēnenken), with a phrase from 53:4 LXX, "our sins" (τὰς ἁμαρτίας ἡμῶν, tas hamartias hēmōn). Peter personalizes the quotation for the Christian community by taking "our sins" from 53:4 in place of "the sins of many" in 53:12. Thus, Peter speaks to his readers as those for whom Isaiah's Suffering Servant bore sin. And just so there will be no misunderstanding about specifically how Jesus Christ has borne our sins, Peter adds two prepositional phrases, "in his body" and "on the tree," an explicit reference to the death of Jesus by crucifixion. The latter phrase may be an allusion to Deut. 21:23, where God's curse is invoked on the one who is hung on a tree (probably, in the historical context of Deuteronomy, a reference to being impaled for display, not crucified; cf. 2 Sam. 21:9). In the context of Roman practices, the reference to crucifixion is a reminder that Jesus was executed unjustly as a criminal; Peter's readers might be similarly accused. The purpose of Christ's vicarious bearing of the judgment for sin has ethical implications for the lives of Peter's readers: "so that having no part in sins, we might live in righteousness" (2:24). Peter's understanding of Christian ethics is thoroughly grounded in the Christology of suffering.

In the fourth relative pronoun in this passage, Peter writes, "You are healed" (2:24), where both the LXX and the Hebrew have "We are healed" (Isa. 53:5). The use of the second-person plural pronoun, "you," is characteristic of the style of 1 Peter, occurring 83 times in 1 Peter, with the first plural, "we/our/us," used only 4 times (1:3 [2x]; 2:24; 4:17). This disproportionate use of the second-person plural pronoun can be compared with 2 Peter, where the first plural occurs 15 times and the second plural 21 times. In the epistles that bear Paul's name, the first plural occurs 400 times and the second plural 713 times. As a matter of style, Peter seems deliberately to change the pronouns from the wording of Isa. 53:5 LXX, which he otherwise follows. If his readers are primarily Gentiles, perhaps he is underscoring their inclusion in the people of God by excluding himself as a Jew. In other words, Peter is saying, "The Suffering Servant died not just for *us* Jews, but also for *you* Gentiles." On the other hand, in this occurrence Peter may simply revert back to the second-person plural pronoun to signal his return to the household code, since the description of Christ's suffering is introduced by the thought of *you* slaves being beaten unjustly (2:20). The fatal, physical wounds of the Suffering Servant that heal fatal, spiritual wounds become the transition back to the present perspective of Peter's readers.

The thought in Isa. 53:5 that the wounds of the Suffering Servant heal is followed in 53:6 by the statement "We all have wandered like sheep. . . ." Peter picks up the same imagery in the same sequence, but again changes the first-person plural pronoun to second-person plural: "For you were like sheep going astray. . . ." However, those wandering sheep have now returned to the Shepherd (ποιμήν, *poimēn*) and Overseer (ἐπίσκοπος, *episkopos*) of their souls. A reference to the Shepherd also occurs in Isa. 40:10–11 LXX, where the Shepherd is none other than the Lord himself:

> See, the Lord comes with strength,
>   and his arm with authority;
> see, his reward is with him,
>   and his work before him.
> He will tend his flock like a shepherd,
>   and gather lambs with his arm,
>   and comfort those that are with young. (Isa. 40:10–11 *NETS*)

The joining of shepherding and overseeing in the context of Diaspora is also found in Ezek. 34:11–13 LXX, where God promises:

> I will seek out my sheep and will oversee [*episkepsomai*] them. As the shepherd seeks his sheep in the day on which there is darkness and cloud, . . . so I will seek my sheep, and I will bring them back from every place where they were scattered [διεσπάρησαν, *diesparēsan*]. . . . And I will bring them out from the Gentiles.

Elements of this passage from Ezekiel correlate so well with elements of 1 Peter that it is tempting to conclude that Peter deliberately alludes to

Ezekiel here and elsewhere in his letter. The exact language of shepherding and overseeing is again picked up in 1 Pet. 5:2 to describe the ministry of elders (see comments on 5:1–6). The motif of scattered Christians (cf. 1:1), converted from the Gentiles (cf. 1:2), who were sought after by the Shepherd and who have returned to the *episkopos* of their souls (2:25), aptly echoes Ezekiel's prophecy. This is probably a further example of how Peter understands the purpose of prophecy given by the Spirit of Christ in relation to the Christian church (cf. 1:10–12).

The imagery of sheep following after the shepherd, following in his footsteps so to speak, forms a conceptual inclusio with 2:21, framing the entire christological exposition with the image that walking in Jesus' footsteps, even through unjust suffering, is nevertheless the Shepherd's path of safety, protection, and deliverance.[5]

Peter's insight that unjust suffering is to be expected by the Christian community also finds grounding in Isaiah's prophecy. The Suffering Servant of Isaiah has often been interpreted not as one person but collectively as the people of Israel.[6] In fact, Isa. 41:8–11 LXX identifies the nation of Israel as Yahweh's Suffering Servant:

> But you, Israel, my servant, Jacob, *whom I have chosen*, the offspring of Abraam, whom I have loved; *you whom I took hold of from the ends of the earth*, and I called you from its mountain peaks, and I said to you, "You are my servant [*pais*], I have chosen you and not forsaken you." Do not fear, for I am with you; do not wander off, for I am your God, who has strengthened you; I have helped you and I have made you secure with my righteous right hand. See all who oppose you shall be ashamed and disgraced; for they shall be as though they were not, and all your adversaries shall perish. (*NETS*, emphasis added)

The fluid image of Isaiah's Suffering Servant allows its different elements to be identified with both the nation and an individual (Isa. 52:13–53:12). This is congenial to Peter's insight into the nature of unjust Christian suffering as that of a kind with Christ's suffering. Peter identifies the Christian community as "a chosen people, a royal priesthood, a holy nation, God's special possession" (2:9)—phrases used in the OT to refer to the nation of Israel in Isaiah. Both the obedient Servant and the holy nation suffer.

Once Peter has realized that Jesus is the Suffering Servant of Isa. 53, he finds in the corporate elements of Isaiah's prophecy the justifica-

---

5. Compare the similarity of this image to Matthew's image of true disciples following Jesus into the boat and directly into a life-threatening storm (Matt. 8:18–27).

6. Palestinian Judaism may have had heightened messianic expectations in the first century, while Hellenistic Judaism of the Diaspora did not (Hess and Carroll 2003; Evans and Flint 1997; Harl, Dorival, and Munnich 1994: 220; Thompson 1966: 75). If this distinction is true, the messianic tradition that allowed Isa. 53 to be identified with Jesus may support a Palestinian origin for the author of the letter.

tion that allows him also to identify the Christians to whom he writes as members of the corporate Suffering Servant of Isa. 41. Interpreters have long puzzled over whether Peter's original readers were Gentiles or Jews who had become Christians. Although most today believe the original readers were predominantly Gentile, Peter speaks to his readers as if they are Jews. Because Peter sees the Christians of Asia Minor to be part of the suffering nation of God, he addresses them throughout without differentiating their background or origin. If Peter is indifferent to whether his readers are Jewish or Gentile converts, it is a consequence of his understanding that it was the Spirit of Christ who mediated the prophetic revelation of the OT (1 Pet. 1:11). Therefore, the language used to describe Israel served as a proleptic description of the Christian church. As Achtemeier (1993: 187) points out, Peter's "total appropriation of the language of Israel" for Christians is quite a different use of the OT than the prefiguration of Hebrews, the typological events found in Paul, or specific examples of the life of Christ fulfilling prophecies as found in Matthew.

Peter uses Isaiah's words to explain that suffering unjustly because of faithfulness to Christ is actually evidence that, like the Messiah, they have been chosen of God. If Isaiah's words can be interpreted as speaking directly to Christians, God says to Peter's readers through the words of Isa. 41:8–11, "You are my servant, I have chosen you and not forsaken you. Do not fear, for I am with you; do not wander off, for I am your God, who has strengthened you, and I have made you secure" (Isa. 41:9 *NETS*). What words of exhortation and encouragement for the Asian Christians facing threat from a world that would grow increasingly hostile to Christianity! Peter lets Isaiah speak directly to their situation. Don't be afraid of the unjust suffering you are experiencing. It is not evidence that God has forsaken you; to the contrary, it is evidence that God has chosen you. Do not wander off from Christ, for God will strengthen you to face life as a Christian. God has made you secure because Jesus has suffered the ultimate injustice and yet he lives. You have been born again into that living hope.

Additional Notes

2:18. In the debate over the existence of the imperatival (or commanding) participle, examples from 1 Peter are often cited as evidence. The imperatival participle is one that stands in the nominative case, is not syntactically subordinate to a finite verb, and cannot be considered part of an elided periphrastic phrase. It stands in an independent clause where one would expect a finite verb. Moulton (1985: 180) argues from constructions found in the papyri that this independent use of the participle to command was a development of the Greek language in the Hellenistic period. Daube (in Selwyn 1958: 467–88) argues, in a lengthy appendix to Selwyn's commentary, that Moulton has misconstrued the data from the papyri and that the imperatival participle is a Semitism that originates from Tannaitic Hebrew. Edwin Mayser (cited in Thurén 1990: 20) argues that we need look no further than the fact that the author of 1 Peter was simply using very poor

Greek. From studies done by Moulton, Daube, Meecham, Zerwick, and Turner, Thurén observes that there are only six participles in 1 Peter that everyone agrees are imperatival (2:18; 3:1; 3:7ab; 3:9ab), and there is no consensus on which other participles in 1 Peter are imperatival. Snyder's (1995) more recent reexamination of the issue concurs with this list.

However, not all recent scholars are convinced. Achtemeier (1996: 194) argues that the participles in 2:18; 3:1; and 3:7a are in fact syntactically subordinate to the imperatives of 2:17, specifying the manner in which those general commands are to be accomplished within society's most basic unit, the household (also T. Martin 1992a: 205). Boyer (1984: 174) agrees in principle but subordinates them to the imperative of 2:13, ὑποτάγητε (hypotagēte, submit). B. Campbell (1998: 124) regards the participles of 2:18–3:12 to be circumstantial, attending to all of 1 Pet. 2:11–17 rhetorically, and to ἀπέχεσθαι (apechesthai, to abstain) in 2:11 grammatically. This study raises the question of whether the participles in 2:18 and 3:1 (nominative plurals in the middle voice) could not be understood as periphrastic expressions where the imperative of the verb *eimi* has been elided: "be subject." But regardless of the origin of these six forms or how they are labeled, their immediate context makes clear the imperatival sense they carry.

2:19. The noun συνείδησις (syneidēsis) can refer either to conscious awareness of something (as the NIV, TNIV, NRSV translate) or to the inward, moral conscience (as the KJV, NKJV, NASB, NLT translate). The variant readings of this phrase in early manuscripts might suggest that the ambiguity in sense is very long-standing. In 3:16 syneidēsin occurs with the adjective ἀγαθήν (agathēn, good), where it more clearly carries the sense of "a good conscience," and that instance may have motivated the insertion of the adjective in 2:19, creating the variant readings attested. The two senses of the noun are closely related in 2:19, and one can be derived from the other. For, a "consciousness of God" means not merely the awareness that God exists but also "sensitivity to the divine will concerning conduct" (J. H. Elliott 2000: 519), the violation of which would wound the conscience. Therefore, bearing the pain of unjust suffering because one is conscious of God's will is almost indistinguishable in meaning from doing so for the sake of a conscience toward God (NASB).

2:21. There are variant readings for one verb, the choices being ἔπαθεν (epathen, suffered) and ἀπέθανεν (apethanen, died), variants that also occur in 3:18. While not denying that Christ's suffering terminated in death, Peter uses the suffering of Christ as a paradigm for his readers. *Epathen* is strongly attested in early manuscripts and is most likely the original reading. The variant *apethanen*, so similar in spelling, is more easily understood as either a scribal misreading of the verb or a deliberate change because of veneration for the death of Christ, especially under the influence of the same confusion in 3:18.

b. Instructions to Christian Wives and Husbands (3:1–7)

Because the call to faith in Christ is a call for life-changing, personal realignment, the conversion of either spouse in the Greco-Roman marriage held the potential for serious problems both between the couple and between the couple and society. Depending on how the believing spouse behaved, the situation could also provoke criticism of the Christian religion if its practices were perceived to subvert and disrupt the social order so necessary for the well-being of the empire. Converted spouses also no doubt experienced confusion about how their new identity in Christ should affect their relationship to their unbelieving spouse, and whether new life in Christ necessarily implied a change of one's role within the social hierarchy.

    i. Instructions to Christian wives (3:1–6)
    ii. Instructions to married men (3:7)
    iii. The significance of Peter's teaching today

Exegesis and Exposition

[1]In the same way [i.e., with all respect (2:18)], wives, be subject to your own husbands, so that even if some reject the word, through the way of life of their wives they will be won over without a word, [2]when they observe your holy and respectful way of life. [3]Let [your beauty] not be the outward braiding of hair and adorning with gold or wearing fine clothes, [4]rather, the inner person of the heart adorned by the unfading quality of the gentle and quiet spirit, which is of great value in God's sight. [5]For in this way also in times past the holy women who hoped in God adorned themselves, submitting to their own husbands, [6]as Sarah obeyed Abraham, calling him "lord." You are her children by doing good and not fearing any intimidation. [7]Husbands, in the same way [i.e., with all respect (2:18)] live according to knowledge with the female as a weaker vessel, showing honor to her as even a fellow heir of the grace of life, so that your prayers will not be hindered.

i. Instructions to Christian Wives (3:1–6)

Just as Peter begins his instruction that slaves submit themselves to their masters in all fear of the Lord (2:18), he begins his instructions to believing wives with the same qualification: "Likewise [with all respect], wives, be subject to your own husbands" (3:1; see additional note on 2:18 for a discussion of the imperatival participle). The wife's reverence for God is her motivation for submitting to her husband, regardless of whether the husband is harsh or kind. The antagonism her faith might produce is to be endured for the sake of Christ and for the possible conversion of her husband. Why would a wife's conversion likely provoke antagonism from her husband? In Greco-Roman society it was expected that the wife would have no friends of her own and would worship the gods of her husband (Plutarch, *Advice* §19). If this expectation is applied to a Christian wife, it might result in trouble for several reasons. First, the very fact that a woman would adopt any religion other than her husband's violated the Greco-Roman ideal of an orderly home (Oborn 1939: 133). Because prosperity and well-being were seen as dependent on religious forces, disorder in the home was a threat not only to the family but to society. Christians were frequently blamed as the cause of public calamity because they introduced a new god, upsetting the religious status quo of the empire (Oborn 1939: 137; Colwell 1939; Frend 1967).

Second, the husband and society would perceive the wife's worship of Jesus Christ as rebellion, especially if she worshipped Christ exclusively. If the wife persisted in her new religion to the extent that others outside the household learned of it, the husband would also feel embarrassment and suffer criticism for not properly managing his household. This could seriously damage his social standing, even to the point of disqualifying him for certain honors and offices. Third, the wife's attendance at Christian worship would provide the opportunity for her to have fellowship with other Christians who possibly were not her husband's friends. Depending on the specifics of social expectations, a wife's conversion to Christ could potentially have far-reaching implications for her husband and family.

It is significant that Peter does not directly address any of these particulars. For instance, he neither orders the wife to attend Christian worship nor gives her permission to stay home and worship privately in her heart. He instructs her simply to submit to her own husband's wishes; depending on individual proclivities, the result may or may not have been the same as the expectations of society at large.

It is an important point that Peter leaves the specifics of this matter strictly between husband and wife. The Christian wife is to submit not to the expectations of any and all men in general but to her own husband. Peter opens the door for social transformation by leaving it to husband and wife to work out the specific way her submission is to be expressed. As mentioned above, the writings of the Greek moral philosophers do not usually address women (and slaves), but here Peter does so. Moreover, Peter affirms wives' (and slaves') choice to leave their former way of pagan life while at the same time instructing them to remain within their most basic relationship.

The metamessage of Peter's instructions is probably not lost on the husband, who could see in it two points: (1) This apostle of Jesus Christ instructs the Christian slave and wife, a role that is normally the prerogative of the husband. (2) This direct instruction to slaves and wives implies that both have a measure of moral responsibility and choice unprecedented in Greek thought. The husband or slave master cannot object, since Peter does indeed affirm the man's authority. On the other hand, he also sees in this affirmation that his wife's or slave's submission is motivated no longer by the expectations of Roman society or the principles of Greek moral philosophy but instead by the authority and example of the crucified and resurrected Christ. In a masterful move, Peter both upholds and subverts the social order.

Peter's concern that Christian wives continue to submit to their own husbands not only shields Christianity from the accusation that it is a social evil but is also clearly motivated by evangelistic intent. The unbelieving husband observes virtues in the wife's good demeanor that are motivated by her relationship with Christ, virtues not inferior to those motivated by Greek moral philosophy. Observing this, the man himself may be won to Christ "without words," for in that culture it is shameful for the wife to presume to instruct her husband (which may also be a concern in 1 Tim. 2:11–12). Here is a situation where silence is the more effective means of communication.

Peter further instructs Christian women that their beauty is to be the inner quality of a gentle and quiet spirit, which is of great worth in God's sight, and not the costly adornment of elaborate hairstyles, fine clothing, and gold jewelry, which are, of course, of great worth in society's sight. This implies that at least some among the "foreigners and resident aliens" of Asia Minor actually have enough wealth to make this instruction meaningful (contra the theory of J. H. Elliott 1981). Peter's view on this point is not distinctively Christian, for it agrees both with the values of the OT (e.g., 1 Sam. 16:7) and with the Greek moral philosophers, who also extolled inner virtues over outer appearance. The OT focuses the exemplary woman's inner virtue on fear of the LORD: "Charm is deceptive, and beauty is fleeting; but a woman who fears the LORD is to be praised" (Prov. 31:30 NIV). In contrast, the Greek ideal focused on the virtues. For Xenophon, a woman adorns the world by the daily practice of the virtues (Xenophon, *Oeconomicus* 7.43). For Aristotle, a woman's self-control in all she does and her inclination toward an honorable and well-ordered life with patience and gentleness are her true beauties (Aristotle, *Oeconomica* 3.1). Conversely, outward adornments were often perceived as instruments of seduction (Philo, *On the Virtues* 7.39; Plutarch, *Advice* §30), and a woman's use of cosmetics was viewed as an attempt to deceive; both were unnecessary if a woman stayed at home

(Xenophon, *Oeconomicus* 10.2). A similar thought is seen in Plutarch's comment that most women stay indoors if you take from them gold-embroidered shoes, bracelets, anklets, purple, and pearls (*Advice* §30). In light of these common attitudes, Peter's instructions against outward adornment make sense if a Christian wife is attending Christian worship outside her home, and especially if doing so without her husband. Society would perceive that act alone as questionable. By leaving her home unadorned, her intent to attend worship and not a tryst would presumably be all the more clear.

Peter's reference to Israel's holy women of the past, and specifically the example of Sarah (3:6), is of particular interest in contrast to the Greek writings. Peter presents Sarah as a paradigm of submission because she called her husband "lord." In Gen. 18:12 LXX Sarah refers to Abraham as her κύριος (*kyrios*, master, lord), though she does not directly address him by that term. This noun is the only lexical connection between the story of Sarah and Peter's claim, for the LXX does not use any verb meaning "obey" with respect to Sarah's relationship with Abraham. To the contrary, the Genesis story has Abraham obeying his wife three times (Gen. 16:2, 6; 21:12), which apparently embarrassed both Philo and Josephus, Jewish writers living in Greco-Roman society (Sly 1991). Nevertheless, the submission of Sarah to Abraham was a long-standing element of Jewish tradition.

As Spencer (2000: 113) points out, if the emphasis is to be on Sarah's obedience, Gen. 12:13 is perhaps the passage of greater relevance, for it is a key place where Sarah implicitly obeys Abraham by cooperating with his deceptive ruse in Pharaoh's court (cf. 20:5, 13). Spencer sees Sarah and Abraham as parallels to the Christian wife called to suffer and the husband who disobeys the word. For Spencer, the significance of Peter's reference reflects Sarah's Christlike decision to save her husband's life by being willing to suffer for his sake, while Abraham's conduct exemplifies a husband disobedient to the word.

Even though the only lexical link is to Gen. 18:12, Kiley (1987: 692) sees the motifs of Gen. 12 and 20 to be the relevant background. In these episodes, Sarah submits to the albeit questionable wisdom of her husband "*in an unjust and frightening situation in a foreign land/hostile environment*" (emphasis original). In this way Sarah's situation parallels that of the Christian wives Peter addresses, living as foreigners and resident aliens in a hostile society.

T. Martin (1999: 146) argues that the Testament of Abraham is the most likely literary background because "it contains specific situations where Sarah addresses Abraham as 'lord' and obeys him. This text also contains the idea of Sarah as the mother of the elect and connects good deeds with fearlessness," all of which are also elements of 1 Pet. 3:6. Martin is probably right that the Testament of Abraham preserves some of the traditions about Sarah shared by its author and the author of 1 Peter, though not necessarily through any direct literary dependence.

The apostle Peter is most likely simply drawing on Jewish interpretive tradition and would not have intended a choice of any one passage from Genesis or any other text in order to understand his reference to Sarah. In Jewish tradition Sarah is a virtuous woman, and virtuous women are understood to be obedient to their husbands.

Apparently Peter is providing a role model of a virtuous woman from Israel's founding tradition as a replacement for role models known in the Greek writings. Plutarch holds up examples of admired Greek women renowned for their virtue (*Advice* §48). Xenophon points to the unnamed wife of Ischomachus (*Oeconomicus* 7.1–10.13), who in a textual variant of one edition also calls her husband "lord and master" (Wedderburn and Collingwood 1876: 45).

Peter instructs Christian women, who may have been familiar with the Greek role models, to look instead to the founding "first lady" of God's covenant people in the tradition that they now embrace as their own. By virtue of being born again into the living hope of the gospel, Sarah has become their spiritual ancestor. In Christian thinking that motivates wifely behavior, the Greek moral philosophers are now to be replaced with the writings of Yahweh's prophets. This is another way Peter subtly subverts Greco-Roman culture.

The Christian women of Asia Minor are "daughters" of Sarah if they do what is right and do not give way to the kind of fear that results in hatred and hostility. Therefore, Christian women married to unbelieving men are not to despise and reject their husbands, making the household climate one of hostility, but to subject themselves even to unjust treatment because of their faith in Christ, and in so doing accomplish God's better way.

The exhortation for wives to be subject to their own husbands in proximity to the discussion of Jesus as the model for Christian suffering immediately raises the question of whether women should stay in marriages where there is physical abuse. There is nothing in this passage of Scripture that would either sanction the abuse of wives or suggest that women should continue to submit themselves to that kind of treatment. The nature of the suffering that Peter is addressing is primarily verbal abuse and loss of social standing. Slaves were commonly beaten, not because they were Christian, but because they were considered property (though their Christian faith may have exacerbated hostility from unbelieving masters; 2:20). Peter wants Christians to conduct their relationships in a way that would be considered a good witness to unbelieving society. Because even Greco-Roman statutes did not sanction spousal abuse, a woman who endured domestic violence would not necessarily have been considered a virtuous wife (de Silva 2000: 39). Peter is speaking specifically of suffering that may come from standing for an unpopular belief and doing what is good and right in the name of Christ. In fact, Peter delicately prohibits domestic violence in the exhortation to husbands that immediately follows.

ii. Instructions to Married Men (3:7)

In his household code, Peter addresses last those who have the most power and authority. He begins his exhortation to husbands with the same qualification as for slaves and wives: "likewise [with all respect (2:18)], live with your wives according to knowledge" (3:7). Achtemeier (1996: 217) considers this participle, as well as those in 2:18 and 3:1, to be subordinate to the imperatives of 2:17, "Respect all people. . . . Fear God," by specifying the manner in which those commands are to be accomplished within society's most basic unit, the household. In any case, the context makes the imperatival sense clear (see additional note on 2:18 for a discussion of the imperatival participle).

It is too often and too quickly assumed that Peter here addresses the Christian husband of a believing, Christian wife (Beare 1970: 157; Best 1971: 127; Boring 1999: 127; Davids 1990: 122; J. H. Elliott 2000: 582; McKnight 1996: 185; Michaels 1988: 169, though entertaining the possibility that the wife may not be Christian). Fewer argue that the wives in view are, in fact, not Christian (Gross 1989). Moreover, as some have observed, the Greek word used in the instructions to men here is not the noun usually used to refer to a wife (γυνή, gynē), as in 3:1, but is the adjective γυναικεῖος (gynaikeios, female) used substantivally. The singular article may refer to a class, the female, and not necessarily to one woman. In the context of the household, "the female" would refer primarily to the wife but also suggests a broader reference, possibly to all the women living within the household under the authority of the husband (Achtemeier 1996: 217; Grudem 1988: 77; Reicke 1964: 102).

The Christian conversion of a married man would have raised issues within the marriage relationship whether or not the wife also became a true believer, and Peter's exhortation would be applicable in either case. Peter directly addresses the general Greco-Roman attitude of the inferiority of women by pointing out that the female also is a coheir of grace and therefore not excluded from the same privileges of grace enjoyed by the male.

Interpreters perhaps often assume that the female in view is the believing wife of a Christian husband because Greco-Roman mores expected a wife (indeed all members of the household) to follow the religion of the male head of the household. Because of social conditioning, it may have been true that the wife typically followed the Christian conversion of the husband with at least outward compliance to his new religion, and if she experienced true, heartfelt conversion to Christ, so much the better. Nevertheless, the situation of a Christian husband with a reluctant, unbelieving wife is not outside the purview of this exhortation.

The Christian conversion of a man with a pagan wife would probably not provoke the same social concerns as the conversion of a wife with a pagan husband. However, the extent to which the pagan wife openly resists Christian worship and practices may bring embarrassment on the husband for not properly managing his household. This would be especially acute for men of social standing and power, for, as Plutarch (*Advice* §43) writes, "A man therefore ought to have his household well harmonized who is going to harmonize State, Forum, and friends" (Babbitt 1971: 333). A similar concern likely motivates the apostle Paul when he discusses qualifications for the elders and deacons of the church in 1 Tim. 2–3. Nevertheless, husbands are not encouraged to be despotic tyrants with their wives; rather, as Plutarch (*Advice* §47) continues, "The husband ought to show no greater respect for anybody than for his wife" (Babbitt 1971: 337). Peter also recommends respect for the wife, apparently without differentiating between the couple who are both Christians and the Christian husband with a nominally Christian, but inwardly pagan, wife.

The reference to the wife as coheir of the gracious gift of life may at first glance seem to prohibit an understanding that she is not a Christian. However, the *hōs kai* (3:7) may be read "*as even* a coheir." This would then indicate that the husband is to treat his wife as if she were a sister in Christ. The unbelieving wife is to be accorded the same respect as a fellow Christian (since society would assume she shared her husband's religion) with the hope of winning her to authentic faith. The believing wife, on the other hand, deserves to be treated as a fellow believer despite her gender. If she is a Christian, her status as a coheir levels the spiritual ground between the believing husband and believing wife, opening the door wider for social transformation.

Peter's description of the female as the "weaker vessel" reflects similar descriptions in the Greek writings that should perhaps inform our understanding here. Aristotle (*Oeconomica* 1.3.4) understands that weakness to be both in body and in courage: "For Providence made man stronger and woman weaker, so that he in virtue of his manly prowess may be more ready to defend the home, and she, by reason of her timid nature, more ready to keep watch over it" (Armstrong 1936: 333). Xenophon (*Oeconomicus* 7.23–28) also discusses the different attributes of men and women:

> [God] made the man's body and mind more capable of enduring cold and heat, and journeys and campaigns; and there imposed on him the outdoor tasks. To the woman, since he has made her body less capable of such endurance, I take it that God has assigned the indoor tasks. . . . And since he imposed on the woman the protection of the stores also, knowing that

for protection a fearful disposition is no disadvantage, God meted out a larger share of fear to the woman than to the man; and knowing that he who deals with the outdoor tasks will have to be their defender against any wrong-doer, he meted out to him again a larger share of courage. (Marchant 1938: 421)

According to the prevalent understanding of the time, God impartially gave memory, attention, and the power to practice self-control to both man and woman. Gender-differentiated aptitudes make the husband and wife mutually dependent because the one is competent where the other is deficient.

In the context of 1 Peter, the weaker vessel is primarily understood as physical weakness relative to men's strength. Therefore, Peter's exhortation indirectly addresses the issue of physical abuse. However, the immediate context makes it clear that the female is also weaker in the sense of social entitlement and empowerment. Peter teaches that men whose authority runs roughshod over their women, even with society's full approval, will not be heard by God.

This concept is certainly consistent with OT teaching. Yet because Peter is engaging the Greco-Roman worldview, he probably alludes here to the thought, common in ancient society, that the prayers of the male head of household to the gods are important for the prosperity and well-being of the household and therefore contribute to the well-being of the city (Xenophon, *Oeconomicus* 5.19–20). Peter points out that the well-being of the Christian household depends on the man recognizing the female as a coheir in Christ and living with her respectfully, even though he is the physically stronger and socially empowered male. In this way Peter delicately prohibits domestic violence in the Christian household.

iii. The Significance of Peter's Teaching Today

The reader who does not understand Peter's intent in his instruction of slaves, wives, and husbands will not understand the message of 1 Peter. Within this passage Peter grounds his ethical teaching on the Christian life rightly lived after the example of Christ's suffering. How shortsighted it is to use this passage as if it were a marriage manual simply addressing the relationship between husbands and wives! And how ironic it is that the words that first-century slaves and wives would have read as affirming and empowering are criticized by some today as enslaving and oppressive. When read within its original historical setting, these verses become a call to social transformation within the Christian community, allowing it to become an alternate society based on God's redemptive plan. The Christian's willingness to suffer unjustly out of reverence for God in order to follow in the footsteps of Jesus Christ is a radical break with social expectations of that day just as it is in our own day. Peter affirms aspects of the cultural expectations of his day, yet he does so for theological reasons that masterfully subvert traditional social structures. Where other Jewish writers, such as Philo and Josephus, accept the household ethic code of Hellenistic society as compatible with Jewish tradition (Balch 1981: 73; Sly 1991), Peter—also a Jewish writer—creatively points to a new way traced out by the footsteps of Christ.

These instructions to slaves, wives, and husbands appear in a unit of discourse that begins with the exhortation for Christians to live such good lives among the pagans that they might ultimately glorify God (2:11). They are to submit to every human authority so that ignorant talk about Christians will be silenced (2:13). It may be surmised, therefore, that one of Peter's primary concerns is that Christian behavior should not give Christ a bad name among unbelievers. Peter encourages his readers to conduct themselves in a way that would be both recognized and respected by Roman rulers and society as good, silencing the criticism, slander, and persecution of unbelievers.

Peter emphasizes the evangelistic and apologetic value of submission within the household. Paul, in contrast, roots the submission of the wife to the husband in the relationship between Christ and the church and in the creation of marriage as a one-flesh union (Eph. 5:21–33). The Christian man must love his wife as Christ loved the church (5:25) and as he loves himself (5:33). The Christian wife must submit to her own husband (5:22) and must respect her husband (5:33). While we must not simply conflate Peter's thought with Paul's, we also must not conclude that Peter's teaching on submission is simply posturing to win favor for Christianity in the eyes of pagan society.

Although both the Greek moral philosophers and the NT speak of "submission," the apostolic definition of it and foundation for it are completely different. The Greco-Roman worldview was concerned with the pragmatic benefits of social stability; the Christian view of submission is concerned with honoring transcendent theological values that ought to capture the heart of believers and transform them within all of their relationships.

Paul's household code in Eph. 5:21–6:9 provides a model of mutual submission and love in marriage that is theologically, rather than apologetically, grounded. In contrast to Peter's one-verse instruction to husbands, Paul develops the theological basis for the husband's relationship to his wife that defines the character of the wife's submission (5:25–33). Christian marriage is understood as a lifelong commitment in an exclusive one-flesh union that mirrors the profound mystery of Christ and the church (5:32). On this model of Christ's love for his church and the church's submission to Christ, marital love is understood as the resolve to live one's entire life totally committed to the well-being of one's spouse in every decision. When "submission" of the wife becomes the central issue, the image of Christian marriage has already been distorted. A well-known evangelical leader is quoted as saying, "I believe in a wife submitting to her husband, but I don't believe the husband ever has the right to demand it. . . . In fact, I know when I am unworthy of it, she does not. My responsibility as a husband is to be worthy" (quoted in Mc-Knight 1996: 192). Peter, unlike Paul, is addressing the situation where the husband is not a Christian and does not love his wife as Christ loved the church. His demands are not necessarily worthy of submission. Yet Peter instructs the Christian wife to submit to her unbelieving husband and to respect him, yet without renouncing her faith, even though she may suffer for her Christian principles. Peter's instruction is almost certainly based on the same theological understanding of marriage as Paul's, but it also happens to formally correspond with what would be expected of the wife by her society, which has no such theological grounding for its expectation. Peter's point is that Christians must be ready to suffer unjustly because of their relationship to God in Christ.

While the foundation for Christian submission in marriage is deeply rooted in theology, the specific expressions of submission relate to the times in which we live. What counts as submission today may be quite different from what counted as submission in the first century, because social expectations differ over time and from place to place. But this does not mean that Peter's instructions are no longer relevant to Christians today since our society generally does not uphold the hierarchical model of marriage as it was practiced in the first century.

How should Peter's instructions for order in the household be applied today? According to Crouch (1972: 158), the significance of a NT household code "derives from its original situation and at the same time transcends the historically conditioned form of its exhortations," calling believers to live out the gospel in the givenness of the historical moment into which they have been placed. This allows the modern believer to reject slavery where the NT does not *explicitly* do so, because the given social order within which most of today's believers are called to live and witness rightly disallows the practice of slavery. Moreover, many Christians today live under governments where there is a mechanism for change—unlike the dictatorial regime of the Roman emperors—and Christians can work to change their social order for justice and equity in accord with biblical principles. And so the NT household codes that instruct slaves to submit to that institution in the first century do not warrant Christians supporting slavery today or being indifferent to it in those parts of the world where it is yet practiced.

Similarly, the society in which we live accords different status and privileges to women than the first century did. Accordingly, Christian men and women are called by the household codes to live out their marriages in a way that honors the gospel in today's social order. Peter wanted the first-century wife and husband to relate to each other in a manner that reflected the biblical view of marriage. It would still be wrong for a Christian husband or wife to misrepresent the character of the gospel by living in a way that is inconsistent with the biblical character of marriage. For instance, spousal abuse, infidelity, or malicious neglect violates both biblical standards and the higher ideals of social expectations. And the apologetic value of Christian behavior emphasized by Peter is still a concern. Churches must consider how their position on the role of women within the Christian community speaks to the larger social order.

Therefore, the specific expressions of appropriate submission must be culturally defined. A woman who is active outside the home or a married woman appearing in public without the escort of her husband or other male relative does not scandalize our society as it did in the first century. Peter wisely did not spell out in specific terms what it means for a Christian wife to submit to her husband or for a Christian husband to live considerately with his wife. The apostle laid down the principles and then left the details to be worked out between the spouses. The church today is right to uphold a biblical order within marriage that mirrors the relationship of Christ and his church, but it should also follow Peter's wisdom and refrain from trying to specify what that must look like in every case.

B. The Inner Qualities of Righteous Living (3:8–12)

This passage summarizes Peter's teaching on the qualities of Christian character needed to sustain the Christian community as it responds rightly to the hostility of an unbelieving society. First Peter 2:11–17 provides instruction about how the Christians of Asia Minor are to relate in general to the structures of their society, and 2:18–3:7 guides their conduct within their households. Now Peter continues to list qualities that should be evident in relationships primarily between Christian believers in the wider community. These exhortations define the character needed to respond to evil and insult, whatever its source (3:9–12).

1. Christian virtues that sustain community (3:8)
2. Christians called to return blessing in response to evil (3:9)
3. The Lord is against even Christians who do evil (3:10–12)

Exegesis and Exposition

⁸Finally, all of you be like-minded, understanding, showing brotherly love, compassionate, and humble. ⁹Do not repay evil for evil or insult for insult, but to the contrary, bless, because to this you have been called in order that you may inherit blessing. ¹⁰For

> whoever wishes to love life
>   and to see good days
> must stop the tongue from evil
>   and the lips from speaking deceit.
> ¹¹They must turn from evil and do good,
>   and seek peace and pursue it.

¹²This is because "the eyes of the Lord [are] upon the righteous and his ears [are] toward their prayers, but the Lord's face [is] against those who do evil."

1. Christian Virtues That Sustain Community (3:8)

Balch's claim that 3:8–12 constitutes a summary of the household code, such that the "all of you" refers only to slaves, wives, and husbands, does not enjoy wide support (Balch 1981: 88). The larger discourse structure suggests that these instructions, while certainly including the slaves, wives, and husbands he has just addressed, are for all members of the Christian community, as verses that open this major unit of discourse (2:11–17) address all. Most of Peter's readers probably are slaves, wives, or husbands. But all members of the community are to learn from what has just been said specifically to slaves, wives, and husbands, for these roles provide the basis for social unity (cf. 3:9 with 2:23).

The Christian community is to be an alternate society where believers should not have to face the same kinds of insult and hostility that come from those outside the church (cf. comments on 2:1). However, in order for the Christian community to really be a place of support and refuge, certain qualities must characterize its members. In 3:8 Peter lists five adjectives that should characterize believers in their relationships toward one another. These terms, particularly "brotherly love" (φιλάδελφος, *philadelphos*) and "compassion" (εὔσπλαγχνος, *eusplanchnos*), were used with reference to kinship obligations (Pilch and Malina 1993: 28–115). Peter feels free to apply to the Christian community terms commonly used of family relationships, apparently following the thought that their new birth generated by God the Father (1:3–4) makes the Christian community into a family. Peter suggests that his readers have kinship obligations to one another that are expected of biological kin in that society. Given the importance of the family unit as the basis of Greco-Roman society, the application of kinship terms to the relationship between Christian believers may be viewed as inappropriate or even threatening to the social order by those outside the church. However, the NT in general and 1 Peter in particular never endorses animosity for one's biological family members who are not Christians. The priority to be given to Christ over one's own family applies only when the family rejects Christ and pressures the believing member to do so as well. Therefore, while Christianity may have been perceived as divisive within families (and may still be), the rejection of one's family is not a constitutive value of the Christian community, as Peter's household code makes clear.

A comparison of 1 Pet. 3:8–12 with Rom. 12:10–17 has been offered as evidence that 1 Peter is dependent on Paul here (Beare 1970: 160). The same values are found in both passages, although not in the same order and with somewhat different wording. Many interpreters deny, or at least seriously question, that literary dependence accounts for both the similarities and the differences (Achtemeier 1996: 221; Best 1971: 129; J. H. Elliott 2000: 602; Gundry 1966–67: 342; Kelly 1969: 135; Michaels 1988: 174–75; Piper 1978–79: 218–19). The evidence, rather, suggests that this list of character traits was common in the Christian tradition, probably going back to the teachings of Jesus himself (Selwyn 1958: 189), and that Peter and Paul both drew on that tradition and put it in a form suitable for their own individual purposes.

Peter's list of virtues necessary for building up the Christian community would also be esteemed in the Greek ethical tradition. Goppelt (1993: 230) suggests that the five adjectives in 1 Pet. 3:8 "consistently reproduce in Hellenistic formulation what is stated in Romans 12 in a more OT-Jewish manner" because some of these same adjectives are found in the common Hellenistic ethical vocabulary. However, Peter is concerned not with building up society at large but specifically with character and relationships among Christian believers. This list of virtues is intended to reinforce the Christian's cohesion not with society at large but with the countercultural society of the Christian community.

For instance, the first term, "like-mindedness" (ὁμόφρων, *homophrōn*), refers to sharing "a common heritage of faith and ethical tradition" (Selwyn 1958: 189) that is valued by Greco-Roman society because it produces the cohesion needed to sustain a community. Even though like-mindedness was valued by society at large, Peter calls the Christian community to a like-mindedness that does not reinforce their cohesion with society at large but actually subverts it. As defined by the apostle, the like-mindedness implicitly calls them to reject the religion and ethical tradition that has informed their former "useless" way of life inherited from their ancestors (1 Pet. 1:18) and to embrace apostolic teaching. Like-mindedness is perhaps the foundational value of the Christian community that unifies people from various races and religions joined together in belief in Christ.

The second quality mentioned, humility (ταπεινόφρων, *tapeinophrōn*), was disdained in first-century Greco-Roman society and would have been quite a countercultural value. As J. H. Elliott observes (2000: 605): "In the highly competitive and stratified world of Greco-Roman antiquity, only those of degraded social status were 'humble,' and humility was regarded as a sign of weakness and shame, an inability to defend one's honor. Thus the high value placed on humility by Israelites and Christians is remarkable." Therefore, even though Peter uses the ethical terminology of Greco-Roman society, he brings it to bear on forming a cohesive Christian community that will exhibit distinctive qualities in the relationships among believers and between believers and those outside the community.

"Be like-minded, understanding, showing brotherly love, compassionate, and humble." Such qualities are essential for a truly Christian life, but how do they compare with the values of the society in which we live? These are qualities that presume a high commitment to the stability and well-being of the community. Modern Western concepts of individualism tend to trump commitment to community. Where commitment is found, it is often evaluated in terms of individual needs. An individual whose needs are no longer met by a community terminates the "commitment" and seeks a new and more obliging group. Such thinking runs counter to the qualities of 3:8. Like-mindedness implies a willingness to conform one's goals, needs, and expectations to the purposes of the larger community.

The quality of understanding demands deferentially seeing things from another's point of view. The emphasis on brotherly love often falls on "love" rather than on "brother," which sometimes leads to a misunderstanding that affection is more important than the resolve to do right by others with whom we are substantially related by faith in Christ.

The quality of compassion in modern society is, according to Pilch and Malina (1993: 31), "an aspect of pity which implies sorrow for another's suffering or misfortune and sometimes connotes mild contempt because the object of pity is regarded as weak or inferior." People in our society tend to be generously compassionate toward victims of fires, floods, and other disasters, but the virtue of compassion was understood differently in the first century, which used it in mentioning kindness shown to family members. Its appearance in Peter's Christian virtue list implies that the Christian community should understand itself as a type of family. In the first century humble people did "not threaten or challenge another's rights, nor [did] they claim more for themselves than [had] been duly allotted them in life" (Pilch and Malina 1993: 107). Of particular relevance to the Christian readers of 1 Peter, to humble oneself was to "declare oneself powerless to defend one's status." These are qualities that ran counter to the trends of first-century society, as they do in our own today. But Peter is saying that, like Jesus, his readers do not need to use the same tactics as the world to defend who they are as heirs of God in Christ.

2. Christians Called to Return Blessing in Response to Evil (3:9)

In 3:9 Peter turns his attention to the reason that apparently has precipitated his letter: the relationship of his readers with hostile people outside the Christian community. He introduces the topic that extends through 4:19, how his readers are to live out the gospel in a world that is suspicious of Christians and even hostile to them: "Do not repay evil for evil or insult for insult, but to the contrary, bless, because to this you have been called in order that you may inherit blessing." As a transition to the problem facing his readers, this verse is an important indication for the kind of hostility that must be characterizing Christians' relationships with unbelievers. Citing Malina (1993: 28–62), J. H. Elliott (2000: 607) identifies the expressions of hostility as insult, defamation of character, and verbal abuse, the "weapons typically employed in an agonistic honor-and-shame society for challenging the honor of others and publicly shaming and discrediting those who are different or regarded as one's competitors." So understood, the Christian response of nonretaliation would be startling within that culture. Peter instructs Christians to forgo the usual verbal retaliation that would be necessary to successfully defend one's honor and the reputation of one's community. Given the tendency of human nature to retaliate, coupled with the social expectation to do so, the Christian who refrains from verbal retaliation and instead offers blessing would give unbelievers pause.

In 2:23 the example of Jesus' refusal to retaliate for unjust accusations broke the vicious cycle of escalating conflict that is so familiar within communities, and provides the basis for a similar course of action by those following in his footsteps. While 3:9 is no doubt directed primarily to insult and abuse from outside the Christian community, it also answers to the problem of strife within the church when believers lodge charges and countercharges against each other. As he did within the household code, Peter here again subtly subverts first-century social expectations by showing that Jesus Christ opens a better way in which Christians are to follow.

As J. H. Elliott (2000: 603) points out, to the extent that Peter reflects the ethical teaching of Jesus, it further implies that Jesus must serve as an ethical model for all believers. However, as the basis for the Christian's ethical model, Peter notably points not to Jesus' teaching but to his response to the undeserved suffering that led to the cross (2:21–25). Nevertheless, Peter's exhortation of nonretaliation can be compared to what Jesus teaches his disciples about how to treat enemies. It has sometimes been debated whether Jesus' atoning sacrifice or his teachings are at the heart of Christianity. This passage eloquently demonstrates that the two cannot be separated.

The parallels between Luke, Paul, and 1 Peter are well recognized, even though the explanation of the parallels is highly debated (e.g., Gundry 1966–67; Gundry 1974; Best 1969–70). The closest parallel of 3:9 to the words of Jesus is found in Luke 6:27–28: "But to you who are listening I say: Love your enemies, do good to those who hate you, bless those who curse you, pray for those who mistreat you" (TNIV). Peter applies Jesus' general teaching to the specific situation where Christians face hostility for no reason other than that they are Christians.

It is imperative here to understand what "loving" one's enemies means in contrast to modern ideas of "love." Such modern ideas led one student to ask in exasperation, "How can Jesus expect me to love my enemies when I don't even like them?" "Loving" in modern culture refers primarily to an emotional attachment of a greater intensity than merely "liking." But Peter clearly interprets Jesus' command to love to refer not to emotions but to acting rightly toward one's adversaries, regardless of whatever emotions may or may not be involved (cf. Jesus' teaching on loving one's neighbor as presented in the parable of the good Samaritan in Luke 10:25–37). Acting rightly toward one's adversaries is defined in 1 Pet. 3:9 as not responding in kind to their insults, slander, and evil intents. It means having the inner fortitude to break the cycle of evil that spirals ever downward.

But as if nonretaliation were not hard enough, the Christian is to respond to evil and insult with blessing! In the Greek world the word εὐλογέω (*eulogeō*, bless) meant to publicly speak well of someone. While that may be in view here, it is probably the Jewish and Christian use of the term, meaning to invoke God's favor on someone, that is primarily intended. The self-control implied in this command is truly a supernatural fruit of the Holy Spirit (Gal. 5:23). For it is exactly when we are insulted and treated with malicious intent that we are most tempted to respond in kind by gossip, exaggerating the extent of the fault, or with outright slander. Those who are able not simply to clench their teeth and remain silent but to maintain an inner attitude that allows one to pray sincerely for the well-being of one's adversaries, are truly a witness to the life-changing power of a new identity in Christ.

When I asked students in class one day to come up with specific, practical examples of how someone might bless an adversary, the story was shared of a Christian soldier living in a barracks with his unit. Each evening, when he would read his Bible and pray before retiring, he was reviled and insulted by the soldier across the aisle. One night a pair of muddy combat boots came flying at the Christian. The next morning, the hostile soldier found his boots at the foot of his bed, cleaned and polished and ready for inspection. Several soldiers in this company eventually became Christians as a result of the inner strength of one who could return blessing for insult.[1]

If it is difficult enough simply to refrain from retaliation, it may seem superhuman to return blessing for evil and insult. However, this is the path for the Christian who wishes to follow in the Lord's footsteps, because to this (ὅτι εἰς τοῦτο, *hoti eis touto*) you have been called. The position of the prepositional phrase "to this [*eis touto*] you were called" raises the question of what readers are called to: to return blessing for insult or to inherit a blessing? Is the referent of the prepositional phrase *eis touto* the preceding thought, "repay evil with blessing," or the subsequent clause, "in order that you may inherit blessing"? In other words, does Peter say, "You have been called to bless those who insult you" (reading the referent as what precedes)? Or, "Bless those who insult you because you know that a blessing most certainly awaits you" (reading the referent as what follows)?

1. With appreciation for my students in RS112: General Epistles, spring 2002, Westmont College, who in every class stimulated good thoughts and insights.

Grammatically speaking, the prepositional phrase (*eis touto*) can point either to what just preceded or to what immediately follows. Interpreters are divided whether to take it as preceding (Achtemeier 1996: 224; Best 1971: 130; Clowney 1988: 141–42; J. H. Elliott 2000: 609; Grudem 1988: 147; Michaels 1988: 178; Piper 1978–79: 224) or following (Davids 1990: 127; Goppelt 1993: 234; Kelly 1969: 137; Selwyn 1958: 190). This prepositional phrase occurs two other times in 1 Peter (2:21; 4:6). Almost identical syntax is found in 4:6, where the phrase *eis touto* points to the immediately preceding reason given ("they will give an account to the one prepared to judge the living and the dead") for why the gospel is preached. The *hina* clause (ἵνα, in order that) in 4:6 indicates the purpose of the preaching ("they might nevertheless live"). The other occurrence of the phrase *eis touto*, in 2:20–21 in this same unit of discourse, clearly has a backward reference: the calling in view is to suffer for doing good. It therefore is more probable that in 3:9 Peter picks up the call to suffering and expands it from slaves to all believers with the reminder that the purpose of blessing those who insult the name of Christ is that blessing might be the believer's inheritance. Returning evil for evil only perpetuates a vicious cycle.

Some interpreters object to taking the preceding phrase as the antecedent of "to this you were called" because they read this to mean that the promised inheritance is contingent on blessing enemies in return for evil. It may sound like salvation by works: "You have been called to return blessing for insult in order that you might inherit a blessing [be saved]." That understanding—so antithetical to the teaching in the rest of the NT and 1 Peter—has been the largest motivation for reading the prepositional phrase as pointing forward. However, as Kistemaker (1987: 128) points out, the text doesn't say that believers *earn* a blessing; they *inherit* it, and an inheritance is never earned.

Others avoid this problem by arguing that the inherited blessing refers to this life and not to eschatological salvation (Grudem 1988: 147–49). Clowney (1988: 142) argues that the referent of *eis touto* precedes it, but does not think that Peter is advocating a works religion based on earning merit by guarding our tongues. Rather, he explains, "God who calls us to inherit his blessing calls us to follow the path of peace that leads to blessing (3:11). The Christian's knowledge of the blessing that he will receive from the Lord encourages and enables him to bless others, even his enemies." Peter is teaching that those who have been called to return blessing for evil and insult have themselves inherited the blessing of life in Christ. Therefore, they are called to a course of ethical behavior that does not stoop to the level of pagans, even though pagan behavior constitutes the acceptable social norm. Peter's exhortation is not a call to what modern psychologists refer to as passive aggression: active blessing rather than passive hostility is the necessary course of action. Those who resolutely refuse this call to follow in Jesus' footsteps and continue to behave as the pagans thereby call into question their new identity in Christ, on which their eschatological blessing (salvation) depends.

3. The Lord Is against Even Christians Who Do Evil (3:10–12)

The use of Ps. 33 LXX (34 Eng.) in 1 Pet. 3:10–12 as the grounds of Peter's exhortation further supports taking the phrase that precedes "to this you were called" as its referent. The previous quotation of this same psalm, Ps. 33:9 LXX (34:8 Eng.), in 1 Pet. 2:3 and Peter's extensive allusions to that psalm indicate that it is an important scriptural foundation for his thinking about Christian ethics, much as Isa. 53 forms the basis of his Christology (see Jobes 2002). In Ps. 33:13–15 LXX the psalmist writes: "Whoever wishes to love life and to see good days must stop the tongue from evil and the lips from speaking deceit. They must turn from evil and do good, and seek peace and pursue it." In the psalm the implicit call is a turn from evil to good that involves the way the mouth is used to respond. A similar sequence is reflected in Peter's exhortation to his readers that they are called "to this" (*eis touto*), to return blessing for evil and insult. Therefore, the use of Ps. 33 LXX corroborates the reading that takes the referent of the prepositional phrase "to this [*eis touto*] you were called" to be the preceding thought, return blessing for insult.

Psalm 33 LXX (34 Eng.) appears pervasively throughout the paraenetic sections of 1 Peter as a scriptural basis for Christian ethics. First Peter follows the Greek translation of Ps. 33, which is quite faithful to the Hebrew text (Ps. 34). However, the LXX translator(s) did interpretively render one expression that made this psalm of deliverance quite congenial to 1 Peter's exile motif (cf. 1 Pet. 1:1; 5:13). The plural Hebrew noun in Ps. 34:5, מְגוּרוֹת (*mĕgûrôt*, terrors, fears, 34:4 Eng.), is rendered in the Greek translation by παροικιῶν (*paroikiōn*, sojournings, 33:5 LXX), the same word used in 1 Pet. 1:17 to refer to the trying situation of Peter's readers as a "sojourn." The LXX translator interpreted the troubles of David from which the Lord delivered him (as shown in the superscription of the psalm) to be the fears that arose during his sojourn among the Philistines, when David was living in exile, away from Judah. This is a good example of the LXX translator contextualizing the translation for the Greek Jews who were also facing particular fears presented by the pagan society in which they were living in Diaspora, away from Jerusalem. Because the author of 1 Peter has framed his letter with the Diaspora motif (cf. 1:1; 5:13), this particular psalm of deliverance is particularly well suited to his purposes, and it extensively informs his thought.

In addition to the two direct references to Ps. 33 LXX in 2:3 and 3:10–12, the language of Ps. 33 LXX (34 Eng.) echoes throughout the first half of Peter's letter:

1. Both start with blessing God:

Psalm 33:2 (34:1 Eng.)	εὐλογήσω τὸν κύριον ἐν παντὶ καιρῷ	1 Peter 1:3	εὐλογητὸς ὁ θεὸς καὶ πατὴρ τοῦ κυρίου ἡμῶν Ἰησοῦ Χριστοῦ
	eulogēsō ton kyrion en panti kairō		*eulogētos ho theos kai patēr tou kyriou hēmōn Iēsou Christou*
	I will bless the Lord at all times		blessed be the God and Father of our Lord Jesus Christ

2. The result of seeking the Lord was deliverance from all David's sojournings (παροικιῶν, *paroikiōn*):

Psalm 33:5 (34:4 Eng.)	καὶ ἐκ πασῶν τῶν παροι-κιῶν μου ἐρρύσατό με	1 Peter 1:17	ἐν φόβῳ τὸν τῆς παροικίας ὑμῶν χρόνον ἀναστράφητε
	kai ek pasōn tōn paroikiōn mou errysato me		*en phobō ton tēs paroikias hymōn chronon anastraphēte*
	and from all my sojourn-ings he delivered me		in fear [of God] live out your time of sojourning

3. The absence of shame, highly valued in ancient society, is found in both Ps. 33 and 1 Peter. In 1 Pet. 2:6, Peter is quoting from Isa. 28:16 LXX, which shares with Ps. 33 the theme of no shame for the righteous:

Psalm 33:6 (34:5 Eng.)	προσέλθατε πρὸς αὐτόν, . . . καὶ τὰ πρόσωπα ὑμῶν οὐ μὴ καταισχυνθῇ	1 Peter 2:6	ὁ πιστεύων ἐπ᾽ αὐτῷ οὐ μὴ καταισχυνθῇ
	proselthate pros auton, . . . kai ta prosōpa hymōn ou mē kataischynthē		*ho pisteuōn ep' autō ou mē kataischynthē*
	come to him [the Lord], . . . and your faces shall never be put to shame		the one who trusts in him [the Lord] shall never be put to shame

4. The benefits to those who fear the Lord are found in both the psalm and the epistle:

Psalm 33:8 (34:7 Eng.)	παρεμβαλεῖ ἄγγελος κυρίου κύκλῳ τῶν φοβουμένων αὐτὸν καὶ ῥύσεται αὐτούς	1 Peter 1:17	ἐν φόβῳ τὸν τῆς παροικίας ὑμῶν χρόνον ἀναστράφητε
	parembalei angelos kyriou kyklō tōn phoboumenōn auton kai rhysetai autous		*en phobō ton tēs paroikias hymōn chronon anastraphēte*

	the angel of the Lord camps around those who fear him and he will deliver them		in fear [of God] live out your time of sojourning
Psalm 33:10 (34:9)	φοβήθητε τὸν κύριον, οἱ ἅγιοι αὐτοῦ, ὅτι οὐκ ἐστιν ὑστέρημα τοῖς φοβουμένοις αὐτόν	1 Peter 2:17	τὸν θεὸν φοβεῖσθε
	phobēthēte ton kyrion, hoi hagioi autou, hoti ouk estin hysterēma tois phoboumenois auton		*ton theon phobeisthe*
	fear the Lord, you his holy ones, because those who fear him have no want		fear God
Psalm 33:12 (34:11)	φόβον κυρίου διδάξω ὑμᾶς		
	phobon kyriou didaxō hymas		
	I will teach you the fear of the Lord		

5. The responsiveness of God to the suffering of the righteous:

Psalm 33:18 (34:17 Eng.)	ἐκέκραξαν οἱ δίκαιοι, καὶ ὁ κύριος εἰσήκουσεν αὐτῶν καὶ ἐκ πασῶν τῶν θλίψεων αὐτῶν ἐρρύσατο αὐτούς	1 Peter 3:12	ὀφθαλμοὶ κυρίου ἐπὶ δικαίους καὶ ὦτα αὐτοῦ εἰς δέησιν αὐτῶν
	ekekraxan hoi dikaioi, kai ho kyrios eisēkousen autōn kai ek pasōn tōn thlipseōn autōn errysato autous		*ophthalmoi kyriou epi dikaious kai ōta autou eis deēsin autōn*
	the righteous cried out, and the Lord heard them and from all their affliction he delivered them		the eyes of the Lord are upon the righteous and his ears [are turned] toward their prayer

6. The "many afflictions" from which the righteous are delivered are mentioned in both:

Psalm 33:20 (34:19 Eng.)	πολλαὶ αἱ θλίψεις τῶν δικαίων, καὶ ἐκ πασῶν αὐ- τῶν ῥύσεται αὐτούς	1 Peter 1:6	ὀλίγον ἄρτι εἰ δέον [ἐστὶν] λυπηθέντες ἐν ποικίλοις πειρασμοῖς
	pollai hai thlipseis tōn dikaiōn, kai ek pasōn autōn rhysetai autous		*oligon arti ei deon [estin] lypēthentes en poikilois peira- smois*
	many are the afflictions of the righteous, and from all of them he will rescue them		though it is necessary for a little while to suffer many kinds of trials

7. The redemption of the servants of the Lord:

Psalm 33:23 (34:22 Eng.)	λυτρώσεται κύριος ψυχὰς δούλων αὐτοῦ	1 Peter 1:18	οὐ φθαρτοῖς, ἀργυρίῳ ἢ χρυσίῳ, ἐλυτρώθητε
	lytrōsetai kyrios psychas doulōn autou		*ou phthartois, argyriō ē chrysiō, elytrōthēte*
	the Lord will redeem the lives of his servants		not with perishable things— silver or gold—you have been redeemed
		1 Peter 2:16	ὡς θεοῦ δοῦλοι
			hōs theou douloi
			[live] as servants of God

As these citations demonstrate, Peter does not simply proof-text from Ps. 33 LXX but grounds his points in the original sense of the Hebrew psalm as it has been contextualized in the LXX for the Diaspora. Although the psalm originally referred to David, Peter directly applies the hopes and promises of Ps. 33 LXX to his contemporary readers. His logic appears to be that just as God delivered David from his sojourn among the Philistines, God will deliver the Asian Christians from the afflictions caused by their faith in Christ, because they are no less God's covenant people than was David.

In Ps. 33:9 LXX (34:8 Eng.) the tasting of God's goodness is related to putting hope in him: "O taste and see that the Lord is kind; Happy the man who hopes in him" (*NETS*; cf. 1 Pet. 2:3). That hope in Ps. 33 LXX is specifically for deliverance from shame (33:6 [34:5]), affliction (33:7 [34:6]), and want (33:10–11 [34:9–10])—the very things Peter's readers are facing as sojourners in their own society. Peter's extensive application of the concepts, theology, and language of Ps. 33 LXX to his Christian readers is an example of what he has claimed in 1 Pet. 1:25: the word of the Lord abides forever, defining truth anew for each generation.

The reference to "loving life" and seeing "good days" in 3:10 may suggest that those who suffer through bad days are not righteous in God's sight. However, the words of the psalmist in their original context "make it clear that those who are called to bless Yahweh are not those who are beyond suffering and pain" (G. Wilson 2002: 574). In fact, those who are delivered in the psalm "are the ones who *in the midst of their trouble* experience the blessing of Yahweh" (emphasis original, G. Wilson 2002: 574). Should the references to "life" and "good days" in the psalm quotation in 3:10 therefore be taken as references to this life or to the eschatological future?

Goppelt (1993: 236–37) is probably right to resist choosing between the two. He construes "life" to refer to the entire existence of the Christian with the Creator, both the temporal present and the eschatological future, which has been given to believers as an inheritance. "Good days" for the Christian are those that enjoy the fellowship of God, days that are already present in this life because of the eschatological new birth in Christ. The point of the psalm quotation is to show that people who have been born again into the good days of new life with God are called to bless when insulted and to return good for evil. Their calling does not assure them an exemption from insult and evil.

The command to return blessing and good for insult and evil is truly a call to a transformed character. It is the character of a people who refuse to allow their enemies to define them but who seek their definition in Christ (Volf 1994: 21). It may be possible to clench our teeth and do something good for someone who has insulted and hurt us, all the while bearing ill will toward them in our hearts. But as Piper (1978–79: 230) points out, this would not be true obedience to 3:9, for "one cannot truly bless while inwardly desiring someone's hurt." He diagnoses the problem of harboring ill will as a failure to hope fully (1:13) in the life-transforming grace of Jesus Christ by reverting back to ungodly attitudes. The command of 3:9 calls us not to a legalistic and begrudging compliance but to a confidence in the transforming power of the new birth, which allows Christians in all sincerity to speak and act toward adversaries from a heart that truly desires their blessedness (Piper 1978–79: 230).

When faced with unjust insult and evil, Peter's readers must decide whether to respond in kind out of the old nature and perpetuate strife or to demonstrate the power of God's grace through radically new conduct. Although Peter is primarily addressing insults and verbal abuse coming from those outside the church, sadly all too often members within the Christian community become entangled in the downward spiral of insult for insult and evil for evil. The psalm cited is a reminder that God's face has always been against those who do evil, whether that evil is perpetrated by members of the covenant community or by those outside. Therefore, the Christian's choice in how to respond to others in every situation is a choice whether to be blessed by God or opposed by God. Each such choice is a microcosm of life or death.

C. Suffering Unjustly for the Name of Christ (3:13–4:11)

After instructing his readers to live rightly in response to the animosities of Greco-Roman society, the apostle Peter now gives encouragement and exhortations that address the unjust suffering of his Christian readers, which is probably the primary reason he is writing the letter. Christ is again the example, but in this section his final victory and authority over all powers provide an example for conduct and the basis for encouragement. Given the example of Christ, who chose to suffer rather than to disobey, Christians are to put behind them the way of life that is antithetical to God's purposes, even though it may mean suffering the pain of self-denial as well as ridicule and persecution from others.

1. Suffering for Doing Good (3:13–17)

The theme of the afflicted sojourner who nevertheless lives rightly was introduced through the quotation of Ps. 33 LXX (34 Eng.) in 3:11. Phrases from that psalm echo throughout this unit as well and shape Peter's thought at least through 3:17 with themes of a good conscience and good conduct (3:16) and the preference to suffer for doing good rather than evil (3:17). Here again, as in 2:12, it appears that Peter sees enough common ground in the definition of "doing good" between the Christian and society in first-century Asia Minor that unjust suffering is not a universal and inevitable threat to the Christian believer.

Exegesis and Exposition

¹³And who is going to harm you, if you become zealous to do good? ¹⁴But even if you should suffer because of righteousness, you are blessed. "Do not be afraid of them or be troubled," ¹⁵but revere the Lord Christ in your hearts. Be prepared at all times [to give] a defense to everyone who asks you about the hope [alive] among you, ¹⁶but [do it] with humility and respect, having a good conscience so that when you are spoken against, those who malign your good conduct in Christ might be put to shame. ¹⁷For it is better to suffer [even] while doing good, if the will of God wills [it], than to suffer because of doing evil.

The apostle addresses the problem of unjust suffering directly, which is here understood to be a potential problem for all Christians, not just those in slavery (2:20–21). First Peter 3:13 follows closely on the thought of 3:12 in the previous unit, as indicated by the asserverative καί (*kai*, and) that introduces the rhetorical question: "And who is going to harm you if you become zealots of good?" Peter's rhetorical question may be an allusion to Isa. 50:9 LXX: "Look, the Lord helps me; who will harm me?" (*NETS*). The implied answer, particularly since the question comes immediately after the image of God's attentive gaze in 1 Pet. 3:12, is that no one can truly harm those who do good out of devotion to God.

As discussed above, the virtues the apostle commends in 3:8 (as well as those later in 4:3) were generally affirmed by Greco-Roman culture, perhaps with the exception of humility, which may have been viewed as a sign of weakness. The mere fact of being a Christian was apparently not yet widely perceived as evil, much less illegal. Peter's earlier instructions not to cause unnecessary offense suggest that Christianity was still new enough that it was effectively on trial by Greco-Roman society to see if and how it would match the cultural and social values of the polytheistic, pluralistic first-century Roman world. Worshipping a man who had been executed as a criminal but was reported to be alive may have seemed absurd to most, but even such an absurd belief might have been tolerated as long as its adherents continued to function as good citizens and members of society.

This irenic tenor of 1 Peter implies a time before the great persecutions arose against the church and before innocent Roman Christians suffered tortuous deaths at the order of Emperor Nero. Nero's intense persecution and slander of Christians in Rome (in 64–67) was a localized event that did not directly touch Asia Minor (as far as extant records go). Nevertheless, it would have influenced the disposition of provincial governors and the population at large toward Christians, who by Nero's action had been defined as traitors and enemies of the state. It is easier to understand Peter's optimism if he wrote before this watershed event occurred than afterward. For if Peter had asked during or after the persecutions of Nero, "And who is going to harm you if you are zealous to do good?" everyone in the room would probably have shouted, "Nero!" While it might be argued in light of Matt. 10:28 that even a martyr's death does not ultimately harm the believer, the verb κακόω (kakoō, treat badly, 1:13) as used in the NT most frequently refers to persecution and ill treatment in this life (also Acts 7:6, 19; 12:1; 14:2; 18:10). This is probably the intended sense of the verb here, for Peter's point is that even though God's eyes are on the righteous, it may nevertheless be God's will that the righteous suffer at the hands of those who are offended by righteousness. Even the Matthew passage does not deny the possibility of suffering under the power of those who can in fact kill the body.

Even though Peter affirms the general expectation that no harm comes to those who do good, the very reason Peter writes is that some of his readers have in fact been the targets of accusations (1 Pet. 2:12), ignorant talk (2:15), evil and insult (3:9; 4:14), threats (3:14), and malicious talk (3:16). Christians commonly, even if sporadically, experienced such expressions of social marginalization and alienation everywhere from the death of Jesus onward, as the book of Acts documents. In 3:14a Peter concedes that suffering is possible even when doing what is right. He uses the present optative form, πάσχοιτε (paschoite, you may suffer), indicating that though such suffering is a real possibility, it is, generally speaking, not a present one. Achtemeier (1996: 230) understands the optative to express "sporadic reality" and explains that "while Christians are not undergoing continuous suffering, they do live in an environment charged with suspicion and hostility, which has erupted and can erupt into violence and persecution at any time." Goppelt (1993: 241) thinks Peter chooses the optative here to emphasize "the openness of the situation in order to protect the Church from fatalistic resignation." Such protection from fatalistic resignation may be needed especially for those in the church who are too quick to paint themselves as martyrs and who construe every slight offense as an act of persecution. While persecution for Christ is a potentially real danger, and perhaps even inevitable from time to time, it is not to be expected at every turn.

Peter's concession that one may suffer for doing what is right qualifies his previous statement that there is enough common definition of "good" for Christians to get along in their society. Here he concedes that his readers may run up against those who do not like or agree with the Christian definition of what it means to live righteously. He later acknowledges in 4:3–4 that by abstaining from socially acceptable practices because they are not right, the Christian indicts a society that approvingly practices them. Peter observes the result: those who feel accused and indicted by right-living Christians "heap abuse on you."

Precisely in this situation—when Christians are abused simply for refusing to participate in ungodly practices of their society—Peter describes them as "blessed." The words "blessed" and "suffering" do not seem to go together, and so one can well wonder in what sense Peter can claim that those who suffer for doing good are blessed. Michaels (1988: 186) defines "blessed" in this passage as indicating those "privileged recipients of divine favor," and Goppelt (1993: 242) suggests "participants in God's salvation." Peter pronounces his readers "blessed" only twice, here and in 4:14, where in a similar context the believer is being insulted because of the name of Christ. Peter's use of the word "blessed" is almost certainly another echo of Jesus' teaching, this time as recorded in Matt. 5:10: "Blessed are those who are persecuted because of righteousness, for theirs is the kingdom of heaven" (TNIV).[1] Blessing may encompass the joys and riches of life, but for Peter the privilege of living rightly because of Christ and suffering for it is nothing less than a blessing, a sign of God's favor and evidence of one's salvation.

The Christian's response to unjust suffering is stated both negatively and positively: (1) do not be afraid of the opposition, and (2) remain faithful to Christ ("revere the Lord Christ in your hearts"). By invoking an exhortation from Isa. 8:12 in 3:14b, Peter reminds his readers that they are not the first of God's people to experience threat: "Do not be afraid of them or be troubled." Peter is quoting Isa. 8:12 LXX, Isaiah's prophetic encouragement to the southern kingdom of Judah not to fear the allied kings of Israel and Aram (Syria) or the great power of Assyria, which will sweep both neighboring adversaries away. Isaiah warns the nations opposing Jerusalem, "And whatever counsel you take, the Lord will scatter it; and whatever word you speak, it will not remain for you,

---

1. For discussion of how 1 Peter echoes the teachings of Jesus while not being dependent on the Synoptic Gospels, see Gundry 1966–67; Gundry 1974; Best 1970.

because the Lord God is with us" (Isa. 8:10 LXX, *NETS*, emphasis added). The Lord exhorts Isaiah and his hearers not to fear the threat, for the Lord God is with them, and so it is the Lord they are to fear (Isa. 8:13). First Peter takes the quote up in an entirely different historical context, but with the same purpose of encouraging his readers in the face of threat, applying it to Christians who are not facing hostile powers beyond their borders but adversaries from within their own society.

In 1 Pet. 3:14 the quotation of Isa. 8:12 literally reads, "Their fear do not fear," which requires a context to disambiguate the word modified by the possessive pronoun "their." Does it mean "Do not fear the things these people fear" or "Do not be afraid of these people"? In both the Hebrew and the Greek versions of Isaiah, the first meaning is intended, for the words modified by "their" is "these people," referring to Isaiah's compatriots in Jerusalem and Judah who are overwhelmed by their fear of Aram and Israel. The Lord spoke to Isaiah, warning him not to cave in to the same fears. But the quote sits differently in 1 Peter, with an altered sense.

Although 1 Peter reproduces the quote faithfully, a minor change from a singular pronoun to a plural contextualizes it for a completely different situation. The third-person singular pronoun αὐτοῦ (*autou*, of it), whose antecedent in the OT text is "this people," has been replaced by the third-person plural αὐτῶν (*autōn*, of them), modifying an unspecified entity but presumably referring to the members of society at large. Therefore, the sense of the fear in 3:14 changes to "Do not be afraid of what these people threaten," that is, those who may harm you even if you are eager to do good (3:13–14).

The LXX of Isa. 8:12–13 instructs readers to "sanctify the Lord himself" (κύριον αὐτὸν ἁγιάσατε, *kyrion auton hagiasate*). But Peter makes one insertion that significantly changes the quotation. Rather than fearing their adversaries, the Asian Christians are to revere the Lord—whom Peter identifies as Christ by substituting τὸν Χριστόν (*ton Christon*, the Christ) in the quotation where the LXX reads αὐτόν (*auton*, himself): κύριον δὲ τὸν Χριστὸν ἁγιάσατε (*kyrion de ton Christon hagiasate*). There is some grammatical ambiguity about whether the construction should be read as predicative (revere Christ as Lord) or appositional (revere the Lord, namely, Christ). The syntax is constrained by that of the LXX quotation into which Peter introduces Christ, but probably without intending to change the sense of the quotation; hence, preference should be for the appositional reading. If so, this is an example where a NT writer freely identifies Jesus Christ with the Lord, Yahweh of the OT (see additional note on 3:15).

Such changes to the LXX quotations have been made by the author of 1 Peter in order to contextualize the quotation for a new theological and sociopolitical situation. Christ is identified as the Lord whom the readers are to revere. The nature of the threatening adversaries is different, but the basis for the command not to fear remains the same, because "the Lord God is with us" (Isa. 8:10 LXX). If they trust in the Lord and remain faithful to his calling in their lives, Christ will be for them a sanctuary, but if not, they will stumble and fall (cf. 1 Pet. 2:7–10).

Peter's exhortation in 3:15 has been used to justify Christian philosophy and apologetics: "Be prepared at all times [to give] a defense to everyone who asks you about the hope in you." While that is a legitimate application of this verse, the apostle Peter did not have in mind the professional or academic field of Christian apologetics. Nor does the term "defense" (ἀπολογίαν, apologian) necessarily imply that the Christians to whom Peter writes are being tried in a court of law (though it was construed in that sense by previous interpreters who assumed that formal persecution was the historical background). Rather, Peter is concerned that Christian believers be able humbly and respectfully to defend their hope in Christ to anyone who might ask, even if legal charges are in view for some.

"Hope" in 1 Peter is a term referring to the future aspect of salvation, for it is into a living hope that Christians have been reborn through the resurrection of Christ (1:3). It is this very hope that separates and alienates them from pagans and invites the kind of conflict that Peter has in view. The "hope in you [pl.]" (ἐν ὑμῖν, en hymin) should be understood not so much as the hope within an individual believer but as the hope that is among believers, namely, their shared belief in the gospel of Jesus Christ that defines and unites them as Christians.

Peter's vision for how the Christian is to relate to even a hostile social situation is thought provoking. He does not advocate a withdrawal from society for safety's sake or a hostile counterattack on society. Rather, as Goppelt (1993: 243) puts it, "Faith does not close doors to relationships with other people out of either fear or hate. It turns, rather, in openness to others just as it turns to God." The Christian community may be a colony in a strange land, but as Achtemeier (1996: 234) observes, "Cultural isolation is not to be the route taken by the Christian community. It is to live its life openly in the midst of the unbelieving world, and just as openly to be prepared to explain the reasons for it."[2]

This verse raises the question of how many Christians today could make an articulate statement of the reasons for their faith in Christ in terms that would be understood by modern society. Most "testimonies," when given at all, are given in a Christian gathering, using the jargon of the church, which makes perfect sense to the converted, but in terms that have little meaning for those who are not already believers. While such practice is an important part of a Christian's development, according to

2. Those living where Christianity is a capital offense must of course be cautious about their application of this passage in such a hostile setting that is unlike Peter's original context.

Peter, believers must be able to relate the Christian faith to unbelievers by addressing their questions in terms they find meaningful.

It is interesting that Peter finds it necessary in 3:16 to admonish believers that they must keep a clear conscience when testifying to the reason they hope in Christ. This speaks to at least two issues: walking the talk and talking rightly. First, an effective testimony requires a clear conscience regarding one's personal integrity before the Lord. One cannot explain the hope we have in Christ while living in ways that contradict that hope. Second, even the best-intentioned testimony must be conducted in an appropriate manner. If offense is to be taken, it should be over the content of the gospel message, not because the message was offered in a manner that invalidates Christ's love for seekers. The Christian testimony must reflect humility and respect for the hearer.

Achtemeier (1996: 234) understands that the "respect" (φόβος, *phobos*, fear, 3:16) Peter mentions is reverence toward God, not respect for others. But Peter elsewhere teaches that one way fear of God is expressed (1:17; 2:17) is by respecting others (2:18; 3:1, 7). Here in 3:16a the phrase "with humility and respect" (μετὰ πραΰτητος καὶ φόβου, *meta praütētos kai phobou*) qualifies the manner in which the explanation for Christian hope is to be offered, and therefore *phobou* (fear), like humility, refers to an attitude toward others that is rooted in one's attitude toward God.

The purpose of a respectful defense of Christianity when spoken against is so that "those who malign your good conduct in Christ might be put to shame" (3:16). In modern society, shame most often refers to the emotion that is akin to embarrassment or guilt. But the Christian's testimony is not intended to embarrass those to whom it is offered. In the OT and Jewish writings, shame connotes a social status, often in reference to utter defeat and disgrace in battle. Shame means "to be overthrown and left at the mercy of one's enemies" (Michaels 1988: 190–91). Scripture often promises that those who are faithful to God will not in the end be shamed, but their opponents will be. This does not refer to emotion but to standing. Rather than being intimidated by whatever opposition his readers encounter in their society, Peter wants them to respond with a positive and effective explanation of the gospel. Instead of allowing fear to drive them to use the same tactics of insult and malicious talk against their opponents, they are to respond in a way that is beyond reproach. The humble and respectful testimony of believing Christians defeats the malicious talk of those who would malign the faith.

Even so, Peter is well aware that the Christian cannot expect to be exempt from suffering. And so Peter continues in 3:17, "For it is better to suffer even while doing good, if the will of God wills it, than to suffer because of doing evil." Although the immediate outcome may be suffering, the Christian is called to live constantly by a higher ethical standard than quid pro quo (tit for tat). Being mistreated or maliciously slandered because one is a Christian does not give license for a response in kind. It is exactly at those moments when a believer may feel the least like responding with a gracious testimony of hope in Christ that it is most important to do so.

First Peter 3:17 makes the interesting statement that "it is better" to suffer for doing good than for doing evil. This "better than" proverbial form is found in OT Wisdom literature and also in Jesus' teaching in the Synoptic Gospels, as in Matt. 5:29, "It is better for you to lose one part of your body than for your whole body to be thrown into hell" (TNIV). A thought similar to 1 Pet. 3:17, albeit in a different form, is also part of the common Greek wisdom tradition (Achtemeier 1996: 237–38). For instance, Plato writes that suffering injustice is less shameful than doing injustice (Plato, *Gorgias* 474c). It is often difficult to determine whether NT writers are thinking from the traditions of Judaism or of Hellenism or even whether a sharp distinction can be made between the two. As the household codes show (see comments on 2:18–3:7), Peter does affirm some elements of Greek moral philosophy and may be referring to that tradition here. However, the presentation of eschatological alternatives is not completely absent because Scripture defines the terms used, even if expressed in Greek wisdom forms. In other words, what Plato means by acting "unrighteously" and what the apostle Peter means by it are no doubt quite different. The apostle's teaching is not defined by the wisdom of great thinkers, such as Plato, but is based on the eschatological reality spoken of in Scripture as ultimately revealed in Christ.

Such sayings in the form "It is better to . . . than to . . ." often present eschatological alternatives (Michaels 1988: 191–92). Michaels (1966–67: 398) paraphrases 3:17 to emphasize its eschatological implication: "If it should be God's will that we suffer, it is better to suffer now, as doers of good at the hands of evil men, than on the day of visitation, when these same evil-doers shall receive their just punishment from the eternal Judge of all men."

First Peter 3:17 also raises the important question of whether a loving God truly wills the Christian to suffer (see also 4:19). The Greek of 3:17 seems rather explicit: εἰ θέλοι τὸ θέλημα τοῦ θεοῦ (*ei theloi to thelēma tou theou*, if the will of God wills), but again the verb (*theloi*) is in the present optative. Just as the possibility of suffering for doing good (3:14) is expressed in the optative mood, meaning that suffering is a possibility but not a certainty, the will of God might possibly will a Christian to suffer for doing good. Peter affirms that it is not God's purpose to make Christians suffer. But the very fact that at least some of the Christians of Asia Minor (and many others since) *have* suffered unjustly for living rightly implies that it was in some sense God's will for them at that moment in that situation. J. H. Elliott (2000: 635) expresses it well: "The qualification, *if this should be God's will*, refers to suffering *for doing what is right* and not simply suffering per se. The point is not that God wills suffering but that God *wills doing what is right* rather than doing what is wrong . . . , even if and when this results in suffering" (emphasis original). Elliott correctly emphasizes that God wills for his people to live faithfully and to do what is right even if the response of an unbelieving world causes them to suffer. This is a quite different concept from "God causes Christians to suffer in this life for their spiritual well-being" (Kistemaker 1987: 137). While the thought that God's will may include suffering could raise issues of theodicy for some, Peter's affirmation is meant to be taken as an encouragement. If suffering is within God's will, it is also within God's sovereign control. And thus Christian suffering is determined not by the will of one's adversaries but by the will of one's heavenly Father.

The apostle Peter is therefore confident that even if it may be necessary (δέον, *deon*) for Christians to suffer various trials, it is only "for a little while" (1:6–7), after which God will restore and strengthen (5:10). Peter acknowledges that suffering because one is a Christian is inevitable (necessary) whenever genuine Christian faith encounters hostile opposition, a reality that prevails until the Lord returns. It is not God's purpose that Christians suffer per se; it is God's will that Christians remain faithful and obedient even if suffering results. The encounter of Christian faith with hostility therefore becomes a test that must be faced by Christians. If a Christian turns away from Christ in order to avoid suffering insult and alienation from unbelieving friends, neighbors, or colleagues, then that person's faith is thereby shown to be lacking. God wills the Christian to suffer in the sense that God wills the Christian to remain faithful even if suffering is the consequence. Such a testing situation allows Christians to see their faith for what it is—or is not.

There was a time in my young Christian life when I thought that vicarious atonement meant vicarious suffering—that because Jesus suffered, I didn't have to! The idea that God would never will anyone to suffer for doing right and that all suffering must be contrary to God's will is an idea that must be discarded if Peter's message is taken seriously. Christians are to follow in Christ's footsteps. Since God willed Christ to suffer, then intentional and purposeful suffering can also be expected to lie along the path of the believer. But Peter encourages such sufferers again with the example of Christ in 3:18–22. Christ suffered purposefully and only for a time. His suffering was the way to his victory over all beings and authorities. Those who share in Christ's suffering because of their faith in him will not be defeated but will also share in Christ's victory.

Additional Note

3:15. G. Howard (1977: 80–81) presents an interesting idea that considers the word "Christ" (Χριστόν, *Christon*) to be a secondary change made by scribes. He proposes that the author of 1 Peter originally used the Hebrew Tetragrammaton at this place in the quotation as, he argues, was the custom. At some stage of textual history, the Tetragrammaton here and throughout the NT (and the LXX?) was replaced by the Greek word κύριος (*kyrios*, Lord), which had already been used in Christian tradition to refer to Christ. Howard concludes it was not Peter's intention to identify Christ with Yahweh. Rather, such identification was a later mistaken construal made possible by the ambiguous use of *kyrios* to refer both to God and Christ. Howard's theory must presume that all LXX manuscripts were similarly handled, for *kyrios* is frequently found throughout the Greek OT where the Hebrew has the Tetragrammaton. In any case, Peter's theology is untouched, for he claims the divinity of Christ throughout the letter.

2. Christ's Victory over Unjust Suffering (3:18–22)

In a previous section of the letter (1 Pet. 2:18–25), the apostle points to Christ's unjust suffering in the flesh as the example for Christian living. This passage explains that it is better to suffer for doing good than for doing evil (3:17) because Christ, by the power of his resurrection and ascension, has defeated all the powers of evil and will destroy them along with all who practice evil (just as in the days of Noah). Therefore, suffering unjustly for doing good is evidence that one is on the right side of the eschatological divide. Unjust suffering for doing good, as God defines good, means that one is living out that pledge to God taken at baptism for a lifetime devoted to serving him. Just as Christ's unjust suffering led to his vindication, Peter encourages his readers that the unjust suffering they experience will not be the final word, for they have already been vindicated when Christ arose from death.

a. The difficulties of this passage
b. Christ leads us to God through death in the flesh to life in the Spirit (3:18)
c. Christ's proclamation to the spirits (3:19–20a)
d. The Noah story in Asia Minor
e. The development of the alternative interpretations
f. Noah and Christian baptism (3:20b–21)
g. Christ's ascension as victory (3:22)

Exegesis and Exposition

[17][For it is better to suffer even while doing good . . . than to suffer because of doing evil] [18]because Christ also ⌜suffered⌝ once and for all for sins, the righteous one on behalf of the unrighteous, so that he might bring you to God. He was put to death in [the realm of] the flesh but made alive in [the realm of] the Spirit. [19]In [this realm] also he went and proclaimed to the spirits in prison [20]who in times past disobeyed when the patience of God waited in the days of Noah while the ark was being built, in which a few—that is, eight people—were saved through water. [21]This [flood] also symbolizes baptism, ⌜which⌝ now saves you—not putting off the filth of flesh, but rather the pledge of a good conscience to God—through the resurrection of Jesus Christ, [22]who is at the right hand of

God, having gone into heaven, with angels and authorities and powers subject to him.

a. The Difficulties of This Passage

As Goppelt (1993: 247) observes, this is the third christological passage in 1 Peter (see 1:18–21; 2:22–25), and all three take as their starting point the suffering and death of Jesus. Whereas 2:22–25 emphasizes the redeeming power of Christ's crucifixion, this passage highlights the conquering power of his resurrection and ascension. Moreover, it grounds the believer's willingness to suffer unjustly for the sake of Christ in the fact of Christ's willingness to suffer unjustly for the sake of believers so that he might bring them to God.

This passage in 1 Peter is the one most debated and written about; from the earliest days of the church, it has been understood in very different ways. Even the usually dogmatic Martin Luther commented as he struggled with this passage, "This is a strange text and certainly a more obscure passage than any other passage in the New Testament. I still do not know for sure what the apostle meant" (Pelikan 1967: 113). Even among today's interpreters this passage has the reputation for being perhaps the most difficult in the NT. Certainly the passage assumes a familiarity with images and traditions alien to modern culture. Moreover, there are an unusual number of textual and lexical difficulties within these few verses.

One common understanding of the passage is enshrined in the Apostles' Creed in the words "he descended into hell," which by virtue of their placement within the creed suggests it happened between Jesus' crucifixion and resurrection. However popular the Apostles' Creed may be—unlike the Nicene Creed, which contains no such statement (Scharlemann 1989: 311)—it was not written or adopted by any early official church council (Williams 1999: 81). The phrase first appeared around AD 400 in Rufinus's exposition of a Roman creed that included the phrase "he descended into hell" instead of the phrase "and was buried." It therefore appears that the "descent" was at one time merely a graphic way of referring to burial, or the "descent" into the grave, and it is still so understood by the Westminster Larger Catechism (Q & A 50; Williams 1999: 81–82). Many modern editions of the Apostles' Creed omit the statement in recognition of its redundancy now that the consensus of scholarship has largely abandoned the *descensus* interpretation (explained below; see Williams 1999: 89–90 for a discussion of confessional integrity on this matter).

A second ancient understanding is that the preincarnate Christ preached repentance through Noah to the sinful people of that generation, who were about to be judged by the waters of the flood. But since the appearance of Dalton's (1965) magisterial work *Christ's Proclama-*

tion to the Spirits, the passage has been understood a third way by the majority of commentators: that it refers to Christ's victory proclamation following his resurrection as he ascended to take his rightful place in heaven as the ruler over all.

This intriguing passage is fraught with problems that obscure its interpretation—text-critical problems, grammatical ambiguities, lexical uncertainties, theological issues, as well as the question of what literary and theological background the author is assuming. Surveys of the passage's convoluted history of interpretation can be found in Dalton (1965: 15–41), Reicke (1946: 7–51), and most recently in Feinberg (1986: 309–12).

The exegetical questions basically come down to these: Where did Christ go? When did he go? To whom did he speak? What did he say? Even if this passage is more obscure than we might wish, two clear points anchor the point of the text: (1) Being linked with 3:13–17 by ὅτι καί (*hoti kai*, because also, 3:18), the 3:18–22 passage is intended to ground the immediately preceding claim that it is better to suffer for doing good than for doing evil. (2) Even though Christ suffered unjustly to death for doing good, that suffering was not the defeat it may have appeared to be but was instead a victory over all angels, authorities, and powers (3:22). Suffering unjustly for doing good is therefore not the final judgment about who is in the right. Moreover, Peter is keen to impress on his readers that nothing that can come against them is beyond the control of the risen and living Christ (3:22). Hence, if they suffer for being Christians, it is within God's will (3:17). Therefore, this passage, as obscure as its details may be, functions as a word of encouragement to Christians oppressed by the powers they faced. The interpretation of its obscurities and ambiguities should be governed by its function within this immediate context in the letter.

b. Christ Leads Us to God through Death in the Flesh to Life in the Spirit (3:18)

First Peter 3:18 provides the reason for Peter's claim in 3:17 that it is better to suffer for doing good than for doing evil: "Because Christ also suffered once for sins, the righteous one on behalf of the unrighteous, so that he might bring you to God. He was put to death in the realm of the flesh but made alive in the realm of the Spirit" (see additional note on 3:18). The suffering Christ had previously been held up as an example for the Christian in 2:19–25. By his suffering death, Christ "brings you" (*hymas prosagagē*) to God. Previously in the letter, Peter emphasized the need for Christians to follow in the footsteps of Jesus (2:21). Therefore, Christ's death opens the way for Christians to follow him through death and into the presence of the Father. Peter here exhorts Christians to identify with the heroic and victorious Christ if they intend to follow in his footsteps. It is better to suffer for doing good, as Christ did, because that is the way to follow Christ to victory.

Christ's suffering included his death (see additional note on 3:18 for a discussion of the textual problem here), which was once for all (ἅπαξ, *hapax*, once) and served the redemptive purpose "to bring you to God" (3:18). The implication of the connection between 3:17 and 3:18 is that even if a Christian were to suffer to the point of unjust martyrdom for the sake of Christ, such suffering is both purposeful and victorious because death is not the final word. Christians follow in Christ's footsteps through death to victory. Although the death of Christ was uniquely redemptive, those who suffer and even die unjustly simply because they are Christians are on the right side of the mysterious way in which God has willed to work out his redemptive plan throughout history. It therefore is better to suffer for doing good and be right with God than to suffer for doing evil. Consequently, the "persecution of believing Christians is a victory, not a defeat" (Dalton 1965: 85).

The emphasis on Christ's suffering in this letter is remarkable when its source is considered, for Peter the disciple has previously so adamantly rejected any thought of a suffering Messiah when Jesus announced what lay ahead (Mark 8:32; Matt. 16:22). But Peter the apostle has come to understand that Christ's suffering of death was "once for sins so that he might bring you to God." The phrase περὶ ἁμαρτιῶν (*peri hamartiōn*, for sins) is used repeatedly throughout the LXX of the Pentateuch to refer to the sin offerings of the sacrificial system. Peter has come to understand Christ's suffering to death as a unique sin offering that provides access to God, making it possible to be born again into the living hope that Christ's resurrection to eternal life has accomplished (1:3). While the world may have viewed Jesus as a common criminal executed by Roman authority with probable cause, Peter describes him as δίκαιος (*dikaios*, righteous) and undeserving of the death he suffered. But Jesus did not die just an undeserved death. Jesus died a vicarious death on behalf of the unrighteous. The unrighteous who recognize the atoning nature of Christ's sacrificial death and become Christians must therefore live righteously, which means that it is better to suffer unjustly if necessary (3:17). In this way the Christian believer identifies with Christ, who stands alive forevermore on God's side of the moral divide between righteousness and evil.

First Peter 3:18–19 continues to explain Christ' victory. Christ was "put to death in flesh but made alive in spirit" (θανατωθεὶς μὲν σαρκὶ ζῳοποιηθεὶς δὲ πνεύματι, *thanatōtheis men sarki zōopoiētheis de pneumati*). The sense of the opening prepositional phrase in 3:19, ἐν ᾧ καί (*en hō kai*, in which also, at which time also), is crucial to the three different interpretations of when Christ preached. The sense of these dative phrases (temporal? locative?) in verses 18 and 19 will determine which of the three basic interpretations of the passage is adopted.

In order to adopt the first interpretation, that Christ preached through Noah to Noah's generation, the phrase "made alive in spirit" must somehow refer to Christ's preincarnate state while doing justice to the emphatic contrast with "put to death in flesh." In a second view, if Christ preached during the three days when his body was in the tomb, that flesh-spirit contrast must refer to the two components of Christ's human being: his human body, which was put to death, and his human soul (or spirit?), which went to preach. If so, in what sense was his soul "made alive" when his body was put to death? One could argue that his soul remained alive, but that is not what the text says.

A third interpretation has emerged as the consensus view of modern interpreters: the flesh-spirit contrast is not between Christ's body and soul but between his two states of existence—in the realm of earthly human life before his death and in his glorified state of existence after the resurrection. Notice, however, that the answer to the question of when Christ preached does not completely settle the other questions of where he preached, to whom he preached, or the content of his preaching. Moreover, within each of the three basic interpretations, different answers to each of these questions can be found, resulting in a labyrinth of exegetical options, each of which has no clearly overwhelming claim to certainty (see J. H. Elliott 2000: 648–50 for a detailed enumeration of the several major possibilities). Erickson (1995: 137) calculates 180 different exegetical combinations, in theory.

The interpretation that the preincarnate Christ preached through Noah to those of Noah's generation has a long and venerable tradition within the history of interpretation. It was taught by Augustine, was repeated by Aquinas (Dalton 1965: 35), and was current during the Reformation (Feinberg 1986: 311). Augustine offered this interpretation in response to the other competing interpretation enshrined in the Apostles' Creed—that Christ descended into hell between his death and resurrection—because that interpretation was raising the theological problem of possible postmortem conversion (people being saved after death). Augustine, a Latin father, could not read the Greek NT well and was not primarily interested in exegesis; he was concerned with protecting the theology of the finality of death with regard to a decision for conversion. So it was his rejection of postmortem conversion that motivated his search for an alternate understanding. He offered the interpretation that Christ preached through Noah's lips to Noah's contemporaries. In our times this has become a minority position but continues to be defended (Clark 1972: 130; Erickson 1995: 140; Feinberg 1986; Grudem 1986). The idea that Christ spoke through Noah does accord well with 1:11, which speaks of the Spirit of the preincarnate Christ preaching in times past through the prophets. But the test of its viability must be how adequately it addresses the syntax of 3:18 and the opening phrase of verse 19.

The syntax of 3:18 forms a contrasting parallel between two passive participles, θανατωθείς (*thanatōtheis*, put to death) and ζῳοποιηθείς (*zōopoiētheis*, made alive), each respectively followed by contrasting datives, σαρκί (*sarki*, in flesh) and πνεύματι (*pneumati*, in spirit). This contrast qualifies the purpose clause in 3:18, "so that he might bring you to God." The particles μέν (*men*, on the one hand) and δέ (*de*, but) indicate that the contrast is probably to be understood as concessive (*although* he was put to death in flesh, he was made alive in spirit). Moreover, the parallel syntax suggests that both datives following the participles have the same sense. There are, however, at least four ways of construing them: (1) as locatives: "in flesh, . . . in spirit" (Grudem 1988: 156); (2) as datives of respect or reference: "with respect/reference to flesh, . . . with respect/reference to spirit" (Clowney 1988: 157; Michaels 1988: 204; Scharlemann 1989: 316; Selwyn 1958: 196); (3) as instrumental: "by flesh, . . . by the Spirit" (Achtemeier 1996: 239); or (4) as a simple conjunction: "wherein," "thereby," or "thus" (Goppelt 1993: 255; Westfall 1999: 131). Some, however, argue that the first dative is locative and the second is agency (Clark 1972: 126; Kistemaker 1987: 140). The structure of the syntax suggests that the contrast must be understood not as simply between the nouns "flesh" and "spirit" but between the entire phrases: "put to death in flesh" but "made alive in spirit."

Grudem (1986: 21) takes the datives as locatives and reads the phrase "made alive in spirit" to be a reference not specifically to the bodily resurrection of Christ but to the realm into which he was resurrected. The phrase *en hō* in 3:19, then, refers back to this spiritual realm, which he assumes to be the same spiritual realm in which the preincarnate Christ was active when he preached through Noah.

Feinberg (1986: 315, 319), who also defends the interpretation that Christ preached through Noah, understands the phrase "made alive in spirit" to be a specific reference to the bodily resurrection of Christ, which was achieved by the Holy Spirit. He takes the *en hō* of 3:19 to be a reference back to the Holy Spirit, in whom or by whom the preincarnate Christ preached through Noah to Noah's contemporaries. This understanding, however, violates the parallel syntax of the datives, for although one could argue that Christ was made alive *by* the Holy Spirit, he was not put to death *by* the flesh. This interpretation also involves taking "flesh" and "spirit" as two modes of Christ's personal existence, during the incarnation and outside it. Achtemeier (1996: 239), who disagrees with the position held by Grudem and Feinberg, nevertheless takes the datives as instrumental, or agency, and contrasts the implied subjects of the passive participles: humanity puts Christ to death, but the Spirit raises him (also Goppelt 1993: 255). It seems, however, that in context the emphasis is not between the agents of the action but between the two states of Christ's existence. Just as Christ emerged from suffering and death into resurrection life, so will Peter's oppressed readers, which is a thought more apt to Peter's purposes.

A second ancient understanding of this passage supports the view of the Alexandrian fathers, Clement and Origen, sometimes referred to as the *descensus ad inferos*, or the "harrowing of hell," that Christ descended into hell during the time between his crucifixion and his resurrection.[1] In its earliest form, this view arose not through exegesis of 3:18–22 but as an answer to two theological questions: (1) How could the saints of the OT times be redeemed by Christ, since they lived before his time? (2) Where and what was Jesus Christ doing between his death and resurrection? In fact, this passage in 1 Peter was only much later brought in to provide some biblical defense for the *descensus* view (Dalton 1965: 16). To defend this interpretation, one must take the contrast in 3:18 to be between flesh (*sarx*), understood as "body," and spirit (*pneuma*), understood as "soul." Of the six times *sarx* is found elsewhere in 1 Peter, only two occurrences might possibly be construed as a reference to the physical body (3:21; 4:1); the rest refer to the realm of earthly life. *Pneuma* occurs seven other times in 1 Peter, but only two might possibly be understood as a reference to the human soul—in 3:4, where it more likely means attitude or temperament, and in the highly debated 3:19, which has been understood by some as disembodied human spirits after death. More often *pneuma* in 1 Peter refers to the divine Spirit of God (4:14), Christ (1:11), or the Holy Spirit (1:2, 12).

The word pair σῶμα (*sōma*, body) and ψυχή (*psychē*, soul) were the terms used in Greek vocabulary to distinguish between the material body and the immaterial soul, not *sarx* and *pneuma*. The word *psychē* is found five times in its plural form in 1 Peter (1:9, 22; 2:25; 3:20; 4:19), referring to the whole person or to a person's life. Peter does not seem to speak elsewhere in terms of a body-soul dichotomy. The understanding that 3:18 refers to a body-soul dichotomy arose later where the Greek Platonic dualism held sway, particularly in Alexandrian interpretation.

If only the two individual nouns *sarx* and *pneuma* are contrasted, the lexical data may seem inconclusive. But these nouns occur in two syntactically parallel phrases. More important, the body-soul contrast required by the *descensus* interpretation does not do justice to the contrast between the full phrases "put to death in flesh" and "made alive in spirit." In what sense could Christ's soul be said to have been made alive in contrast to the death of his body? Even granting that Peter could refer to the doubtful body-soul contrast with *sarx* and *pneuma,* the soul would have remained alive and active, but the text says Christ "was made alive in spirit." Christ in his entirety was put to death at the crucifixion and in his entirety was made alive at the resurrection. Since the two participles explain the phrase "so that he might bring you to God," it

---

1. For some of the art this doctrine has inspired, see Hornik and Parsons 2003.

is more likely that the contrast refers to two aspects of the redemptive event: Christ's death and subsequent resurrection. This is corroborated by clear reference to his ascension in 3:22, which completes the redemptive sequence: crucifixion ("put to death"), resurrection ("made alive"), and ascension ("gone into heaven").

The verb zōopoieō (make alive) occurs elsewhere in the NT ten times, all with God, Christ, or the Holy Spirit as subject. It is sometimes found in parallel with ἐγείρω (egeirō, raise; e.g., Rom. 8:11), suggesting that here its sense is synonymous with being raised to life. Michaels (1988: 205) explains, "If 'flesh' is the sphere of human limitations, of suffering, and of death (cf. 1 Pet. 4:1), 'Spirit' is the sphere of power, vindication, and a new life." Therefore, the majority of recent commentators understand the contrasting phrases "put to death in flesh" but "made alive in spirit" to refer either to two spheres of Christ's existence (the earthly sphere versus the eschatological) or to two modes of his personal existence (in human form before his death and in glorified form after his resurrection) (Achtemeier 1996: 249; Brooks 1974: 303; Clowney 1988: 158; Dalton 1965: 14; Davids 1990: 138; J. H. Elliott 2000: 647; France 1977: 268; Goppelt 1993: 253; Hiebert 1982: 149; Hillyer 1992: 114; Horrell 1998: 70–72; Kistemaker 1987: 139–40; Marshall 1991: 121–23; Michaels 1988: 205; Williams 1999: 85). It is a tricky question whether or not to capitalize "Spirit" in 3:18. If so, it is to be understood as a reference to the eschatological reality that the Spirit completes with the resurrection of Christ.

c. Christ's Proclamation to the Spirits (3:19–20a)

A third participle in 3:19, πορευθείς (poreutheis, going), is grammatically linked to 3:18 by the phrase en hō kai. These three participles form a series: Christ was put to death, he was made alive, he went. After intervening verses, the participle poreutheis is repeated resumptively in 3:22 to refer to the ascension. Thus, the three elements of the redemptive event are in view in 3:18–19: the crucifixion, the resurrection, and the ascension. The relationship between the "going" of 3:19 and the death and resurrection of 3:18 is specified by the prepositional phrase en hō, where the antecedent of the relative pronoun is pneumati. The phrase can be understood as locative ("in the realm of the Spirit he went"), temporal ("at the time the Spirit made him alive he went"), or instrumental ("by the [power of] the Spirit he went"). Achtemeier (1996: 252–53) understands it as instrumental: "In addition (καί) to being raised from the dead by the (power of the) Spirit, Christ went, by that same Spirit, and in risen form" (emphasis added). Today most interpreters take it to be temporal with respect to the resurrection, meaning that at the time when Christ was made alive in spirit or was in that state, he went and preached (Boring 1999: 140; Dalton 1965: 14; Davids 1990: 138; J. H.

Elliott 2000: 652; Michaels 1988: 205; Reicke 1964: 109; Selwyn 1958: 197). If the phrase "in the spirit" of 3:18 is taken to mean at or immediately after Christ's resurrection, there is little difference between the locative, temporal, or instrumental sense of the prepositional phrase *en hō* in 3:19. But since the participles seem to define a sequence of events by which Christ "led you to God" (his death, resurrection, and, as will be argued, ascension), a temporal sense seems most apt.

First Peter 3:19–20 forms the exegetical crux of this passage: "In which also he went and proclaimed to the spirits in prison who in times past disobeyed when the patience of God waited in the days of Noah while the ark was being built, in which a few—that is, eight people—were saved through water." This statement raises the questions of where Christ went, who were the "spirits in prison," and what he said to them. Although the Apostles' Creed preserves church tradition referring to the "descent" of Christ, the verb in the text is notably not καταβαίνω (*katabainō*, descend) but the more general verb πορεύομαι (*poreuomai*), which simply means "to go." It might still be legitimate to understand Christ's going as a descent if the text itself located the "prison" below, but it does not. In the absence of background knowledge contemporaneous with 1 Peter, the Western church used its own traditional understanding of hell as located below and inferred the "going" to be a descent. It should be noted, however, that none of the titles used at that time to describe the place of the dead—Hades, Tartarus, Sheol—are found in this text. Furthermore, the place of dead people is not elsewhere in the NT referred to with the word "prison" (φυλακή, *phylakē*). Moreover, it is highly debated whether "the spirits" are the souls of deceased people or demonic beings.

The answers to the questions of where and to whom Christ preached and how this connects to the Noah story may be found in Jewish tradition as preserved in the pseudonymous book of 1 Enoch. However, the language and imagery of 1 Enoch are so bizarre and unfamiliar to modern readers that while it no doubt provides the background to 1 Pet. 3:19–20, it hardly resolves the mystery of these verses. The original readers, likely more familiar with the Enoch traditions than we, would probably not have been so mystified. According to Gen. 5:21–24, Enoch, the seventh generation from Adam, "walked with God," and then God "took him away." Despite only this passing reference in Genesis, Enoch developed into a prominent figure in ancient Jewish tradition, and at the time the NT was written, there was a highly esteemed book allegedly written by him. The book of 1 En. 12.1–2 explains that when Enoch was taken away from the earth, he went to dwell with "the Watchers and the holy ones" (Isaac, *OTP* 1:19). The tradition of the Watchers is apparently an embellishment of the mysterious story of Gen. 6:1–4, where "the sons of God went to the daughters of men and had children by them" (6:4

LXX). In Genesis, this story immediately precedes the Noah narrative and appears to give justification for the flood.

First Enoch tells a similar but more elaborate tale. The Watchers were the fallen angels who had abandoned heaven (12.4), slept with human women (15.3), and produced children, referred to as "giants" from whose bodies "evil spirits" have come (15.9). These evil spirits have taught people "deeds of shame, injustice, and sin" (13.2) and will continue to corrupt the earth until "the day of the great conclusion, until the great age is consummated, until everything is concluded" (16.1). The Watchers appeal to Enoch to intercede with God on behalf of themselves and the evil progeny they have produced. Enoch obliges and returns with God's proclamation to the Watchers: "[You will] not be able to ascend into heaven unto all eternity, but you shall remain inside the earth, imprisoned all the days of eternity." Moreover, the Watchers would see the destruction of their sons (referred to as "the spirits") because the petitions for themselves and for their sons (the spirits) will not be heard by God (14.5–6). These "spirits" that came from the bodies of the giants fathered by the Watchers through human women were the cause of the human evil that led to the great flood during the time of Enoch's grandson, Noah.

This tradition as documented in 1 En. 12–16 appears to offer a background that fits well with 1 Pet. 3:19–20. Both involve spirits who receive a proclamation from God and who are closely associated with the story of Noah, which immediately follows in both Gen. 6:9–9:29 and 1 Pet. 3:20. If this is the assumed tradition behind 1 Pet. 3:19, then the spirits to whom Christ preached should be understood as fallen angels and/or demonic spirits.[2] Their imprisonment represents in spatial terms God's restraining power over them, and the message Christ preached to them is the confirmation that "the day of the great conclusion," first announced by the flood, is now upon them. Christ's ascension itself may have been the proclamation of their defeat (Bandstra 2003). In other words, the apostle Peter is identifying Jesus Christ as the victor over all evil in both the spirit and the human worlds forevermore.

Despite the several apt parallels between 1 Pet. 3:19–20 and the Enoch-Noah tradition, some interpreters question using it as a background for exegesis, since Peter does not mention Enoch explicitly (see the first additional note on 3:19). Furthermore, the book of 1 Enoch would have to have been well known among Peter's readers for an allusion to it to be recognized, which some think is unlikely (Grudem 1986: 16–18). Some believe it is unlikely that Peter's (presumably) Gentile readers, who stood outside the Jewish religious tradition, would have known 1 Enoch, especially because the geographical range of its importance

2. For a discussion of "two or three frames of discourse or associated bundles" in the exegesis of this passage, see Westfall 1999: 125–29.

beyond the Ethiopian church is unknown. However, Peter's allusion to the tradition of the Watchers does not necessarily require a literary knowledge of the book of 1 Enoch. The book of 1 Enoch may preserve a tradition that was more generally and widely known. Many people today who are familiar with the concept of purgatory are neither Roman Catholic nor able to cite the religious texts in which that doctrine is stated. Only a general knowledge of the role of the evil spirits in Noah's flood story would have been sufficient to make Peter's point. Moreover, other evidence suggests the importance of the flood story to Asia Minor, since that is where Noah's ark allegedly settled on dry ground (see discussion below). The fact that Peter neither refers to Enoch nor quotes from 1 Enoch shows that he is not interested in accrediting or exegeting 1 Enoch but is simply using a tradition that would have been familiar to his readers.

For those who knew the Enoch-Noah tradition of the condemnation of the Watchers and the evil spirits that came from their progeny, Peter's point is that Christ's resurrection and ascension have given him victory over them and the evil they incited on earth. And it is certain that the residents of Asia Minor, whether Jew or Gentile, were familiar at least with the Noah tradition. For, in addition to the biblical account found in Genesis, there are four extant accounts of a great flood that were indigenous to Asia Minor (Trebilco 1991: 88–90).

d. The Noah Story in Asia Minor

The four indigenous flood stories of Asia Minor disagree with the biblical account to the extent that it is almost certain that they descended from an independent tradition. Sometime after a large Jewish population arrived in Asia Minor around 205 BC as colonists in newly founded Seleucid towns, they observed that the name of a town in central Asia Minor, Apamea Kibotos (modern Dinar), included the Greek word for "ark" (κιβωτός, kibōtos) as found in the LXX of the Genesis flood story. From this they inferred that the town's name must have preserved the location where Noah's ark had come to rest, probably on the nearby mountain. While this inference was probably incorrect (Trebilco 1991: 90–91), Noah was nevertheless the most prominently known biblical figure in Asia Minor even among Gentiles. His enduring fame is attested by an amazing series of Noah coins minted over the reigns of five Roman emperors from Septimius Severus (AD 193–211) through Trebonianus Gallus (251–53). The coins depict Noah and his wife on one side, with the image of the Roman emperor on the other (Trebilco 1991: 86–88). Given the lexical connection between the LXX and Apamea Kibotos in the centuries before Christ and the remarkable interest in Noah during the later Roman period in Asia Minor, it seems likely that even Peter's

Gentile readers knew enough about the traditions of what caused the flood to understand 1 Pet. 3:19–20.

Moreover, Trebilco points out that Noah holds a prominent place in the Sibylline Oracles 1.128–29 (which may have been written in Asia Minor between 30 BC and AD 70). In them Noah is described as a preacher of righteousness and repentance. Consistent with the Greek tradition that the Sibyls were female prophets, there is a tradition that these oracles were originally given by Noah's daughter or daughter-in-law (Momigliano 1987: 138). The oracles contain sermons preached by Noah that focus not on conversion to the Israelite religion but on righteous living (Trebilco 1991: 98). Noah's authority over the people of Asia Minor is bolstered when one oracle (Sib. Or. 1.261–67) declares that Noah was in fact the Apamean flood hero who had first settled there and from whom they themselves descended. Therefore, the Asian readers of these oracles "should now repent, stand in awe of the Great God, propitiate him and live a holy life, avoiding the sins of their ancestors, who sneered at Noah rather than responding to his preaching" (Trebilco 1991: 99).

If Trebilco's analysis is correct, the previous associations of Noah as a preacher of righteousness and repentance with the residents of Asia Minor are congenial to Peter's message of holy living written to an audience in the same geographical region.[3] Peter brings Noah into his letter at this point not because it is a baptismal homily that needs a reference to water, as past interpreters have claimed (see "Noah and Christian Baptism" below), but in order to connect Christ's victory to the Noah tradition so prominent in the culture in which his readers lived. Peter further reinforces the connection between Noah and Christianity by drawing the analogy between Noah's deliverance from the floodwaters and Christian baptism (see discussion below).

Both Enoch and his grandson, Noah, delivered a message of condemnation to those directly involved in the evil that provoked the flood. The very act of building the ark was a condemnation of the wicked generation in which Noah lived. "By faith Noah, when warned about things not yet seen, in holy fear built an ark to save his family. By his faith he condemned the world" (Heb. 11:7 TNIV). By analogy with Enoch and Noah, it is consistent that Christ delivered the final verdict of condemnation to the spirits when he ascended to the throne of God—a condemnation previously predicted in the Enoch story.[4] The practical value of Christ's victory over all spirits and all evil is that the forces of evil that opposed God and brought the unjust suffering of Peter's readers were also subjected to Christ's rule.

---

3. The dating of the various Sibylline Oracles is difficult to ascertain. If the oracles are second-century, it may have been the influence of 1 Pet. 3:19–20 on the Noah tradition that generated the claims that Noah was a preacher of righteousness and repentance.

4. For a discussion of the function of this passage as an analogy, see Westfall 1999.

Peter wishes to connect the sins of angelic beings in the ancient past, the victorious proclamation of the risen Christ, and the lives of Christian believers "now." He uses the flood as a type of God's catastrophic judgment, which happened only after God's restrained patience, and he poses the survival of Noah from that divine judgment as a type of Christian salvation, which involves the tamed waters of baptism. His point is that just as there were only a few saved from the flood, they were nevertheless and certainly saved. Therefore, despite their small numbers the Christians of Asia Minor are not lost to God's concern in the mass of pagan humanity, and God saves the righteous in spite of their small number (cf. Gen. 18:22–32). Moreover, though the pagans of Noah's time spurned his warning to repent, God's patience did not imply God's indifference. Just as the rain eventually began to fall for forty days and forty nights, the final judgment of God will also overtake scoffing unbelievers in the future. The God who saved Noah is the same God who will save Christian believers. These points were meant to be words of encouragement to the Christians of Asia Minor who, like Noah, were being derided and maligned by their society because of their faith.

e. The Development of the Alternative Interpretations

If the Enoch-Noah tradition so aptly forms the background against which 1 Pet. 3:19–20 is to be understood, how is it that for much of the church's history the passage was understood to refer to Christ's descent into hell between Good Friday and Easter Sunday? The book of 1 Enoch, which preserves the tradition of Enoch's proclamation of condemnation to demonic beings in written form, seems to have been lost after the second century until an Ethiopic copy was rediscovered late in the eighteenth century (although fragments exist in Aramaic, Greek, and Latin; Isaac, *OTP* 1:6). Without this knowledge, interpreters began to read the passage against a different background, the theory of Christ's descent into hell, which had already begun to develop independently.

The *descensus* theory apparently developed from such theological questions as the following: How did the OT saints gain salvation? What was Jesus doing in the time between his death and resurrection? Could people be saved after death, especially those who had not heard the gospel? Clement of Alexandria (ca. AD 150–220) may have been the first to use 1 Pet. 3:19–20 as support for the idea of postmortem conversion. Since conversion could come only through hearing the preaching of the gospel, it must be that those who died without that opportunity in this life would hear it either from Christ or from his deceased apostles in the place of the dead. Clement of Alexandria was already familiar with the *descensus* doctrine as he approached 1 Pet. 3:19–20. This allowed him to construe Christ's "going" as a descent, the "spirits" as the souls of Noah's generation that perished in the flood (or more widely, all

OT-era people), and the "prison" as the place that later developed into the doctrine of purgatory. Origen and St. Cyril of Alexandria followed Clement, and this interpretation continued to enjoy favorable standing in the Eastern church. Even today, those who support a postmortem opportunity for conversion point to Christ's descent in 3:19 as a precedent that opens the door to the possibility, often reading 4:6 in the same light (Goppelt 1993: 258–59). A. Hanson (1982: 103) demythologizes the descent into hell but believes it was the originally intended meaning of 1 Pet. 3:18–22:

> What we can learn from the *descensus* doctrine is the universality of God's redemption in Christ. . . . All those who have had no true opportunity of knowing God in Christ will be given such an opportunity in God's providence. Thus this apparently bizarre concept does in fact relieve us of the awful conclusion accepted by so many Christians down the ages, that all those who have not known God in Christ are damned. . . . And this is perhaps why the "he descended into hell" is still worth keeping in our creeds.

Christians today continue to disagree on how wide God's mercy actually is, but the text of 3:19–20 specifically limits Christ's preaching to the "spirits" that were disobedient at the time of Noah. If one wishes to argue that these spirits are the souls of the deceased being offered salvation, the question arises why only that generation received the privilege of Christ's postmortem gospel offer. Jewish interpretation of the flood story may offer a possible answer: because that generation was thought to be the most vile of all humanity, beyond any hope of repentance or restoration, or else God would not have destroyed them all in the flood (Beare 1970: 172). Later Christian interpreters saw Christ's mercy as so great as to have been extended even to those previously thought unredeemable (Goppelt 1993: 259). Nevertheless, the text of 3:19–20 limits Christ's preaching to that generation, and one is left with the problem of finding a biblical basis for broadening a postmortem offer of salvation beyond that limit to all who lived before Christ, much less to universalism.

Clement's doctrine that postmortem conversion is possible troubled Augustine, who believed it was a clear principle of Scripture that one's eternal destiny is determined in this life. Augustine could not read Greek well, and living in the fourth century, he may not have known the Enoch tradition. Therefore, doing his best with a difficult passage and probably influenced by 1 Pet. 1:10–12, he offered the interpretation that the preincarnate Christ preached to Noah's contemporaries *while they were still alive*, but they were dead at the time Peter wrote and thus "spirits in prison." A variation on Augustine's interpretation is that the imprisonment refers to the spiritual state of Noah's generation during their lifetime as slaves to sin. This interpretation also does not do justice to the Greek syntax of 3:18 and 3:19b, but not being proficient in Greek, Augustine was more concerned with the theological implications of the passage. He did, however, believe that Jesus Christ was wholly put to death and wholly raised; hence, he rightly rejected the Greek body-soul dichotomy the Alexandrian interpreters saw in verse 18 (Dalton 1965: 35n114). Without the knowledge of the Enoch-Noah tradition preserved in 1 Enoch, Christ's preaching through the lips of Noah became a theologically acceptable interpretation as an alternative to postmortem conversion.

Calvin also was troubled by the concept of postmortem conversion, and so he reinterpreted the *descensus* tradition as a final proclamation of salvation to the godly souls of the deceased and as damnation to the reprobate (*Institutes* 2.16.8–9). He took the clause of the Apostles' Creed referring to Christ's descent as an essential part of redemption and not simply a restatement of Christ's burial. In Calvin's view, the descent to hell is a graphic image that speaks of the tortures of condemned and ruined humankind, which Christ vicariously bore in his own soul (*Institutes* 2.16.8–9). In his commentary on 1 Pet. 3:19–21, he argued that Christ proclaimed salvation to the souls of those who were godly people before the flood. Calvin could read Greek, and he notes the difficulty of this understanding when the text of 3:20 so clearly says Christ preached to those who disobeyed, who were not godly, at the time of Noah. And so he offers the explanation that the true servants were "mixed together with the unbelieving, and were almost hidden on account of their number" (Calvin 1963: 294). The "prison" was actually a refuge to protect them, a watchtower from which they looked for the promised salvation (Calvin 1963: 293). Between Christ's death and resurrection, he proclaims his victory, which is good news to these godly spirits that their salvation is now secured, but a final word to the reprobate of their exclusion from salvation (*Institutes* 2.16.9; Calvin 2000: 442). Hillyer (1992: 115) points out that a similar view was held in the early church by Tertullian, who taught that the phrase "spirits in prison" "is not restricted to the wicked dead but includes all who under the OT dispensation were confined to Sheol/Hades, the place of the dead, until Christ's own triumph over death."

One might ask of the *descensus* interpretation, however, whether Christ's proclamation of victory, if delivered between the crucifixion and resurrection, was not a bit premature, for it is not until the resurrection and ascension—and some would add Pentecost—that the vindication and victory of Christ was fully achieved. Of course, in some sense, the certainty of Christ's victory was established even before creation, as Peter himself teaches (1:20). But if Christ is understood to have proclaimed victory between Good Friday and Easter Sunday, the temporal specificity seems just a bit premature. The ascension of Christ marks the final stage of accomplishing redemption and is more apt as a proclamation of Christ's victory.

Once the interpretive tradition of Gen. 6:1–4 preserved in 1 Enoch was lost, theological issues, not exegesis, drove the interpretation of 1 Pet. 3:19–21. Today, theological issues continue to shape the interpretation of those who still defend the *descensus* view and understand it to be a mythology that communicates the universal offer and scope of salvation (Beare 1970: 172; Goppelt 1993: 259; A. Hanson 1982: 102; Hill 1982: 59; Selwyn 1958: 314–62).

Goppelt (1993: 255–63) is the contemporary interpreter who defends this view in most detail. He (1) takes *en hō* in 3:19 to be a simple conjunction that has no temporal meaning; (2) assumes that the verb κηρύσσω (*kēryssō*, preach, proclaim) implies an offer of salvation, which could not apply to fallen angels and therefore must refer to the souls of the deceased; (3) points out that the fallen angels were disobedient long before Noah, so the spirits must be human beings who were disobeying while the ark was being built; and (4) takes 3:19 to be referring to the same event as 4:6 (see comments on 4:6). According to Goppelt, the point of the passage is that Christ offers the gospel to even the most lost of humanity.

The verb *kēryssō* in 1 Pet. 3:19 is often used for the preaching of the gospel in the NT (e.g., Matt. 4:23; Mark 1:14; 6:12; Acts 9:20; Rom. 10:14; 2 Cor. 1:19; Gal. 2:2; 1 Thess. 2:9). However, its semantic range is broader, and it is also used to mean "proclaim" in both the NT and the LXX (e.g., Gen. 41:43; Exod. 36:6; 2 Kings 10:20; Esth. 6:9; Jon. 1:2; Luke 4:19; 8:39; Rev. 5:2). Notably, the verb more specific to preaching the gospel, εὐαγγελίζομαι (*euangelizomai*, preach the good news) is not used of Christ's proclamation in 1 Pet. 3:19.

Any theory that understands the *pneumata* (spirits) of 3:19 to refer to the souls of deceased people faces the important lexical problem of whether that noun without further qualification was used to refer to deceased souls in contemporary literature. On the basis of lexical studies, many NT commentators today claim it was not (Achtemeier 1996: 255; Bandstra 2003: 123; Best 1971: 143; Boring 1999: 140; Davids 1990: 140; J. H. Elliott 2000: 656; France 1977: 269–70; Kelly 1969: 154; Kistemaker 1987: 143; McKnight 1996: 217; Michaels 1988: 208; Selwyn 1958: 198; Stibbs 1979: 143). In the NT and in 1 Enoch (Swete 1925), the word *pneuma*, especially in its plural form, is used overwhelmingly to refer to malevolent supernatural beings. The souls of deceased people are typically referred to with the term *psychē* in the NT. The one reference where *pneuma* in its plural form clearly refers to human beings (Heb. 12:23) is qualified by a substantive adjective, "spirits of the righteous," and it is not completely clear that this is a reference to the deceased. When *pneuma* is used to refer to deceased humans in 1 Enoch, it is always qualified (e.g., 20.6, "spirits of humans"; 22.3, "spirits of the souls of the dead"; 22.7, 9, 11–13; Swete 1925). Both the lexical data and the congruence of this passage with established tradition concerning Enoch's connection to the Noah story tilt toward understanding the imprisoned spirits as the fallen angels and the spirits of their degenerate offspring (see the second additional note on 3:19).

One objection against interpreting *pneumata* as fallen angels and/or their progeny, despite lexical support, is the argument that only human beings were disobedient while Noah was building the ark. The fallen angels who produced demonic offspring by human women did so well before Noah was even on the scene. Furthermore, according to Gen. 6:5, it was human wickedness, not demonic, that provoked God to flood the earth. These objections may be formally true and must be taken seriously because they appeal to the specificity of the text. Even so, the temporal conjunction ὅτε (*hote*, when) need not be understood so specifically to mean that God's patience waited *only* while Noah was building the ark, but rather is a reference to the whole episode found in Gen. 6, including both the fallen angels and Noah. In both Gen. 6 and in the extrabiblical Enoch-Noah traditions, the narrative of the fallen angels is the preface to the Noah story. In Gen. 6 there is no intervening material, so that logically, the extreme and irremediable wickedness of humanity in Noah's generation that motivated their disobedience even while the ark was being built was caused by the corrupting influence of the fallen angels and their degenerate progeny.

f. Noah and Christian Baptism (3:20b–21)

The discovery of the Noah coins and the existence of four extant flood stories indigenous to Asia Minor show the importance of Noah to the culture of that region (Trebilco 1991: 86–88). First Peter is addressed explicitly to Christians of that area, claiming that the risen Christ has authority over all evil—even that committed in long ages past at the time of Noah. Peter further associates the Christian gospel with Noah by using a typology between Noah's flood and Christian water baptism.[5] Peter writes in 3:20–21,

> who in times past disobeyed when the patience of God waited in the days of Noah while the ark was being built, in which a few—that is, eight people—were saved through water. This also symbolizes baptism that now saves you—not of flesh putting off filth, but rather the pledge of a good conscience to God—through the resurrection of Jesus Christ.

It was once believed that the water imagery provided by the reference to Noah's flood was introduced in this passage because 1 Peter was

---

5. Typology is the analogy between two events, people, or institutions in history, where the former (type) foreshadows the latter (antitype) in one or more definite and notable ways.

originally a homily (Perdelwitz 1911; Windisch 1930) or liturgy (Preisker 1951) for water baptism plausibly administered on Easter (Cross 1954) or that it at least preserved fragments of baptismal hymns (Boismard 1961). That theory is no longer widely accepted today, for several reasons (Dalton 1965: 68–70). Reconstruction of the underlying hymn has not been convincing (Hill 1982: 56). More importantly, the identification of this passage as a hymn arose from the assumption that the body of 1 Peter was baptismal liturgy, a theory now largely discarded. There is only one explicit reference to baptism (3:21), which embarrasses any theory that makes the performance of the sacrament central. Moreover, there are no well-defined criteria that would distinguish such a genre. Most scholars today are convinced of the unity of the epistle and its integrity as a letter.

The discovery of the Noah coins and the four extant flood stories in Asia Minor show that 3:19–21 is intended to connect the cultural heritage of the region to which Peter writes with the Christian faith of his readers living there. Noah's flood was an OT event that displayed God's salvation of the righteous few and his judgment on, and destruction of, an entire society that refused to repent. It was, and still remains, a type of the eschatological judgment that has been fulfilled in Christ but yet still looks to the future for its consummation in history. When Jesus taught about the coming of the Son of Man, he too used the Noah story, not to spotlight Noah's virtue but to underscore the suddenness of the coming eschatological judgment:

> As it was in the days of Noah, so it will be at the coming of the Son of Man. For in the days before the flood, people were eating and drinking, marrying and giving in marriage, up to the day Noah entered the ark; and they knew nothing about what would happen until the flood came and took them all away. That is how it will be at the coming of the Son of Man. (Matt. 24:37–39 TNIV//Luke 17:26–27, 30)

Peter's readers will be among those who escape the second "flood" of judgment because they have already passed through the waters of Christian baptism, which saves them by virtue of the vindicating resurrection of Jesus Christ.

The typological correspondence of the floodwaters to the water of baptism would suggest taking the δι' ὕδατος (di' hydatos, through water, 1 Pet. 3:20) as instrumental rather than locative (see additional note on 3:20), since Peter uses the instrumental sense that "baptism saves you" (3:21). The very water that threatened to kill Noah and his family was at the same time the means of their deliverance. The two corresponding *dia* phrases are not "through [*dia*] water" and "through [*dia*] baptism" but "through water" (3:20) and "through the resurrection of Jesus Christ" (3:21). The parallelism of the syntax supports taking *dia* as instrumental in both phrases. The ambiguity of *dia* assists Peter's transition from the OT story (where the *dia* could sensibly be construed as locative) to its typological application (where it could not; Davidson 1981: 324–25; France 1977: 273). Either construal leaves Peter's point intact.

Not only is the case of the relative pronoun in dispute (*ho*, 3:21; see additional note on 3:21), so also is the identity of its antecedent. Interpreters have argued that the antecedent is ὕδατος (*hydatos*, water) in 3:20 (Achtemeier 1996: 266; France 1977: 273; Michaels 1988: 213–14); or ἀντίτυπον (*antitypon*, antitype), which follows in 3:21 (J. H. Elliott 2000: 668); or the entire thought of 3:20b (Beare 1970: 174; Cook 1980: 77; Goppelt 1993: 266). The three respective translations are close in sense:

1. "were saved through water, which also now saves you" (Achtemeier 1996: 240);
2. "were saved through water. Corresponding to this, baptism now saves you too" (J. H. Elliott 2000: 637);
3. "were saved through water. In the counterpart to this, baptism now saves you also" (Beare 1970: 170).

Selwyn's (1958: 203) argument—based on "the rhythm of the Greek sentence," takes ὑμᾶς (*hymas*, you) as the antecedent, forming the typology between Peter's readers and Noah—has not been widely accepted: "And water now saves you too, who are the antitype of Noah and his company, namely the water of baptism."

Although water is the symbol that typologically associates the flood with Christian baptism, Peter's correspondences appear broader than the water element alone (Davidson 1981: 325–32). Regardless of how the grammatical difficulty with the relative pronoun is resolved, J. H. Elliott (2000: 669) points out the corresponding parallels of the typology:

3:20	3:21
a few	you
were saved	baptism now saves
through water	through the resurrection of Jesus Christ

The observation that the two corresponding *dia* phrases contrast "by water" with "by the resurrection of Jesus Christ" mitigates the problem that may immediately leap to mind: Does Peter here endorse the principle of baptismal regeneration in his statement that "baptism now saves you"? Such a view maximizes the typological correspondence between the flood and Christian baptism, but having made the transition from the OT story to the present, Peter quickly qualifies it. He adds the important prepositional phrase "baptism now saves you *through the resurrection of Jesus Christ*" and also the clause "not putting off the filth of flesh, but the pledge of a good conscience to God." These two qualifying clauses join the objective basis of salvation in Christ's resurrection with the subjective basis in the believer's experience.

The first qualification of the phrase "baptism now saves you" in 3:21 is structured as a contrast: "the baptism that now saves you" is not this but (ἀλλά, *alla*) that. Each clause of the contrast is difficult to understand, and both present lexical problems. The first phrase, "not putting off the filth of flesh," has been understood as a reference to mere religious ritual involving external washing (Beare 1970: 175; Boring 1999: 141; Calvin 1963: 296; Davids 1990: 144; J. H. Elliott 2000: 679; France 1977: 274; Goppelt 1993: 268; Reicke 1964: 114), or as an allusion to Jewish circumcision (Achtemeier 1996: 269; Dalton 1965: 217–18), or more generally as spiritual cleansing (Clowney 1988: 165; Michaels 1988: 216).

The words of the phrase are unusual. The noun ἀπόθεσις (*apothesis*, putting off) occurs elsewhere in the NT only in 2 Pet. 1:14, where Peter speaks of soon "putting off" his tent, a metaphor for his body, in referring to his death. The noun is related to the verb ἀποτίθημι (*apotithēmi*, put off, remove), which is used in 1 Pet. 2:1 to refer to "putting off all evil and all deceit and hypocrisies and jealousies, and all backbiting." Evidence suggests that this verb was used in early Christian baptismal catechesis (J. H. Elliott 2000: 677; Selwyn 1958: 204). If so, Peter uses a lexical echo to remind his readers of the present implications of their baptism.

The noun σάρξ (*sarx*, flesh) is often assumed (probably wrongly) to be synonymous with "body," and the "removal" therefore is taken to be a form of washing, leading to the interpretation that an external religious ritual is in view. If so, Peter would be contrasting the nature of Christian baptism, which is an external ritual involving water, with other religious rituals, probably those of Jewish tradition, and saying that Christian baptism is not simply a ritual but something much more.

However, the noun ῥύπος (*rhypos*, filth) is a strong word that occurs only here in the NT. In the LXX it occurs four times (Job 9:31; 11:15; 14:4; Isa. 4:4), where three of those occurrences refer to moral filth. The nuance of *apothesis* and *rhypos*, together with the contrast between "flesh" and "a good conscience," suggests that Peter is referring here not to mere external washing or religious ritual (much less circumcision) but to the moral filth characteristic of a carnal (fleshly) existence. Therefore, the apostle is saying that the baptism that saves does not remove moral filth from Christians in such a once-and-for-all way that Christians need not care about how they live after being baptized. In fact, he uses the cognate verb of *apothesis* in 1 Pet. 2:1 to admonish them to put off the characteristics that impede their spiritual nourishment, and in 2:11 he exhorts them to abstain from the desires that war against the soul. Many, perhaps all, of Peter's readers had presumably already been baptized in water. This stands as a reminder to them that water baptism is not a "ticket to heaven" that exempts them from subsequent issues of morality.

Rather (ἀλλά, *alla*), Christian baptism is a pledge to God of a good conscience—a pledge to live rightly ever after. This clause also presents lexical problems. The word συνείδησις (*syneidēsis*), though often translated "conscience," has a broader semantic range than does the English word, a range that includes "consciousness" in the sense of awareness about something. The two ideas are not unrelated, since a consciousness or awareness of moral standards adjudicates between a bad or good conscience. The word *syneidēsis* here probably refers to a disposition or attitude about life in light of one's awareness of God in Christ, with an element of loyalty in view (France 1977: 275).

The second word in question, ἐπερώτημα (*eperōtēma*, pledge, request), also occurs only here in the NT but is a cognate to the verb ἐπερωτάω (*eperōtaō*, ask or request), which occurs over fifty times in the NT. Under the influence of the verb, this noun is taken to mean a request. By this understanding, through the sacrament of water baptism, Christians "appeal" to God to give them a good conscience and cleanse them from the guilt of sin. While this interpretation may be attractive, it does not fit the context quite as well as taking *eperōtēma* to mean "pledge," a meaning attested in the papyri (e.g., P.Cair.Preis. 1.16, cited by Selwyn 1958: 205). The noun *eperōtēma* is found in the papyri on the occasion of sealing a legal contract to refer both to a formal question of willingness from one party *and* a positive response from the other (France 1977: 275; Hill 1982: 59; Hillyer 1992: 116; Kistemaker 1987: 148; G. Richards 1930: 77). If this second-century lexical evidence is allowed, it makes good sense of the contrast and fits the larger context as well. Peter is reminding his readers that when they were baptized, a question was asked about their faith in Christ, to which they gave a positive response. They were then baptized in water as a sacrament of that pledge of faithfulness made to God. Peter reminds them of that pledge as they face suffering because of Christ and the temptation to turn away.

Some wish to take *eperōtēma* as simply a declaration of an appropriate awareness of Christ as Lord (e.g., Brooks 1974: 293–94). Although baptism may be thought of as a declaration, it is a declaration that constitutes an implicit pledge of a continuing relationship to God in Christ, which thereafter calibrates the moral compass by which one lives. As Selwyn (1958: 205) explains, the idea that baptism is a seal of contract between the believer and God is not far removed from that which led to the adoption of the Latin word *sacramentum* (military oath) to refer to baptism and the Eucharist.

Putting all of this together, Peter is therefore saying that baptism in itself does not remove moral filth once and for all so that Christians need not be concerned with how they live. Rather, he reminds his readers that at baptism they pledged to live in relationship with God, which would result in a good conscience before him. Therefore, he can exhort them to continue to live, even under persecution, in a way that honors their baptism. The reference to baptism is important in Peter's argument that it is better to suffer unjustly for doing good than to suffer for doing evil. But this reference to baptism does not support the theory that 1 Peter was originally a baptismal homily or liturgy.

The efficacy of water baptism is completely dependent on Christ's resurrection (3:21), and so the three redemptive elements of Christ's death, resurrection, and ascension (see below) frame this passage. Therefore, the discourse on baptism is not a digression from Peter's main point (e.g., B. Campbell 1998: 184–85; Lindars 1981: 299; cf. Westfall 1999) but is where the objective accomplishment of redemption is brought to bear on the very real and pressing life situation of Peter's readers.

g. Christ's Ascension as Victory (3:22)

Although 3:18–22 ranges through several topics—from Christ's resurrection to his victory over the spirits to Noah's flood to Christian baptism and its moral imperative—the unity of the passage rests on its Christology in relation to God's people. With these words Peter encourages his readers by teaching glorious truths of Christology. The elements of the redemptive event frame this passage:

> 3:18 Christ suffered once for sins,
> the righteous on behalf of the unrighteous,
> so that he might bring you to God.
> Christ was put to death in the flesh.
> He was made alive in the Spirit.
> 3:19 He went [πορευθείς, *poreutheis*] and preached to the spirits.
> 3:22 He went [πορευθείς, *poreutheis*] into heaven.
> Angels and authorities and powers are subject to him.

The content and form remind one of 1 Tim. 3:16:

> Beyond all question, the mystery from which true godliness springs is great:
>
> > He appeared in a body,
> > was vindicated by the Spirit,
> > was seen by angels,
> > was preached among the nations,
> > was believed on in the world,
> > was taken up in glory. (TNIV)

The sequence and formulaic style of 1 Pet. 3:18–19 and 3:22 have led some to see in these words an early Christian creed, possibly in the form of a hymn, already fixed at the time Peter wrote (Goppelt 1993: 247–50; S. Johnson 1960: 49). Some have even suggested that Peter begins to recite the creed, then digresses into tangential comments about Noah and baptism. The three participles—θανατωθείς (*thanatōtheis*, put to death, 3:18), ζῳοποιηθείς (*zōopoiētheis*, made alive, 3:18), and πορευθείς (*poreutheis*, went, 3:19)—link the sequence of redemptive events in such a way that the repetition of *poreutheis* in 3:22 is meant to resume the sequence. If so, the "going" in 3:22, explicitly and clearly a reference to the ascension ("having gone into heaven"), corroborates that interpretation of 3:21 as Christ's ascension that is both a going and a proclamation. Therefore, the doctrine of the *descensus* of Christ into hell cannot be defended on the basis of 1 Pet. 3:19. (Other NT passages usually cited to support such a doctrine can be understood differently as well: Acts 2:27, 31; Rom. 10:6–8; Eph. 4:8–10; see also John 5:25–29; Matt. 27:52).

But as J. H. Elliott (2000: 653) points out, even the so-called digression has a structure where redemptive events of Christ's life frame the salvation of the righteous:

3:19a   Christ went [*poreutheis*] to the spirits in prison.
　　3:20   Noah and family were saved through water.
　　3:21   Water baptism now saves you through the resurrection of Jesus Christ.
3:22   Christ went [*poreutheis*] into heaven, with cosmic powers subjected to him.

Dalton (1965: 115) helpfully outlines the logic of the theology found in this difficult passage:

First stage: By water God saves . . . Noah and his family from the evil world which lies under the domination of evil spirits. Unbelievers and their angelic instigators are punished.
Second stage: God's definitive act of salvation is done through the passion and resurrection of Christ. . . . As risen Lord, Christ proclaims the definitive defeat of the evil spirits.
Third stage: By water, through the resurrection of Jesus Christ, God saves the Christian believer from the evil world. . . . The evil world, which does not believe and cannot be baptized, is doomed to condemnation.
Fourth stage: The Christian suffering persecution from the pagan world is confident because he knows that it has no power over him: the evil angelic forces behind it have been overthrown.

The typology Peter sets up is between the sacrament of Christian baptism and Noah's flood. It does not require that Christ descended into hell between his death and resurrection or that he preached by the Spirit through the lips of Noah, as Grudem and others continue to defend. However, some of the implications of Peter's teaching for Christian self-understanding as enumerated by Grudem (1988: 160–61) still stand even if one rejects his interpretation of 3:19:

- Noah and his family were a minority surrounded by hostile unbelievers; so are Peter's readers (3:13–14; 4:4, 12–13).
- Noah was righteous in the midst of a wicked world. Peter exhorts his readers to be righteous in the midst of wicked unbelievers (3:13–14, 16–17; 4:3–4).
- Noah witnessed boldly to those around him by believing God and building the ark. Peter encourages his readers to be good witnesses to unbelievers around them (3:14, 16–17).
- Noah realized that judgment was soon to come upon the world. Peter reminds his readers that God's judgment is certainly coming, perhaps soon (4:5, 7).
- At the time of Noah, God patiently waited for repentance from unbelievers before he brought judgment. So it is also in the situation of Peter's readers.
- Noah was finally saved with only a few others. Peter thus encourages his readers that, though perhaps few, they too will certainly finally be saved, for Christ has triumphed and has all things subject to him (3:22; 4:13, 19; 5:10).

This passage presents the sweeping scope of the efficacy of Christ's victory in his resurrection and ascension. Christianity is not a parochial religion that is (or was) valid for only a limited time of history in a certain region of the world. If Peter's claim is true that Christ's resurrection and ascension have dealt with even the primordial evil of fallen angels in uncountable prior centuries of human history, then Christ is victorious over all evil—even the most depraved—for all time.

Additional Notes

3:18. Two verbs, ἔπαθεν (epathen, suffered) and ἀπέθανεν (apethanen, died), are attested in the several confusing manuscript readings of this verse. In spite of the very strong manuscript evidence for "died," it is more likely that "suffered" was original because it better fits the context and provides a reason later scribes would change it to "died." Peter uses the verb πάσχω (paschō, suffered) twelve times, but there are no uncontested occurrences of apethanen (died). Where the verb is in reference to Christ (2:21; 3:18; 4:1), all occurrences suffer the same verb confusion in the manuscripts. Because throughout the letter Christ is the paradigm for the believer's suffering, this major theme indicates that paschō was the original verb also in reference to Christ (Achtemeier 1996: 247; Dalton 1965: 119; J. H. Elliott 2000: 640; Goppelt 1993: 250; Michaels 1988: 201). The statement "Christ suffered for sins" is unique in the NT and is sometimes used as an argument against this reading. However, the force of this objection derives from taking the expression out of its immediate context. For this passage gives an explanation of 3:17, why it is better to *suffer* for doing right than for doing wrong. Furthermore, 4:1 continues the theme of choosing to suffer rather than to sin. If so, it is easy to understand why scribes, who were copying phrase by phrase and were not reading each occurrence in context, changed the verb to *apethanen* (died) in veneration for the crucifixion.

3:19. In 1763 William Bowyer Jr.'s edition of the Greek NT proposed a textual emendation that read Ἐνώχ καί (Enoch also) instead of ἐν ᾧ καί (*en hō kai*, in which, at which time) in 1 Pet. 3:19a. This proposal was in turn accepted by both Moffatt and Goodspeed in their translations of the NT made in 1913 and 1923 respectively. The emendation would read, "Christ was made alive in the spirit. Enoch went in spirit to preach." This proposal has been almost universally rejected by contemporary scholars, and rightly so, for it completely lacks manuscript evidence, and the abrupt shift to Enoch does not fit well in the context. (For its defense, see Goodspeed 1954.) Even so, the rejection of this textual emendation does not mean that familiar elements of the Enoch tradition are not the background for the passage.

3:19. The lexical evidence concerning the use of *pneuma* to refer to the human soul continues to be debated, but only a few interpreters take it as a reference to the souls of deceased people (e.g., Erickson 1995: 140; Feinberg 1986: 336; Grudem 1988: 206–20; Perkins 1995: 65). Grudem gives the most detailed defense of this view, claiming that even in 1 Enoch *pneuma* is indeed used to refer to the souls of the deceased (Grudem 1988: 208–9). When the Greek text (*Apocalypsis Henochi Graece*, Black 1970) is examined, even the verses cited as evidence by Grudem are arguably ambiguous. Where *pneuma* is clearly used in 1 Enoch to refer to the continued existence of the dead (e.g., 22.9), the attributive adjective νεκρῶν (*nekrōn*, of the dead) is specified, observing the same pattern as in the NT. In the sections of 1 Enoch that parallel 1 Pet. 3:19–20, *pneuma* without a qualifier clearly refers to supernatural beings, not deceased souls. For the two occurrences of *pneuma* in the LXX that occur in a context of death (Ps. 145:4 [146:4 Eng.]; Eccles. 12:7) one could argue that even there the word refers to the breath, not the soul.

For some, however, the distinction between human souls and fallen angels is not particularly significant. Reicke (1964: 109) and A. Hanson (1982: 102), who both hold to a *descensus* interpretation, argue that Christ preached both to the souls of deceased people and to fallen angels, and Selwyn (1958: 199) also allows for that possibility. Reicke (1964: 109) makes the remarkable claim that "in speaking about persons of remote antiquity, no sharp distinctions were made between angels and men." The question turns on whether the Enoch-Noah tradition is the background for the passage, where *pneuma* clearly refers to malevolent angelic beings.

3:20. The eight persons in the ark were saved either "through the midst of water" (taking δι᾽ ὕδατος, *di' hydatos*, as locative) or "by water" (taking it as instrumental). "Through the midst of water" captures the nuance that the floodwaters were a threat *through* which the eight were safely brought. Cook (1980: 76) argues for the unlikely sense that this refers to the rising floodwaters through which Noah and his family waded (up to their ankles? up to their necks?) to enter into the ark, though in the text they were not delivered from the flood until all its waters receded and were no longer a threat. Moreover, it is not clear that the rain began to fall before they entered the ark (Gen. 7:13). Cook errs by pressing the sense of motion that the preposition "through" can sometimes, though not necessarily, convey. Contra Cook, the preposition "through" sometimes means agency with no thought of motion. Goppelt (1993: 265) argues that only the locative nuance does justice to the sense of the verb διεσώθησαν (*diesōthēsan*, they were delivered out of). The parallelism of the two corresponding *dia* phrases in 3:20–21, "through [*dia*] water" and "through the resurrection of Jesus Christ," supports taking *dia* as instrumental in both phrases (BDAG 225).

3:21. The more difficult nominative form of the relative pronoun ὅ (*ho*, which), which appears in virtually all manuscripts, is more likely to be the original reading. The emendation to the dative case, ᾧ (*hō*)—as proposed by Erasmus and followed by no less a textual critic than Hort as well as a few modern commentators (Beare 1970: 174; J. H. Elliott 2000: 668)—is based on an oral confusion of the two forms in the earliest days of its transmission history. It is understandable why a scribe would change the difficult nominative relative pronoun to the more expected dative; it is more difficult to imagine a motivation for the reverse that would have occurred as widely as the manuscript evidence attests. Therefore, in this case the more difficult reading is more likely to be the original.

3. Living Out Christ's Victory in an Unbelieving World (4:1–6)

The objective of Peter's epistle is to instruct his readers about who they are in Christ, so that a new way of seeing themselves might both encourage them and motivate their behavior and life choices. In the previous section Peter explained that suffering—even suffering to death—is no sign of weakness or defeat. Now the apostle exhorts his readers to arm themselves with the same resolve and way of thinking that Jesus Christ had, so that they might abstain from the carnal desires that war against them (cf. 1 Pet. 2:11). Previous to their commitment to Christ, they had already spent enough time doing the things that unbelievers ("Gentiles") like to do. Now, because of faithfulness to Christ, they have ceased to do such things. They live somewhat apart from society's ways, as visiting strangers and resident aliens might be expected to do. As a result, they are taking heat for no longer indulging in those things, and their withdrawal from former practices implicitly indicts those who continue in them.

    a. Be willing to suffer rather than sin (4:1–2)
    b. Suffering abuse from unbelievers (4:3–4)
    c. The universal scope of God's judgment (4:5–6)

Exegesis and Exposition

[1]Therefore, because Christ suffered in the flesh, you must also arm yourselves with the same resolve: that the one who suffers in the flesh is through with sin. [2]This will equip you to live out the rest of your time in the flesh no longer [motivated] by human desires but instead by the will of God. [3]For the time past was [more than] enough to do what the Gentiles like to do, as you went along with acts of abandon, lust, drunkenness, revelry, carousing, and licentious idolatries. [4]In this they are surprised that you have stopped running with them into the same flood of debauchery and they malign [you]. [5]They will give an account to the One prepared to judge the living and the dead. [6]For this reason, the gospel was preached even to the dead, so that although they were condemned in the flesh by human judgment, they might nevertheless live in the Spirit by God's judgment.

a. Be Willing to Suffer Rather Than Sin (4:1–2)

Pagans of the first century viewed Christians as killjoys who lived gloomy lives devoid of pleasure (Colwell 1939; Frend 1967; Sherwin-White 1974). The pleasures from which Christians of the first century typically abstained were the popular forms of Roman entertainment: the theater with its risqué performances, the chariot races, and the gladiatorial fights with their blood and gore. Christian lifestyle also condemned the "pleasures" of an indulgent temper, sex outside marriage, drinking, slander, lying, covetousness, and theft (Colwell 1939: 61). These attitudes toward contemporary Roman customs and morals, combined with the Christians' refusal to burn incense to the emperor—a gesture of civic gratitude intended to assure the well-being of the empire—earned Christians the reputation of being haters of humanity and traitors to the Roman way of life.

This problem of withdrawal from old behaviors and lifestyles continues to be an issue today, especially for those new to Christian commitment. New converts must frequently decide which friends "BC" (before conversion to Christ) they can keep and to which they must become as strangers for the sake of their new life. Even though they may be criticized for abandoning their past ways, Peter reminds his readers that human judgments are not the last word because God will judge *everyone*, not just those who believe in him. Because a day of reckoning is coming, the gospel of God's forgiveness was preached "to the dead" to prepare them for meeting their Judge. Although Peter's readers may have been condemned by merely human opinion (an allusion to official process and possibly martyrdom?), they nevertheless live according to God's judgment. With this, Peter encourages his readers to continue to abstain from the things that society deems acceptable, even though by their abstinence they condemn such conduct and thereby possibly incur the anger of those who indulge in such things. As Achtemeier (1996: 277) points out, "It is a problem that will recur whenever Christians are forced by their faith to oppose cultural values widely held in the secular world within which they live."

Exegetical problems and ambiguities continue in this passage, particularly in 4:1 and 4:6. The startling claim presented in 4:1 that "the one who suffers in the flesh is through with sin" has generated a number of interpretations. The resumptive οὖν (*oun*, therefore) picks up the thought of 3:18, that Christ suffered once for all to deal with sin so that "he might bring you to God." Since this is the case, the Christian is to be armed with the same *resolve* (ἔννοια, *ennoia*) that Jesus Christ himself had (cf. Phil. 2:5). In the LXX Proverbs the noun *ennoia* often refers to that mind-set or disposition that issues in right moral action (e.g., Prov. 2:11; 3:21; 16:22; 23:19). Therefore, Peter exhorts his readers to have the same resolve that characterized Christ.

The conjunction ὅτι (*hoti*, because, that) can be understood either as causal, giving the reason for the imperative to arm (arm yourselves with the same resolve Christ had *because* the one who suffered in the flesh is through with sin; as Beare 1970: 178; Clowney 1988: 169; J. H. Elliott 2000: 714; Goppelt 1993: 280; Michaels 1988: 225; Reicke 1964: 116); or as epexegetical, specifying the content of the resolve (arm yourselves with the same resolve Christ had, *that* the one who suffers in the flesh is through with sin; as Achtemeier 1996: 278; Calvin 1963: 298; Davids 1990: 147). Given the flow of Peter's argument, it is more likely epexegetical. The participle παθόντος (*pathontos*, suffered) in the opening genitive absolute seems best construed as causal ("*because* Christ suffered in the flesh") and therefore already provides sufficient grounds for the imperative that follows: "Therefore, because Christ suffered in the flesh, you must also arm yourselves with the same resolve: that. . . ." Moreover, in extrabiblical Greek, when *hoti* follows the noun *ennoia*, it is most often giving the content of the resolve (Achtemeier 1996: 278).

However, the sense of the *hoti* clause is not unrelated to the referent of ὁ παθών (*ho pathōn*, the one who suffered/suffers) in the phrase that follows. A few interpreters, going back at least as far as Erasmus, have understood the referent of the one who suffered to be Christ himself (Clowney 1988: 169–70; Davids 1990: 149; Michaels 1988: 226–29; Thurén 1995: 166). But most take the referent to be the Christian believer (Achtemeier 1996: 280; Beare 1970: 179; Best 1971: 151; Calvin 1963: 298; J. H. Elliott 2000: 714; Goppelt 1993: 282; Reicke 1964: 116; Selwyn 1958: 209). Neither interpretation is without difficulty.

If the referent of the phrase "the one who suffered" is Christ, it is obliquely repeating what was said in the first clause, "*because* Christ suffered in the flesh, . . . arm yourselves *because* the one who suffered. . . ." Some have objected to taking Christ as the referent of the phrase "the one who suffered is through with sin" because it implies that Christ must once have been a sinner if he ceased from it. This objection is answered by understanding the phrase "is through with sin" as referring to the present situation that has resulted from Christ dealing once for all with sin and not to the personal experience of Jesus himself (as Clowney 1988: 170). Another objection is that the phrase *ho pathōn* is surrounded by references to Peter's readers: "*You* must arm yourselves . . . , so as to live out the rest of *your* time in the flesh. . . ." It seems disruptive to some to take *ho pathōn* as a reference to a third party. Michaels (1988: 223, 229) attempts to resolve this problem by taking the clause "for he who suffered in the flesh is through with sin" as a parenthesis and by setting it off in dashes in his translation. If so, this repeats the thought in the initial genitive absolute, "since Christ has suffered in the flesh," and adds the further thought "he is through with sin."

Perhaps discourse analysis offers the weightiest objection to taking Christ as the referent of *ho pathōn*. Peter has already moved from a christological section into a hortatory section. The topic of how to live in the face of unjust suffering is introduced in 3:8–17. The christological basis for that exhortation is found in 3:18–22. The second-person plural imperative in 4:1 (ὁπλίσασθε, *hoplisasthe*, arm yourselves) signals the return to exhortation that is further unpacked in the rest of the chapter. Therefore, it seems more apt to the immediate context that Peter is exhorting his readers to be prepared to accept unjust suffering, as even Christ did, by arming themselves with the same mental disposition that allowed Christ to do so.

If the individual believer is the referent of *ho pathōn*, then the aorist substantive participle *pathōn* is gnomic and therefore translated into the English present tense to convey the general sense of "whoever suffers in the flesh is through with sin." Taking the phrase in this way presents at least three ways of answering the question of how suffering eliminates sin in the life of the believer. Some have suggested that Peter is here quoting a Jewish proverb that physical suffering is somehow a purifying experience and perhaps even atones for sin in some sense (cf. 1 En. 67.9; 2 Macc. 6:12–16; 2 Bar. 13.10). While it might be argued that suffering the due consequence for one's own sin pays the penalty for it and is in that sense atoning, Peter is here explicitly speaking of *unjust, undeserved* suffering. Moreover, the thought that physical suffering is necessarily a purifying experience or that suffering presents less opportunity for the sufferer to sin is highly questionable. In fact, the experience of suffering may present even more opportunity to become embittered and sin in one's heart against God (cf. the book of Job) and to lash out at others. Furthermore, such an interpretation requires taking the phrase "in the flesh" (*sarki*) as synonymous with "in the body" (*sōma*), which is questionable in light of Peter's use of the phrase elsewhere. The expression in 4:1 is identical with that of 3:18, where "in the flesh" refers to this realm of earthly life that Christ entered in his incarnation. Because Peter is attempting to present Christ's suffering during his incarnation as a rationale for Christian suffering in this life, the occurrence of the term in 3:18 and 4:1 should probably be taken with the same sense: suffering in this earthly life. This is corroborated by 4:2, where Peter admonishes his readers to live out the rest of their time in the flesh (*sarki*) for God's will rather than for ungodly human desires, clearly meaning the rest of their natural lives. Although it is true that both Christ in his incarnation and the Christian believer must live in this earthly realm in a body, that is not the point of 3:18, where life before resurrection (*sarki*) is contrasted to life thereafter.

A second understanding of the clause ("whoever suffers in the flesh is through with sin") probably also misinterprets Peter's use of *sarx* under the influence of Pauline theology (Calvin 1963: 298–99). Romans 6:5–7 states that in baptism the Christian has been united with Christ in his death, and therefore the power of sin in the Christian's life has been broken. While one should expect the theology of the great apostles to have much common ground, it is a mistake to assume that Peter's wording must always be interpreted in light of Paul's theology. Paul uses the word *sarx* (flesh) differently than Peter, as a pejorative reference to the totality of fallen human nature, equivalent to the "old nature" of Rom. 6:5–7 (ὁ παλαιὸς ἄνθρωπος, *ho palaios anthrōpos*). For Paul, it is not possible to live by the Spirit while at the same time living in the "flesh" (cf. Gal. 5:16). In marked contrast, Peter in this section of his discourse (3:18; 4:1, 2, 6) consistently uses the term to refer to the time of earthly life before death.

Therefore, (1) Peter's analogy between Jesus' suffering and that of the believer, (2) his use of *sarx*, and (3) the hortative nature of the discourse resumed in 4:1—these all indicate that Peter's reference to "the one who suffers is through with sin" is the Christian believer armed with the same resolve as Christ. The question remains: In what sense can Peter claim that the suffering Christian is *through with sin* if both the idea of purification by suffering and the Pauline thought is rejected here?

This study concludes that those who suffer unjustly because of their faith in Christ have demonstrated that they are willing to be through, or done, with sin by choosing obedience, even if it means suffering. Although it is true that sin eventually but inevitably leads to suffering, obedience to God may lead to unpleasant consequences as well. This is sometimes overlooked by those who understand following Christ as only the path to blessing, if not to health and wealth. Peter's readers face the choice of either taking the path of least resistance—going along with the values, norms, and practices acceptable and expected by their society—or being obedient to God and suffering the consequences of criticism and condemnation by unbelieving family and friends. Their willingness to suffer this way therefore demonstrates that they have resolved to be through with sin.

This understanding of the relationship between suffering and obedience flows from Peter's Christology, which is centered on Jesus' human experience of suffering and death as the means of redemption and the basis for Christian living (1 Pet. 1:3, 18–19; 2:21–25; 3:18; 4:1). Jesus consistently chose to obey God, even though it meant suffering various kinds of trials and in the end led to his excruciating death. It would not do justice to the fully human nature of Jesus Christ to assume that he fulfilled God's redemptive plan for his life without thought, deliberation, or decision. Jesus' agony in Gethsemane indicates otherwise. In fact, throughout his human development Jesus had consciously to embrace his calling and commitment to his relationship to the Father (Luke 2:52; Heb. 5:8). Hebrews 5:8 is particularly telling: "Son though he was, he learned obedience from what he suffered" (TNIV). Repeatedly throughout his life, Jesus deliberately had to embrace his calling even though it meant the suffering of being misunderstood, rejected, and finally tortured to death. His full humanity meant that although he was tempted to sin and thereby to renounce his calling, he constantly had to decide to obey God and suffer the consequences.

Peter has already instructed his readers that they, too, are called to suffer unjustly, because of this example set by Christ (2:21). In order to follow in the footsteps of Jesus, to embrace their calling, and to face daily a society unfriendly to their values, Christians must be armed with the same disposition and resolve that allowed Jesus to set his face resolutely toward the cross. Suffering for their relationship with God in Christ then becomes something to be expected and not something to be avoided. Therefore, the content of the resolve enjoined on Christians, the same resolve that Jesus had, is *that* (*hoti*) those who suffer unjustly for their faith in God have demonstrated that they are through with sin to the extent that they would choose to suffer rather than to sin. And because they would rather suffer than sin, they can live out the rest of their time in the flesh no longer motivated by human desires but instead by the will of God (4:2). The fact that they are suffering demonstrates the true nature of their resolve. They have not just resolved to cease from sin that presents itself; they have in this case actually ceased from it, or they wouldn't be suffering for righteousness. This interpretation fits the overall theme of the letter—suffering for being a Christian—as well as the immediate context of 4:2–4, which exhorts believers to abstain from the things they once approvingly participated in, even though it might bring the disapproval and abuse of their unbelieving associates.

b. Suffering Abuse from Unbelievers (4:3–4)

The thought of 4:2–4 divides the Christian's life into two segments: life lived as a pagan before conversion to Christ, and life lived after conversion but still "in the flesh." Choosing to suffer rather than to sin means that for the time remaining "in the flesh," the Christian is no longer to be motivated by ungodly human desires but by God's will. Peter rather sarcastically points out that whatever time previously spent in doing what the "Gentiles" (ἔθνη, *ethnē*) wish to do has been more than enough time for such ungodly living. This rule of Christian ethics repeats what was introduced in 1:14: "As obedient children [i.e., after conversion], do not be conformed as previously to the desires of your ignorance; instead, corresponding with the holiness of the one who called you, you too be holy in [your] whole way of life."

The reference to human desires in 4:2 (ἀνθρώπων ἐπιθυμίαις, *anthrōpōn epithymiais*) is specified in 4:3 as desires contrary to the will of God, listed as various acts of "abandon, lust, drunkenness, revelry, carousing, and licentious idolatries." The first five items involve unrestrained desires for sex, food, and drink; the last refers to wanton acts commonly practiced within the religious ritual of pagan worship.

Acts of abandon (ἀσελγείαις, *aselgeiais*) means any behavior lacking moral constraint, particularly sexual acts but also acts of violence. *Lusts* (ἐπιθυμίαις, *epithymiais*) in 4:2 refers to all human impulses that tend toward immorality, but in this list (4:3), it probably refers more specifically to excessive indulgence in sex or other acts of self-gratification. Three of the terms (οἰνοφλυγίαις, *oinophlygiais*; κώμοις, *kōmois*; πότοις, *potois*) refer to excessive acts of eating and drinking, such as would be practiced at the Bacchus (Dionysus) and Saturnalia festivals. All five terms refer to practices that have in common a lack of self-control, a character flaw leading to behaviors that are a self-destructive violation of God's standards and are harmful to others.

Achtemeier (1996: 282) makes the interesting observation that the final term, "licentious idolatries," is not used by secular writers to describe religious activities, even religions of which they do not approve. In the first-century polytheistic culture, some religions may have seemed distasteful, but their practice was not considered immoral or a violation of divine mandate. Only the Judeo-Christian tradition (including Islam, which later developed from it) has a concept of idolatry, which is one reason why Jews and Christians have been the objects of social persecution throughout the centuries. Few in the polytheistic first century cared if Christians wanted to worship Jesus, but it was highly offensive for the apostles to label other religions as idolatrous and inconsistent with the true worship of God. In our pluralistic age of globalization, issues of multicultural pluralism are creating an ethos similar to that of the polytheism Peter faced: everything spiritual seems acceptable except the exclusive claims of the gospel of Jesus Christ.

It is striking that Peter refers to all unbelievers as "Gentiles" (*ethnē*) when writing to Christian readers who themselves may have been ethnically Gentile (as Paul also does in Eph. 4:17). The apostles used terms, familiar to the Jewish tradition, that divided all humanity into God's covenant people and the rest of humanity, who were referred to as *ethnē*, the nations, or Gentiles. The Christian apostles kept the language but redrew the line, redefining God's covenant people to be those who believe in Christ and referring to all others as "Gentiles." In this letter Peter writes to Christian readers *as if they were* Jews who are now scattered among the nations (Gentiles), as the ethnic Jews had historically been in the Diaspora (1 Pet. 1:1). This helps to explain why modern interpreters have been unable to decide with certainty whether the original readers were Jewish or Gentile converts; Peter wants his readers to think of themselves as God's true covenant people without distinction. If the original Christian readers had been deported from Rome because of their participation in the Jewish sect of *Chrestus* (Christ), they had been treated as Jews regardless of their ethnicity (see "Roman Colonization and the Origin of 1 Peter" in the introduction).

Peter writes that his readers had once participated in the ungodly activities listed in 4:3. This has been taken by most interpreters to imply that Peter's readers were ethnically Gentiles, for it is argued that Jews would never have lived liked that. One might expect that knowledge of the Torah would indeed have provided a moral restraint deterring Jews from such ungodly behavior. But the inference that Jewish people would never participate in such unbridled practices reflects perhaps an idealized and romanticized view of Jewish devotion and piety rather than historical and sociological possibility. The Pentateuch itself records instances of ancient Israel indulging in pagan ways that sound much like the ungodly vices of 4:3. For instance, the golden-calf incident of Exod. 32 shows Israel's tendency to idolatry even before the ink was dry, so to speak, on the covenant. Their idolatry involved eating, drinking, and revelry not unlike the behaviors listed in 1 Pet. 4:3. Closer to the time of 1 Peter, the Testament of Judah, written in the second century BC and translated into Greek probably not later than AD 50, grieves that Israel practices *aselgeia* (licentiousness)—the same word heading the list in 4:3—as well as witchcraft and idolatry (T. Jud. 23.1). In first-century Galilee, wealthy Jewish patrons displayed their acculturation to the Greco-Roman world by commissioning decorative art for the synagogues of Galilee that displayed the astrological zodiac, Hercules, Medusa, and scenes reminiscent of the Dionysus cult (Baumgarten 1999: 73, 82). Although these aesthetic artifacts don't necessarily imply pagan behavior among the Jews of Galilee, they count as evidence for that possibility. Moreover, the fact that other contemporary Jews defaced such symbols suggests that some passionately disapproved. If that was the situation in Galilee, one could imagine that in Asia Minor acculturation may have been even more prevalent. The fact that Peter's readers once participated in the practices listed in 4:3 did not prevent Calvin (1963: 300–301) from concluding that the book was written primarily to Jewish Christians, for Peter views any religion apart from Christ as empty (cf. 1:18) and ungodly. It is therefore questionable whether 4:3 offers any conclusive evidence concerning the readers' Jewish or Gentile origins.

The apostle Peter is not saying, of course, that *every* non-Christian, whether Jew or Gentile, lived in the manner of 4:3. In fact, both pagan and Jewish Greek writers outside the NT also condemn lack of self-control (e.g., Seneca, *Ep.* 83.16–26; Philo, *Drunk.*; *Plant.* 160–66). There no doubt were many non-Christians who led exemplary moral lives. The Christian life Peter enjoins would have been compatible with the highest ideals recognized by Greek moral philosophy, even though the actual practices of Greco-Roman society were characterized by excessive indulgence and debauchery. Such is often the case; our modern society often does not live by its highest ideals either.

Even if Peter's exhortation may be consistent with the ideals of the Greek moral philosophers, he does not appeal to Greek thought as the moral basis of his exhortations but to the will of God. To the extent possible, Christians are to live in a manner that will be recognized as "good" by their society (2:12–17, 18–20; 3:1–8). However, Christians are to become as foreigners and resident aliens to their society when the condoned and normalized practices of that society are indulgent and destructive excesses, which are inconsistent with the virtues of new life in Christ. So Peter teaches that Christians are to remain within the social structures of their society (2:11–3:7) yet not participate in institutionalized practices that are recognized as contrary to God's will. As Davids (1990: 151) points out, "Acts of abandon, lust, drunkenness, revelry, carousing and idolatry may well have characterized family religious celebrations, official meetings of the trade guilds, and civic holidays." In such a culture, there would be plenty of opportunity to suffer abuse for the name of Christ by refusing to participate in the rituals of culture and thereby alienating oneself from friends, family, and business associates.

The response of unbelievers is surprise—accompanied by dismay, disappointment, and even anger—that their Christian friends no longer "run with them into the same flood of debauchery," and they malign the Christians (4:4). Writing about Thessalonica, J. M. G. Barclay (1993: 515) explains the strong sense of betrayal felt by non-Christians when Christians declined participation in normal cultural activities:

> Family members who broke ancestral traditions on the basis of their new-found faith showed an appalling lack of concern for their familial responsibilities. Christians deserted ancestral practices, passed on since time immemorial, for a novel religion (if such it could be called) of recent manufacture. The exclusivity of the Christians' religion—their arrogant refusal to take part in, or to consider valid, the worship of any God but their own—deeply wounded public sensibilities. Such an unnatural and ungrateful attitude to the gods even branded them as "atheists." Moreover, it was highly dangerous for even one segment of the community to slight the gods, whose wrath was ever to be feared. Civic peace, the success of agriculture, and freedom from earthquake or flood were regularly attributed to the benevolence of the gods.

The word ἀνάχυσις (*anachysis*, outpouring, 4:4), occurring only here in the NT, refers figuratively to the indulgent outpouring of excesses in the pagan lifestyle. Rather than following the Christians' good example, pagan friends malign them because they do God's will, and thereby pagans implicitly blaspheme God. In his ancient commentary on 1 Peter, Oecumenius writes: "Not only do the Gentiles wonder at the change in you, not only does it make them ashamed, but they also attack you for it, for the worship of God is an abomination to sinners" (Bray 2000: 113). Just as Noah's obedient faith implicitly condemned his generation when he built the ark (Heb. 11:7), the Christians of Asia Minor pass judgment on society by refraining from the evil practices in which they once indulged with society's approval. Therefore, the abuse and slander they suffer is a righteous suffering for the sake of Christ. By persecuting Christians, their opponents are siding against God, and for that reason they will come under God's judgment.

c. The Universal Scope of God's Judgment (4:5–6)

The merism in 1 Pet. 4:5, "the living and the dead," indicates the universal scope of God's purview. The claim, so popular in today's intellectual milieu, that truth is socially constructed opposes ideas of universal truth. When applied to religious thought, it implies that a given religion is true only for those who believe it. But 1 Peter teaches here that the gospel of God's forgiveness and judgment in Christ is true not only for believing Christians but for all people as well. The universal claim to truth was as offensive to first-century Greco-Roman thought as it has become in today's pluralistic culture. The apostle teaches here that no one escapes God's judgment, which will either acquit or condemn based on response to Christ, the Living Stone or the stumbling stone (2:7–8).

Peter notes that those who blaspheme God by maligning Christians for their righteous living will have to give an account of themselves "to the One prepared to judge the living and the dead" (4:5). Although elsewhere in the NT and in Christian creeds Christ is often identified as the judge of humankind, it is more likely that the phrase "the One prepared to judge the living and the dead" here refers to God the Father because 1 Peter has Christ taking the role of the exemplary believer. Christ does not take judgment into his own hands "but instead trusted the One who judges justly," that is, God the Father (2:23). Following the example of Christ, it is likewise to their Creator that Peter instructs his readers to look for vindication (4:19).

Since the time of the ancient church, the enigmatic thought of preaching to the dead in 4:6 has prompted two general interpretations. Those who support a postmortem opportunity for conversion take 4:6 as a broader instance of Christ preaching to the spirits in 3:19. Others take it to refer to those who are spiritually dead even though physically alive. In the immediate context, Peter's point is that death does not exempt a person from God's coming judgment. Accountability after death was not widely taught in the pagan world. With such an assumption, a pagan critic could reasonably question what good the gospel is, since it seems so restrictive of behavior in this life, and then the believer dies like everyone else. Peter, however, teaches that *because* people will be judged even *after* physical death, contra pagan expectation, the gospel message of forgiveness and judgment that has been preached to those who are now dead—whether they became believers or not—is still efficacious. Death does not invalidate either the promises or the warnings of the gospel of Jesus Christ. Peter's claim not only would warn the unbeliever but would also encourage Christians concerning believers who may have passed on. Peter reassures his readers that the efficacy of the gospel continues after physical death to be the basis for God's judgment, and therefore a decision to live for Christ in this life is truly the right decision, even despite appearances to the contrary as judged by the world's reasoning. As Calvin (1963: 302) eloquently puts it in his commentary on this verse,

> We see . . . that death does not hinder Christ from being always our defender. It is a remarkable consolation to the godly that death itself brings no loss to their salvation. Even if Christ does not appear as Deliverer in this life, yet His redemption is not void, or without effect, for His power extends even to the dead.

The fact that some of those to whom Christ was preached have died is therefore no basis for judging the value of the gospel. God will judge rightly. The Christian dead may have indeed been judged by human standards in this life and may have been found wanting, whether by popular opinion or by official action. Nevertheless, judged by God's standards, they are alive in the eternal realm of the Spirit.

Because this verse is sometimes used to support the possibility of conversion after death, the reasons for rejecting this interpretation deserve further consideration. The referent of "the dead" (νεκροῖς, *nekrois*) in 4:6 must be informed by the use of the same term in 4:5, where it forms half of a merism that refers to all humanity in all ages, whether physically alive at the moment or physically dead. Therefore, the understanding, ancient though it may be, that 4:6 refers to the spiritually dead is unlikely. Hilary of Arles (ca. AD 401–449) expresses this understanding and the possible connection to 3:19: "The gospel is preached to the Gentiles who are dead in sin, but this may also refer to the fact that when the Lord was buried in the tomb he went to preach to those who live in hell" (Bray 2000: 113). If even ancient commentary allowed that *nekrois* might refer to the physically dead, it raises the question of who these dead were and specifically if they were the same beings that Christ preached to in 3:19. Those who understand 3:19 to be a reference to a descent into hell, where Christ preached the gospel in a postmortem offer of salvation, have construed 4:6 to be a broadening of that principle, even though the verses have few points of contact. S. Johnson (1960) argues for this interpretation based on a rather artificially constructed chiasm and overlooks the fact that the two verses do not occur within the same discourse unit. The immediate contexts of 3:19 and 4:6 should take priority in informing their respective interpretations. This is especially true since the two verses are only superficially similar. In 3:19 Christ is the one who proclaims, but in 4:6 the verb is passive and implies that Christ is the content of the preaching. This problem has sometimes been answered by broadening the postmortem preaching to extend to preaching done by the deceased apostles. Furthermore, the verbs are not the same in both verses, for the more general verb κηρύσσω (*kēryssō*, proclaim) stands in 3:19, but εὐαγγελίζομαι (*euangelizomai*, preach good news) is a more specific reference to preaching the gospel in 4:6. The weightiest reason the two verses are not directly related is that the audience in 3:19 is "the spirits" (*pneumata*), not "the dead" (*nekrois*) as in 4:6, and the two words are not synonymous. It was the assumption that Christ descended to Hades, as stated in the Apostles' Creed, that gave rise to the theory of postmortem conversion in 4:6 (see comments on 3:18–22).

Goppelt (1993: 289) is one of the few interpreters who argues that the wording of 4:6 "suggests that proclamation of the gospel is encountered by the dead *when they are dead* and that their death here, as in v. 5, is literal" (emphasis added). He reads 4:6 in the context of 3:19 as an eschatological event where the proclamation of Christ applies not only "to the most lost but to all the dead" (1993: 289). Therefore, in his judgment both 3:19 and 4:6 are mythological images that should be understood "as a kerygmatic confession, without trying to objectify it as an order of salvation for the dead or as a portrayal of a Hades proclamation."

Most contemporary interpreters no longer claim an association between 4:6 and 3:19 (Achtemeier 1996: 291; Bandstra 2003: 123; Dalton 1965: 42–51; Dalton 1979; Davids 1990: 154; J. H. Elliott 2000: 730–31; Hillyer 1992: 122; Kistemaker 1987: 163–64; Michaels 1988: 237–38). First Peter 4:6 is not speaking of two groups of people, but one. The dead in 4:6 who have been judged by human standards in the flesh are the same ones who are alive in the realm of the Spirit as judged by God's standards, and they therefore do not need an offer of salvation. Moreover, the phrase εἰς τοῦτο γάρ (*eis touto gar*, for this reason) closely joins 4:5 and 4:6.

First Peter 4:5 claims that pagans who reject the gospel of Christ and mock Christians for living out their faith will have to answer to God, the one who judges the living and the dead. As noted above, "the dead" in 4:6 should be understood to have the same referent as in 4:5, for there is no syntactic or lexical marker that would suggest otherwise. Therefore, the claim of 4:5 is that there is a judgment of God coming and that being dead does not excuse one from having to give an account for what was done before death. First Peter 4:6 begins "for this reason," that is, for the reason that there is a judgment coming, the gospel was preached to the dead, meaning to those who are *now* dead (but who heard the gospel while living, as the TNIV makes clear). The whole point of evangelism is to prepare people for the day they must give an account of themselves to their Judge. Physical death does not exempt those who reject the gospel in this life from judgment, nor does it render the gospel ineffective for those who committed themselves to it when they heard it in this life. The gospel was preached because judgment is coming (4:5), *so that* (4:6, ἵνα, *hina*) people may live in the realm of the Spirit (*pneumati*) as judged by God's standards, regardless of how they were judged by human standards during this life (*sarki*, in the flesh). This understanding of 4:6 is consistent with Peter's use of the terms *sarki* and *pneumati* in 3:18 and 4:2 to refer, respectively, to this earthly life before physical death and the life of the believer after God's judgment.

First Peter 3:19 and 4:6 are not referring to the same proclamation, but both nevertheless do make universal claims for Jesus Christ. In both verses Christ is presented as the victor over both present and ancient evil, who has full authority over both fallen angels and human souls. He is also presented as the basis on which God's judgment will be carried out.

Summary

In 4:1–6 Peter addresses the problem afflicting his readers and gives instructions intended to change their self-understanding so that they may be better prepared to live as Christians within a society that is not sympathetic to their faith. By consciously adopting the same resolve that Jesus had as he embraced his calling and faced his opponents, Christians are to be prepared to suffer as necessary, identifying with their Lord and equipping themselves to engage their society as visiting strangers and resident aliens. Just as foreigners characteristically do not fully participate in the culture and customs of their host land but may live by the values and practices of their homeland, Christians may find themselves at odds with the values and practices of the society in which they reside. Although Peter gives an apt reminder for all believers, this passage is an especially relevant encouragement for new Christians who may be taken by surprise at the intensity of the negative reaction their faith provokes from unbelieving friends. When peer pressure comes into play, the church's role as an alternate society, a Christian colony in a strange land, provides a social context in which Christians should seek and find the support and kinship they once found through engaging in practices contrary to the will of God. Each season of life brings new and different challenges to the Christian believer. Hence, Peter's message of being prepared to suffer unjustly for one's faith if necessary provides a lifelong corrective against tendencies to compromise with cultural expectations and to assimilate the values and practices of those who reject God.

4. Living Out Christ's Victory in the Christian Community (4:7–11)

With this passage Peter continues to reshape his readers' self-understanding in Christian terms by providing an eschatological perspective for living out their faith in Christ: they are living in view of the end of all things. Throughout the NT, as here, teaching about the future is offered as the basis for how Christians are to live now. What one believes about the future shapes how one lives today. A belief that the future is full of hopelessness, despair, and futility becomes a self-fulfilling prophecy when people live today as if that future were true. On the other hand, hope in a future that is meaningful and assured produces the confidence to live each day with that future in view.

a. Thinking rightly in view of the end (4:7)
b. A love that "covers" sin (4:8)
c. Gracious hospitality (4:9)
d. Gifts of grace as acts of service (4:10–11a)
e. Peter's doxology (4:11b)

Exegesis and Exposition

[7]The end of all things is near. Therefore, be self-controlled and clear-minded for prayers. [8]Above all, have earnest love for one another, because "love covers a multitude of sins." [9]Be graciously hospitable to one another without complaining. [10]Inasmuch as each one has received a gift of grace, serve one another with it as good stewards of the many forms of God's grace. [11]If anyone speaks, [you should speak] as words of God; if anyone serves, [you should serve] from the strength that God supplies, so that by everything [you do] God might be glorified through Jesus Christ, to whom belong the glory and the dominion forever and ever! Amen!

a. Thinking Rightly in View of the End (4:7)

This passage constitutes the final unit in the letter's body that extends from 2:11 through 4:11 and reinforces the apostle's expectations for life in the Christian community. It forms an inclusio with the initial statement of the body (2:11–12):

Dear friends, I urge [you] as resident aliens and visiting foreigners to abstain from the carnal desires which war against your soul and maintain a good life among the Gentiles, in order that although they speak against you as evildoers, because they recognize your [way of life] from your good works, they will glorify God on the day of [his] visitation.

First Peter 4:7–11 echoes the themes in 2:11–12 of abstention from evil and an exemplary way of life that results in glory to God in view of the end. The doxology of 4:11 punctuates the closing of this major section of the letter, functioning like doxologies in Rom. 11:36; Eph. 3:21; Phil. 4:20; and 1 Tim. 1:17. The vocative ἀγαπητοί (agapētoi, dear friends) in 1 Pet. 4:12 signals, as it did in 2:11, the beginning of a new section that will close this letter.

Peter makes a bold claim about the future, a claim that is intended to shape the behavior of his readers. "The end of all things is near" (πάντων δὲ τὸ τέλος ἤγγικεν, pantōn de to telos ēngiken). The word order of the Greek places "all things" (pantōn) as the first word, emphasizing the comprehensive sweep of Peter's statement. This brief statement is nevertheless enigmatic. The untranslated conjunction δέ (de) indicates that this passage is loosely connected to the preceding thought: the judgment of God. Even if society judges the Christian gospel to be undesirable or irrelevant, everything will be judged in reference to the resurrected Christ, and that judgment is near because the resurrection has already happened. Therefore, the Christian is to live in light of the nearness of "the end" as it is defined by Christ's resurrection. One implication of this truth is that Christians are not to be rooted in this world (Calvin 1963: 302), as the description of them as visiting strangers and resident aliens already implies (1:1; 2:11). The Christian's sense of value, self-worth, and identity are to be rooted instead in the eschatological hope into which they have been born again (1:3).

How, then, is "the end" (τὸ τέλος, to telos) to be construed? While modern readers may immediately think of the end of the world, the semantic range of the word telos suggests more than mere termination and may refer to the last stage of a process as well as to its outcome or goal. Peter is saying that because of the resurrection of Jesus Christ, his readers are living in the last stage of God's great redemptive plan, and the goal of that plan is being realized. The collocation of to telos with the verb ἐγγίζω (engizō, to be near) in its perfect form (ἤγγικεν, ēngiken) reinforces this eschatological sense. The same perfect form of this verb occurs repeatedly in the Synoptic Gospels, in the preaching of John the Baptist (Matt. 3:2) and in Jesus' teaching about the "nearness" of the kingdom of God (e.g., Mark 1:15; Matt. 4:17; 10:7; Luke 10:11; 21:8). The consummation of the kingdom of God will involve the return of Christ and the end of history as we know it because those events are necessary for God to achieve his telos, the redemption of humanity. Therefore, "the end is near" signifies the final stage of that redemptive process, which leads to its consummation in the return of Christ.

This understanding is consistent with Peter's statement in 1 Pet. 1:20 that Jesus Christ has been made known "during the last of times" (ἐπ' ἐσχάτου τῶν χρόνων, *ep' eschatou tōn chronōn*). "The last of times" indicates the final stage in God's redemptive plan, inaugurated by the resurrection and ascension of Christ. Therefore, Peter's statement that "the end is near" is not precisely equivalent to saying that the end of the world will happen soon. While "the end" is certainly a future-oriented concept, Peter is not referring to one termination point in time. He rather has in mind the period of time after which Christ, who all along has been sovereign over all things, has finally been revealed as such in the resurrection. Peter's description of his readers in 5:10 as those who have been called into the age of God's glory in Christ corroborates the idea that a period, rather than point, of time is in view. An exclusively temporal interpretation has misled some to point out that Peter (and Jesus!) must have been wrong, since two thousand years later the world still goes on. The NT writers may or may not have been surprised that two thousand years would pass without the return of the Lord, but that is somewhat beside the point of what Peter is saying. We, too, are living in the last stage of God's redemptive process; it is no more or less true that "the end is near" today than it was when Peter first said it.

Peter is saying that because his readers are living in the last stage of a divinely initiated process, whose outcome has already been assured by the resurrection of Jesus Christ (1:3; 3:22), their behavior should reflect that reality. The end of all things is the basis (οὖν, *oun*, therefore) for four exhortations that flesh out in practical terms the resources needed for the Christian community to be an alternate society in which its members may take refuge from the rejection of a hostile society. Peter gives four practical ways that his readers are to live out Christ's victory in Christian community:

1. Think rightly and be clear-minded so you can pray.
2. Persist in a love for one another that "covers" sin.
3. Be graciously hospitable to fellow believers without complaining.
4. Serve one another with the gifts of grace you have received.

Peter wants his readers to live in light of the reality he has just asserted in 4:7, that *everything* (*pantōn*) is coming to its final outcome as judged by the revelation of Jesus Christ. Nothing and no one is exempt from the redemptive process that will bring deliverance to some and condemnation to others. Therefore, the Christian worldview vitally involves *all things*. The Christian faith is not merely an anthropological phenomenon that by custom is exercised on Sunday morning in a church building. The gospel of Christ is a reality of cosmic scope that touches everyone and everything on the planet. Peter's readers are to allow this reality to govern the way they think and live. Rather than acting out of turmoil and confusion concerning spiritual matters, Peter says they must think rightly and be clear-minded (σωφρονήσατε οὖν καὶ νήψατε, *sōphronēsate oun kai nēpsate*). The two verbs are similar in meaning, and their collocation here may form a hendiadys that expresses one thought, not two (Achtemeier 1996: 294). It clearly commends mental preparation that restates the command opening the letter in 1:13: "Fully set your hope on the grace to be brought to you when Jesus Christ is revealed by making your mind ready for action by being self-controlled."

The first verb, "be self-controlled" (*sōphronēsate*), is found also in the exhortation of Titus 2:6. The second, "be clear-minded" (*nēpsate*), contrasts with a drunken state in which one lacks self-control and in that sense can refer to sobriety. Peter uses this verb twice elsewhere in his letter in similar exhortations to live a disciplined life (1:13; 5:8). In this instance, the two verbs function as a hendiadys that refers to the mental state Peter wishes for his readers. Because the end of all things is near, one is to be fully in control of one's thoughts. The Christian is accurately to perceive the reality that Christ's resurrection has inaugurated, and that perspective is to motivate a sound and self-controlled way of life. This exhortation for a clear and sober mind stands in sharp contrast with the lifestyle from which Peter's readers have come, as described in 4:3, where their minds were dulled by excessive drinking and sex and confused by debauchery and idolatry.

Right thinking and being clear-minded are to result in prayers (εἰς προσευχάς, *eis proseuchas*). The preposition *eis* indicates purpose. This is an interesting association, since one might expect clear-mindedness to be necessary for preparing a sound defense against one's critics or for making wise decisions as threatening circumstances present themselves. However, Peter's first concern is prayer. The knowledge that Peter's readers live in the final stage of God's redemptive plan should motivate prayers, not a complacent fatalism ("Well, God's going to do what God's going to do"). Nor should it move them to abandon their responsibilities and relationships with each other and with their society. Rather, the knowledge of God's final stage of redemption, rightly apprehended, should motivate a prayerful engagement with others. As Davids (1990: 156–57) explains, this is not the prayer "based on daydreams and unreality, nor the prayer based on surprised desperation, but the prayer that calls upon and submits to God in the light of reality seen from God's perspective and thus obtains power and guidance in the situation, however evil the time may be." The first resource for living out Christ's victory in the Christian community is the believer's prayer life. However, maintaining a vital prayer life is easier said than done, as most Christians know from experience. It is especially difficult to pray if others' reactions to one's faith are generating a hostility jeopardizing one's social standing, livelihood, and well-being as many of Peter's readers apparently are facing. The jumble of conflicting emotions and thoughts that arise in that situation can obscure the reality of Jesus Christ's victory, provoking behavior and decisions contrary to Peter's command to return blessing for insult (3:9). Prayer itself may be seen as futile or "not working" as hostilities continue and even worsen. If one's Christian identity is the source of the problems, the temptation could be strong to disassociate from the church and fellow Christians. In fact, Jesus himself predicted that when trials came, "the love of many [Christians] will grow cold" (Matt. 24:12). He used the same phrase (*eis telos*, 24:13) to teach that persistence in faith *to the end* is needed for salvation.

b. A Love That "Covers" Sin (4:8)

Perhaps echoing Jesus' warning that the love of Christians may grow cold in times of trial, Peter exhorts his readers that because the end of all things is near, they must persist in their love (ἀγάπη, *agapē*) for one another (4:8). This love is described by the adjective ἐκτενῆ (*ektenē*, earnest) and is the object of the present participle ἔχοντες (*echontes*, having). "Having an earnest love for one another" is, in Peter's mind, *above all* (πρὸ πάντων, *pro pantōn*) else. "Earnest" implies an intent that is steadfastly pursued. "Earnest love" speaks not so much of emotional intensity but is, in this context, a love that persists despite difficulties because it is a love that also "covers a multitude of sins."

The phrase "covers a multitude of sins" is apparently from a saying familiar to Peter's readers, probably coming from Prov. 10:12 (cf. James 5:20). Peter is probably not here quoting the text of a biblical verse, for the wording he uses matches neither the Masoretic text nor the LXX, which he has clearly used extensively in other quotations throughout the letter. A paraphrase of Prov. 10:12 in Hebrew probably circulated in Greek among Greek-speaking Jews and/or Christians, and Peter may just be using that familiar expression, which most likely predated both of its NT occurrences (as also Achtemeier 1996: 295; Boring 1999: 150; Davids 1990: 158; Goppelt 1993: 297).

What does it mean that love "covers" sins? In the full proverb in both the Hebrew text and the LXX, love's covering is put in antithetic parallelism to "hatred stirring up dissension and quarrels": "Hatred stirs up dissension, but love covers over all wrongs" (Prov. 10:12 NIV). Since "hatred" is the antonym of "love," the phrase "covers a multitude of sins" in this antithetic parallel suggests that the sense of "covering" and "stirring up dissension" are also opposites. If so, the love that covers sins is probably best understood as a forbearance that does not let wrongs done within the Christian community come to their fullest and most virulent expression. This was the way Clement of Rome understood 1 Pet. 4:8 in the late first century. In his letter to the Corinthians (1 Clem.

49.5) he explains this covering love as "love [that] endures everything, is long-suffering to the last" (Kleist 1961). The downward spiral is broken when someone in loving forbearance breaks the cycle of acting on hard feelings and doing wrong (as also Achtemeier 1996: 296; Boring 1999: 150; Davids 1990: 158; Reicke 1964: 122). As White (1919: 543, 546) explains, a person who is under the control of godly love acts,

> when a private personal injury has been done to him, as though nothing had occurred. In this way, by simply ignoring the unkind act or the insulting word, . . . he brings the evil thing to an end; it dies and leaves no seed. . . . This consideration gives dignity and worth inestimable to the feeble efforts of the most insignificant of us to make love the controlling principle in our daily lives.

So understood, Peter is not making a theological statement about sins being forgiven ("covered") by God. Nor is he saying that sin in the church should be ignored or denied ("covered up"). Peter is concerned with behaviors that could destroy the Christian community; such behaviors must be extinguished if the church is to survive.

This understanding that love covers sins by not responding in kind to behavior that destroys community is consistent with the exhortation of 1 Pet. 1:22: "From your heart love one another earnestly, for you have been born again." The requirements of such love are further explained in 2:1 as "putting off all evil and all deceit and hypocrisies and jealousies, and all backbiting." And in 3:9 Peter further commands that blessing is to be returned for insult. By Peter's definition, "love" is not a warm, fuzzy feeling but means treating others in the Christian community in such a way as to promote unity and to avoid or overcome behaviors that destroy relationships. Clearly, living in community with other believers for a sustained period of time—especially in a hostile society—gives plenty of opportunity for such "sins" to occur that hurt members of the community, sow seeds of bad feelings, and fuel ongoing cycles of evil, deceit, hypocrisies, jealousies, and backbiting. This is why 4:8 calls not merely for love but for an earnest love that persistently continues to cover, to suppress, the potential for the destruction of the community. Such behavior actually extinguishes sin and its effects within the community by not retaliating in kind, thereby realizing in the context of community the claim of 4:1 that Christians must be through with sin.

Exercising this kind of love that covers all sin, Peter says, is above all else (πρὸ πάντων, *pro pantōn*). In other words, the fundamental characteristic that enables a Christian community to survive is the willingness and ability of its members to love in this way. Why was this such a paramount virtue? In our times we see churches split and congregations alienated over trivial issues. Although this is a painful situation, such discord does not destroy the Christian presence in our society because there are so many Christian congregations in virtually every town. However, at the time Peter wrote, the Christian church was tiny, with perhaps only a handful of believers in towns widely separated across Asia Minor. If relationships in that community were destroyed, the disaffected believers had nowhere to turn, and the witness to the gospel in that place was extinguished. As state pressure grew against the Christian church, the threat of destruction from without increasingly pressed upon the infant churches. How tragic if they were destroyed from within by their own inability to live in harmony with other believers! Such love in the church was the primary resource for the preservation of the Christian community as an alternate society.

c. Gracious Hospitality (4:9)

The third of Peter's exhortations in 4:7–11, hospitality, is not possible without the kind of love he calls for throughout his letter. When writing on the connection between the Christian virtues, Clement of Alexandria called hospitality akin to love (*Strom.* 2.9). Because Christians have been reborn by God into a new and living hope that characterizes the final stage of God's redemptive plan, they are to be graciously hospitable to one another. The adjective φιλόξενοι (*philoxenoi*, hospitable) functions with imperatival force, "[be] hospitable." The use of an adjective rather than an imperative or participial form may suggest that Peter wishes to both recognize the extent to which hospitality is being practiced and also urge it at the same time (Achtemeier 1996: 296).

Most commentators construe hospitality at the time Peter wrote to mean that Christians are to welcome fellow believers into their homes as overnight guests (Davids 1990: 159; J. H. Elliott 2000: 753; Michaels 1988: 248; Reicke 1964: 122). Because suitable inns were few and far between in the first century, this form of hospitality was no doubt both a practical necessity and a mutual courtesy. And since Peter is addressing believers scattered all over Asia Minor, they probably have opportunity to assist traveling Christians from other towns and provinces in this way, especially perhaps the courier who will carry Peter's letter. However, there is nothing in the immediate context to suggest that such hospitality specifically focuses on hosting overnight guests. In fact, the repetition of the reciprocal expressions in 4:8, "for one another" (εἰς ἑαυτούς, *eis heautous*); 4:9, "to one another" (εἰς ἀλλήλους, *eis allēlous*); and 4:10, "serve one another" (*eis heautous*), suggests a hospitality that functions within and among the local community of believers. If so, Peter may be expecting his readers to open their homes for the purpose of Christian worship and fellowship, since at that time the local church had to meet in the homes of its members. This form of hospitality could be quite costly if it marked the family as a target for anti-Christian persecution. Furthermore, to welcome all Christian believers into one's home without grumbling requires one to maintain a certain openhearted-ness toward all. The exercise of love that Peter says is above all would be necessary if the local church was to have a place for all believers to gather together.

It is this quality of openheartedness toward one another that is the basis for a Christian hospitality willing to minister to other believers even in the absence of warm feelings and even when relationships are strained. Moreover, such openheartedness toward fellow believers would allow the opportunity for hospitality beyond the official meetings of the church. If their pagan friends and even their own families are os-tracizing Christians, those distressed believers are to find a warm wel-come in the homes of other members of the Christian community. The church is to be that alternate society where Christians find a place when shunned by unbelievers who live by different values. In a hostile world, the church is to be a place of safety and well-being for its members, a place where common beliefs unite more than differences divide. The Christian community is a colony of the holy nation of God among the nations of the world.

d. Gifts of Grace as Acts of Service (4:10–11a)

The final resource for the preservation of the Christian community is the stewardship of gifts of God's grace they have received for the pur-pose of serving others (4:10–11). Again the emphasis is on others within the Christian community benefiting from what each has received from God. Peter uses the same word, χάρισμα (*charisma*, gift), that Paul uses to refer to specific spiritual gifts such as healings, miraculous powers, and speaking in tongues (e.g., 1 Cor. 12:4, 9, 30–31). Here the word refers more generally to the gifts of God's grace in the fullest sense (cf. Rom. 5:15–16; 6:23). Peter implies that each Christian believer, by defi-nition, has received a gift of God's grace. That experience of grace is to be directed toward service to others, as Paul also teaches the specific *charismata* should be used (1 Cor. 12:1–31). There is no reason to think that the specific spiritual gifts delineated by Paul are excluded from Peter's thought, but neither is Peter concerned with those particular manifestations of God's grace. In fact, he mentions that expressions of God's grace may take various forms (ποικίλης, *poikilēs*) as members of the congregation serve one another (1 Pet. 4:10). The manifold forms of God's grace to be ministered within the Christian community answer to the many kinds of trials (also *poikilēs*) suffered by his readers, which Peter mentioned in the opening of the letter (1:6).

Peter goes on to say that those who speak and those who serve should do so recognizing that they are stewards of the gift of God's grace (4:11). "Speaking" and "serving" represent the whole of one's activities. Paul expresses a very similar thought in Col. 3:17: "Whatever you do, whether in word or deed, do it all in the name of the Lord Jesus, giving thanks for God the Father through him" (TNIV).

The elliptical expression in 4:11, "if anyone speaks, as words of God [ὡς λόγια θεοῦ, *hōs logia theou*]," should probably be taken to mean that those who teach about Christ and offer counsel in his name must understand themselves to be representing God's words to the community. Therefore, those who speak must understand that they are engaged in serious business that restrains them from positing merely their own human speculation. Instead, they must speak in accordance with the revelation that God has given in the OT and through the apostles of Christ. As Goppelt (1993: 304) explains, "Whoever passes on the gospel should be intentional about speaking not from narrow individuality, but from a posture of having listened to God. . . ." Christian teaching and counsel is to reflect the truth of the living hope into which they have been reborn, thereby encouraging, edifying, and rebuking each other in love.

God also provides the strength for their service (4:11). It is often said with reference to finances, "God's work never lacks God's supply." God's supply with respect to finances can be debated, but 4:11 implies that God supplies strength for the task at hand for those who serve others in the Christian community. This is not limited to those in an official capacity (though that is certainly not excluded) but refers to believers offering what they can to meet the needs of others within the community.

There seems to be somewhat of a sequence to Peter's logic in 4:7–11. First, Christians must have a perspective on life that is informed by the understanding that they live in the final stage of God's redemptive work. That realization must be met with a mental state that rightly apprehends this situation so that prayers can take their proper place in the Christian's life. Thinking rightly and praying in a manner consistent with God's redemptive work enables a love for one another that persists even when one is hurt by wrongs within the community. When one has correctly apprehended reality, is centered on prayer, and is able to break the cycle of wrongs, one can also speak words that are consistent with God's revelation and serve others with a strength that he supplies.

When the full range of activities in the Christian community is done with love, then in *all* things (ἐν πᾶσιν, *en pasin*) God is glorified through Jesus Christ. The unity and well-being of the community of people who bear Christ's name are preserved; right living in the Christian community displays God's redemptive plan, and therefore God is glorified *through* Jesus Christ. Peter's readers cannot glorify God in speech or actions that are not consistent with Christ's gospel.

e. Peter's Doxology (4:11b)

This passage, which ends the body of the letter, appropriately closes with a doxology of praise, "to whom is the glory and the dominion forever and ever. Amen!" This doxological clause begins with the relative pronoun ᾧ (*hō*, to whom), presenting the ambiguity of whether the antecedent is God or Christ. Word proximity suggests that Christ is the intended antecedent (Michaels 1988: 253; Selwyn 1958: 220). Furthermore, the doxology of 2 Pet. 3:18 clearly ascribes glory to Jesus Christ, so if Petrine authorship—or at least Petrine tradition—can be assumed, that doxology may shed light on the thought here. Moreover, the shorter doxology of 1 Pet. 5:11 clearly ascribes glory to Christ.

Most of the sixteen doxologies in the NT are offered to God, but some of these also seem ambiguous. The argument is made that since God is glorified *through* Christ in 4:11 it would be contradictory for the same doxology then to glorify Christ. For this reason, many interpreters understand the antecedent of the pronoun to be God the Father (Achtemeier 1996: 299; Calvin 1963: 306; Davids 1990: 162; J. H. Elliott 2000: 762; Kelly 1969: 181–82; Goppelt 1993: 306). However, as Michaels (1988: 253) points out, this argument cuts both ways, for it sounds redundant "to ascribe glory to God twice in succession." In either case, the apparent ambiguity of the antecedent of the relative pronoun does not seem to trouble the author as much as it does modern interpreters, perhaps because he understands Christ and the Father to share such praiseworthy attributes. Even though Peter's readers may feel powerless within the hostile situations they face, the doxology reminds them that all power belongs to the God they serve in the name of Christ.

The glory that comes to God is distinctively Christian, in that it comes from people who bear Christ's name even though doing so jeopardizes their standing in their society, their livelihood, and in some cases possibly their very lives. Although the experience of Peter's readers has been hard, he encourages them in this passage by insisting that they do indeed have the resources to live out Christ's victory within their Christian community, for it comes not from themselves but from God, who is the limitless supply.

IV. Consolation for the Suffering Flock (4:12–5:11)

The apostle Peter finishes his letter with consoling thoughts for his readers, who are facing some degree of grief and suffering for the name of Christ. He has already encouraged them to maintain holy lives in the face of pressure to return to a pagan lifestyle (1:13–2:10). He has followed that with advice about how to avoid unnecessary conflict by maintaining good relationships in the civic arena (2:11–17), in the household (2:18–3:7), and in the Christian community (3:8–3:12). When conflict cannot be avoided, he has instructed them how to respond (3:13–4:11). He draws the letter toward its close with some thoughts of consolation for those who, despite their best efforts, will nevertheless find themselves suffering because of their faith in Jesus Christ.

IV. Consolation for the Suffering Flock (4:12–5:11)
➤ A. Two Final Thoughts about Suffering for Christ (4:12–19)
   B. Final Exhortations to the Community (5:1–11)

A. Two Final Thoughts about Suffering for Christ (4:12–19)

Although we intuitively know that suffering is somehow not the way life is meant to be, Peter makes the startling claim that suffering should come as no surprise to the Christian. In fact, when suffering comes for the right reasons, it is actually an opportunity for joy and blessing. Peter explains that to suffer for being a Christian is to suffer according to the will of God. This indicates that the one who chooses to suffer for being a Christian rather than turning aside from following Christ is already undergoing the eschatological judgment that will in the end separate God's people from those who reject him.

1. The blessing of suffering (4:12–16)
2. Suffering now as eschatological judgment (4:17–18)
3. Trusting God even while suffering (4:19)

Exegesis and Exposition

[12]Dear friends, do not be surprised by the fiery ordeal among you that is taking place to test you, as [if this were] something strange happening to you. [13]Rather, to whatever extent you share the sufferings of Christ, rejoice, so that also when his glory is revealed you will exuberantly rejoice. [14]If you are vilified because of the name of Christ, [you are] blessed, because the Spirit of glory and of God rests upon you.⌐ ¬ [15]For let none of you suffer as a murderer, or a thief, or an evildoer, or [even] as a meddler. [16]But if [anyone suffers] as a Christian, let that one not be ashamed, but let them glorify God because of this name. [17]Because [it is] time for the judgment to begin with the house of God; and since [it begins] first with us, what will be the end of those who disobey the gospel of God? [18]And since the righteous person is saved with difficulty, where will the ungodly and the sinner appear? [19]So then, let even those who suffer according to the will of God entrust their lives to the faithful Creator by doing good.

1. The Blessing of Suffering (4:12–16)

A previous generation of scholars argued that the doxology in 1 Pet. 4:11 concludes an original work that later was joined to 4:12–5:14 (Perdelwitz 1911; Windisch 1930; Moule 1955–56; Reicke 1964; Beare 1970). But the thematic and lexical echoes between this section and chapter 1 attest the unity of the text as it now stands (see "Literary Unity and Genre" in the introduction). The trying fiery ordeal of 4:12 echoes the refining fire of 1:7. The theme of rejoicing amid trials in 4:13 in anticipation of the final consummation of joy resumes the same theme from 1:6–7. The presence of the Spirit with suffering believers in 4:14 further defines the sanctifying work of the Spirit in 1:2. The concept of appointed times in 4:17 and 5:6 echoes the wording of 1:5, 11.

In his final statement Peter makes two points about suffering for being a Christian. He opens with the thought that such suffering is to be expected, and he closes with the admonition that the one who suffers is to continue to live righteously as an expression of abiding trust in God despite circumstances.

First, in 4:12 Peter makes the startling claim that unjust suffering is not to come as a surprise. This thought runs counter to modern sensibilities that consider suffering and hard times to be an abnormal state of life that should be avoided if at all possible. And if they can't be avoided, they should be dealt with expeditiously so that "normal" life can resume as quickly as possible. In some first-century Greek thought, however, consolation could be found in the knowledge that whatever the misfortune one encountered, "nothing unexpected has happened" (Holloway 2002). In this way of thinking, misfortune is more bearable if it is understood to be a normal part of the workings of the universe. Even today some clergy offer consolation for bereavement in the thought that death is simply a normal part of life and therefore to be taken in stride.

Misfortune and death are certainly "normal" in the sense that they are universally experienced, but they are not normal when viewed from God's intention in creation and his plan in redemption. The idea that normal life should always be harmonious and free from suffering, despite universal suffering and death, remains a lingering echo of life in Eden as God created it before the fall. It is also a longing for the time when there will be no more tears, suffering, pain, and death (Rev. 21:4). From either the prefall or the eschatological perspective, suffering and death are abnormal. But Peter's letter is pastoral, addressing the needs of people who live in this world, where evil, sin, and suffering are pressing realities of life. Therefore, such fiery trials are not to take Christians by surprise but are to be expected. Because evil and sin targeted the perfect human being, Jesus Christ, those who follow in his footsteps should not be surprised to find themselves also targets of the forces of evil and sin that came against Jesus. Christ's suffering, rejection, and execution normalize suffering for the Christian in this world. But to suffer because one is a Christian is at the same time to be blessed, because it marks one as belonging to God's obedient followers, upon whom his Spirit rests (4:14). As Jesus himself taught, "Woe to you when everyone speaks well of you" (Luke 6:26 TNIV), for such universal acclaim suggests that one has in some way compromised the testimony of God's truth in order to please.

Peter's statement that Christians should not be surprised when they are vilified and slandered because they are Christians must be properly framed by its sociopolitical setting. Peter was speaking in a time when Christian values and the resulting way of life contrasted markedly with Greco-Roman society. In that setting, one could hardly be an uncompromising Christian and remain unrecognized as such. Modern Western society has for many centuries been so largely shaped by the Judeo-Christian ethic that acceptable values of Christians and of unbelievers have not necessarily conflicted so sharply. From the time of Constantine to rather recently, at least a nominal Christian profession was socially acceptable and in many places even the social norm. Therefore, Western Christians may not be able to relate to the theme of suffering for Christ in 1 Peter, since most have not lived in a social situation similar to its original readers. But from that time until this, the church has always been persecuted in some part of the world, and some believers live with the daily threat of persecution for their faith. To them, 1 Peter is a precious letter of pastoral encouragement from the heart of an apostle, helping them understand their calling as followers of Christ.

If suffering for Christ should be the believer's experience, Peter reframes it as a reason not for bitterness or despair but for joy (4:13). The thought that suffering produces joy is as strange as Peter's earlier statement that those who suffer are "blessed" (3:14). This does not mean that the believer should enjoy suffering per se, but undeserved suffering because of Christian faith is evidence of future eschatological deliverance, which will bring the ultimate joy a human being can experience. Society may judge the gospel to be irrelevant or even evil, but it is God's judgment that ultimately will stand. The Christian who stands fast and suffers for the gospel is responding to an eternal reality that will outlast death and even history itself. The joy prompted by recognizing this is but a foretaste of the joy that Christians will experience when the glory of Christ is fully and universally revealed (4:13) and their faith is vindicated at last. Peter consoles his readers that it is therefore better to stand by one's faith now, even though it results in suffering, than to deny Christ for present relief only to suffer much worse in the coming judgment as one who has denied and rejected Christ. This thought is all the more poignant coming as it does from Peter, the disciple who denied Jesus three times the night he was arrested.

Those who suffer for Christ, Peter says, are blessed. The blessing is not in the suffering itself but because the presence of the Spirit of glory and of God is present (4:14). The idea that suffering is a blessing in disguise because it builds character, whether true or not, is probably not Peter's thought. He does not suggest that suffering for the name of Christ is beneficial to the believer in any way other than as evidence of genuine faith. The blessing comes not because of an opportunity for self-improvement but because of the presence of God.

The idea that God blesses misfortune and suffering may also seem strange. All too often, when believers suffer and face hard times, they question where God is. Have they displeased God? Has God left them to their own resources? Is their suffering a sign of God's disfavor or even his anger? Although the human heart naturally tends to view suffering in that way, Peter's teaching corrects his reader's understanding of their experience. First, suffering that comes because one is living for Christ should not be a surprise; Jesus' suffering normalized (and dignified) it. And second, the Spirit of glory and of God rests upon the believer who suffers rather than sins. For it is only by the power of the Spirit that one finds the resolve and strength to live an uncompromising life in a society that is hostile to one's fundamental convictions and values. One's willingness to suffer rather than compromise indicates the inner transformation of the sanctifying work of the Spirit (1:2) that has set one apart as a living stone in the spiritual house of God (2:5). God has not abandoned the Christian who suffers; to the contrary, God is powerfully present in the experience of suffering for Christ.

The phrase "the Spirit of glory and of God rests upon you" (τὸ τῆς δόξης καὶ τὸ τοῦ θεοῦ πνεῦμα ἐφ᾽ ὑμᾶς ἀναπαύεται, *to tēs doxēs kai to tou theou pneuma eph' hymas anapauetai*) is probably an allusion to Isa. 11:2 LXX (see additional note on 4:14 for a discussion of the longer reading). The LXX of Isa. 11:1–2 is a messianic prophecy:

> And a staff shall come out of the root of Iessai [Jesse],
>   and a blossom shall come up out of his root.
> And the spirit of God shall rest on him,
>   the spirit of wisdom and understanding,
>   the spirit of counsel and might,
>   the spirit of knowledge and godliness. (*NETS*)

Peter understands that it was the Spirit of Christ who spoke to the prophets, such as Isaiah, revealing the sufferings of the Messiah and the glories that would follow (1 Pet. 1:10–12). In 4:14, Peter claims that the same Spirit of God predicted to rest upon the Messiah also rests on the believer who is willing to suffer for Jesus Christ. Peter consoles his readers that because the same Spirit of glory and of God rests upon them, their current suffering is as Christ's was, a prelude to the glory to follow.

Peter is quick to distinguish the kind of suffering that marks the believer destined for glory from suffering that results from one's own bad behavior: "For let none of you suffer as a murderer, or a thief, or an evildoer, or [even] as a meddler" (4:15). This list denotes egregious misconduct that seems to be ordered from the greater to the lesser.

Murder and theft are prohibited by the Ten Commandments and were prosecuted under Greco-Roman law as well. But it is not necessary to infer that some of Peter's readers have actually violated the Roman laws implied by the four terms. Some of his readers may have been accused of various kinds of evildoing (2:14–15), and for that reason it is very important that they not be found in fact to be what they have been accused of being.

The first three terms, "murderer," "thief," and "evildoer," are introduced as one syntactical unit by ὡς (hōs), joining them as behaviors that Peter expects all would agree to be wrong. There is no honor or glory in suffering that comes from committing murder, theft, or evildoing, of course. Hōs is repeated again before the fourth and final term, ἢ ὡς ἀλλοτριεπίσκοπος (ē hōs allotriepiskopos), which both sets it apart from, and joins it to, the preceding three with the sense "or [even] as a meddler" (see additional note on 4:15 for a discussion of the meaning of this term). There is no glory or honor in suffering that results from even the lesser misconduct of becoming inappropriately involved in another person's affairs. Meddling may be a problem among Peter's readers, for it is a peculiar word with which to end a vice list if it has no specific relevance to them. Perhaps Peter singles out meddling because his readers may not have recognized that at least some of their suffering could be coming from meddling in a way that did not seem obviously wrong or inappropriate to them. J. H. Elliott (2000: 788) describes what such meddling may have involved in the social context of the original readers: "Censuring the behavior of outsiders on the basis of claims to a higher morality, interfering with family relationships, fomenting domestic discontent and discord, or tactless attempts at conversion." The prohibition against meddling accords well with Peter's teaching elsewhere that Greco-Roman social roles and boundaries are to be respected, though not to the point of denying Christ (2:12–13, 17; 2:18–3:7). Peter wants his readers to avoid attracting hostility if at all possible, without renouncing their faith in Christ.

Whether or not Peter's readers were actually involved in meddling (or engaged in any of the other behaviors listed), he clearly assumes that they might be capable not only of meddling but also of the more egregious conduct of evildoing, theft, and murder. Despite the span of their severity, all four of these misbehaviors are grouped together as one over against being a Christian:

> 4:15 Let none of you suffer as a murderer, thief, evildoer, or [even] as a meddler.
>
> 4:16 But if anyone suffers as a Christian . . .

Knox (1953: 188) has suggested that what lies behind this structure is the possibility that Christians were often "placed in the false position of being *punished*" for such crimes even though they were innocent (emphasis original). In this case, Peter is instructing his readers to live in such a way that the only "crime" against the state or society for which they are guilty is their Christian faith. Although Peter's instructions are appropriate in the context of formal charges, there is no reason to think they are limited to that situation.

If you suffer for being a Christian (Χριστιανός, *Christianos*, 4:16)—for living in word and deed consistently with the gospel of Jesus Christ—then do not be ashamed if society rejects and reviles you, whether through social ostracism or official prosecution. You are blessed (4:14) and God is glorified when you suffer simply for bearing the name of Christ—not for being a Christian murderer, a Christian thief, a Christian evildoer, or even a Christian meddler. Peter thereby calls his readers to assess realistically what is actually causing their suffering, while affirming that they may be suffering simply for living as God wills them to live as a Christian.

In 4:16 Peter contrasts glory with shame when one is suffering for the name of Christ (Bechtler 1998; B. Campbell 1998: 234, 239). Those so suffering were no doubt tempted to think that perhaps their faith in Jesus Christ is ill-founded or that perhaps they should be ashamed of themselves for believing something that so offended their society. The insults and slander of unbelievers are perhaps intended to shame and thereby to marginalize those who believed in something so outrageous as the resurrection of the dead. In a culture where one's standing is based on honor or shame, shame is no doubt a major issue for Christians who offend their society by their beliefs or lifestyle. But Peter wants his readers to understand themselves on very different terms. He provides "an alternative way of calculating honor within their alternative, liminal communities of faith" (Bechtler 1998: 203–4). Faith in Christ is nothing to be ashamed of, even when society says it is. What is more, suffering for Christ is actually a mark of honor, and in 4:17a Peter provides a mysterious reason why this is so.

2. Suffering Now as Eschatological Judgment (4:17–18)

Do not be ashamed of your faith in Christ, Peter writes, "because it is time for the judgment to begin with the house of God." The reference to the "house of God" picks up the image of Christians as living stones in a spiritual house of God (2:4–5). Peter joins this image with the OT tradition that God's judgment begins with God's own people. This may seem to be a strange concept to Christians today who feel that because of Christ they are not subject to the judgment of God, much less due any suffering or penalty. And certainly there is unanimous teaching among the NT writers that there is no condemnation for those who believe in Christ and that they will be delivered from the destiny that is coming to those who disobey God by rejecting the redemption he provides in Jesus Christ. But there is ample teaching that Christians will nevertheless be judged and that it is their standing with Christ that will bring this judgment to a good end (e.g., Rom. 14:10).

Peter assumes that his Christian readers will be judged along with the rest of humanity. Moreover, his thought is informed by the tradition in Judaism that when God judges, he will begin with his own people, and in fact with the elders at the temple (Jer. 25:29 [32:29 LXX]; Ezek. 9:5–6; Amos 3:2; Zech. 13:9; Mal. 3:1–5). Because of the lexical affinity the prepositional phrase ἀπὸ τοῦ οἴκου τοῦ θεοῦ (apo tou oikou tou theou, from the house of God) in 4:17a has with Ezek. 9:5–6 LXX, Schutter (1987) has argued that the tradition based on the Ezekiel passage is the primary background for understanding 1 Pet. 4:17a (also McKelvey 1969: 133). On the other hand, D. Johnson (1986: 292) argues that Zech. 13:9 and Mal. 3:1–3, which both refer to God's fiery presence, are more relevant for Peter's imagery than the Ezekiel passage, for they "provide the pattern for the escalation of eschatological judgment as it moves out from the house of God to those outside the covenant." Two passages are in view:

This third I will bring into the fire [διὰ πυρός]; I will refine them [καὶ πυρώσω αὐτούς] like silver and test them like gold. They will call on my name and I will answer them; I will say, "They are my people," and they will say, "The LORD is our God." (Zech. 13:9 NIV)

"See, I will send my messenger, who will prepare the way before me. Then suddenly the Lord you are seeking will come to his temple; the messenger of the covenant, whom you desire, will come," says the LORD Almighty. But who can endure the day of his coming? Who can stand when he appears? For he will be like a refiner's fire [πῦρ χωνευτηρίου] or a launderer's soap. He will sit as a refiner and purifier of silver; he will purify the Levites and refine them like gold and silver. (Mal. 3:1–3 NIV)

The fiery judgment of God in these passages is alluded to with the phrase "fiery ordeal" of 1 Pet. 4:12. Some interpreters have taken the image of the fiery ordeal as an allusion to physical torture and martyrdom. Some have even suggested that news of Nero's torching of Christians in Rome reached Peter's ears at this very point while he was writing and that the phrase is a direct allusion to it. This imaginative interpretation goes well beyond the data. Moreover, the image of smelting precious metals in a refining fire was widely applied. Seneca, for instance, uses the metaphor in his proverb *Ignis aurum probat, miseria fortes viros* (Fire tests gold, affliction tests strong men; *Ep., On Providence* 5.10; for further discussion see "Date and Authorship" in the introduction and comments on 1:7). The image is also found in Jewish writings outside the canon in the context of enduring suffering (e.g., Sir. 2:1–5). However, the OT images of God's presence as a refining fire that judges, starting with his own people, are the most likely source of Peter's thought here, because 4:17 introduces the idea of God's judgment.

The original context of the passages from Ezekiel, Zechariah, and Malachi do not fit Peter's use, for they are pronouncing God's judgment on his people for violating the covenant. Peter here is saying exactly the opposite. Peter's readers are suffering because they are living for Christ and not because God has abandoned them (as in Ezek. 9) or is punishing their sins (as in Jer. 25:29). Furthermore, when Peter quotes OT passages elsewhere in the letter and applies them to his readers, he consistently preserves the original context (e.g., Ps. 33 LXX; Isa. 53). Moreover, the lack of precise lexical correspondence to any one of these passages suggests that Peter is not referring to any of them but is drawing on a familiar tradition in Judaism to make a somewhat different point for his Christian readers. That is, the suffering that Peter's readers are experiencing is an integral part of God's eschatological judgment, which all human beings must face, but because of their faith in Christ they need not fear it.

How can suffering caused by unbelievers be an integral part of God's eschatological judgment? There is a startling mystery in Peter's logic when he closely associates, if not actually identifies, God's judgment with pagan hostilities. Bechtler (1998: 145) states the mystery: "Paradoxically, the hostility of the larger society toward Christians (4:16) is here symbolized as God's judgment, and the difference between Christians and non-Christians is pictured in the following verse (4:18) not as a categorical distinction but as a difference of degree." The logic that Bechtler points out, but does not develop, reveals how Peter understands the nature of the judgment (τὸ κρίμα, to krima) to be God's judgment. Peter says that it is "time for the judgment to begin with the house of God." His association of pagan hostility and God's judgment is by inference and is not explicit. The presence of the definite article (to krima) and the allusion to the prophetic tradition of fiery eschatological judgment implies that the judgment in view is God's. Moreover, the phrase ὁ καιρός (ho kairos, the time) suggests that "now," at the time Peter writes, is the appointed time for God's judgment to begin. The presence of the article strengthens that construal, but even if the article is not original, as variant readings may indicate, Peter's use of kairos in 1:11 indicates that Peter has in mind the appointed times of God's redemptive work. Therefore, the judgment of 4:17 should be understood as eschatological judgment.

But how can eschatological judgment intrude into history? Does not eschatological judgment mean that which occurs following the last days of history? The suffering of God's people in the end times is a familiar theme of Christian eschatology, sometimes called the "messianic woes" preceding the (return of) the Messiah, or the "birth pangs," or the Great

Tribulation. This has led many interpreters to construe Peter's reference to eschatological judgment as a temporal indicator that he believes the return of Christ is near because his readers are beginning to suffer the persecution that is expected to immediately precede the return of Christ. But the fact that Peter understands the persecution of his readers to be the beginning of eschatological judgment does not necessarily mean that he thinks the return of Christ is imminent. Although he may believe that, his reference to persecution as God's judgment makes a different point intended to comfort and console his readers.

The English word "judgment" may at first connote condemnation and the penalty or punishment that consequently follows. This is in fact the sense of *to krima* as it is used in Rom. 3:8; Gal. 5:10; 2 Pet. 2:3; Jude 4; and Rev. 17:1. If this were the sense of the word as used in 1 Pet. 4:17a, the statement would mean that the hostility of pagans causing Peter's Christian readers to suffer is a punishment or penalty on those Christians, who apparently have been judged by God and found culpable. Nothing like this is mentioned elsewhere throughout the letter. Furthermore, this sense does not fit Peter's point, which is exactly the opposite: suffering for Christ does not imply the guilt of the sufferer and in fact brings glory to God.

The phrase *to krima* can also refer to "the action of a judge" (BDAG 567) with no assumed penalty or punishment in view. This is more likely the sense of *to krima* in 1 Pet. 4:17a. God will begin his process of judging humanity with his own people, to see which are truly Christ's. (Compare a similar teaching about God's judgment in Jesus' parable where he first judges the sheep and then the goats in Matt. 25:31–46.) This understanding of *to krima* is corroborated when the suffering of pagan hostility that is identified as God's judgment in 4:17 is previously described in 4:12 as a fiery ordeal that is happening "to test you."

Peter is saying that eschatological judgment, understood as the sorting out of humanity, begins with God's house, defined in 2:4–5 as those who come to Christ and are built as living stones into a spiritual house. The contrast in 4:17b is between "those who reject the gospel of God" and "us," a group in which Peter probably includes himself and all whom he considers to be genuine Christians. Those who profess Christ are the first ones to be tested in God's judging action, and it occurs during their lives and throughout history. The Great Tribulation of the final days immediately preceding the return of Christ is the most severe form of this testing. The testing that persecution because of Christ presents, wherever and whenever it occurs, is of one piece with the final eschatological judgment, because persecution sorts out those who are truly Christ's from those who are not. The hostile reaction of unbelievers to their Christian associates is at the same time God's plumb line, testing the mettle of those who profess faith in Christ, that their faith may be proved as genuine as smelted gold and silver. For this reason Peter says—because this trying situation of persecution is a judging—Christians should stand firm and unashamedly bear the name of Christ (4:16). By doing so, they bring glory to God. Therefore, the suffering they bear for the name of Christ, which is shaming them in the eyes of society, becomes their badge of honor as one of the living stones in God's spiritual house. Although Peter's logic is obscure and based on an unfamiliar tradition, he is consoling his readers by explaining why they should see rejection by society actually as honor and not shame.

This interpretation of Peter's logic also makes good sense of the enigmatic thought that immediately follows in 4:18, that "the righteous person is saved with difficulty" (quoting Prov. 11:31 LXX; see additional note on 4:18). The concept of the difficulty of salvation originated with Jesus, who taught that the distressful last days are shortened for the sake of the chosen (Mark 13:20) and that those who find the narrow door are but few of the many who seek to enter (Luke 13:23–24). Peter's point is not that salvation is difficult for God to achieve, though the sufferings of Christ were certainly no easy means of atonement. The hostility of those who rejected Jesus was ironically the means that took him to the cross, by which the atonement he offered to them was made. Peter sees the situation faced by his readers to be analogous. The thought is that the world's response makes it difficult for Christians to remain faithful to Christ to the end. Will Peter's readers have the resolve and the stamina to persevere to the end? Or will the insults, abuse, ostracism, and even more serious and threatening pressures drive them to deny Christ, renounce the faith, and return to pagan beliefs and living, thus rejecting the gospel of God as surely as those who never made a profession? In this sense it is difficult for even the righteous person to persevere to the end and be saved.

The difficulty of being saved that Peter observes may not be fully appreciated by modern Western Christians for whom society has not (yet) drawn a line in the sand. Even so, how sad it is that many who once professed Christ eventually turn away under peer pressure. If that happens in a society that has a relatively great tolerance for Christianity, imagine the difficulty of living for Christ in a society where today it is illegal to be a Christian.

Peter further consoles and encourages his readers with the contrast between them and those who persecute them (4:17b):

εἰ πρῶτον ἀφ' ἡμῶν,   τί τὸ τέλος τῶν ἀπειθούντων τῷ τοῦ θεοῦ εὐαγγελίῳ;

ei prōton aph' hēmōn,   *ti to telos tōn apeithountōn tō tou theou euangeliō?*

If first with us,   what will be the end of those who reject the gospel of God?

Peter groups himself with his readers in contrast to those who reject the gospel of God. If in God's testing those who embrace his gospel have to suffer so first, what magnitude of suffering will the end bring for those who reject the gospel and make no pretense to serve or obey God? In 4:16, the motivation to faithfulness was positive, pointing out the opportunity Christians have to glorify God by remaining faithful to Christ in the midst of suffering and thereby demonstrating that God is worthy of their suffering. Here in 4:17b–18, Peter makes the negative point that those who reject the gospel of God will suffer much more than anything the Christian will endure during the hardships and persecution of this life. Therefore, it is better to suffer a little now as a Christian than to become one of those who reject Christ and will suffer much more later.

3. Trusting God Even While Suffering (4:19)

So, if God is testing his people when he allows them to suffer persecution from pagan hostility, what is the correct response to this situation? In 4:19 Peter continues: "Let even those who suffer according to the will of God entrust their lives to the faithful Creator by doing good." It is easiest to entrust one's life and loved ones to God when life is going well and things are good. But Peter wants even those who suffer to trust God when they are suffering "according to the will of God," that is, not for being murderers, thieves, evildoers, or meddlers. We seem to assume that God knows what he is doing when we are happy and well. But trouble and difficult times raise hard questions about our relationship with God and about his intent and character. It is harder to entrust our lives to God when we are suffering, and especially when that suffering is unjust and is the consequence of living obediently for him!

Here Peter alludes to the theme of following in Jesus' footsteps, for what did Christ do when he was reviled and suffered? He entrusted himself to the one who judges justly (2:23). This example of trusting God even unto death is the example Jesus left that Christians might follow in his footsteps (2:21). Therefore, Peter exhorts his readers to entrust their lives to the faithful Creator, who is the one who has the authority and power to judge all humanity justly. Neither human society nor human governments can pass the final judgment on Christians, and so in the long run those judgments are irrelevant.

First Peter 4:19 counts God being Creator as the basis for his prerogative to execute eschatological judgment. God will sort out all humanity, separating those who are his from those who reject his gospel. Christians need not fear this process but should trust their lives to God in all circumstances, including difficult ones, recognizing them as part of God's own work.

How is this trust expressed when one is suffering? By continuing to do good (ἐν ἀγαθοποιΐᾳ, en agathopoiïa). It is easiest to do good when things are going well, when we are prospering and healthy. But when we suffer as the consequence of doing good (i.e., living for Christ with all that it implies), how unreasonable it seems to continue to do the very things that are causing pain. Continue to live as a Christian; continue to observe appropriate social relationships; continue to minister to one another in the Christian community. Do not let persecution and suffering deflect you from your calling in Christ, because they are a part of this calling.

Suffering because one is a Christian is, therefore, neither unexpected nor shameful, because the nexus of suffering and honor is embodied in Jesus Christ himself. Suffering is an opportunity to glorify God and a badge of honor for the living stones in the house of God. Joy rather than surprise. Blessing rather than insult. Glory to God rather than shame. The Christian is called to enduring commitment to Christ's gospel amid suffering caused by that very commitment.

Additional Notes

4:14. NA[27] rejects as a secondary gloss the phrase included in the majority of manuscripts at the end of 4:14: κατὰ μὲν αὐτοὺς βλασφημεῖται, κατὰ δε ὑμᾶς δοξάζεται (*kata men autous blasphēmeitai, kata de hymas doxazetai*, [the Spirit] . . . blasphemed by them but glorified by you). Michaels (1988: 265) supports the reading as original, arguing that it is consistent with Peter's style elsewhere, in 1 Pet. 3:18 and 4:6, and noting that it most likely dropped out of manuscripts due to homoeoteleuton (ἀναπαύεται . . . δοξάζεται). Rodgers (1981: 93) argues that because the phrase is attested in one Old Latin manuscript, T, the reading is in fact ancient, but he does not discuss the possibility that the Old Latin manuscript was simply "corrected" to agree with a Greek manuscript that included the secondary phrase. He further argues that it is original because it is an allusion to Isa. 52:5 LXX that sits well in the context of 1 Peter: τάδε λέγει Κύριος. Δι' ὑμᾶς διὰ παντὸς τὸ ὄνομά μου βλασφημεῖται ἐν τοῖς ἔθνεσιν (*tade legei Kyrios, Di' hymas dia pantos to onoma mou blasphēmeitai en tois ethnesin*, Thus says the Lord, "Because of you my name is always being blasphemed among the Gentiles"). Rodgers takes this allusion to imply that Peter's readers are Jewish, but in so doing, he overlooks the power of allusion to speak into a new context. He points out that if the phrase is original, it functions to encourage Peter's readers by affirming that their suffering is not blaspheming their Lord's name; rather, it is the unjust behavior of their adversaries that does so. However, the so-called allusion shares only one verb with Isa. 52:5 LXX, calling into question whether it is truly an intentional allusion at all. Furthermore, the absence of the phrase in the earliest and best manuscripts of 1 Peter has swayed modern English translations (except the NKJV) and virtually all interpreters to agree with NA[27] and omit it from consideration as original to Peter's letter.

4:15. The meaning of ἀλλοτριεπίσκοπος (*allotriepiskopos*; variant reading, ἀλλοτρίοις ἐπίσκοπος, *allotriois episkopos*) remains uncertain. The word occurs only here in the NT. Thiede (1988: 179) suggests it may be a word coined by Peter, possibly as an allusion to Nero. According to Beyer (*TDNT* 2:620–22), other constructions with the *allotrio-* prefix consistently refer to one who has something else in mind, such as ἀλλοτριοπραγέω (*allotrioprageō*, to pursue matters of another, which do not concern one). Following this etymological pattern, ἀλλοτρίου (of another) + ἐπίσκοπος (overseer) would appear to mean "overseer of another." Erbes (1919–20) argues that in the context of 1 Peter it refers to one who is an irresponsible bishop. The negative sense of *allotriepiskopos* in Pseudo-Dionysius the Areopagite (*Epistles* 8) derives not from the word itself but from the context, where it clearly refers to a bishop who is "intruding into an alien sphere of office" (Beyer, *TDNT* 2:620–21n12). However, the immediate context of 1 Pet. 4:15 does not indicate that an ecclesiastical meaning is intended. Moreover, it occurs in a list of misconduct of a more general nature. Bischoff (1906) offers that the term means an insurrectionist or traitor. Based on the translation of the word in one Latin manuscript, Achtemeier (1996: 312) supports the sense that *allotriepiskopos* means a defrauder who misuses a position of agency or executor "for personal enrichment through embezzlement." In the absence of conclusive lexical data, most English translations reflect its etymological sense, "to oversee another," and translate it as "meddler" (NASB, NIV, TNIV, ASV, ESV) or "busybody" (KJV, NKJV) or "mischief maker" (NRSV). The more periphrastic translations amplify the word into a phrase: "prying into other people's affairs" (NLT); "overseer of other people's matters" (J. N. Darby); or "inspector into other men's matters" (R. Young). The doubt that this sense is the precise meaning of *allotriepiskopos* lingers because another word was available to convey this sense (ἀλλοτριοπράγμων, *allotriopragmōn*). Some have concluded that the author of 1 Peter coined this term for the rhetoric of the occasion (J. H. Elliott 2000: 785). It is clear that all known forms of the *allotrio* compounds denote an activity that is not the concern of the doer, and that in 1 Pet. 4:15 this behavior should be avoided. Therefore, "meddler" remains the best inferred sense from the currently available data (for more extensive discussion of the lexical data, see Achtemeier 1996: 311–13; J. H. Elliott 2000: 785–88).

4:18. The Greek adverb μόλις (*molis*), translated here as "with difficulty," in the quotation of Prov. 11:31 has no proper correspondence with the Hebrew text, which reads, "If the righteous receive their due on earth [בָּאָרֶץ, *bāʾāreṣ*], how much more the ungodly and the sinner" (NIV). The Peshitta and an Arabic version follow the LXX; the Vulgate and the Targum follow the Hebrew Masoretic Text (Barr 1975). Barr argues against S. R. Driver's explanation that the LXX and Peshitta are based on a (mis)construal of the pointing of the consonantal text that read it as a word in the Samaritan dialect meaning "coerced" or "compelled." Instead, Barr argues that the LXX translator read a transposition of two consonants, as if the word was בְצַר (*bṣr*) or בְצַרא (*bṣrʾ*), even though this sense is "in straits" rather than "with difficulty." The LXX reading of Prov. 11:31 cannot be explained with certainty. But regardless of how the thought of the difficulty of salvation expressed in the LXX reading came to be there, it is this thought that Peter takes up in his argument in 4:18.

IV. Consolation for the Suffering Flock (4:12–5:11)
    A. Two Final Thoughts about Suffering for Christ (4:12–19)
➤   B. Final Exhortations to the Community (5:1–11)

B. Final Exhortations to the Community (5:1–11)

Peter draws his letter to a close with instructions to the elders and to the "younger" and then exhorts all of them to humble themselves under what they are experiencing, for it is God's hand upon their lives. He cautions them once again to think clearly so they may not be caught unawares by their adversary, the devil. Peter's final exhortation is that they stand firm in the true grace of God. He leaves them with the encouraging thought that they are not alone in their suffering but that all their fellow Christians throughout the world are subject to the same testing. Moreover, Peter reminds them once again that their travail will be short-lived and that God himself will set all things right.

1. Christ Shepherds His Flock through the Elders (5:1–5)

In this passage Peter instructs his readers about the type of shepherd-leadership that is needed to assure the survival of the church in trying times of persecution. The leaders must oversee the church in a godly way, shepherding the flock rather than domineering it. The pastoral motif of the shepherd caring for and seeking the weak and the wandering even while jeopardizing himself provides the background against which these final instructions to the church are to be read. In this final section of the letter, by encouraging the elders to shepherd and the others to submit to that leadership, Peter underscores the importance of responsible church structure for seeing the Christian community safely through the fiery ordeal of testing.

a. Instructions to the elders (5:1–4)
b. Instructions to "the younger" (5:5)

Exegesis and Exposition

[1]Therefore, the elders among you I earnestly urge—[I,] your fellow elder and witness of the sufferings of Christ, [and] one who also shares in the glory about to be revealed. [2]Shepherd the flock of God among you, ⌜overseeing⌝ [them] not as forced, but willingly, according to God; not for greedy gain, but eager to be of service; [3]not domineering those allotted [to you] but being role models for the flock. [4]And when the chief shepherd appears, you will obtain the amaranth crown of glory. [5]Similarly, you who are younger submit to the elders. And all of you clothe yourselves in humility with regard to one another, because God opposes the arrogant but gives grace to the humble.

a. Instructions to the Elders (5:1–4)

The exhortation to the elders (πρεσβύτεροι, *presbyteroi*) among Peter's readers follows upon Peter's explanation in 4:17–19 that persecution of the church is the beginning of the sorting process by which those who are truly God's are separated from those who are not. It is better, Peter explains, to suffer persecution according to God's will for being a Christian than to renounce Christ in order to avoid trouble for this moment only and then face a worse judgment later. Those who are suffering for the faith should entrust themselves to their faithful Creator and continue to do good. As noted above, 4:17 has the most direct lexical affinity with Ezek. 9:5–6 LXX, where judgment begins with the elders who are in front of the temple. Perhaps it is coincidental, but Peter's mind is moving in the same direction, for he, too, speaks of judgment beginning in the house of God, followed immediately by a reference to elders. This suggests that the disputed οὖν (oun, therefore) of 5:1 is possibly original to Peter's logic, joining the specific instructions for elders to the thought that in God's house they are judged first. Therefore, the elders especially should not draw back from shepherding the people, for it is God's will that they willingly lead the church, even though by doing so they may make themselves a larger target of persecution. Peter reminds them that regardless of what they suffer now, they will receive the amaranth (i.e., unfading) crown of glory when the Chief Shepherd, Jesus Christ, appears. (The adjective "amaranth" refers to a red flower whose color was unfading.)

First Peter 5:1 is the most extensive self-description given by the author in this epistle. Peter describes himself with two phrases in apposition: first, the fellow elder and witness of the sufferings of Christ; and second, one who will also share in the about-to-be-revealed glory. Peter's self-description as ὁ συμπρεσβύτερος (ho sympresbyteros, the fellow elder) indicates his solidarity with those whom he exhorts, making them aware that their ministry of church leadership is an extension of his own and thereby deriving the authority of the elders from that of the apostles. The definite article combined with the preposition sym- (a form of syn, with) may be understood as a possessive, "your fellow-." Peter personally understands their responsibilities, their fears, and the pressures that assail them because he also bears the responsibilities of an elder. The apostle embraces his calling as a leader in the church, a calling that will lead to his martyrdom in Rome. He is not asking them to do anything that he himself is not also doing.

Some interpreters see this self-description as an indication that the apostle Peter could not have written this letter, on the assumption that an apostle would not describe himself as simply a "fellow elder" (Beare 1970: 198). Norbert Brox (cited in J. H. Elliott 2000: 817) assumes pseudonymous authorship, arguing that this is a self-reference to the actual author of 1 Peter, who was in fact an anonymous elder. However, the terms "apostle" and "elder" were not necessarily mutually exclusive even during the lifetime of the apostles. In fact, it is difficult to imagine that an apostle would not also be considered an elder both in the local church where he resided and throughout the church at large. The author of the letter has already established his apostolic authority in 1:1, and self-reference to being a "fellow elder" is appropriate if his purpose here is to empathetically express his solidarity with those he is consoling and encouraging (as also J. H. Elliott 2000: 818). The term "fellow elder" may in fact argue against pseudonymous authorship, since it

1. Christ Shepherds His Flock through the Elders

seems more likely that a pseudonymous author consistent in his guise would simply reassert Peter's apostolic authority here as the basis for exhorting the leaders of the church.

In the same syntactic unit governed by the definite article, ὁ (*ho*, the), Peter also describes himself as a "witness of the sufferings of Christ." At first it may seem that the term μάρτυς (*martys*, witness) refers to an eyewitness, alluding to Peter's personal experience with Jesus. Against this understanding, some interpreters point out that Peter himself was not actually present to see Jesus die on the cross (Best 1971: 168; Davids 1990: 177; J. H. Elliott 2000: 819). However, that observation unnecessarily presses the precision of the phrase. From the time that Peter recognized Jesus as the Messiah and heard him predict his own rejection and death in Jerusalem, he was a witness of the sufferings of Jesus (Matt. 16:13–23; Mark 8:27–33; Luke 9:18–22). Peter witnessed the tide of popular support turn against Jesus. He saw how Jesus' ministry alienated him from his earthly family. Peter witnessed how the Jewish leaders rejected Jesus' claims, and he knew of the plots against Jesus, ate the last Passover meal with him, and observed his agony in the garden of Gethsemane, the betrayal of Judas, the arrest, and the questioning before the high priest, which led to his execution. The penetration of the nails was the final, lethal blow, but whether Peter witnessed the precise moment of crucifixion or not, he could legitimately claim to be a witness to the sufferings of the Messiah.

But does the term *martys* necessarily indicate an eyewitness? The syntax suggests otherwise. The words "fellow elder" (*sympresbyteros*) and *martys* are governed by one definite article and joined by a copulative καί (*kai*, and), imparting the sense of the preposition *sym-* to both terms. As a fellow elder, Peter also shares the role of a fellow witness (as also Davids 1990: 177; Goppelt 1993: 342–43; Michaels 1988: 280–81). This understanding is further reinforced by the καί (*kai*, also) in the second descriptor as a fellow heir of glory, indicating that the theme of joint participation extends throughout the apostle's self-description as a fellow elder, a fellow witness, and a fellow heir of glory. This is the more likely construal in the immediate context, since the semantic range of *martys* allows reference to any witness who testifies to what he or she believes to be the truth.

Even though *martys* here need not be a reference to Peter's eyewitness experience of Jesus' suffering, it also need not be taken as evidence of pseudonymous authorship, much less as a reference to Peter's own martyrdom (Beare 1970: 198; Best 1971: 168). Nor does it imply that Peter was not an eyewitness of the sufferings of Christ. Rather, Peter is intent here to motivate church leadership that continues the witness of the apostles, whose testimony to the truth is indeed based on eyewitness experience.

The courageous act of leading the church in perilous times rather than renouncing Christ is itself a form of witness that Peter shares with local church leadership. The apostle willingly embraces apostolic leadership of the church, making himself vulnerable to the same hostile forces that killed Jesus. Those who follow in the footsteps of Jesus (2:21) witness to the truth of his message as they share in the suffering of rejection he experienced. This construal of *martys* coheres well with the major theme of 1 Peter: all believers are called to suffer as necessary for their faithfulness to Christ. Here Peter is the apostolic role model for his fellow elders, who are being called upon in turn to be role models (5:3) for all in the Christian community.

Peter presents suffering for Christ and the glory of eternal life as two sides of the same coin, and so he immediately describes himself in a second phrase in apposition as "one who also shares in the glory about to be revealed." Given the explicit future cast of the adjectival participle that qualifies "glory" (μελλούσης, *mellousēs*, about [to be], 5:1), it is unlikely that the glory refers directly to the transfiguration or the resurrection of Christ (contra Selwyn 1958: 228). The phrase anticipates the promise in 5:4 that those who, like Peter, entrust themselves to God and continue to faithfully serve the church will receive the unfading (i.e., immortal) crown of glory when Jesus appears.

The terms *presbyteroi* (elders, 5:1) and *episkopountes* (overseeing, 5:2) have both been offered as evidence for dating this letter much later than the lifetime of the apostle Peter, on the grounds that these terms reflect an ecclesiastical structure that did not exist in the apostle's own lifetime. However, the use of the term *presbyteroi* is of no help at all in dating the letter, for its use spans centuries in Jewish writings (see "Date and Authorship" in the introduction). In the third century BC the LXX used *presbyteroi* in referring to leaders of ancient Israel (e.g., Exod. 24:1) and religious leaders during Maccabean times (e.g., 1 Macc. 14:20); then the NT used it for Jewish leaders in Jerusalem at the time of Christ (e.g., Mark 15:1). Following Jewish tradition, the Christian church from its earliest days adopted the term *presbyteroi* to refer to leaders of a local group of believers (e.g., Acts 14:23; 15:2) who were probably heads of households where house churches met (R. Campbell 1994). At the earliest stage of the church in any given locale, elders probably were not officeholders in the formal sense of later ecclesiology but men who, by virtue of their age and the prestige of their families, exercised "an authority that is informal, representative, and collective," based on their seniority in relationships that already existed (R. Campbell 1994: 4, 64). In the sociology of the day it was quite fitting for such men to be appointed a leadership role in the Christian church, a role that became more formalized and official as the needs of the church developed. These sociological factors may have been the basis on which Paul and Barnabas chose elders (e.g., Acts 14:23) but may have played an even stronger role in churches that developed without direct apostolic oversight.

The qualifying participle *episkopountes* is sometimes claimed to offer greater evidence of a late date for 1 Peter than *presbyteroi*; starting in the early second century, its cognate noun ἐπίσκοποι (*episkopoi*, overseers) referred to the office of bishop. But both the verb and the noun also have a long history of usage both before and after being later adopted by the Christian church (R. Campbell 1994). In 1 Pet. 5:2 the service performed by the *presbyteroi* is specified by the verb ποιμάνατε (*poimanate*, shepherd), which is qualified by the adverbial participle *episkopountes*. Only the action of the *presbyteroi* is in view. The apostle Paul also uses *presbyteroi* and *episkopoi* interchangeably in Acts 20:17, 28 as he exhorts the Ephesian elders (*presbyteroi*) to shepherd (*poimainein*) the people of God because they are overseers (*episkopoi*). This is clear evidence that in the earlier stages of the church, no distinction between *presbyteroi* and *episkopoi* was intended (R. Campbell 1994: 173). Apparently, the term *presbyteroi* came from the Jewish Greek tradition and *episkopoi* from the lexicon of secular Greek, but there was no clear distinction in the office to which it referred in the NT writings (Beyer, *TDNT* 2:615–20). At the end of the first century, Clement of Rome refers to only two church offices, using *episkopoi* and *presbyteroi* interchangeably alongside *diakonoi* (1 Clem. 42.4; 44.4–5). The early second-century writings of Ignatius (ca. AD 106) distinguish between three offices, where the elders (*presbyteroi*) and deacons (*diakonoi*) serve below an *episkopos* (e.g., Ign. *Magn.* 6.1; 13.1; Ign. *Trall.* 3.1). Therefore, like *presbyteroi*, the use of the term *episkopountes* also does not allow 1 Peter to be dated with certainty. However, the use of both terms to refer to the same office supports an earlier rather than a later date.

It was perhaps the later adoption of the term *episkopountes* to refer to the service of bishops in distinction from elders that provided a motivation for the omission of the participle *episkopountes* from many manuscripts of 1 Pet. 5:2 (see additional note on 5:2). After the office of bishop (*episkopos*) developed in the early second century, the term *episkopountes* as used in 5:2 may have caused confusion because it would have been read in that context to refer to the same service elders performed within a local group. Since the participle is somewhat redundant in 5:2, scribes may have deliberately dropped it rather than allow the confusion.

The collocation of *episkopountes* with the verb "shepherd" (ποιμάνατε, *poimanate*) should probably be taken as one of Peter's many allusions to the LXX rather than as a reference to an ecclesiastical office. In 2:25 Peter referred to his readers in their pre-Christian state as wandering sheep. The shepherd motif was widely known in Jewish tradition, but because of the heavy concentration of quotations and allusions to Isa. 53 LXX in 1 Pet. 2:21–25, it is likely the wandering-sheep image in 1 Peter has as its immediate background Isa. 53:6 LXX: "All we like sheep have gone astray; each has strayed in his own way, and the Lord gave him [the Suffering Servant] over to our sins." Peter sees the formation of the Christian community as a fulfillment of God's promise to seek out the scattered sheep and to oversee (*episkepsomai*) them (Ezek. 34:11 LXX). They are to follow the footsteps of Christ even as sheep follow their shepherd.

It is not surprising that Peter is drawn to the shepherding motif in Isaiah and Ezekiel, when one remembers his reconciliation with Christ in John 21:15–19, where Jesus asks Peter to feed and care for his sheep as an undershepherd. Jesus, the great Shepherd, commissions Peter in his role as undershepherd; Peter in turn commissions fellow elders as undershepherds, shepherding and overseeing the Christian believers in their locale. He assures them that just as Jesus was glorified in resurrection life, they too will receive that crown of immortality for faithfully fulfilling their calling when Jesus appears.

In 1 Pet. 5:2–3, Peter describes how the *presbyteroi* are to shepherd the flock of God. The adverbial participle "overseeing" (*episkopountes*), which modifies the verb "shepherd" (*poimanate*), is then further qualified by three sets of opposing adverbial qualifiers:

1. overseeing them not as if forced,
   but willingly, according to God;
2. overseeing them not greedy for gain,
   but eager to be of service;
3. overseeing them not as domineering,
   but being role models for the flock.

In the first of the three qualifying phrases, the adverb ἀναγκαστῶς (*anankastōs*, under compulsion) is opposed to ἑκουσίως (*hekousiōs*, voluntarily, 5:2). The *presbyteros* is to shepherd the flock of God by overseeing them voluntarily, not as if forced, raising the question of what kind of compulsion might be in view. Goppelt (1993: 345) assumes from the admonition against compulsion that *presbyteroi* were chosen and appointed by others, exposing the appointees to hardships and dangers that might disincline one from assuming the position willingly. The cognate noun ἀνάγκης (*anankēs*, compulsion) appears in Paul's warning to the Corinthians not to give money to the church under compulsion, for God loves a cheerful giver (2 Cor. 9:7). Peter is saying something similar with regard to service in church office. Regardless of the mechanism for appointing elders, begrudging service is not to be offered, for leadership so motivated will ultimately not be pleasing to God.

The elder should oversee the church "according to God" (κατὰ θεόν, *kata theon*, 5:2). But does this mean that oversight of the church is God's will? Or that the oversight is to be done in a manner consistent with

God's will? Or that the oversight is to be done as God himself oversees the flock? All three are good thoughts that could fit well in the context. But because Peter has been instructing his readers not to follow the ways of Greco-Roman society, perhaps "according to God" is meant in contrast to overseeing the church according to the norms of society or the dictates of Roman rule. Some interpreters take it to mean that the elder must oversee the flock willingly and after the pattern of the Lord himself. This sense coheres well with the general principle in 1 Peter that believers are to follow in the footsteps of the Lord, who is referred to as a "shepherd" and "overseer" in 2:25. Moreover, it also coheres with the echoes of Jesus' teaching that his chosen leaders must serve as he himself served. The concept that the leaders of God's people are themselves undershepherds of God the Great Shepherd is already present in OT tradition based on Jer. 23:1–4, where God indicts the leaders of his people for being poor shepherds, who scattered the flock and drove them away. God promises through Jeremiah that he will place good shepherds over the people when he raises up to David a righteous Branch (23:5–6). In the time of stress and persecution in which Peter writes, the leaders of the Lord's people must oversee the flock in a way that gathers, pastures, and defends it, if the Christian community is to survive and thrive in the face of social pressures.

In the second qualifying phrase, "overseeing them not greedy for gain, but eager to be of service," the adverb αἰσχροκερδῶς (*aischrokerdōs*, greedily) is opposed to προθύμως (*prothymōs*, eagerly, 5:2), a term often used in secular writings to characterize the benefactor of a city who enthusiastically provides time and money for civic duties. *Presbyteroi* are to oversee the flock, not motivated by greed for financial gain but from a spirit of eagerness to serve others. The practice of financially compensating church leadership in some form apparently arose early in the church (e.g., 1 Cor. 9:7; Gal. 6:6), but abuse of the privilege also arose with it (1 Tim. 3:3; 6:5; Titus 1:11; 2 Pet. 2:3; Jude 11). The term *aischrokerdōs* implies a dishonest attempt to gain financially, which suggests that the leaders who oversaw the Christian community sometimes misappropriated its resources for their own gain. The proper attitude of an elder is an eagerness to give, not a desire to get.

The third qualifying phrase (5:3) echoes the teaching of Jesus himself, who said to the men he had chosen as apostles:

> You know that the rulers of the Gentiles lord it over them, and their high officials exercise authority over them. Not so with you. Instead, whoever wants to become great among you must be your servant, and whoever wants to be first must be your slave—just as the Son of Man did not come to be served, but to serve, and to give his life as a ransom for many. (Matt. 20:25–27 TNIV//Mark 10:42–45; Luke 22:25–27)

Peter exhorts the *presbyteroi* that they must not lord it over the people, but rather their attitude must be an example for others in the community to follow. In a culture where status is cherished and authority is asserted to preserve honor, this call to humbly serve others is no doubt a special challenge (see 5:5 and comments on 3:8).

The genitive object of κατακυριεύοντες (*katakyrieuontes*, lord it over) is the peculiar word κλήρων (*klērōn*, those allotted). In context *klērōn* corresponds to *poimnion* (flock) in 5:2, and both words refer to the people who have been allotted in God's providence to the *presbyteroi*. The noun *klēros* was used to refer to a marked object, similar to dice, that was cast to make decisions as well as to the assignment that resulted from casting the die, or lot (e.g., Matt. 27:35; Acts 1:26). It is often translated "share" or "portion" and is found frequently in the Greek translation of the OT to refer to what God had ordained, apportioned, and distributed (e.g., Num. 33:54; Josh. 14:2; 18:6). The use of this peculiar word is possibly a metaphor suggesting the idea of divine appointment of these particular people to the care of these particular elders. The *presbyteroi* need to recognize the Christian believers "among them" (5:2) as the sheep assigned by God to their care, and similarly the believers need to acknowledge the *presbyteroi* as their allotted leaders.

Those who bear the burden of faithfully shepherding God's flock willingly, eagerly, and as role models will receive the unfading crown of glory when Christ, the Chief Shepherd, is revealed (5:4). The noun ἀρχιποίμενος (*archipoimenos*, Chief Shepherd) is attested at least twice in extant texts from the Roman period and was a title that apparently would have been familiar to Peter's readers (Deissmann 1927: 99–100). The *archipoimenos* was the overseer of the shepherds when a flock was too large to be attended well by one. The *presbyteroi* are not simply to follow the example of Christ as independent agents when shepherding God's people; instead, they are to recognize themselves as underlings of Christ the Chief Shepherd, to whom they will be held responsible. Christ will recognize those who worked for him and not for themselves (Goppelt 1993: 349).

The reward of faithfully shepherding the flock of God will be a crown of glory that never fades (5:4). Literally, the Greek expression is τὸν ἀμαράντινον τῆς δόξης στέφανον (*ton amarantinon tēs doxēs stephanon*, the amaranth crown of glory), where the adjective *amarantinon* refers to the quality of the amaranth flower, a red blossom whose color was unfading. The crown is an image well known to the first-century Greco-Roman world, for a wreath of leaves worn on the head was commonly awarded to those who won athletic competitions. A similar wreath, but made of gold, was frequently given as the reward for civic benefactors (Llewelyn 1994: 240). In using this imagery, Peter encourages the *presbyteroi* to faithful service in trying times. But their victory is sure, for it depends on the appearing of Christ, not on their own efforts. The victory they attain through perseverance is an unfading (everlasting) glory. This image of a crown of unfading flowers contrasts with the withering and falling flowers of all human glory acquired apart from Christ (1:24).

b. Instructions to "the Younger" (5:5)

In a much briefer form in 5:5, Peter exhorts the νεώτεροι (*neōteroi*, younger) to submit to the *presbyteroi*, who have been commissioned to shepherd them. In such a brief span of discourse, it is unlikely that *presbyteroi* refers here in 5:5 only to older people in the church when in 5:1 it clearly refers to leaders in the church (contra Selwyn 1958: 227). The adverb ὁμοίως (*homoiōs*, similarly) probably modifies the verb παρακαλῶ (*parakalō*, I exhort) in 5:1, making this exhortation to the *neōteroi* correspond to that in 5:1–4.

The term *neōteroi* is the comparative form of the adjective νέος (*neos*, new or young) and was never used to refer to an office of the church. The contrast is not between the older men and the younger men of the church—for which νεανίας (*neanias*) or νεανίσκος (*neaniskos*) would be expected. Rather it is between those who have the seniority and the commensurate standing that qualifies them to be *presbyteroi* in contrast to those who, for whatever reason, do not. Official elders of the church were naturally chosen from those who held seniority in the faith, which most often also corresponded to physical age. Those not (yet) qualified to be elders were "younger" in standing in the church. The term *neōteroi* therefore refers "to those who were not elders, that is to say all other church members" (R. Campbell 1994: 206).

This address to elders (*presbyteroi*) is somewhat strange, for there is no other explicit reference in the letter to church structure or to issues of church authority. In fact, the word "church" (ἐκκλησία, *ekklēsia*) is never mentioned in 1 Peter. If there are organized local churches in the areas to which Peter writes, he has chosen not to address them as such (cf. the openings of the apostle Paul's letters). This may be simply because Peter has chosen to frame his letter in the metaphor of a united though scattered Christian Diaspora rather than to highlight the individual units of Christian believers within Asia Minor. Or perhaps it is because Peter knows the recipients of his letter are not in well-established churches, as would be the case if they had been relocated from elsewhere into communities (or colonies) where no well-established church organization yet existed (see "Recipients" in the introduction).

In any case, this reference to *presbyteroi* does suggest Christian groups with at least a developing structure of leadership. The instruction in 5:2 that elders are to shepherd the church and in 5:5 that others are to submit to the elders would be a bit odd if addressed to a long-standing, well-ordered church hierarchy because it would seem to be stating the obvious. The apparent need to define the authority of the *presbyteroi* may suggest an early stage in the development of church structure in these areas.

The phrase in 5:1, "elders among you" (πρεσβυτέρους ἐν ὑμῖν, *presbyterous en hymin*), where "elders over you" might be expected, contributes to the impression of a somewhat fluid church organization. It suggests not a well-designated and fixed group but those elders who happen to be among the community of believers at the time Peter writes (Achtemeier 1996: 323; J. H. Elliott 2000: 815). J. H. Elliott (2001: 555) sees them as heads of household churches. Michaels (1988: 279) translates the phrase "any elders among you" in an attempt to reflect the anarthrous noun. The same prepositional phrase "among you" (*en hymin*) in 5:2 refers to any believers who are known to the elders at this time.

If this phrasing does imply a peculiar, more fluid situation, it could be explained if the church in the regions to which Peter writes was still in its embryonic stage. This passage may be the first apostolic commissioning of elders in northern Asia Minor, where no apostle was ever physically present as far as extant tradition attests. If Peter's readers were recently displaced to Asia Minor, there may well have been a vacuum in church leadership that the apostle is here addressing. Some of Peter's readers may have been previously recognized as elders in the locale from which they had come. But what is now their function and responsibility when they are displaced to a foreign location and brought into contact with other Christians who have similarly been displaced from other locations? Peter is instructing the *presbyteroi* that they must begin or resume their function as elders of the Christian believers in their new location. This scenario does justice to the ingressive sense of the aorist *poimanate*, as identified by interpreters (Beare 1970: 199; Davids 1990: 178; Goppelt 1993: 343), for its sense would be "begin to shepherd." However, the simple unmarked use of the aorist (as Achtemeier 1996: 325) would not preclude the same scenario.

The hypothesis that church leadership is here being established in the embryonic churches of northern Asia Minor also does justice to the "similarly" (ὁμοίως, *homoiōs*) in 5:5, where the apostle enjoins submission for the Christian community that corresponds to the commissioning of its elders. Christians who have been displaced from other places and have perhaps once submitted to other elders are now to recognize the authority and leadership of new elders in this new situation. The emphasis in the letter on the unity of Christian believers as living stones in one spiritual structure (2:4–5) corroborates the need for believers to see themselves as one with fellow Christians regardless of where they reside.

Peter previously ended his instructions to specific groups in 2:13–3:7 with general instructions to all in 3:8–12, and he does so here as well. Peter instructs that "all" (πάντες, *pantes*) his readers, whether *presbyteroi* or *neōteroi*, are to clothe themselves in humility with regard to one another because "God opposes the arrogant but gives grace to the humble" (5:5). Arrogance, whether by domineering *presbyteroi* or by contemptuous *neōteroi*, evokes God's opposition. The challenge of mutual humility is especially great in a time of persecution, for the consequences at stake may incite elders to abuse their power or believers to rebel against church leadership. But God gives grace to those who are willing to humble themselves for the sake of Christ and his flock, allowing the church to survive and thrive even in times of persecution.

The concept of "clothing" oneself in the Christian virtues is a common image in the NT (e.g., Rom. 13:12, 14; Eph. 6:11, 14; Col. 3:12, 14; 1 Thess. 5:8). However, the verb ἐγκομβόομαι (*enkomboomai*, put on, tie around) is found only here in the NT and not at all in the LXX or Apostolic Fathers. Various attempts have been made to define more specifically the term as donning the apron of a slave, or the symbolic dress of a religious man (Harris 1919), or, possibly picking up the shepherd motif, the apron a herdsman would tie around himself (Davids 1990: 185). The point nevertheless seems clear that humility in relationships is a paramount Christian virtue.

First Peter 5:5b (cf. James 4:6) is an exact quotation of Prov. 3:34 LXX, other than the substitution of θεός (*theos*, God) for the LXX's κύριος (*kyrios*, Lord): "God opposes the arrogant but gives grace to the humble." Because Peter in his letter consistently uses *kyrios* to refer to Jesus Christ, the substitution of *theos* preserves the sense of the quotation in its original context, where *kyrios* refers to Yahweh. This quotation grounds Peter's exhortation in the authority and normativity of Scripture. His instruction to the Christians of Asia Minor is not ad hoc but reflects the attitude God has instructed his people to have whenever and wherever they have lived. Humility is truly the wise way of life, even though it was taken as a sign of "lowly slave mentality" in Greco-Roman society, unworthy of a free citizen (J. H. Elliott 2000: 847; Goppelt 1993: 253). However, Peter's readers are to regard themselves not as citizens of their society but as visiting strangers and resident aliens (1 Pet. 1:1; 2:11) who live by the standards of a different kingdom. True humility, as opposed to a contrived, self-degrading humiliation, flows from recognizing one's complete dependence on God and is expressed by the acceptance of one's role and position in God's economy. With such humility one is freed from attempts to gain more power or prestige. Instead, humility expresses itself in the willingness to serve others even beyond one's self-interest.

The precarious situation of Peter's readers demands the leadership of "courageous and competent" elders who can shepherd the flock in a way that maintains social cohesion and commitment to the gospel of Jesus Christ (J. H. Elliott 2001: 557). Even though the origin of the church in northern Asia Minor is shrouded by our ignorance of its founders, this area became the cradle of Christian doctrine in the first four centuries of the church, hosting the great early councils. By the second century, there were flourishing, well-established churches in the areas to which Peter wrote. It is no stretch of the imagination to infer that these earliest Christians of Asia Minor took the apostle Peter's message of consolation and encouragement to heart, rising to the challenge of leading the church through perilous times, generation after generation, with the humility, strength, and grace that only the Lord can supply.

Additional Note

5:2. As NA²⁷ indicates by bracketing [ἐπισκοποῦντες] (*episkopountes*, overseeing), there is considerable doubt about its presence in the original text. The important witnesses ℵ* and B omit it, but 𝔓⁷², ℵ², and A include it. It is almost certainly an echo of ἐπίσκοπον (*episkopon*, overseer) in 1 Pet. 2:25, which also follows a reference to wandering sheep in need of a shepherd, the Lord himself. If the participle was not original, it is difficult to imagine a motivation for adding it, because of its redundant sense with the main verb, *poimanate*. It is somewhat easier to imagine it being deliberately omitted at a later stage, because the term came to have such a narrow ecclesiastical reference to the service of bishops, not elders, that it would have been confusing in this context. Since it is somewhat redundant with the main verb, it could be safely dropped without substantially altering the sense. This seems somewhat more likely, and the balance of both external evidence and transcriptional probabilities tilts slightly in favor of the participle being the original reading (as also Davids 1990: 178n11; J. H. Elliott 2000: 824n665; Michaels 1988: 276). However, it remains a difficult call. Fortunately, neither omission nor inclusion substantially changes the meaning of Peter's admonition.

2. Accepting Difficult Times, Standing Fast, and Trusting God (5:6–11)

Peter rounds off the body of his letter with admonitions followed by encouragement. He wants his readers to accept the difficult times they are facing as from God's hand but yet to be on guard against the devil's evil desire to take advantage of their circumstances to their own destruction. Peter's readers are not alone in their plight, which is shared by Christians throughout the world. Because God is sovereign over even the hardships they suffer, they can trust him to put things right, strengthening, empowering, and securing them.

    a. Accepting difficult times as from God's hand (5:6–8a)
    b. Standing fast against the devil (5:8b–9)
    c. Trusting God to put things right (5:10–11)

Exegesis and Exposition

⁶Be humbled, therefore, under the mighty hand of God, in order that he might exalt you at the appointed time, ⁷casting upon him your every anxiety, because he cares about you. ⁸Be clear-minded and on the alert. Your adversary the devil paces around as a roaring lion, seeking [someone] to devour. ⁹Take your stand against him, firm in faith, knowing that the same type of sufferings are being experienced by your fellow Christians throughout the world. ¹⁰But the God of all grace, who called you into his eternal glory in Christ ⌐ ⌐, after you have suffered a little while, will himself put things right, strengthen, empower, [and] secure [you]. ¹¹To him be the dominion forever! Amen!

a. Accepting Difficult Times as from God's Hand (5:6–8a)

Three imperatives form Peter's concluding exhortation: (1) be humbled, therefore, under God's mighty hand; (2) be clear-minded and on the alert; and (3) take your stand against the devil. Variations of the phrase "the mighty hand of God" (τὴν κραταιὰν χεῖρα τοῦ θεοῦ, *tēn krataian cheira tou theou*) are used repeatedly in the exodus story to refer to the power that God displayed when he delivered his people from Egypt and brought them into their own land (LXX: Exod. 13:9; Deut. 3:24; 4:34; 5:15; 7:19; 9:26; 11:2). First Peter 5:6 is the only occurrence of the phrase in the NT, though "the hand of God" without the adjective is mentioned in the NT to refer to a manifestation of God's power in other contexts (Luke 1:66; Acts 4:30; 11:21; 13:11). The gospel of Jesus Christ is God's deliverance from the bondage of sin in this age into his eternal glory, portrayed in biblical theology as a second exodus (Heb. 3:7–4:13; Dillard and Longman 1994: 66–67; Sahlin 1953). Because of their participation in this deliverance of God in Christ, Peter's readers are experiencing a degree of humiliation that might incite them to retaliate against their critics. The natural human urge to fight back and defend one's rights is strong.

Peter has already explained that (1) persecution comes to faithful Christians and is not apart from God's will (1 Pet. 3:17), (2) they should recognize painful trials as a normal part of Christian life (4:12), and (3) these experiences are God's purifying fire of judgment (1:7; 4:17–19). To "be humbled" implies a decision to remain faithful to Christ even knowing that humiliation will result. As Achtemeier (1996: 338) explains, "The point is not that Christians have a choice of whether they humble themselves; that happens to them simply because they are Christians." The point is how Christians respond when, because of their faith, their social status has suffered and their situation has become difficult. The command to be humbled *under God's mighty hand* is a command to accept, though not to seek, difficult circumstances as a part of God's deliverance, neither railing against God ("Why did this happen to me?" "What did I do to deserve this?") nor raging against those causing the difficulty, but rather blessing those who insult and injure (3:9). As Achtemeier (1996: 338) explains, "Christians are to acknowledge that such status conforms to God's will and to accept it for that reason, since it is the path God wishes Christians to take, a path that will lead finally to God's exaltation of them." An example of the acceptance of even extreme social humiliation is found in the martyrs who resolutely went to tortured deaths, understanding it as both God's plan for them and a witness to his redemption before the world.

But acceptance of the lowly status of Christians in society is not the end of the matter. Peter continues the thought with a purpose clause introduced by ἵνα (*hina*, in order that). Their willingness to submit to God's mighty hand now is purposeful: "that he may exalt you at the appointed time" (5:6). Given Peter's previous references to the coming glory when Christ is revealed (1:7; 4:13; 5:1, 4), this is probably also a similar reference to the future vindication of Christians who have been demeaned and humiliated by their society because of their faith. Allowing themselves to be humbled in their present situation by adhering to their faith in Christ, they will certainly be exalted when he appears and the whole world sees its folly in rejecting his gospel. This thought is Peter's exposition of Prov. 3:34, "God . . . gives grace to the humble," which he quotes in 1 Pet. 5:5. Those who allow themselves to be humbled under God's mighty hand are those who will find grace when Jesus Christ appears.

2. Accepting Difficult Times, Standing Fast, and Trusting God

Although their exaltation is yet future, God does not leave his people unsupported as they face humbling circumstances now. The adverbial participle ἐπιρίψαντες (*epiripsantes*, casting upon, 5:7) is an attendant circumstance to the imperative "be humbled." Be humbled and cast upon him all your anxiety, because he cares about you.

Many anxieties result from professing faith in Christ in a polytheistic society that is hostile to the exclusive claims of the gospel. The loss of status and respect, loss of family standing, loss of friends, perhaps even loss of one's livelihood and, in extreme cases, of one's life—these are real possibilities for the Christians of Asia Minor. Peter instructs his readers to cast these anxieties on God (5:7), another way of saying they must entrust themselves to their faithful Creator and continue to do good (4:19). Jesus taught that anxiety about life is one of the impediments that can choke out God's word (Mark 4:19). For God's word to be fruitful, there must be a self-forgetfulness that is based on trust in God regardless of circumstances. "Worry, anxiety for oneself and striving to secure one's own life, which are marked by fear, is lifted from those who are called to faith," lifted by knowledge of God's personal care and concern for them (Goppelt 1993: 359). God is neither unaware nor unconcerned about what his people are going through in order to remain faithful to Christ.

Peter's second and third imperatives come in rapid succession, and both pertain to one's mental state, so they can be considered as one unit of thought: "Be clear-minded and on the alert" (1 Pet. 5:8). Twice Peter has already used the first of the two verbs, νήφω (*nēphō*, be self-controlled, 1:13; 4:7). It is an antonym for the state of mind caused by drunkenness and is used more broadly in 1 Peter to refer to spiritual sobriety, a clear-minded and self-controlled mental state that is free from confusion and driving passions. The second verb, γρηγορέω (*grēgoreō*, be on the alert) presupposes the state of mind of the first, for one cannot be alert in a mental state that resembles drunkenness. This verb occurs often in the NT, referring both to readiness for the Lord's return (e.g., Matt. 24:42–43; 25:13; Mark 13:35, 37; Rev. 3:3; 16:15) and to watchfulness that avoids moral jeopardy (e.g., Matt. 26:41; Mark 14:38; Acts 20:31; 1 Thess. 5:6; Rev. 3:3).

b. Standing Fast against the Devil (5:8b–9)

The only reference in the epistle to spiritual powers of darkness is found here in 5:8 with a reference to the devil (διάβολος, *diabolos*), portrayed as a pacing lion looking for prey. Peter states these two imperatives with no conjunction joining them to his thought about the devil. Later scribes made the implied logical connection explicit by joining the clauses with ὅτι (*hoti*, because). Spiritual sobriety and alertness are necessary *because* the threat of destruction is real and the devil is a true adversary. Fierce animal imagery is also used in Daniel and Revelation to symbolize world systems deformed by the powers of darkness and sin. Peter may be implying with the lion imagery that satanic powers are at work in the sociopolitical system of the Roman Empire, under which his readers are suffering. The roar of a lion would scatter a flock of sheep in panic, so this threatening image coheres well with the shepherd-flock motif in 5:1–5. When a lion is on the prowl, neither the shepherd nor the sheep sleep, but both are alert and watchful. Peter's readers are to understand that the persecution they feel is "not only individual deceit and malice, but also a supra-individual orientation in society, which is called into question by Christians and is, thereby, provoked" (Goppelt 1993: 362). The goal of the devil is to devour, a graphic depiction of his desire to annihilate the Christian and, collectively, the church by assimilating them back to the evil ways of the world.

The connection between the devil as a pacing, roaring lion and the persecution faced by the Asian Christians is only implied. This introduces a mysterious tension into Peter's thinking. He has previously said that the difficult circumstances his readers are experiencing are to be understood as God's judgment beginning with God's house (4:16–19), the intrusion of the eschatological sorting of the sheep from the goats. Such persecution and difficulty are therefore an unavoidable part of God's redemptive work in the world. But here Peter brings the devil into the picture as the immediate threat. This implies that, in Peter's understanding of their suffering, God is using the threat that Satan presents through the hostility of society and government to prove those who are truly God's (cf. Job 1:6–12).

Although at first glance this concurrence of God's purposes with Satan's devices may seem incongruous, it is really the continuation of the dynamics in the garden of Eden. God had given Adam and Eve his word in the form of a command not to eat the fruit of a certain tree. Satan in the form of the serpent confronted Eve and Adam not with a threat but with a temptation—"You will be like God" (Gen. 3:5 NIV). In that moment, Adam and Eve were presented the opportunity to be clear-minded and alert and thus to stand firm against the devil, who slithered about like a venomous snake, looking for someone to poison. But they were not alert and firm, and consequently they succumbed to the spiritual death of bondage to sin. The dynamics between God, the devil, and God's people remain the same until the Lord returns, but in Christ believers have regained the power to take their stand against the prowling lion, despite the consequences, and to show themselves to be the true and faithful people of God.

Peter's third and final imperative exhorts his readers to take a stand against the devil by standing firm in their faith. As Achtemeier (1996: 341) explains:

The opposition the Christians face from their non-Christian contemporaries is not something they can avoid by modifying their behavior or adapting their beliefs in such a way as to escape such opposition. Only by completely abandoning the gospel and the community shaped by it, only by submitting to the satanic forces that stand in total opposition to God, can they escape the persecutions they otherwise face.

If the gospel is to survive in Asia Minor, these beleaguered Christians must not allow themselves to be scattered by the threat but must take their stand against the devil by holding fast to the gospel and their place in the Christian community.

Moreover, because the threat they perceive and the persecution they experience are caused by their very presence as Christians in the world, the same type of adversity is suffered by Christians throughout the "world." Robinson (1976: 160) argues that the phrase ἐν κόσμῳ (*en kosmō*, 1 Pet. 5:9) is a Latinism that was used in Rome to refer to all regions of the empire outside the imperial city. But it is doubtful that the apostle wishes to distinguish believers in Asia Minor from those in Rome. Rather, Peter wishes his readers to see themselves not as isolated, scattered individuals but as part of God's holy nation wherever they may reside and to draw encouragement and strength from their solidarity with believers around the empire. Resistance to some degree is to be expected wherever a Christian community takes seriously its commitment to God, because the Christian church is the emergence of God's victory over the powers of darkness. Until Christ returns, the battle between good and evil will persist, and suffering for faith in Christ will be the norm for the Christian calling. The believer shares in what is the common experience of all Christians and is not alone in this.

c. Trusting God to Put Things Right (5:10–11)

Peter concludes the body of his letter with a strong note of hope and doxology (5:10–11) that echoes the opening in 1:1–7. God is described as the God of "all grace," reminding readers that there is no other source of mercy in life. This all-gracious God has called Christians into eternal glory in Christ. Throughout the letter Peter uses the word "glory" to refer to the state of being that was accomplished by the sufferings and resurrection of Christ (1:11), yet to be fully revealed at his return (4:13), and of which new life in Christ is even now a part (1:3). That new realm of being is eternal, making the adversities of this present age comparatively fleeting (cf. 1:24–25).

Although Peter acknowledges the inevitability of Christian suffering according to God's will (1:6; 2:21; 3:9, 14, 17; 4:12), he also affirms the relative brevity of it: "after you have suffered a little [ὀλίγον, *oligon*]" (5:10). Although *oligon* here could be a reference to the severity of suffering, it is probably meant to be construed as temporal, especially in comparison with 1:6 and in contrast to the "eternal glory" of 5:10a (Achtemeier 1996: 336; Davids 1990: 188; J. H. Elliott 2000: 845). Moreover, the references to suffering are general, and the extent and severity would likely have varied from place to place and in different situations. At first glance, this phrase may seem to say that the times when a believer is aware of suffering for Christ will be sporadic and brief. But this statement is probably to be read from an eschatological, not an existential, perspective. If the cause of Christian suffering cannot be avoided without renouncing Christ, then the threat of suffering is always present throughout the entirety of the Christian's life. And the threat of potential suffering that can at any time erupt into overt suffering is, in itself, a burden that Christians must carry. Therefore, Peter is more likely saying here that in the light of the eternal (αἰώνιον, *aiōnion*) glory, which believers have in Christ, a lifetime in this body is but a little while (*oligon*).

Peter uses four nearly synonymous verbs to describe what God himself will do for the benefit of the faithful Christians after that little while has passed: God "will himself put things right, strengthen, empower, and secure you." Peter probably uses these four as a rhetorical crescendo to refer to the complete act of God at the consummation of all things. God will put things right (καταρτίσει, *katartisei*). A world where Christians can expect to suffer simply because of their faith in God is not a world as God created it. In the time and place of eternal glory, there will be no suffering, for God will put things right, eliminating its source. God himself will strengthen (στηρίξει, *stērixei*) you, in the sense of causing one to become "more firm and unchanging in attitude or belief" (BDAG 945). Certainly, when Christ is revealed and faith becomes sight, the Christian's belief in the gospel will reach its full certainty. In the meanwhile, God's grace enables believers to remain firm and unchanging. "Although you have not seen him, you love him; although you do not see him now, you believe in him" (1:8). God himself will empower (σθενώσει, *sthenōsei*) you. In any society that gets away with persecuting Christ's followers, Christians are truly in a position of weakness. But the time will come when Christ is revealed as the true Lord of the earth, and the believer's faith in him will be vindicated. At that time Christians will be the empowered people. Finally, God himself will secure (θεμελιώσει, *themeliōsei*) you. This verb alludes back to the spiritual house metaphor, as it refers to securing a foundation for a building as well as providing a basis for a belief (BDAG 449). By virtue of their faith in Christ, Christians are being built into a spiritual house whose cornerstone is the Living Stone (2:4–5). The foundation of that spiritual house will be found secure when Christ is revealed.

In these ways God is already working in the lives of those who through faith are being kept until salvation is revealed (1:5). All four verbs are intended to strengthen, empower, and secure Peter's readers in this present life as they continue to face their fiery trials for a little while; Peter is assuring them of what God himself is doing that will be completed in the end. Resources for living life today are found in the knowledge of the ultimate end. Although God himself will do these things in the ultimate sense when Christ is revealed at the parousia, Peter reminds his readers of them because their new lives in Christ (1:3) partake of that future glory in the here and now. Although Christians may face unjust circumstances that are never put right in this life, those circumstances can be given up to God with the confidence that he will indeed make all things right. Despite appearances, God's Spirit indeed strengthens, empowers, and secures Christians, imparting the courage and confidence to live well through this "little while" of suffering. Because what we believe about our future shapes how we live today, Peter concludes the body of his letter with an eschatological statement that puts all of today's realities into the perspective of eternity.

Peter's final word in this closing unit is a doxology, "To him be the dominion forever! Amen!" At the time Peter wrote these words, to all human appearances it must have seemed that to Rome instead belonged the dominion forever. Roman rule had brought the *pax Romana* (Roman peace) that ended regional wars and unified the empire, generally improving life around the Mediterranean. But the price of that "peace" was the iron-fisted power of Roman might that tolerated not even the suspicion of a threat to its glory. The supernatural nature of the Christian church is perhaps best revealed by the historical fact that until the conversion of Constantine, all of the might of Rome stood against the infant church. Annihilating power stood ready to come against any whose allegiance to the kingdom of God and to his Christ took priority over the kingdom of Caesar. Just the threat of Roman power would have been sufficient to annihilate Christianity had it been based on anything other than or less than the reality of the resurrection of Jesus Christ. In the face of Roman might, Peter ends his epistle by confessing that to God alone belongs eternal might (κράτος εἰς τοὺς αἰῶνας, *kratos eis tous aiōnas*), which makes Roman glory look like a withered flower (1:24). God's eternal might constitutes his eternal dominion, for no other power can conquer or thwart his sovereign purposes.

This is the second occurrence of *kratos* (κράτος, dominion), previously used in Peter's doxology of 4:11, where God's eternal glory and dominion are identified with Jesus Christ. Its adjectival form, κραταιάν (*krataian*, mighty), describes God's hand, his manifestations of power in history that deliver his people from the oppression of persecution (5:6). To call Christ Lord and proclaim God to be King is to be humbled under God's mighty display of eternal power rather than to cower before the pale might of any earthly ruler.

Additional Note

5:10. NA[27] includes the variant reading Ἰησοῦ (*Iēsou*, Jesus), though Metzger (1994: 627) indicates that the shorter text is preferable because of the scribal tendency to add rather than omit sacred names. When the pattern of the Lord's sacred name in 1 Peter is examined, Metzger's view is supported. Χριστός (*Christos*, Christ) occurs twenty-one times elsewhere in the letter. Even when three instances are omitted because they also have variant readings, a clear pattern emerges. *Christos* stands alone nine times; when it is combined with the name *Iēsous*, it occurs eight times, and in every occurrence *Iēsous* stands before *Christos*. Since Peter does not once elsewhere refer to *Christos Iēsous*, the variant reading of 1 Pet. 5:10 is most likely a later scribal addition.

V. The Letter Closing: Final Words and Greetings (5:12–14)

The major theological statement of the closing is Peter's apostolic affirmation that what he has written is the true grace of God, in which they are to take their stand (5:12). Peter's readers have been given new birth into a living hope through the resurrection of Jesus Christ. By definition that living hope puts them at odds, to some extent, with the society in which they must live. And yet in the midst of whatever they might suffer because of their faith in Christ, they also have great joy and peace that come only from being right with God, the Creator and Judge of all.

A. Silvanus—amanuensis, courier, or both? (5:12a)

B. She in Babylon chosen with you (5:13)

C. Stand fast in the true grace of God (5:12b)

Exegesis and Exposition

[12]Through Silvanus, whom I consider to be your faithful brother, I have written to you briefly, exhorting [you] and confirming, This is the true grace of God. Stand fast in it! [13]She in Babylon chosen with you and Mark, my son, greet you. [14]Greet one another with a kiss of love. Peace to you all who are in Christ.

A. Silvanus—Amanuensis, Courier, or Both? (5:12a)

In this closing Peter gives the general reason for his letter of exhortation: to confirm the true grace of God. The closing echoes the greeting of the opening verses (1 Pet. 1:1–2):

1 Peter 1:1–2	1 Peter 5:12–14
Peter	I
to the chosen	she chosen with you
Diaspora	Babylon
peace to you	peace to you

Peter mentions three others associated with him: Silvanus, Mark, and "she in Babylon chosen with you." This presents two exegetical enigmas: (1) What is the role of Silvanus—amanuensis or courier (or both)? (2) To whom is Peter referring when he sends greetings from "she in Babylon chosen with you"?

Most interpreters who date this letter within the lifetime of the apostle Peter consider the Greek vocabulary and style to be too good for what could be expected of a Galilean fisherman. The traditional answer is to understand Silvanus as Peter's amanuensis, apparently assuming that Silvanus, being a Roman citizen, could have produced Greek of this quality (W. Barclay 1976: 275; Cranfield 1958: 121; Davids 1990: 198; Kelly 1969: 215; Kistemaker 1987: 207; Reicke 1964: 133). The several assumptions that attend the inference that the Greek is too good for someone like the apostle Peter to have written it need to be critically examined (see the excursus).

What's more, Peter's explicit reference to Silvanus as the one "through" whom he wrote (διά Σιλουανοῦ . . . ἔγραψα, dia Silouanou . . . egrapsa) more likely describes the role of a courier than of an amanuensis (Achtemeier 1996: 350; Clowney 1988: 221; Davids 2002; J. H. Elliott 2000: 870; Grudem 1988: 200; Michaels 1988: 306; Perkins 1995: 81; E. Richards 2000; Robinson 1976: 168). The idiom γράφειν διά τινος (graphein dia tinos, to write by way of someone) is attested elsewhere in the NT (Acts 15:23), in first- and second-century papyri letters (BGU 1079; CPR 6.80 lines 9–10; P.Mich. 15.751 lines 4–7; P.Wisc. 2.69 lines 4–5) and in the church fathers (e.g., Ign. Rom. 10.1; Phld. 11.2; Smyrn. 12.1) as one standard way of referring to a courier bearing the letter (see E. Richards 2000 for a survey of much of the data). Uses of διά (dia) plus a genitive proper name with verbs of sending and receiving such as πέμπω (pempō) and ἀποστέλλω (apostellō) also occur in the papyri letters (Llewelyn 1994: 54). The one NT letter that clearly refers to a scribe uses quite different language (Rom. 16:22). The fact that scribes later added a subscript to Romans—referring to Phoebe as the courier of the letter by the phrase ἐγράφη ἀπὸ Κορίνθου διά Φοίβης (egraphē apo Korinthou dia Phoibēs, written from Corinth through Phoebe)—attests that this was a natural idiom used to refer to a courier. There is a single occurrence of the phrase in the letter of Dionysius of Corinth where διά does refer to the author of 1 Clement (Goppelt 1993: 369), but that context is not quite the same as this (Michaels 1988: 306–7). A few claim it may refer to both the writer and the courier (Best 1971: 177; Bigg 1956: 195; Selwyn 1958: 241).

Perhaps the most relevant citation is found in Acts 15:23, where Silvanus is chosen as one of the men who would carry the apostles' letter from the council of Jerusalem back to Antioch. The phrase used there, "wrote through their hand" (γράψαντες διὰ χειρὸς αὐτῶν, grapsantes dia cheiros autōn), parallels the phrase dia Silouavou . . . egrapsa, suggesting that Silvanus is the carrier of Peter's letter. However, even if Silvanus did carry Peter's letter, it does not mean that he, or Mark for that matter, could not have served as an amanuensis if Peter in fact needed one. And so the question of an amanuensis must be decided on other grounds.

Those who argue for pseudonymous authorship of the letter understand this reference to Silvanus as a fictional element meant to give the letter verisimilitude (Boring 1999: 180). However, this ruse would certainly preclude the letter being actually delivered to an original destination, for a pseudonym for its bearer(s) would spoil the intent of the ruse. Pseudonymous authorship must imply that an unknown author in Asia Minor simply presented the manuscript as a long-lost letter that had been rediscovered. Moreover, if the reference to Silvanus is entirely fictional, one wonders why he was chosen rather than someone more widely associated with Peter.

Some object that any one person could not likely have delivered the letter throughout the vast regions listed in 1 Pet. 1:1 (Goppelt 1993: 369). Michaels (1988: 307) answers this objection by taking Cyprian's reference to "The Epistle of Peter to Pontus" as evidence of the possibility that Silvanus delivered the letter only to its port of entry. That could likely have been one of Pontus's port cities on the Black Sea, from which it was distributed in some form (also Cranfield 1958: 121).

Because Silvanus is mentioned by name but with no other information, it would seem that Peter's readers must have known who he was. However, Peter's affirmation that the apostle regards Silvanus as a faithful brother may hint of something that would make such an affirmation advisable, especially if Silvanus is carrying the letter. This suggests that even if the recipients were familiar with Silvanus by reputation, they did not know him personally. Those who take Silvanus as the amanuensis of the letter see in this phrase a validation that he has accurately represented Peter's thoughts (Davids 1990: 199; but note his change of mind about Silvanus as the amanuensis in 2002: 120–51).

Silvanus is probably the same man who accompanied Paul on his travels in Asia Minor and Greece (2 Cor. 1:19) and is listed as a coauthor of 1 and 2 Thessalonians, along with the apostle Paul and Timothy (1 Thess. 1:1; 2 Thess. 1:1). The name Silvanus appears to be the Latinized form of the Greek name Silas, whom Luke refers to as Paul's companion (Acts 16:19, 25, 29; 17:4–15; 18:5); Silas in turn was probably the Greek form of his Aramaic name. Silvanus was among the trusted leaders of the early church in Jerusalem (15:22) and held Roman citizenship (16:37). This companion of apostles was among the well-known core leadership of the first-century church from its earliest days in Jerusalem, through Paul's missionary journeys, and later with Peter and Mark in Rome.

B. She in Babylon Chosen with You (5:13)

The phrase "she in Babylon chosen with you" (1 Pet. 5:13) presents two questions: (1) Who is "she"? (2) How should the reference to Babylon be understood? The feminine article (ἡ, *hē*) turns the prepositional phrase "in Babylon" (ἐν Βαβυλῶνι, *en Babylōni*) into a substantive that can refer to an individual woman or to a collective group represented by an elided noun of the feminine gender. Bigg (1956: 197) stands virtually alone in defending the older understanding that this is a reference to Peter's wife, arguing that the alternative, "the church and Mark, my son" is a more difficult combination than "my wife and Mark, my son." Mark is most likely John Mark (Acts 12:12, 25; 15:37, 39), who was not literally Peter's son but whom tradition identifies as Peter's interpreter (Eusebius, *Ecclesiastical History* 3.39.15). This mitigates Bigg's objection, making it less likely that the phrase "she . . . in Babylon" is literally a reference to his wife. Applegate (1992) proposes that the phrase refers to a specific female leader in the church of Asia Minor who is well known to the readers and is referred to by Peter to help authorize the household code, but this is too imaginative to be preferred to the alternatives.

If an elided noun is to be specified, two have been suggested, yet with little difference in sense. The feminine noun ἡ ἐκκλησία (*hē ekklēsia*, the church) is often assumed (Best 1971: 177; Cranfield 1958: 123; Michaels 1988: 310; Selwyn 1958: 243), although that noun is not used elsewhere in the letter. The nearest feminine noun that would fit the context is ἡ ἀδελφότης (*hē adelphotēs*, the brotherhood, fellow Christians) in 1 Pet. 5:9, and it seems a more probable antecedent (T. Martin 1992a: 145; J. H. Elliott 2000: 882). In 5:9 Peter has pointed to the fellowship of suffering Christians throughout the world; in 5:12 he sends greetings from that part of the Christian fellowship "in Babylon." Regardless of the elided noun to be supplied, the majority of interpreters today understand the phrase to refer to the Christian community with which the apostle Peter is associated (Achtemeier 1996: 353; Boring 1999: 181; Clowney 1988: 224; Davids 1990: 201; Goppelt 1993: 373; Grudem 1988: 201; Kelly 1969: 218; Kistemaker 1987: 208; Reicke 1964: 134).

There is virtually unanimous agreement among modern interpreters that the referent of "Babylon" is actually Rome (Achtemeier 1996: 354; W. Barclay 1976: 278; Best 1971: 178; Clowney 1988: 224; Cranfield 1958: 123; J. H. Elliott 2000: 883–86; Goppelt 1993: 374–75; Grudem 1988: 201; Kelly 1969: 218; Kistemaker 1987: 209; Michaels 1988: 311; Perkins 1995: 81; Reicke 1964: 134; Selwyn 1958: 243). There is less agreement about the significance of this symbol. The reference to Babylon is sometimes offered as evidence for dating 1 Peter to after AD 70, for it was after the Romans destroyed the temple in Jerusalem that subversive apocalyptic writings, such as John's Revelation in the NT, adopted "Babylon" as a code word for Rome. However, this sense cannot be assumed for its occurrence here because the genre of 1 Peter is not apocalyptic and the letter contains nothing overtly subversive about the Roman state (in fact, quite the contrary).

Given the several echoes of the greeting of 1:1–2 found here, the reference to Babylon is clearly to be read in parallel with "Diaspora" in 1:1, a pairing not typically found in apocalyptic where Babylon appears as the great evil city. Nothing is said of Babylon's evil in 1 Peter, leading Michaels (1988: 311) to observe that the only thing wrong with Babylon is that it is not home. Along the same lines, Davids (1990: 203) writes, "So Rome equals Babylon becomes a . . . symbol for the capital of the place of exile away from the true inheritance in heaven." Most likely "Babylon" forms an inclusio with "Diaspora" in the opening verse and thus functions "to identify both the author and his Christian community as sharing with the readers such exile status" (Achtemeier 1996: 354).

As Kelly (1969: 219) astutely observes, if the reference to Babylon functions merely as an inclusio with Diaspora to frame the book in exile language, it is less clear that Babylon is "intended to designate any specific locality at all." He cites the "waters of Babylon" in Ps. 137:1 as a similar reference that Jews of the Diaspora could identify as whatever place in the world they happened to live. The reference to Babylon here might function similarly. In that case, "there would thus be no reference to Rome or any other place in this verse," though Rome might otherwise have been known to be the location of Peter (Kelly 1969: 219). Thiede (1986) argues similarly that Babylon here and the expression in Acts 12:17 that Peter left Jerusalem "for another place" (εἰς ἕτερον τόπον, *eis heteron topon*) are both allusions to being in a state of exile and neither is intended to specify location. The latter phrase, Thiede argues, is an echo of Ezek. 12:3 LXX, the only other place in the biblical corpus where the phrase *eis heteron topon* is used in reference to going into the Babylonian exile. It may be that Rome as the location of the composition of 1 Peter leans much more heavily on tradition than on exegesis.

If so, in 1 Pet. 5:13 Peter is simply sending greetings from the Christian community from wherever he writes, and from his associate Mark. But even if Acts 12:17 is intended only to say that Peter was driven into exile away from Jerusalem, Rome cannot be ruled out as the destination to which he fled. The reference could be intended as a comparison. Just as God's people had been driven out of Jerusalem and sent into exile in Babylon, the capital city of their oppressors centuries before, Peter himself has been driven from Jerusalem by the Roman powers and is sojourning in exile in the capital city of his oppressors.

C. Stand Fast in the True Grace of God (5:12b)

While such exegetical mysteries may never be resolved with certainty, the major theological point of the closing in 5:12 is clear and unambiguous: "This is the true grace of God. Stand fast in it!" The antecedent of the feminine demonstrative pronoun, "this" (ταύτην, *tautēn*), has been understood as the readers' present difficulties (Reicke 1964: 133), the entire way of life described in the letter (Grudem 1988: 201), or the contents of the letter (Bigg 1956: 196). The participles "exhorting" (παρακαλῶν, *parakalōn*) and "confirming" (ἐπιμαρτυρῶν, *epimartyrōn*) suggest that "the true grace of God" is to be understood as all the exhortations and teaching in the letter. Peter has set them forth for his readers to follow, difficult though they may be. These teachings include his apostolic confirmation that suffering for the name of Christ is truly an integral part of the Christian calling to follow him.

The better-attested imperative form στῆτε (*stēte*, stand) in 5:12 sits uneasily with the relative clause, εἰς ἥν (*eis hēn*, into which), but interpreters are virtually unanimous in reading the imperative here as Peter's final exhortation that his readers stand in the truth now confirmed to them (Achtemeier 1996: 348; Best 1971: 177; Bigg 1956: 196; Clowney 1988: 223; Cranfield 1958: 122; Davids 1990: 197; J. H. Elliott 2000: 879–80; Grudem 1988: 201; Kelly 1969: 217; Michaels 1988: 308; Selwyn 1958: 243). Goppelt (1993: 367, 373) sees the difficult syntax with *stēte* as intended to combine an indicative and an imperative, which he understands to mean "in which you may stand."

This final word of Peter's apostolic message in 5:12 both exhorts his readers and confirms to them the truth that, despite their suffering and despite circumstances that may appear to the contrary, they have been born again into a living hope through the resurrection of Jesus Christ. Through his own suffering, Jesus has conquered all evil and has called them to follow his footsteps through life, through death, and into glory. Those who do will be vindicated and glorified by God, just as Jesus was. The only just Judge of humanity is its Creator, who is also the Father of the Lord Jesus Christ and of all chosen to enter into the new covenant in Christ's blood (1:1–2). Therefore, stand fast in that knowledge, for everything else will soon end.

Excursus
The Syntax of 1 Peter:
How Good Is the Greek?

One of the weightiest arguments against Peter's authorship of 1 Peter is that the Greek of the epistle is just too good for an uneducated Galilean fisherman to have written. Those who accept pseudonymous authorship opt for an anonymous author from the Petrine circle in Rome or perhaps a Christian elder in Asia Minor. Those who wish to defend Peter as the author often propose his use of an amanuensis, perhaps even Silvanus (1 Pet. 5:12), writing under the direction of the apostle.

It thus appears that the quality of the Greek of 1 Peter is recognized by both sides of the authorship debate as being too good for Peter himself to have written. This opinion involves many assumptions that need to be critically reconsidered from time to time as more knowledge of the presence of Greek in Galilee becomes available. There seems to be a presumption that Galilean fishermen were uneducated, and relative to other segments of the population, that assumption is probably more true than not. However, the further assumption that only formally educated people can develop a high level of proficiency in a second language probably rings truer to North Americans, who generally acquire a second language through formal academic courses. However, there are pockets of the population, mostly in the borderlands, who live in societies that are in practice bilingual. In those areas, even formally uneducated people can develop a relatively high level of proficiency, especially if exposed to the second language early in life.

Currently available evidence is inconclusive about how pervasive the Greek language was in Galilee, and particularly in that crossroads town of Capernaum, hometown of this fisherman-turned-apostle (Fitzmyer 1979: 28–56). Recent archaeological evidence from the excavation of Sepphoris has indicated that despite its primarily Jewish population, the Greek culture and language may have had more of a presence in Galilee than previously recognized, though its extent is still highly contested (Batey 1992; Batey 2001; Chancey 2001). Corresponding to the debated

An earlier version of this essay appeared under the title "The Syntax of 1 Peter: Just How Good Is the Greek?" in the *Bulletin for Biblical Research* 13.2 (Fall 2003): 159–73, and is used by permission.

prevalence of the Greek language in Galilee is the prevalence of use of the LXX. Previous to recent archaeological work at Sepphoris, Josephus gave the impression that few Palestinian Jews of his day spoke Greek well and that acquisition of good Greek proficiency was looked down on (Fitzmyer 1992). Based on such information, the use of the LXX in Palestine was thought to be minimal at best. However, Josephus also mentions that ordinary freedmen and even slaves could acquire skill in the Greek language if they so desired (Fitzmyer 1992: 59). Moreover, the use of Greek for public announcements in Palestine and on ossuaries from the vicinity of Jerusalem attests, according to Fitzmyer (1992: 59), "to the widespread use of Greek among first-century Palestinian Jews at all levels of society" (also Silva 1980). Fitzmyer (1979: 36) cites the discovery of many documentary papyri written in Greek in Palestine between the two Jewish revolts (AD 70–135), including most surprisingly a letter from Bar Kokhba to his lieutenants—written in Greek! Fitzmyer follows C. F. D. Moule (1959), who understood the Hellenists referred to in Acts (6:1; 9:29; 11:20) as those who spoke only or primarily Greek. Fitzmyer (1979: 37) also lists the numerous hints in the Gospels that Jesus himself—who arguably had no more formal education than Peter—spoke Greek (also Batey 2001: 406).

Although Peter is described in Acts 4:13 as ἀγράμματος (agrammatos, uneducated), in that context the adjective probably means that because Peter had had no formal rabbinic training, his theological statements astounded those who had (Achtemeier 1996: 7). As Achtemeier points out, because Peter's fishing business was located in the crossroads town of Capernaum, he would have had daily contact with foreigners, and conversation with them would have been conducted most likely in the common language of Greek. The Greek name of Peter's brother, Ἀνδρέας (Andreas, Andrew), may suggest some Greek influence even within his own family (John 1:40). Moreover, just as missionaries today make great efforts to learn the language of the people to whom they are called, Peter could certainly have developed greater proficiency in Greek in the decades between Jesus' death and his own, understanding the importance of proclaiming the gospel in the language and style of the lingua franca of the empire. Some such education was apparently available even in Palestine if Josephus could claim that ordinary freedmen and even slaves could learn Greek if they chose to do so. And if Peter spent extensive time in Rome or another large city—a highly debated point—certainly he could there have availed himself of the opportunities for developing proficiency in Greek.

If it can be assumed that Peter began as a disciple of Christ with some proficiency in Greek, the question concerning authorship of 1 Peter changes: Could someone like Peter have developed proficiency in Greek writing to the level exhibited in the epistle? And therefore, the question of just how "good" the Greek of 1 Peter is takes center stage. At this point the definition of "good" needs to be objectified. Although there are many elements of the text of 1 Peter that bear consideration, one point directly relevant to the authorship issue is whether the Greek of 1 Peter shows signs that it was written by a native-Greek speaker or by someone for whom Greek was a second language. The concept of linguistic interference is helpful here. Linguistic, or dynamic, interference

> occurs when features from one language are transferred temporarily into the other language. Interference can occur at any level of language (syntax, phonology, vocabulary) and in either written or spoken language. One example of dynamic interference would be a native English speaker who also has some competence in French using the word *librairie* to mean library whereas it means bookshop. (Baker and Jones 1998: 58)

In his discussion of bilingualism in first-century Palestine, Moisés Silva (1980) cites linguistic studies of modern situations analogous to that of first-century Palestine. In the northeastern region of Spain, Spanish has been imposed as the official language upon a population whose native language is Catalan. The study of linguistic interference between the two languages by A. M. Badia-Margarit concludes that "cultured Catalans cannot generally prevent a series of characteristic features of their natural language from appearing in their Spanish" (Silva 1980: 214). A second study, of the interference between Welsh and English, concludes similarly that the English spoken by native-Welsh speakers contains "a superabundance of features which are possible and comprehensible in English" but that reflect characteristics of their native language (Silva 1980: 214). This concept of linguistic interference led Moulton to conclude that

> the ordinary Greek speech or writing of men whose native language was Semitic . . . brought into prominence locutions, correct enough as Greek, but which would have remained in comparatively rare use but for the accident of their answering to Hebrew or Aramaic phrases. (Silva 1980: 203, 215)

Therefore, Greek writings known to have been produced by native-Semitic speakers can be compared with those known to have been written by native-Greek speakers, and the relative frequency of occurrence of certain elements of style and syntax can be examined for indication of linguistic interference.

Opinion about the quality of the Greek of 1 Peter is apparently often based on the subjective feel of the text, since there have been no quantitative analyses of the Greek syntax of 1 Peter in comparison with other books of the NT or other Greek texts. The present study compares certain elements of the syntax of 1 Peter with that of other writings to gain some perspective on the relative quality of the Greek of 1 Peter. This is not an attempt to defend or refute Peter's authorship of the epistle or an attempt to identify his alleged amanuensis. It is simply an attempt to bring some objective, quantitative perspective to the question of the quality of the syntax of 1 Peter in comparison with other Greek texts, specifically other NT books, Josephus, and Polybius.

Of course, when we speak of proficiency in a language, syntax is only one indicator of the linguistic proficiency of a writer, and quantitative analysis should not end there. The rhetorical elements of 1 Peter are most often cited as revealing that the author "had enjoyed some level of formal education; if not an 'advanced' education in rhetoric or philosophy, at least a 'middle' education" (Achtemeier 1996: 4). It is argued that 1 Peter exhibits the formal elements of the rhetorical structure of deliberative or epideictic oration (Thurén 1990; Thurén 1995; B. Campbell 1998). While this may be true, it is also true that all well-structured arguments, even in contemporary English, could be expected to exhibit structural contours similar to those taught in formal Greek rhetoric because universal principles of logic underlie the structure of a good presentation. All thoughtful speakers or writers introduce their presentation in a way that is intended to engage the audience, then state the context for their argument in general terms, then in increasingly specific terms that get to the heart of the issue. Most provide a concluding summary that is intended to help the audience remember, and perhaps act upon, what they have heard or read. Labeling those contours with Latin names—*exordium*, *narratio*, and so on—does not prove that the author of such a text was deliberately following the outline of formal Greek oration.

On the other hand, the text of 1 Peter does indeed exhibit some elements of rhetorical ornamentation, though not nearly as much as the book of Hebrews. Achtemeier (1996: 3) points out series of words with similar sounds; accumulation of synonyms; the use of anaphora; antithetic and synthetic parallelism; coordinate parallel expressions first negative, then positive; rhythmic structure; and the frequent use of conjunctive participles and relative clauses. However, the claim that these features demonstrate formal training in rhetoric must also, of course, be critically evaluated.

Hence, while an analysis of syntax does not settle the question of how good the Greek of 1 Peter is, syntax is nevertheless a good place to start. The advantage of analysis that starts at the syntactical level is that syntax generally operates for most writers at an unconscious level, flowing from their proficiency with a language, and therefore provides an indicator of proficiency unencumbered by the more deliberate structures of content. Moreover, as the studies cited above show, it is at the level of syntax that interference from a native language frequently and prominently occurs. Therefore, syntactical analysis is useful in showing whether or not the Greek of 1 Peter shows evidence of Semitic interference consistent with what would be expected from a bilingual author whose native language was Aramaic. If it could be determined with some certainty that the

Greek of 1 Peter shows Semitic interference at the syntactical level, the possibilities for authorship would at least be circumscribed.

The quantitative methodology used in this study was developed in my doctoral dissertation to facilitate a direct comparison of the syntax of the Greek texts of the LXX (Jobes 1995: 29–47). Without modification it can be applied to any Greek text, enabling both a graphic profile of the given text to be produced and a numeric quantification of the character of its syntax overall (its S-number). The S-number positions the text on a scale that represents literary texts composed in Greek at one end and texts translated from Hebrew into Greek at the other.

Syntax criticism was a methodology originally formulated by R. A. Martin (1974), who identified seventeen syntactical criteria that he believed indicated Semitic interference in Greek and therefore could be used to distinguish Greek translated from a Semitic source from composition Greek:

Criteria 1–8	The relative frequency of occurrence of eight prepositions with respect to the preposition ἐν: (1) διά with the genitive, (2) διά in all its occurrences, (3) εἰς, (4) κατά with the accusative, (5) κατά in all occurrences, (6) περί in all occurrences, (7) πρός with the dative, and (8) ὑπό with the genitive.
Criterion 9	The relative frequency of occurrence of καί coordinating independent clauses with respect to δέ.
Criterion 10	The percentage of articles separated from their substantives.
Criterion 11	The relative frequency of occurrence of dependent genitives preceding the word on which they depend.
Criterion 12	The relative frequency of occurrence of dependent genitive personal pronouns.
Criterion 13	The relative frequency of occurrence of genitive personal pronouns dependent upon anarthrous substantives.
Criterion 14	The relative frequency of occurrence of attributive adjectives preceding the word they qualify.
Criterion 15	The relative frequency of occurrence of attributive adjectives.
Criterion 16	The relative frequency of occurrence of adverbial participles.
Criterion 17	The relative frequency of occurrence of the dative case used without the preposition ἐν.

Martin's approach has been criticized with the claim that all of the elements he identifies as indicators of Semitic interference can and do occur in Greek written by native speakers. That criticism misunderstands the concept of linguistic interference, which looks for elements of syntax in the second language that happen to be congruent with elements of the speaker's/writer's first language but occur with statistically greater frequency in speech or writing than would be expected of native speakers/writers. Other criticisms of Martin's approach have to do with the effectiveness of individual criteria as indicators of Semitic interference and Martin's use of "raw" frequency counts rather than statistical averages, which appear to make his conclusions arbitrary (Maloney 1989: 379; S. Farris cited in R. A. Martin 1989: 169). My methodology overcomes some of the weaknesses in Martin's analyses by applying some simple descriptive statistics that facilitate direct comparison of the relative frequency of occurrence of each criterion in a text. The methodology also provides a means of comparing its overall syntax as characterized by the criteria with the overall syntax of other texts (Jobes 1995: 40–47). Additional elements of syntax useful as indicators of Semitic interference could be identified, and should be, if the methodology of syntax criticism is to advance (Maloney 1981). To this end, studies of the translation technique exhibited by the various books of the LXX would provide a wealth of such information. In addition to identifying additional elements of syntax that would indicate Semitic interference, further testing of each criterion should be done to see how reliable an indicator of interference it is. One can imagine that there may be other factors affecting the frequency of occurrence of a given element of syntax.

The methodology I developed from Martin's approach is useful for seeing how the syntax of a given Greek text compares with others along the scale from "composition" Greek at one end (Greek composed by Greek speakers with native proficiency) to "translation" Greek at the other (Greek translated from a Semitic source, for which Semitic interference is clearly exhibited). For the purpose of graphing the profile of a text on a numerical axis, -1 represents the norm for composition Greek for each of the seventeen criteria, and $+1$ represents the norm for translation Greek for each of the seventeen criteria. The norm for each of the two poles was calculated by examining the frequency of occurrence of each of the seventeen criteria in texts known to have been composed by highly proficient Greek writers: passages from Plutarch's *Parallel Lives* (325 lines); Polybius, *Histories*, books 1–2 (192 lines); Epictetus, *Discourses*, books 3–4 (138 lines); passages from Josephus's *Against Apion* and *Jewish Antiquities* (215 lines); and selected documentary papyri (630 lines; see R. A. Martin 1974: 18). The norm for translation Greek was calculated by examining the frequency of occurrence of the seventeen criteria in 3,415 lines of text from books of the LXX (Genesis, 1 Samuel, 1 and 2 Kings, both Greek versions of Daniel, and Ezra) for which Hebrew (or Aramaic) source texts are extant and for which Semitic interference from the source can be demonstrated. The average frequency of occurrence of the seventeen criteria as found in the two groups of texts was used to define two norms, one for composition Greek and one for translation Greek. These norms were then normalized to $+1$ and -1, respectively, forming a scale on which the syntax numbers of other texts can be positioned, thereby forming a quantitative basis of comparison.

A Greek text under study, such as the alpha-text of Esther in my dissertation work or the Epistle of 1 Peter in this present study, can then be examined for the frequency of occurrence of each of the seventeen syntactical criteria. The value of each of the seventeen criteria can be plotted on the numerical scale to yield the text's profile. A numeric quantification of the overall syntax of a given text can be represented by the normalized average of those seventeen values, referred to as a text's S-number. The S-number of a given text can then be compared with the norms for composition or translation Greek, as well as with results for other texts. The position of the value of each of the criteria on the scale indicates whether that element of syntax occurs in frequencies that tend toward composition Greek or toward Greek that shows Semitic interference. The value of the S-number relative to that of other texts shows the same tendency in the syntax of the text overall. This methodology allows any one of the seventeen criteria to be compared across various texts. For instance, the relative frequency of occurrence of καί with respect to δέ in the alpha-text of Esther could be compared with Daniel LXX, with 1 Peter, and so on. Furthermore, the overall syntax of a text can be compared with others simply by comparing their S-numbers.

A text written by an author whose Greek syntax is influenced by either a Semitic source text or by interference from a native-Semitic language would be expected to use the elements of syntax identified as criteria with a relative frequency that would fall heavily on the scale between 0 and +1 or higher. A text by an author with no such Semitic influence would exhibit traits that fall heavily on the scale between 0 and –1 or lower.

The Syntactical Profile of 1 Peter

When the text of 1 Peter was examined, only fourteen of the seventeen syntactical criteria occur in sufficient frequency to be included in the profile (criteria 1, 2, and 7 were excluded). (See Jobes 1995: 33–34 for a chart of the minimum number of occurrences of each criterion needed for analysis based on that criterion to be statistically valid.)

Of the fourteen criteria relevant to 1 Peter, nine clearly fall on the side of the scale showing Semitic influence (3, 4, 5, 6, 8, 12, 13, 14, and 17). Five clearly fall on the "composition" side of the scale (9, 10, 11, 15, and 16; see graph 1). Criteria 3, 4, 5, 6, and 8 show that the use of prepositions in 1 Peter has probably been influenced by Semitic syntax. The one preposition ⊐ represents several relationships that are expressed by a variety of Greek prepositions. However, ⊐ is most frequently translated by ἐν in the LXX. Therefore, a relatively high frequency of occurrence of the preposition ἐν compared with texts composed by native-proficiency speakers is understood to be an indicator of Semitic interference. In comparison with 1 Peter, the use of prepositions in Polybius is the Greek of an educated, native-Greek speaker, and the values of criteria 2–8 fall heavily on the scale in the negative range corresponding to native-Greek proficiency (see graph 1). Even Josephus, a significant point of comparison because of his Galilean origins, uses the Greek prepositions more like a native-Greek speaker than does the author of 1 Peter, with the exception of εἰς (criterion 3). This suggests that Josephus had mastered the use of Greek prepositions to near native proficiency, even though his Greek exhibits other signs of Semitic interference. Since prepositions are notoriously the most difficult element of a new language to master, this is one indication that the syntax of 1 Peter reflects an author whose native language is not Greek.

Criterion 12, the frequency of occurrence of dependent genitive personal pronouns, and criterion 13, the frequency of occurrence of genitive personal pronouns dependent upon anarthrous substantives, appear with relative frequency in 1 Peter, which also reflects Semitic interference. R. A. Martin (1974: 76) explains the rationale for criterion 12:

> The genitive personal pronoun is expressed in Hebrew and Aramaic by pronominal suffixes attached directly to the substantive. This suffix must be repeated with each word in a series—he sold his horse, his cow, his cart and his plow. This practice is in contrast to Greek style which often omits the genitive personal pronoun, or uses it only once in a series, or uses a possessive adjective in its place.

R. A. Martin describes the rationale for criterion 13 (1974: 28): "In Semitic languages a noun with a pronominal suffix cannot normally also have an article. It is, by way of contrast, the regular practice in Greek for the substantive to have the article whenever a genitive pronoun depends upon it." The Greek writer influenced by these elements of Semitic syntax tends to use a greater number of dependent genitive personal pronouns as well as a greater number that are dependent on anarthrous substantives. This is certainly the pattern in 1 Peter, where the frequency of occurrence of both criteria 12 and 13 clearly fall on the Semitic end of the scale (see graph 1). In comparison, Polybius uses the style of native speakers, since criteria 12 and 13 have values well below –0.5. Josephus, however, uses dependent genitive personal pronouns in a way that tends toward Semitic syntax, though not nearly with the frequency of the author of 1 Peter (see graph 1).

The position of attributive adjectives (criterion 14) in 1 Peter also indicates Semitic interference. "In Hebrew always and in Aramaic generally an attributive adjective follows the word it qualifies and the Greek translator will usually retain this word order. In original Greek style, however, the attributive adjective precedes as often or more often; that is, Greek style usually prefers the first attributive position" (R. A. Martin 1974: 30). Attributive adjectives in 1 Peter actually more often precede

Graph 1. The Syntax of 1 Peter Compared with Polybius and Josephus

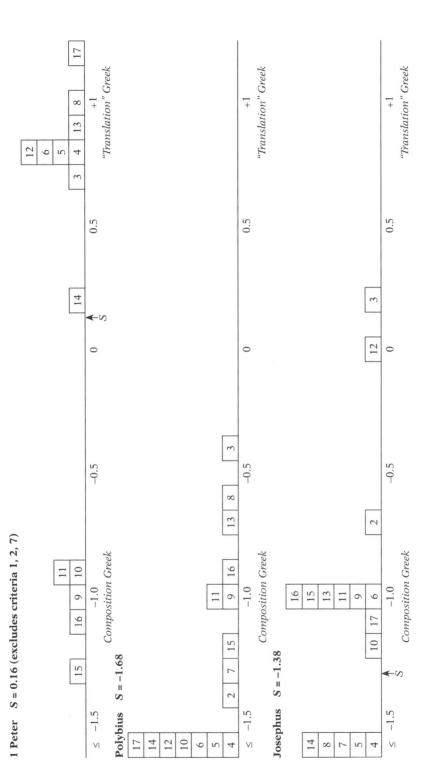

The numbers in the boxes are criterion numbers. The position of the box on the axis indicates the normalized value of the relative frequency of occurrence for that criterion. For instance, the normalized value of criterion 3 is 0.7 for 1 Peter, −0.4 for Polybius, and 0.2 for Josephus. If the normalized value of every criterion equaled the norm for composition Greek, all the boxes for these texts would pile up over −1. The data for Polybius and Josephus come from R. A. Martin (1974).

the word being qualified (22 times) than follow it (16 times). But there are enough following adjectives to bring this criterion into the range of the scale indicating Semitic interference. Even with the number of preceding adjectives, their frequency of occurrence in 1 Peter—when compared with Josephus and Polybius, where criterion 14 is off the scale—shows a clear difference in the positioning of adjectives between Josephus and Polybius, on the one hand, and 1 Peter, on the other.

Finally, the lower relative frequency of the dative case used without the preposition ἐν (criterion 17) also indicates a Semitic influence in the syntax of 1 Peter. In Hebrew and Aramaic, the dative, locative, and instrumental senses are often expressed with the preposition בְּ, which is most often translated into Greek with the preposition ἐν. In native-Greek composition these ideas are often represented by the dative alone or by the use of some other preposition. Therefore, a higher frequency of the presence of ἐν with the dative case, such as is found in 1 Peter, indicates Semitic influence (see criterion 17, graph 1). Such is not the case either in Josephus or, to an even greater extent, in Polybius, where criterion 17 falls below –1 in both writers.

The style of 1 Peter, with its long sentences and rhetorical elements, may suggest someone who has a greater proficiency in Greek than would be expected of a Galilean fisherman. Nevertheless, Semitic interference is indicated by (a) the use of prepositions (criteria 3, 4, 5, 6, 8), (b) the use of the genitive personal pronoun (criteria 12, 13), (c) the position of attributive adjectives, and (d) the use of the dative case with ἐν (criterion 17). A comparison of the syntactical profile of 1 Peter with Josephus and Polybius clearly shows that its syntax, at least as measured by these fourteen syntactical criteria, is not nearly as "good" as Polybius, or even as good as Josephus, if "good" is defined as the Greek style and syntax of a natively proficient speaker.

One of the features of 1 Peter is its extensive use of quotations from the LXX. Given the extent of the quotations relative to the brief length of the letter, the overall syntax of 1 Peter would certainly be expected to exhibit Semitic interference simply from the syntax of the quotations. However, in the data presented above, the quotations have been eliminated from consideration. When the quotations are included in the analysis, the S-number of 1 Peter increases significantly to 0.28, approaching the S-numbers of Greek OT books such as Susanna LXX = 0.28; Esther LXX = 0.33; Alpha-text of Esther = 0.39; Daniel LXX = 0.54; and Theodotion's Daniel = 0.62.

The Comparison of 1 Peter with Other Books of the New Testament

The results of this comparison with Polybius and Josephus lead directly to the question of how the syntax of 1 Peter stacks up against other writers of the NT. Because some argue that Peter used Silvanus (= Silas, 1 Pet. 5:12) as his amanuensis, a comparison with 1 Thessalonians, also associated with Silas (1 Thess. 1:1), is a good place to start. When the syntactical profile of 1 Thessalonians is examined, clear Semitic influence can be seen, as eight of the relevant twelve criteria fall heavily on the Semitic side of the scale. Its S-number is 0.37, indicating even more Semitic interference in its syntax than in 1 Peter. It is interesting that seven of the eight relevant elements of syntax (criteria 3, 6, 8, 12, 13, 14, and 17) occur with similar frequency in both 1 Peter and 1 Thessalonians (see graph 2). Specifically, the prepositions εἰς, περί, and ὑπό with the genitive (criteria 3, 6, 8) occur not only with a similar frequency but with a frequency indicating Semitic interference.

This usage can be compared with the syntax of Heb. 5–9, whose author is reputed to write in the style and syntax of a highly educated Greek speaker. As one would therefore expect, in Heb. 5–9 the relative frequency of those same three prepositions falls in the range of usage similar to Polybius and Josephus.

Criterion 12, the frequency of occurrence of dependent genitive personal pronouns, and criterion 13, the frequency of occurrence of genitive personal pronouns dependent upon anarthrous substantives, occur with a quite similar relative frequency in 1 Peter and 1 Thessalonians. In comparison, when the author of Heb. 5–9 uses genitive personal pronouns, he also tends to make them dependent upon anarthrous substantives in a way that tends toward Semitic style, but he uses genitive personal pronouns with a relative frequency consistent with native proficiency (see graph 2).

Criterion 14, the frequency of occurrence of attributive adjectives preceding the word they qualify, is found to be more toward the style of native Greek in 1 Peter than in either 1 Thessalonians or Heb. 5–9, but not by much and still well within the range of Semitic interference (see graph 2). In all three books, the positioning of the attributive adjective tends toward Semitic style.

And finally, the frequency of occurrence of the dative case used without the preposition ἐν (criterion 17) appears with almost identical frequency in 1 Peter, 1 Thessalonians, and Hebrews.

The contour of the profiles and a comparison of the respective S-numbers clearly show that the syntax of 1 Peter and 1 Thessalonians is more similar than either is to the syntax of Hebrews. The positive arithmetic sign of the S-numbers for 1 Peter and 1 Thessalonians indicates that their syntax tends overall toward the Semitic. The negative sign of the S-number for Heb. 5–9 indicates that the syntax of those chapters tends overall toward Greek without Semitic interference.

Moreover, the profile of Hebrews more closely resembles that of Josephus and Polybius than it does that of 1 Peter and 1 Thessalonians. However, even the high-Greek style of Hebrews displays Semitic tenden-

Graph 2. The Syntax of 1 Peter Compared with 1 Thessalonians and Hebrews 5–9

1 Peter   S = 0.16 (excludes criteria 1, 2, 7)

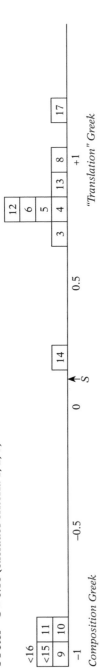

1 Thessalonians   S = 0.37 (excludes criteria 1, 2, 4, 5, 7)

Hebrews 5–9   S = –0.44 (excludes criteria 1, 2, 7)

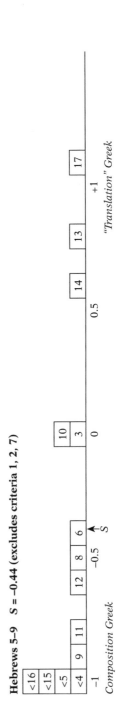

The numbers in the boxes are criterion numbers. The position of the box on the axis indicates the normalized value of the relative frequency of occurrence for that criterion. For instance, the normalized value of criterion 3 is 0.7 for 1 Peter, 1.0 for 1 Thessalonians, and 0 for Hebrews 5–9. If the normalized value of every criterion equaled the norm for composition Greek, all the boxes would pile up over –1.

cies in (a) the frequency of occurrence of genitive personal pronouns dependent upon anarthrous substantives (criterion 13), (b) the frequency of attributive adjectives preceding the word they qualify (criterion 14), and (c) the frequency of the dative case used without preposition ἐν (criterion 17). If the author of Hebrews is Apollos, a native-Greek speaker of Alexandria, these three elements of syntax may indicate traits of the style of Greek in more general use among the Jewish population.

Conclusions

The major conclusion drawn from this study is that the extent of Semitic interference in the Greek of 1 Peter indicates an author whose first language was not Greek. Moreover, the syntax of 1 Peter is comparable to that of 1 Thessalonians but significantly different from that of Heb. 5–9, whose formal elements of rhetoric far surpass those found in 1 Peter as well. These conclusions underline Achtemeier's (1996: 2) warning that despite the admirable features of the rhetoric of 1 Peter, "the quality of its Greek ought nevertheless not be exaggerated." Achtemeier (1996: 7) concluded that the author was probably not the apostle Peter, because he perceived an absence of influence by Hebrew or Aramaic and because of the extensive use of the LXX in the epistle, which he apparently judges to be improbable for a Semitic author. This study has demonstrated quantitatively the presence of Semitic interference in the Greek of 1 Peter and opens the way for considering Semitic authors for whom Greek was a second language. And as for the implications for authorship in 1 Peter's use of the LXX, the debate continues about the pervasiveness of the Greek language in Palestine and, therefore, about the use of the LXX in Palestine. The question remains to what extent the Greek text of 1 Peter demands an author formally schooled in Greek rhetoric, as opposed to someone whose rhetorical skill was acquired by less formal means, and whether someone like the apostle Peter could have achieved that level of proficiency.

Being based on an analysis of syntax, the study presented is not sufficient for determining who the author of 1 Peter was or for concluding that the same author wrote both 1 Peter and 1 Thessalonians, because syntax is shared by all speakers and writers of a given language. The interference in Greek as a second language caused by Semitic syntax could be expected to be similar for all Semitic speakers whose second language was Greek and who had attained equivalent proficiency in the language. It does demonstrate the unlikelihood that the author of 1 Peter was a native speaker of Greek. The discrepancy between Josephus—for whom it might be argued that Greek was also a second language—and the author of 1 Peter probably indicates differing levels of proficiency in the Greek language. This analysis of syntax demonstrates that Josephus had a much better mastery of Greek than did the author of 1 Peter, which is consistent with historical information about him.

This study is intended to demonstrate the advantages of a quantitative textual analysis that moves beyond one's subjective feel for the text. To that end, more objective and quantifiable analyses of various elements of the text of 1 Peter and the other books of the NT are needed to replace the subjective opinions about the quality of the Greek, upon which many theories of authorship are based.

Works Cited

ABD   *The Anchor Bible Dictionary.*
Edited by D. N. Freedman et al. 6
vols. New York: Doubleday, 1992.

Achtemeier, P. J.
1984   Review of John H. Elliott, *A
Home for the Homeless. Journal
of Biblical Literature* 103:130–33.

1989   "Newborn Babes and Living
Stones: Literal and Figurative in
1 Peter." Pp. 207–36 in *To Touch
the Text: Biblical and Related
Studies in Honor of Joseph A.
Fitzmyer.* Edited by M. P. Horgan
and P. J. Kobelski. New York:
Crossroad.

1993   "Suffering Servant and Suffering
Christ in 1 Peter." Pp. 176–88
in *The Future of Christology:
Essays in Honor of Leander E.
Keck.* Edited by A. J. Malherbe
and W. A. Meeks. Minneapolis:
Fortress.

1996   *1 Peter: A Commentary on First
Peter.* Hermeneia. Minneapolis:
Fortress.

Agnew, F. H.
1983   "1 Peter 1:2—an Alternative
Translation." *Catholic Biblical
Quarterly* 45:68–73.

Aland, K.
1961   "The Problem of Anonymity
and Pseudonymity in Christian
Literature of the First Two
Centuries." *Journal of
Theological Studies,* n.s., 12:39–
49.

Alston, R.
1998   *Aspects of Roman History, AD
14–117.* New York: Routledge.

Applegate, J.
1992   "The Co-elect Woman of
1 Peter." *New Testament Studies*
38:587–604.

Armstrong, G. C.
1936   *Aristotle: Oeconomica. Magna
Moralia.* Loeb Classical Library.

Cambridge, MA: Harvard
University Press.

Babbitt, F. C.
1971   *Plutarch's Moralia.* Vol. 2. Loeb
Classical Library. Cambridge,
MA: Harvard University Press.

Baker, C., and S. P. Jones
1998   *Encyclopedia of Bilingualism
and Bilingual Education.*
Philadelphia: Multilingual
Matters.

Balch, D. L.
1981   *Let Wives Be Submissive: The
Domestic Code in 1 Peter.*
Society of Biblical Literature
Dissertation Series 26. Atlanta:
Scholars Press.

1984   "Early Christian Criticism of
Patriarchal Authority: 1 Peter
2:11–3:12." *Union Seminary
Quarterly Review* 39/3:161–73.

1988   "Household Codes." Pp. 25–50 in
*Greco-Roman Literature and the
New Testament: Selected Forms
and Genres.* Edited by D. E.
Aune. Atlanta: Scholars Press.

Bammel, E.
1964–65   "The Commands in I Peter
II.17." *New Testament Studies*
11/3:279–81.

Bandstra, A. J.
2003   " 'Making Proclamation to
the Spirits in Prison': Another
Look at 1 Peter 3:19." *Calvin
Theological Journal* 38:120–24.

Barclay, J. M. G.
1993   "Conflict in Thessalonica."
Catholic Biblical Quarterly
55:512–30.

Barclay, W.
1976   *The Letters of James and Peter.*
Revised edition. Philadelphia:
Westminster.

Barr, J.

1975 "בארץ‎~ΜΟΛΙΣ: Prov. XI.31, I Pet. IV.18." *Journal of Semitic Studies* 20/2:149–64.

Basore, J. W.

1952 *Seneca's Moral Essays.* Vol. 1. Loeb Classical Library. Cambridge: Harvard University Press.

Batey, R. A.

1992 "Sepphoris: An Urban Portrait of Jesus." *Biblical Archaeology Review* 18/3:50–62.

2001 "Sepphoris and the Jesus Movement." *New Testament Studies* 46:402–9.

Baumgarten, J. M.

1999 "Art in the Synagogue: Some Talmudic Views." Pp. 71–86 in *Jews, Christians, and Polytheists in the Ancient Synagogue: Cultural Interaction during the Greco-Roman Period.* Edited by S. Fine. New York: Routledge.

BDAG *A Greek-English Lexicon of the New Testament and Other Early Christian Literature.* By W. Bauer, F. W. Danker, W. F. Arndt, and F. W. Gingrich. 3rd edition. Chicago: University of Chicago Press, 2000.

BDF *A Greek Grammar of the New Testament and Other Early Christian Literature.* By F. Blass, A. Debrunner, and R. W. Funk. Chicago: University of Chicago Press, 1961.

Beare, F. W.

1970 *The First Epistle of Peter.* 3rd edition revised. Oxford: Blackwell.

Bechtler, S. R.

1998 *Following in His Steps: Suffering, Community, and Christology in 1 Peter.* Society of Biblical Literature Dissertation Series 162. Atlanta: Scholars Press.

Bergren, T. A. (ed.)

1991 *A Latin-Greek Index of the Vulgate New Testament.* Atlanta: Scholars Press.

Best, E.

1969 "I Peter II 4–10—a Reconsideration." *Novum Testamentum* 11:270–93.

1969–70 "I Peter and the Gospel Tradition." *New Testament Studies* 16:95–113.

1971 *I Peter.* New Century Bible. Greenwood, SC: Attic.

1986 "A First Century Sect." *Irish Biblical Studies* 8:115–21.

Bigg, C.

1956 *A Critical and Exegetical Commentary on the Epistles of St. Peter and St. Jude.* International Critical Commentary. Edinburgh: Clark.

Bischoff, A.

1906 " Ἀλλοτρι(ο)επίσκοπος." *Zeitschrift für die neutestamentliche Wissenschaft und die Kunde des Urchristentums* 7:271–74.

Black, M. (ed.)

1970 *Apocalypsis Henochi Graece.* Leiden: Brill.

Blevins, J. L.

1982 "Introduction to 1 Peter." *Review and Expositor* 79:401–25.

Blum, E. A.

1981 "1 Peter." Vol. 12 / pp. 209–54 in *The Expositor's Bible Commentary.* Edited by F. E. Gaebelein. Grand Rapids: Zondervan.

Boismard, M.–E.

1961 *Quatre hymnes baptismales dans la première épître de Pierre.* Paris: Cerf.

Boring, M. E.

1999 *1 Peter.* Abingdon New Testament Commentaries. Nashville: Abingdon.

Botermann, H.

1996 *Das Judenedikt des Kaisers Claudius: Römischer Staat und "Christiani" im 1. Jahrhundert.* Stuttgart: Steiner.

Boyer, J.

1984 "The Classification of Participles: A Statistical Study." *Grace Theological Journal* 5:163–79.

Bray, G. (ed.)

2000 *James, 1–2 Peter, 1–3 John, Jude.* Ancient Christian Commentary on Scripture: New Testament 11. Downers Grove, IL: InterVarsity.

Brewster, H.

1993 *Classical Anatolia: The Glory of Hellenism.* New York: Tauris.

Brooks, O. S.

1974 "I Peter 3:21—The Clue to the Literary Structure of the Epistle." *Novum Testamentum* 16:290–305.

Brown, R. E., and J. P. Meier

1983 *Antioch and Rome.* New York: Paulist.

Bruce, F. F.

1959 *Biblical Exegesis in the Qumran Texts.* Grand Rapids: Eerdmans.

CAH *Cambridge Ancient History.* Edited by S. A. Cook, F. E. Adcock, and M. P. Charlesworth. 10 vols. Cambridge: Cambridge University Press, 1934.

Calvin, J.
1963   The Epistle of Paul the Apostle
        to the Hebrews and the First and
        Second Epistles of St. Peter. Calvin's
        New Testament Commentaries.
        Translated by W. B. Johnston. Grand
        Rapids: Eerdmans.
2001   Institutes of the Christian Religion.
        Translated by H. Beveridge. Grand
        Rapids: Eerdmans.
Campbell, B.
1998   Honor, Shame, and the Rhetoric of
        1 Peter. Society of Biblical Literature
        Dissertation Series 160. Atlanta:
        Scholars Press.
Campbell, R. A.
1994   The Elders: Seniority within Earliest
        Christianity. Edinburgh: Clark.
Carson, D. A., D. Moo, and L. Morris
1992   An Introduction to the New
        Testament. Grand Rapids:
        Zondervan.
Casson, L.
1974   Travel in the Ancient World. Toronto:
        Hakkert.
Chancey, M.
2001   "The Cultural Milieu of Ancient
        Sepphoris." New Testament Studies
        47:127–45.
Charlesworth, J. H.
1992   "Has the Name 'Peter' Been Found
        among the Dead Sea Scrolls?" Pp.
        213–23 in Christen und Christliches
        in Qumran? Edited by B. Mayer.
        Regensburg: Pustet.
Chin, M.
1991   "A Heavenly Home for the
        Homeless." Tyndale Bulletin 42:96–
        112.
Clark, G. H.
1972   New Heavens, New Earth: First and
        Second Peter. 2nd edition. Jefferson,
        MD: Trinity Foundation.
Clausing, R.
1925   The Roman Colonate: The Theories
        of Its Origin. New York: Columbia
        University.
Clowney, E.
1988   The Message of 1 Peter: The Way of
        the Cross. The Bible Speaks Today.
        Edited by J. R. W. Stott. Leicester,
        England: Inter-Varsity/Downers
        Grove, IL: InterVarsity.
Colson, F. H., and G. H. Whitaker
1930   Philo: On Drunkenness. Vol. 3.
        Loeb Classical Library. New York:
        Putnam's Sons.
1930   Philo: On Planting. Vol. 3. Loeb
        Classical Library. New York:
        Putnam's Sons.
Colwell, E. C.
1939   "Popular Reactions against
        Christianity in the Roman Empire."
        Pp. 53–71 in Environmental Factors
        in Christian History. Edited by J. T.
        McNeill, M. Spinka, and H. R.
        Willoughby. Port Washington, NY:
        Kennikat.
Congar, Y. M.-J.
1962   The Mystery of the Temple or The
        Manner of God's Presence to His
        Creatures from Genesis to the
        Apocalypse. London: Burns & Oates.
Cook, D.
1980   "1 Peter iii.20: An Unnecessary
        Problem." Journal of Theological
        Studies 31:72–78.
Cranfield, C. E. B.
1958   The First Epistle of Peter. London:
        SCM.
Cross, F. L.
1954   1 Peter: A Paschal Liturgy. London:
        Mowbray.
Crouch, J. E.
1972   The Origin and Intention of the
        Colossian Haustafel. Göttingen:
        Vandenhoeck & Ruprecht.
Dalton, W. J.
1965   Christ's Proclamation to the Spirits.
        Rome: Pontifical Biblical Institute.
1974   "So That Your Faith May Also Be
        Your Hope in God." Pp. 262–74
        in Reconciliation and Hope: New
        Testament Essays on Atonement and
        Eschatology presented to L. L. Morris
        on His 60th Birthday. Grand Rapids:
        Eerdmans.
1979   "The Interpretation of 1 Peter 3,19
        and 4,6: Light from 2 Peter." Biblica
        60:547–55.
1983   Review of John H. Elliott, A Home
        for the Homeless. Biblica 64:442–44.
Dana, H., and D. Mantey
1955   A Manual Grammar of the Greek New
        Testament. Upper Saddle River, NJ:
        Prentice Hall.
Danker, F. W.
1967   "I Peter 1:24–2:17—A Consolatory
        Pericope." Zeitschrift für die
        neutestamentliche Wissenschaft und
        die Kunde der älteren Kirche 58:93–
        102.

1982   *Benefactor: Epigraphic Study of a Graeco-Roman and New Testament Semantic Field.* St. Louis: Clayton.

1983   Review of John H. Elliott, *A Home for the Homeless. Interpretation* 37:84–88.

Daube, D.
1956   *The New Testament and Rabbinic Judaism.* London: Athlone. Reprinted Salem, NH: Ayer, 1984.

Davids, P. H.
1990   *The First Epistle of Peter.* New International Commentary on the New Testament. Grand Rapids: Eerdmans.

2002   "1 Peter." Vol. 4 / pp. 120–51 in *Zondervan Illustrated Bible Backgrounds Commentary.* Edited by C. E. Arnold. Grand Rapids: Zondervan.

Davidson, R. M.
1981   *Typology in Scripture: A Study of Hermeneutical Τύπος Structures.* Andrews University Seminary Doctoral Dissertation Series. Berrien Springs, MI: Andrews University Press.

Deissmann, G. A.
1927   *Light from the Ancient East.* New York: Doran. Reprinted Peabody, MA: Hendrickson, 1995.

de Silva, D.
2000   "1 Peter: Strategies for Counseling Individuals on the Way to a New Heritage." *Ashland Theological Journal* 32:33–52.

de Waard, J.
1965   *A Comparative Study of the Old Testament Text in the Dead Sea Scrolls and in the New Testament.* Leiden: Brill.

Dillard, R., and T. Longman III
1994   *An Introduction to the Old Testament.* Grand Rapids: Zondervan.

Dupont-Roc, R.
1995   "Le jeu des prépositions en 1 Pierre 1,1–12: De l'espérance finale à la joie dans les épreuves présentes." *Estudios bíblicos* 53:201–12.

du Toit, A. B.
1974   "The Significance of Discourse Analysis for New Testament Interpretation and Translation: Introductory Remarks with Special Reference to 1 Peter 1:3–13." *Neotestamentica* 8:54–79.

Elliott, J. H.
1966   *The Elect and the Holy.* Leiden: Brill.

1980   "Peter, Silvanus and Mark in 1 Peter and Acts: Sociological-Exegetical Perspectives on a Petrine Group in Rome." Pp. 250–67 in *Wort in der Zeit: Festgabe für Karl Heinrich Rengstorf zum 75. Geburtstag.* Edited by W. Haubeck and M. Bachmann. Leiden: Brill.

1981   *A Home for the Homeless: A Sociological Exegesis of 1 Peter, Its Situation and Strategy.* Philadelphia: Fortress.

1985   "Backward and Forward 'in His Steps': Following Jesus from Rome to Raymond and Beyond: The Tradition, Redaction, and Reception of 1 Peter 2:18–25." Pp. 184–209 in *Discipleship in the New Testament.* Edited by F. Segovia. Philadelphia: Fortress.

1998   "The Church as Counter-culture: A Home for the Homeless and a Sanctuary for Refugees." *Currents in Theology and Mission* 25:176–85.

2000   *I Peter.* Anchor Bible 37B. New York: Doubleday.

2001   "Elders as Leaders in 1 Peter and the Early Church." *Currents in Theology and Mission* 28:549–59.

Elliott, J. K.
1992   *Essays and Studies in New Testament Textual Criticism.* Cordoba: Ediciones el Almendro.

Erbes, D. K.
1919–20   "Was bedeutet ἀλλοτριοεπίσκοπος 1 Pt 4,15?" *Zeitschrift für die neutestamentliche Wissenschaft und die Kunde des Urchristentums* 19:39–44.

1921   "Noch etwas zum ἀλλοτριοεπίσκοπος I Petr 4₁₅." *Zeitschrift für die neutestamentliche Wissenschaft und die Kunde der älteren Kirche* 20:249.

Erickson, M. J.
1995   "Is There Opportunity for Salvation after Death?" *Bibliotheca Sacra* 152:131–44.

Erling, B.
1999   "The Priesthood of All Believers and Luther's Translation of 1 Peter 2:5, 9." *Lutheran Forum* (Pentecost/ Summer).

Evans, C. A., and P. W. Flint (eds.)
1997   *Eschatology, Messianism, and the Dead Sea Scrolls.* Grand Rapids: Eerdmans.

Feinberg, J. S.
1986   "1 Peter 3:18–20, Ancient Mythology, and the Intermediate State." *Westminster Theological Journal* 48:303–36.

Feldmeier, R.
1992   *Die Christen als Fremde: Die Metaphor der Fremde in der antiken Welt, im Urchristentum und im 1. Petrusbrief.* Wissenschaftliche Untersuchungen zum Neuen Testament 64. Tübingen: Mohr.

Fitzmyer, J. A.
1979   "The Languages of Palestine." Pp. 29–56 in *A Wandering Aramean.* Missoula, MT: Scholars Press.
1992   "Did Jesus Speak Greek?" *Biblical Archaeology Review* 18/5:58–63.

France, R. T.
1977   "Exegesis in Practice: Two Samples" Pp. 252–81 in *New Testament Interpretation: Essays on Principles and Methods.* Edited by I. H. Marshall. Grand Rapids: Eerdmans.
1998   "First Century Bible Study: Old Testament Motifs in 1 Peter 2:4–10." *Journal of the European Pentecostal Theological Association* 18:26–48.

Frank, T.
1927   *An Economic History of Rome.* 2nd revised edition. Baltimore: Johns Hopkins Press. Reprinted New York: Cooper Square, 1962.
1932   *Aspects of Social Behavior in Ancient Rome.* Martin Classical Lectures 2. Oberlin, OH: Oberlin College. Reprinted New York: Cooper Square, 1969.

Frend, W. H. C.
1967   *Martyrdom and Persecution in the Early Church: A Study of a Conflict from the Maccabees to Donatus.* New York: New York University Press.

Gaede, S.
1993   *When Tolerance Is No Virtue: Political Correctness, Multiculturalism and the Future of Truth and Justice.* Downers Grove, IL: InterVarsity.

Garnsey, P.
1974   "Legal Privilege in the Roman Empire." Pp. 141–65 in *Studies in Ancient Society.* Edited by M. I.

Finley. Boston: Routledge & Kegan Paul.

Garnsey, P., and R. Saller
1987   *The Roman Empire: Economy, Society and Culture.* Berkeley: University of California Press.

Gärtner, B. E.
1965   *The Temple and the Community in Qumran and the New Testament.* Society for New Testament Studies Monograph Series 1. Cambridge: Cambridge University Press.

GELNT   *Greek-English Lexicon of the New Testament Based on Semantic Domains.* By J. P. Louw and E. A. Nida. 2 vols. New York: United Bible Societies, 1988–89.

Goodman, M.
1997   *The Roman World 44 BC–AD 180.* With the assistance of J. Sherwood. New York: Routledge.

Goodspeed, E. J.
1954   "Enoch in 1 Peter 3:19." *Journal of Biblical Literature* 73:91–92.

Goppelt, L.
1993   *A Commentary on I Peter.* Translated by J. E. Alsup. Grand Rapids: Eerdmans.

Gross, C. D.
1989   "Are the Wives in 1 Peter 3.7 Christians?" *Journal for the Study of the New Testament* 35:89–96.

Grudem, W.
1986   "Christ Preaching through Noah: 1 Peter 3:19–20 in the Light of Dominant Themes in Jewish Literature." *Trinity Journal,* n.s., 7:3–31.
1988   *1 Peter.* Tyndale New Testament Commentaries. Grand Rapids: Eerdmans.

Gschwind, K.
1911   *Die Niederfahrt Christi in die Unterwelt: Ein Beitrag zur Exegese des Neuen Testamentes und zur Geschichte des Taufsymbols.* Münster: Aschendorff.

Gummere, R. M.
1930   *Seneca: Ad Lucilium epistulae morales.* Vol. 2. Loeb Classical Library. New York: Putnam's Sons.
1934   *Seneca: Ad Lucilium epistulae morales.* Vol. 1. Loeb Classical Library. New York: Putnam's Sons.
1943   *Seneca: Ad Lucilium epistulae morales.* Vol. 3. Loeb Classical

Library. Cambridge, MA: Harvard University Press.

Gundry, R. H.
1966–67 " 'Verba Christi' in I Peter: Their Implications concerning the Authorship of I Peter and the Authenticity of the Gospel Tradition." *New Testament Studies* 13:336–50.
1974 "Further Verba on Verba Christi in First Peter." *Biblica* 55:211–32.
2003 *A Survey of the New Testament.* 4th edition. Grand Rapids: Zondervan.

Guthrie, D.
1970 *New Testament Introduction.* Downers Grove, IL: InterVarsity.

Hanson, A.
1982 "Salvation Proclaimed. I. 1 Peter 3.18–22." *Expository Times* 93:100–105.

Hanson, P. D.
1995 *Isaiah 40–66.* Interpretation. Louisville: John Knox.

Harl, M., G. Dorival, and O. Munnich
1994 *La Bible grecque des Septante: Du judaïsme hellénistique au christianisme ancien.* 2nd edition. Paris: Cerf.

Harris, J. R.
1919 "The Religious Meaning of 1 Peter V.5." *Expositor* 8/18:131–39.
1929 "An Emendation to 1 Peter i.13." *Expository Times* 41:43.

Hemer, C. J.
1977–78 "The Address of 1 Peter." *Expository Times* 89:239–43.
1985 Review of John H. Elliott, *A Home for the Homeless. Journal for the Study of the New Testament* 24:120–23.

Hess, R. S., and M. D. Carroll R. (eds.)
2003 *Israel's Messiah in the Bible and the Dead Sea Scrolls.* Grand Rapids: Baker.

Hiebert, D. E.
1982 "The Suffering and Triumphant Christ: An Exposition of 1 Peter 3:18–22." *Bibliotheca Sacra* 139/554:146–58.

Hill, D.
1976 "On Suffering and Baptism in 1 Peter." *Novum Testamentum* 18/3:181–89.
1982 " 'To Offer Spiritual Sacrifices . . .' (1 Peter 2:5): Liturgical Formulations and Christian Paraenesis in 1 Peter." *Journal for the Study of the New Testament* 16:45–63.

Hillyer, N.
1969a "Spiritual Milk . . . Spiritual House." *Tyndale Bulletin* 20:126.
1969b "The Servant of God." *Evangelical Quarterly* 41:143–60.
1970 "First Peter and the Feast of Tabernacles." *Tyndale Bulletin* 21:39–70.
1992 *1 and 2 Peter, Jude.* New International Biblical Commentary. Peabody, MA: Hendrickson.

Holloway, P. A.
2002 "Nihil inopinati accidisse—'Nothing Unexpected Has Happened': A Cyrenaic Consolatory Topos in 1 Pet 4.12ff." *New Testament Studies* 48:433–48.

Hooker, M. D.
1998 "Did the Use of Isaiah 53 to Interpret His Mission Begin with Jesus?" Pp. 88–103 in *Jesus and the Suffering Servant: Isaiah 53 and Christian Origins.* Edited by W. H. Bellinger and W. R. Farmer. Harrisburg, PA: Trinity.

Hornik, H. J., and M. C. Parsons
2003 "The Harrowing of Hell." *Bible Review* 19/3:18–26, 50.

Horrell, D. G.
1997 "Whose Faith(fulness) Is It in 1 Peter 1:5?" *Journal of Theological Studies* 48:110–15.
1998 *The Epistles of Peter and Jude.* Epworth Commentaries. Peterborough: Epworth.

Hort, F. J. A.
1898 *The First Epistle of St. Peter. I.1–II.17: The Greek Text with Introductory Lecture, Commentary, and Additional Notes.* London: Macmillan.

Howard, G.
1977 "The Tetragram and the New Testament." *Journal of Biblical Literature* 96:63–83.

Isaac, E.
1983 "1 (Ethiopic Apocalypse of) Enoch." Pp. 5–89 in *The Old Testament Pseudepigrapha.* Edited by J. H. Charlesworth. Garden City, NY: Doubleday.

Jenkins, P.
2002 *The Next Christendom: The Coming of Global Christianity.* Oxford: Oxford University Press.

Jobes, K. H.
1995   *The Alpha-Text of Esther: Its Character and Relationship to the Masoretic Text.* Society of Biblical Literature Dissertation Series 153. Atlanta: Scholars Press.
2002   "Got Milk? Septuagint Psalm 33 and the Interpretation of 1 Peter 2:1–3." *Westminster Theological Journal* 63:1–14.

Johnson, D. E.
1986   "Fire in God's House: Imagery from Malachi 3 in Peter's Theology of Suffering (1 Pet 4:12–19)." *Journal of the Evangelical Theological Society* 29:285–94.

Johnson, S. E.
1960   "The Preaching to the Dead." *Journal of Biblical Literature* 79:48–51.
1975   "Asia Minor and Early Christianity." Pp. 77–145 in *Christianity, Judaism and Other Greco-Roman Cults: Studies for Morton Smith at Sixty.* Edited by J. Neusner. Leiden: Brill.

Jones, A. H. M.
1971   *The Cities of the Eastern Roman Provinces.* 2nd edition. Oxford: Clarendon.

Juster, J.
1914   *Les Juifs dans l'Empire romain: Leur condition juridique, économique et sociale.* Paris: Geuthner. Reprinted, Burt Franklin Research and Source Works, New York: Franklin, [1965].

Kaiser, W.
1970   "The Eschatological Hermeneutics of Evangelicalism: Promise Theology." *Journal of the Evangelical Theological Society* 13:94–96.

Kelly, J. N. D.
1969   *A Commentary on the Epistles of Peter and of Jude.* New York/Evanston: Harper & Row.

Kendall, D. W.
1986   "The Literary and Theological Function of 1 Peter 1:3–12." Pp. 103–20 in *Perspectives on 1 Peter.* National Association of Baptist Professors of Religion Special Studies 9. Macon, GA: Mercer University Press.

Kiley, M.
1987   "Like Sara: The Tale of Terror behind 1 Peter 3:6." *Journal of Biblical Literature* 106:689–92.

Kilpatrick, G. D.
1986   "1 Peter 1:11 τίνα ἢ ποῖον καιρόν." *Novum Testamentum* 28:91–92.

Kistemaker, S. J.
1986   *James and I–III John.* New Testament Commentary. Grand Rapids: Baker.
1987   *Peter and Jude.* New Testament Commentary. Grand Rapids: Baker.

Kleist, J. A.
1961   *The Epistles of St. Clement of Rome and St. Ignatius of Antioch.* Westminster, MD: Newman.

Knox, J.
1953   "Pliny and 1 Peter: A Note on I Pet 4:14–16 and 3:15." *Journal of Biblical Literature* 72:187–89.

LaVerdiere, E. A.
1969   "Covenant Theology in 1 Peter 1:1–2:10." *The Bible Today* 42 (April): 2909–16.

Levick, B.
1967   *Roman Colonies in Southern Asia Minor.* Oxford: Clarendon.
1990   *Claudius.* New Haven: Yale University Press.

Lightfoot, J. B.
1893   *The Apostolic Fathers.* London: Macmillan.

Lindars, B.
1981   "Enoch and Christology." *Expository Times* 92:295–99.

Llewelyn, S. R.
1994   *New Documents Illustrating Early Christianity: A Review of the Greek Inscriptions and Papyri Published in 1982–83.* With R. A. Kearsley. New Documents Illustrating Early Christianity 7. [North Ryde], New South Wales: Ancient History Documentary Research Centre, Macquarie University.

MacMullen, R.
1974   *Roman Social Relations 50 BC to AD 284.* New Haven: Yale University Press.

Magie, D.
1950   *Roman Rule in Asia Minor to the End of the Third Century after Christ.* 2 vols. Princeton: Princeton University Press. Reprinted New York: Arno, 1975.

Malina, B. J.
1993   *The New Testament World: Insights from Cultural Anthropology.* 2nd edition. Louisville: Westminster/John Knox.

Works Cited

Maloney, E. C.
1981   *Semitic Interference in Marcan Syntax.* Society of Biblical Literature Dissertation Series 51. Atlanta: Scholars Press.
1989   Review of *Syntax Criticism of the Synoptic Gospels. Catholic Biblical Quarterly* 51:378–80.

Manns, F.
1995   "La théologie de la nouvelle naissance dans la première lettre de Pierre." *Studii biblici franciscani liber annus* 45:107–41.

Marchant, E. C.
1938   *Xenophon: Memorabilia and Oeconomicus.* Loeb Classical Library. Cambridge, MA: Harvard University Press.

Marshall, I. H.
1991   *1 Peter.* IVP New Testament Commentary Series. Downers Grove, IL: InterVarsity.

Martin, R. A.
1974   *Syntactical Evidence of Semitic Sources in Greek Documents.* Cambridge, MA: Society of Biblical Literature.
1989   *Syntax Criticism of Johannine Literature, the Catholic Epistles, and the Gospel Passion Accounts.* Lewiston, NY: Mellen.

Martin, R. P.
1994   "1 Peter." Pp. 87–133 in *The Theology of the Letters of James, Peter, and Jude.* By A. Chester and R. P. Martin. New Testament Theology. Cambridge: Cambridge University Press.

Martin, T. W.
1992a   *Metaphor and Composition in 1 Peter.* Society of Biblical Literature Dissertation Series 131. Atlanta: Scholars Press.
1992b   "The Present Indicative in the Eschatological Statements of 1 Peter 1:6, 8." *Journal of Biblical Literature* 111:307–14.
1999   "The TestAbr and the Background of 1 Pet 3,6." *Zeitschrift für die neutestamentliche Wissenschaft und die Kunde der älteren Kirche* 90/1–2:139–46.

Marucchi, O.
1949   *Manual of Christian Archeology.* Translated and adapted by H. Vecchierello. Patterson, NJ: St. Anthony Guild.

Matera, F. J.
1999   *New Testament Christology.* Louisville: Westminster John Knox.

McCartney, D. G.
1991   " 'λογικός' in 1 Peter 2,2." *Zeitschrift für die neutestamentliche Wissenschaft und die Kunde der älteren Kirche* 82:128–32.

McKelvey, R. J.
1969   *The New Temple: The Church in the New Testament.* Oxford: Oxford University Press.

McKnight, S.
1996   *1 Peter.* NIV Application Commentary. Grand Rapids: Zondervan.

Meecham, H. G.
1953–54   "A Note on 1 Peter ii.12." *Expository Times* 65:93.

Merrill, E. T.
1924   *Essays in Early Christian History.* London: Macmillan.

Metzger, B. M.
1972   "Literary Forgeries and Canonical Pseudepigrapha." *Journal of Biblical Literature* 92:3–24.
1994   *A Textual Commentary on the Greek New Testament.* 2nd edition. New York: United Bible Societies.

Michaels, J. R.
1966–67   "Eschatology in I Peter III.17." *New Testament Studies* 13:394–401.
1988   *1 Peter.* Word Biblical Commentary. Waco: Word.

Mitchell, S.
1993   *Anatolia: Land, Men, and Gods in Asia Minor.* 2 vols. Oxford: Clarendon.

Momigliano, A.
1934   *Claudius: The Emperor and His Achievement.* Translated by W. D. Hogarth. Oxford: Clarendon. Reprinted Cambridge: Heffer & Sons, 1961.
1987   *On Pagans, Jews, and Christians.* Middletown, CT: Wesleyan University Press.

Moo, D.
1996   *The Epistle to the Romans.* New International Commentary on the New Testament. Grand Rapids: Eerdmans.

Moule, C. F. D.
1955–56   "The Nature and Purpose of I Peter." *New Testament Studies* 3:1–11.

1959   "Once More, Who Were the
        Hellenists?" *Expository Times*
        70:100–102.

Moulton, J. H.
1985   *A Grammar of New Testament Greek.*
        Vol. 1: *Prolegomena.* 3rd edition.
        Edinburgh: Clark.

NA²⁷   *Novum Testamentum Graece.* Edited
        by [E. and E. Nestle], B. Aland, K.
        Aland, J. Karavidopoulos, C. M.
        Martini, and B. M Metzger. 27th
        revised edition. Stuttgart: Deutsche
        Bibelgesellschaft, 1993.

Nestle, E.
1898–99 "1 Pet. 1:2." *Expository Times*
        10:188–89.

NETS   *New English Translation of the
        Septuagint.* Edited by A. Pietersma.
        Oxford: Oxford University Press,
        forthcoming.

Noy, D.
2000   *Foreigners at Rome: Citizens and
        Strangers.* London: Duckworth with
        The Classical Press of Wales.

Oborn, G. T.
1939   "Economic Factors in the
        Persecutions of the Christians to AD
        260." Pp. 131–48 in *Environmental
        Factors in Christian History.* Edited
        by J. T. McNeill, M. Spinka, and
        H. R. Willoughby. Port Washington,
        NY: Kennikat.

O'Connor, D. W.
1969   *Peter in Rome: The Literary,
        Liturgical, and Archeological
        Evidence.* New York: Columbia
        University Press.
1975   "Peter in Rome: A Review and
        Position." Pp. 146–60 in *Christianity,
        Judaism and Other Greco-Roman
        Cults: Studies for Morton Smith at
        Sixty.* Edited by J. Neusner. Leiden:
        Brill.

Oesterley, W. O. E.
1925   *The Jewish Background of Christian
        Liturgy.* Oxford: Clarendon.

Oldfather, W. A.
1926   *Epictetus: The Discourses as Reported
        by Arrian.* Vol. 1. Loeb Classical
        Library. Cambridge, MA: Harvard
        University Press.

Osborne, T. P.
1983   "Guide Lines for Christian Suffering:
        A Source-Critical and Theological
        Study of 1 Peter 2,21–25." *Biblica*
        64:381–408.

Oss, D. A.
1989   "The Interpretation of the 'Stone'
        Passages by Peter and Paul: A
        Comparative Study." *Journal of
        the Evangelical Theological Society*
        32:181–200.

Oswalt, J. N.
1998   *The Book of Isaiah: Chapters 40–66.*
        New International Commentary on
        the Old Testament. Grand Rapids:
        Eerdmans.

OTP   *The Old Testament Pseudepigrapha.*
        Edited by J. H. Charlesworth. 2 vols.
        Garden City, NY: Doubleday, 1983–
        85.

Parker, D. C.
1994   "The Eschatology of 1 Peter." *Biblical
        Theology Bulletin* 24:27–32.

Paton, W. R.
1927   *Polybius: The Histories.* Vol. 6.
        Loeb Classical Library. London:
        Heinemann/New York: Putnam's
        Sons.

Pearson, L., and F. H. Sandbach
1965   *Plutarch's Moralia.* Vol. 11. Loeb
        Classical Library. Cambridge, MA:
        Harvard University Press/London:
        Heinemann.

Pelikan, J. J. (ed.)
1967   *Sermons on the First Epistle of St.
        Peter.* In *The Catholic Epistles.* Vol.
        30 of *Luther's Works.* Translated by
        M. H. Bertram. St. Louis: Concordia.

Perdelwitz, R.
1911   *Die Mysterienreligion und das
        Problem des I. Petrusbriefes:
        Ein literarischer und
        religionsgeschichtlicher Versuch.*
        Giessen: Töpelmann.

Perkins, P.
1995   *First and Second Peter, James, and
        Jude.* Interpretation. Louisville: John
        Knox.

Pestman, P. W.
1990   *The New Papyrological Primer.*
        Leiden: Brill.

Pilch, J. J., and B. J. Malina
1993   *Biblical Social Values and
        Their Meaning.* Peabody, MA:
        Hendrickson.

Piper, J.
1978–79 "Hope as the Motivation of Love:
        I Peter 3:9–12." *New Testament
        Studies* 26:212–31.

Poole, A., and J. Maule
1995   *The Oxford Book of Classical Verse in Translation.* Oxford: Oxford University Press.
Porter, S. E.
1992   *Idioms of the Greek New Testament.* Sheffield: JSOT Press.
1993   Review of John H. Elliott, *A Home for the Homeless*, 2nd ed. *Journal for the Study of the New Testament* 51:126.
Preisker, H. (rev.)
1951   *Die katholischen Briefe: Erklärt von Hans Windisch.* 3rd edition. Revised and augmented. Tübingen: Mohr-Siebeck.
Prigent, P.
1992   "I Pierre 2,4–10." *Revue d'histoire et de philosophie religieuses* 72:53–60.
Radice, B.
1969   *Pliny: Letters and Panegyricus.* Loeb Classical Library. Cambridge, MA: Harvard University Press.
Ramsay, W. M.
1890   *The Historical Geography of Asia Minor.* Royal Geographical Society Supplementary Papers 4. London: Murray. Reprinted Amsterdam: Hakkert, 1962.
1893   *The Church in the Roman Empire before AD 170.* New York: Putnam's Sons.
Reicke, B.
1946   *The Disobedient Spirits and Christian Baptism: A Study of 1 Pet. III.19 and Its Context.* Copenhagen: Ejnar Munksgaard.
1964   *The Epistles of James, Peter, and Jude.* Anchor Bible 37. Garden City, NY: Doubleday.
1968   *The New Testament Era: The World of the Bible from 500 BC to AD 100.* Translated by D. E. Green. Philadelphia: Fortress.
Reynolds, J.
1987   "New Evidence for the Social History of Aphrodisias." Pp. 107–13 in *Sociétés urbaines, sociétés rurales dans l'Asie mineure et la Syrie hellénistiques et romaines.* Edited by E. Frézouls. Strasbourg: AECR.
Richard, E.
1986   "The Functional Christology of First Peter." Pp. 121–39 in *Perspectives on First Peter.* Edited by C. H. Talbert. Macon, GA: Mercer University Press.

Richards, E. R.
2000   "Silvanus Was Not Peter's Secretary: Theological Bias in Interpreting διὰ Σιλουανοῦ . . . ἔγραψα." *Journal of the Evangelical Theological Society* 43:417–32.
Richards, G. C.
1930   "I Pet. iii 21." *Journal of Theological Studies* 32:77.
Robinson, J. A. T.
1976   *Redating the New Testament.* Philadelphia: Westminster.
Rodgers, P. R.
1981   "The Longer Reading of 1 Peter 4:14." *Catholic Biblical Quarterly* 43:93–95.
Rolfe, J. C.
1939   *Suetonius.* Vol. 2: *Lives of the Caesars.* Cambridge, MA: Harvard University Press.
Rostovtzeff, M.
1926   *The Social and Economic History of the Roman Empire.* 3 vols. with continuous pagination. Reprinted from corrected sheets of the 2nd edition, Oxford: Clarendon, 1971.
Rutgers, L. V.
1997   Review of Helga Botermann, *Das Judenedikt des Kaisers Claudius.* *Journal for the Study of Judaism* 28:94–99.
Sahlin, H.
1953   "The New Exodus of Salvation according to St Paul." Pp. 81–95 in *The Root of the Vine: Essays in Biblical Theology.* Edited by A. Fridrichsen. New York: Philosophical Library.
Salmon, E. T.
1970   *Roman Colonization under the Republic.* Ithaca: Cornell University Press.
Scapula, J.
1820   *Joannis Scapulae Lexicon Graeco-Latinum.* London: J. F. Dove.
Scharlemann, M. H.
1959   "Why the Kuriou in 1 Peter 1:25?" *Concordia Theological Monthly* 30:352–56.
1989   " 'He Descended into Hell': An Interpretation of 1 Peter 3:18–20." *Concordia Journal* 15:311–22.
Schlatter, A.
1999   *The Theology of the Apostles: The Development of New Testament Theology.* Translated by A. Köstenberger. Grand Rapids: Baker.

Schmoller, A. (ed.)
1989   Handkonkordanz zum griechischen
        Neuen Testament. Stuttgart:
        Deutsche Bibelgesellschaft.
Schutter, W. L.
1987   "I Peter 4.17, Ezekiel 9.6, and
        Apocalyptic Hermeneutics." Pp. 276–
        84 in Society of Biblical Literature
        Seminar Papers. Atlanta: Scholars
        Press.
1989   Hermeneutic and Composition
        in 1 Peter. Wissenschaftliche
        Untersuchungen zum Neuen
        Testament 2. Tübingen: Mohr.
Scott, C. A.
1905   "The Sufferings of Christ: A Note on
        1 Peter I.11." Expositor 12:234–40.
Scramuzza, V. M.
1940   The Emperor Claudius. Cambridge,
        MA: Harvard University Press.
Seland, T.
1995   "The 'Common Priesthood' of Philo
        and 1 Peter: A Philonic Reading of
        1 Peter 2.5, 9." Journal for the Study
        of the New Testament 57:87–119.
2001   "Πάροικος καὶ παρεπίδημος:
        Proselyte Characterizations in
        1 Peter?" Bulletin for Biblical
        Research 11:239–68.
Selwyn, E. G.
1958   The First Epistle of St. Peter. London:
        Macmillan/New York: St. Martin's.
Sherwin-White, A. N.
1974   "Why Were Early Christians
        Persecuted? An Amendment." Pp.
        250–55 in Studies in Ancient Society.
        Edited by M. I. Finley. Boston:
        Routledge & Kegan Paul.
Shimada, K.
1981   "A Critical Note on I Peter 1,12."
        Annual of the Japanese Biblical
        Institute 7:146–50.
Silva, M.
1980   "Bilingualism and the Character of
        Palestinian Greek." Biblica 61:198–
        219.
1994   Biblical Words and Their Meaning:
        An Introduction to Lexical Semantics.
        2nd edition. Grand Rapids:
        Zondervan.
Sleeper, C. F.
1968   "Political Responsibility according
        to I Peter." Novum Testamentum
        10:270–86.

Slingerland, D.
1989a   "Suetonius Claudius 25.4 and the
        Account in Cassius Dio." Jewish
        Quarterly Review 79:305–22.
1989b   "Chrestus: Christus?" Pp. 133–44
        in The Literature of Early Rabbinic
        Judaism: Issues in Talmudic
        Redaction and Interpretation. Edited
        by A. J. Avery-Peck. Lanham, MD:
        University Press of America.
1992   "Suetonius Claudius 25.4, Acts 18,
        and Paulus Orosius' Historiarum
        adversum paganos Libri VII: Dating
        the Claudian Expulsion(s) of Roman
        Jews." Jewish Quarterly Review
        83:127–44.
Sly, D. I.
1991   "1 Peter 3:6b in the Light of Philo
        and Josephus." Journal of Biblical
        Literature 110:126–29.
Smart, J. D.
1965   History and Theology in Second
        Isaiah. Philadelphia: Westminster.
Smith, G. A.
1927   The Book of Isaiah. Vol. 2. Revised
        edition. New York: Harper &
        Brothers.
Snodgrass, K.
1977–78 "I Peter II.1–10: Its Formation and
        Literary Affinities." New Testament
        Studies 24:97–106.
Snyder, S.
1991   "1 Peter 2:17: A Reconsideration."
        Filologia neotestamentaria 4:211–15.
1995   "Participles and Imperatives in
        1 Peter: A Re-examination in the
        Light of Recent Scholarly Trends."
        Filologia neotestamentaria 8:187–98.
Spencer, A. B.
2000   "Peter's Pedagogical Method in
        1 Peter 3:6." Bulletin for Biblical
        Research 10:107–19.
Stanford, W. B.
1945   "St. Peter's Silence on the Petrine
        Claims." Theology 48:15.
Stevenson, G. H.
1939   Roman Provincial Administration.
        New York: Stechert.
Stevick, D. B.
1988   "A Matter of Taste: 1 Peter 2:3."
        Review for Religious 47:707–17.
Stewart-Sykes, A.
1997   "The Function of 'Peter' in I Peter."
        Scripture Bulletin 27:8–21.
Stibbs, A. M.
1979   The First Epistle General of
        Peter. Tyndale New Testament

Commentaries. Grand Rapids: Eerdmans.

Streeter, B. H.
1929   *The Primitive Church.* London: Macmillan.

Swete, H. B. (ed.)
1925   *The Old Testament in Greek according to the Septuagint.* Cambridge: Cambridge University Press.

Sylva, D.
1983   "Translating and Interpreting 1 Peter 3.2." *Bible Translator* 34:144–47.

Talbert, C. H.
1986   "The Plan of 1 Peter." Pp. 141–51 in *Perspectives on First Peter.* Edited by C. H. Talbert. Macon, GA: Mercer University Press.

TDNT   *Theological Dictionary of the New Testament.* Edited by G. Kittel and G. Friedrich; translated and edited by G. W. Bromiley. 10 vols. Grand Rapids: Eerdmans, 1964–76.

Thiede, C. P.
1986   "Babylon, der andere Ort: Anmerkungen zu 1 Petr 5,13 und Apg 12,17." *Biblica* 67:532–38.

1988   *Simon Peter: From Galilee to Rome.* Grand Rapids: Zondervan, Academie Books.

Thielman, F.
2005   *Theology of the New Testament: A Canonical and Synthetic Approach.* Grand Rapids: Zondervan.

Thompson, J. W.
1966   " 'Be Submissive to Your Masters': A Study of I Peter 2:18–25." *Restoration Quarterly* 9:66–78.

Thurén, L.
1990   *The Rhetorical Strategy of 1 Peter.* Åbo: Åbo Academy Press.

1995   *Argument and Theology in 1 Peter: The Origins of Christian Paraenesis.* Society of Biblical Literature Dissertation Series 114. Atlanta: Scholars Press.

Tite, P. L.
1997   *Compositional Transitions in 1 Peter: An Analysis of the Letter-Opening.* San Francisco: International Scholars Publications.

Trebilco, P. R.
1991   *Jewish Communities in Asia Minor.* New York: Cambridge University Press.

Unnik, W. C. van
1954–55   "The Teaching of Good Works in I Peter." *New Testament Studies* 1:92–110.

1969   "The Critique of Paganism in 1 Peter 1:18." Pp. 129–42 in *Neotestamentica et Semitica: Studies in Honour of Matthew Black.* Edited by E. Earle Ellis and M. Wilcox. Edinburgh: Clark.

1980   *Sparsa Collecta: The Collected Essays of W. C. Van Unnik.* Part 2. Leiden: Brill.

Volf, M.
1994   "Soft Difference: Theological Reflections on the Relation between Church and Culture in 1 Peter." *Ex Auditu* 10:15–30.

Warden, D.
1989   "The Prophets of 1 Peter 1:10–12." *Restoration Quarterly* 31:1–12.

Watts, R. E.
1998   "Jesus' Death, Isaiah 53, and Mark 10:45: A Crux Revisited." Pp. 125–51 in *Jesus and the Suffering Servant: Isaiah 53 and Christian Origins.* Edited by W. H. Bellinger and W. R. Farmer. Harrisburg, PA: Trinity.

Wedderburn, A. D. O., and W. G. Collingwood
1876   *The Economist of Xenophon.* London: Ellis and White. Reprinted New York: Franklin, 1971.

Wendland, E.
2000   "Stand Fast in the True Grace of God! A Study of 1 Peter." *Journal of Translation and Text Linguistics* 13:25–102.

Wengert, T.
1996   *A Contemporary Translation of Luther's Small Catechism.* Minneapolis: Fortress.

Wenham, J.
1972   "Did Peter Go to Rome in AD 42?" *Tyndale Bulletin* 23:94–102.

Wentz, A. R.
1959   *Luther's Works.* Vol. 36. Philadelphia: Fortress.

Westermann, C.
1969   *Isaiah 40–66.* The Old Testament Library. Philadelphia: Westminster.

Westfall, C.
1999   "The Relationship between the Resurrection, the Proclamation to the Spirits in Prison and Baptismal Regeneration: 1 Peter 3.19–22." Pp. 106–35 in *Resurrection.* Edited by

S. E. Porter, M. A. Hayes, and D. Tombs. Journal for the Study of the New Testament: Supplement Series 186; Roehampton Institute London Papers 5. London: Sheffield Academic Press.

White, N. J. D.
1919   "Love That Covers Sin." *Expositor* 8:541–47.

Williams, M.
1999   "He Descended into Hell? An Issue of Confessional Integrity." *Presbyterion* 25:80–90.

Wilson, G. H.
2002   *Psalms.* Vol. 1. NIV Application Commentary. Grand Rapids: Zondervan.

Wilson, J.
2001   *For God So Loved the World: A Christology for Disciples.* Grand Rapids: Baker.

Windisch, H.
1930   *Die katholischen Briefe.* Handbuch zum Neuen Testament 15. Tübingen: Mohr-Siebeck.

Winter, B.
1988   "The Public Honouring of Christian Benefactors: Romans 13.3–4 and 1 Peter 2.14–15." *Journal for the Study of the New Testament* 34:87–103.

Yakar, J.
2000   *Ethnoarchaeology of Anatolia: Rural Socio-economy in the Bronze and Iron Ages.* [Tel Aviv, Israel]: Emery and Claire Yass Publications in Archaeology.

Yonge, C. D.
1854   *Athenaeus Deipnosophists.* 3 vols. London: Henry G. Bohn.

Index of Subjects

aliens, resident. *See* foreigners
amanuensis, 6, 319–21
Asia Minor, 13, 19–23, 25–28, 39–41, 66. *See also* colonization, Roman; dating of text
audience, 23–27. *See also* Asia Minor
authority, apostolic, 59–60
authorship, 5–19, 51–53, 319–21, 325–38

"Babylon," 13–14, 34, 321–23
baptism, 54, 251–56. *See also* suffering

Christology, 46–48, 191–200, 256–58, 265–66. *See also* suffering
church structure, 10–11. *See also* authorship
citizenship, 31, 37. *See also* foreigners
Claudius, 29–33
colonization, Roman, 28–32, 38–41. *See also* Asia Minor
conversion, postmortem, 247–49
culture, Christians and. *See* society, Christians in

dating of text, 5–19
deportation, 30–33, 37–38
descensus doctrine, 247–51
descent into hell. See *descensus* doctrine
Diaspora, the, 63–66. *See also* expulsions, Roman
Diaspora letter, 54–55. *See also* genre

Enoch, 243–45
epistles, pseudonymous, 14–17. *See also* authorship
eschatology, 49–51, 290–95. *See also* suffering
ethics, Christian, 49–50
exordium, 79
expulsions, Roman, 30–33, 37–38. *See also* foreigners

fatherhood, God's, 46. *See also* theology, Petrine
fiery ordeal, 8–10, 285–86, 291–92
foreigners, 24–27, 30–31, 37–39, 44–45, 61–66. *See also* society, Christians in

genre, 14–17, 54–55
God, concept of. *See* theology, Petrine
Greek, quality of, 6–8, 325–38

Holiness Code, 114–15. *See also* Old Testament, Jesus and
household codes, 181–87. *See also* society, Christians in

identity, Christian. *See* society, Christians in

Jesus, teachings of. See *verba Christi*
Jesus Christ. *See* Christology
Jewish Christians, 23–24, 32–33
judgment, God's. *See* eschatology

letters. *See* epistles, pseudonymous
Levitical code. *See* Holiness Code
literary unity, 53–54

meddler, 289

Noah, 245–47, 257–58

Old Testament, Jesus and, 52, 77–78, 103–4
ordeal, fiery. *See* fiery ordeal

Paul, Peter's dependence on, 11–13, 51
Pentecost, 27–28
persecution. *See* fiery ordeal
Peter, career of, 8n1, 33–37, 40–41
Petrine group, 5–6
postmortem conversion, 247–49

preexisting material, 55–56. *See also* Paul, Peter's dependence on
priesthood of all believers, 160
pseudonymity, 14–17. *See also* authorship

recipients, 23–27. *See also* Asia Minor
resident aliens. *See* foreigners
resurrection. *See* Christology; eschatology; salvation
rhetoric. *See* Greek, quality of
Rome, Peter in, 33–37

salvation, 48–49, 88. *See also* suffering
self-denial, 5. *See also* suffering
Silvanus, 36–37, 319–21
society, Christians in, 1–5, 42–44, 159, 162, 170–72. *See also* foreigners
soteriology, 48–49, 88. *See also* suffering
source criticism, 55–56. *See also* Paul, Peter's dependence on
structure, church, 10–11. *See also* authorship
suffering, 1–2, 4–5, 45, 285–96. *See also* baptism; Christology; eschatology; salvation; society, Christians in
Suffering Servant, 51, 191–200
syntax, 7–8, 325–38

textual antecedents. *See* Paul, Peter's dependence on
theology, Petrine, 18, 45–46, 51–53, 68–69

unity, literary, 53–54

verba Christi, 17–18

Index of Authors

Index of Greek Words

Index of Scripture and Other Ancient Writings

Old Testament

Genesis

3:5   314
5:21–24   243
6   251
6:1–4   243, 250
6:4 LXX   243–44
6:5   251
6:9–9:29   244
7:13   259
12   205
12:13   205
15:13 LXX   25n4
16:2   205
16:6   205
18:12 LXX   205
18:12   205
18:22–32   247
20   205
20:5   205
20:13   205
21:12   205
23:4 LXX   25n4
23:4   27
23:4 LXX   61, 168
31:42   190
31:53   190
41:43 LXX   250
50:24–25   172

Exodus

2:22 LXX   25n4
3:16   172
6:7   127
12:11   111
13:9 LXX   311
19   160, 161
19:3 LXX   146
19:5   127, 162
19:5–6 LXX   142, 150, 159
19:5–6   146, 162
19:6   158, 161
19:8   72
19:10   123
20:1–17   112
20:6   82

20:20   190
24   59, 72, 161
24:1   302
24:3   72
24:3–8   71, 72
24:7   72
24:8   72
32   268
34:6   82
36:6 LXX   250

Leviticus

11–20   114
11:2   114
11:44   114
12:1   114
14:33–57   115
15:2   114
17:2   114
18:2   114
19:2   114, 115
19:3   115
20:2   114
20:7–8   114
20:26   114
25:23 LXX   25n4
26:12   127

Numbers

6:3   123
19   72
33:54   306
35:34   86

Deuteronomy

3:24 LXX   311
4:34 LXX   311
5:1–22   112
5:10   82
5:15 LXX   311
7:19 LXX   311
9:26 LXX   311
11:2 LXX   311
21:23   197
23:7   25n4

23:8 LXX   25n4
26:17–18   127
28:25   63n2
30:4   63n2

Joshua

3:5   123
14:2   306
18:6   306

1 Samuel

16:7   204

2 Samuel

21:9   197

1 Kings

16:2   118

2 Kings

10:20 LXX   250

1 Chronicles

15:12   123
29:15 LXX   25n4

2 Chronicles

30:17   123

Nehemiah

1:9   63n2
5:9   190

Esther

6:9 LXX   250

Job

1:6–12   314
9:31   254

11:15   254
14:4   254

Psalms

24:8 LXX   137
25:8   137
33 LXX   39, 118, 132, 135, 137, 138, 139, 140, 141, 145, 153, 220, 221, 223, 226, 292
33:2 LXX   221
33:5 LXX   117, 145, 220, 221
33:5–6 LXX   145
33:6 LXX   139, 221, 223
33:7 LXX   139, 223
33:8 LXX   221
33:9 LXX   117, 135, 137, 138, 139, 220, 223
33:10 LXX   222
33:10–11   139
33:10–11 LXX   223
33:12 LXX   222
33:13–15 LXX   220
33:14 LXX   140
33:15 LXX   140
33:18 LXX   222
33:20 LXX   222
33:23 LXX   117, 223
34   39, 107, 117, 118, 137, 138, 145, 153, 220, 226
34:1   221
34:4   220, 221
34:4–5   145
34:5   138, 139, 220, 221, 223
34:6   139, 223
34:7   221
34:8   117, 135, 137, 138, 139, 220, 223
34:9   222
34:9–10   139, 223

New Testament

Old Testament Apocrypha

Old Testament Pseudepigrapha

New Testament Apocrypha

Rabbinic Writings

Qumran / Dead Sea Scrolls

1QH

3.19–23 83

1QS

4.9–11 131
8.8 147
10.21–23 131

4QM[ilik]

130 60

Papyri

BGU

1079 320

CPR

6.80 lines 9–10 320

P.Cair.Preis.

1.16 255

P.Mich.

15.751 lines 4–7 320

P.Wisc.

2.69 lines 4–5 320

Josephus

Against Apion

in toto 330
2.158 183
2.193 183

2.220 183
2.225 183
2.235 183
2.293 183

Jewish Antiquities

in toto 330
19.280–87 33

Philo

On Drunkenness

in toto 268

On Noah's Work as a Planter

160–66 268

On the Virtues

7.39 204
163 170

Classical Writers

Aristotle

Oeconomica
  in toto 181
  1.3.4 208
  1.5.1–2 185
  2.1.1 183
  3.1 204
  3.2 185
  3.3 189
Rhetoric
  3.14 82

Athenaeus

Deipnosophistae
  5.21.12 75
  5.25.10 75
  10.52.27 75
  12.54.11 75
  13.42.17 75
  13.44.3 75

Cassius Dio

Roman History
  60.6.6 32

Catullus

Fifth Epigram
  4–6 85

Dio Chrysostom

On Household Management
  in toto 181

Diodorus Siculus

Bibliotheca historica
  1.4.3 75
  1.83.8 75

4.18.1 75
4.27.3 75
4.67.4 75
9.25.1 75
10.6.2 75
13.27.3 75
19.61.1 75
29.32.1 75
32.15.3 75

Epictetus

Discourses
  2.4.1–8 185n2
  bks. 3–4 330

Galen

On His Own Books
  in toto 16

Herodotus

Histories
  in toto 23n3

Plato

Gorgias
  474c 232
Laws
  8.835E 170
Phaedo
  82.C 170
  83.B 170
Republic
  in toto 181
  4.433A 183
  4.433C–D 183

Church Fathers